Japan's Medieval Population

Japan's Medieval

Famine, Fertility, and

Hungry Ghosts Scroll (*Gaki-sōshi*). Tokyo National Museum. Image:
TNM Image Archives. Source: http://TnmArchives.jp/.

Population

Warfare in a Transformative Age

William Wayne Farris

University of Hawai'i Press   HAWAI'I   Honolulu

Publication of this book has been assisted by a grant from the Kajiyama Bunka Studies Fund at the University of Hawai'i.

Library of Congress Cataloging-in-Publication Data

Farris, William Wayne.
 Japan's medieval population: famine, fertility, and warfare in a transformative age / William Wayne Farris.
     p. cm.
 Includes bibliographical references and index.
 ISBN-13: 978-0-8248-2973-5 (hardcover : alk. paper)
 ISBN-10: 0-8248-2973-5 (hardcover : alk. paper)
 1. Japan—Social conditions—To 1600. 2. Japan—Population—History.
3. Japan—History—1185-1600. I. Title.
 HN723.F37 2006
 304.60952'0902—dc22
                                    2006005763

Designed by University of Hawai'i Press production staff
Printed by The Maple-Vail Book Manufacturing Group

To a beloved mentor, Clif

Contents

–

Acknowledgments

I dedicate this book to Clifton Phillips, Professor Emeritus of History at DePauw University. He served as my undergraduate adviser thirty-five years ago and through his stimulating teaching sparked my interest in Japanese studies. He opened my eyes to a brand-new world. To him I owe more than I can ever repay.

I would like to thank the Japan-U.S. Educational/Fulbright Commission and the Social Science Research Council for money to fund a year-long research stay in Tokyo in 1999. I am especially grateful to Professor Murai Shōsuke for serving as a tireless adviser and to Higashijima Makoto for acting as a patient tutor, putting up with my requests to read first one source and then something completely different. Professors Hongō Kazuto and Hongō Keiko answered many questions and guided me to sources I did not know about. I returned to Tokyo in the summer of 2000, thanks to a Visiting Professorship kindly extended by Tomobe Ken'ichi of Keiō University. Then in the summer of 2001, I was allowed to use the world-class facilities of the Historiographical Institute of Tokyo University, under the sponsorship of Professor Hongō and supported by a research grant from the Northeast Asia Council of the Association for Asian Studies and money from the University of Tennessee. In 2003, I returned once more to Keiō to update my research. Special thanks also go to Kuroda Hideo, Amino Yoshihiko, Ishii Susumu, Tamura Noriyoshi, Fujiki Hisashi, Kitō Hiroshi, Saitō Osamu, Gomi Fumihiko, Kuwayama Kōnen, Hosokawa Shigeo, Kondō Shigekazu, Yoshie Akira, and all the history graduate students at Tōdai for putting up with my unending and sometimes impertinent questions. I would also like to express my deepest gratitude to Conrad Totman, who read the first two chapters and made numerous well-founded suggestions for reorganization; to

Paul Varley, who read chapter 1 and made many helpful comments; to Pat Crosby, the University of Hawai'i Press' Editor Extraordinaire, who went out of her way to help me rewrite the introduction and provided endless encouragement as I struggled to cut the overly long manuscript; to Keith Leber, Managing Editor at the Press; to Bojana Ristich, my copy editor; and to Billy Stevenson, a promising graduate student here at the University of Hawai'i who put the numerous tables and figures into Microsoft Excel format. My thanks are also due to two anonymous outside readers for many interesting and valuable criticisms, not all of which I could incorporate into this book. I feel deep gratitude to Han Chŏng-mi, a graduate student at Tokyo Univeristy who assisted this project in ways so diverse I cannot list them all. Finally, I am grateful for the financial support for publication from the research funds associated with the Sen Chair and the Kajiyama Fund of the History Department at the University of Hawai'i at Manoa.

Any mistakes, of course, are the responsibility of the author.

Introduction

One of the great unexplored topics of Japan's medieval past is its population. This book attempts to describe and explain what happened to Japan's population during the epoch between 1150 and 1600, which I am calling the "medieval" period, and through that lens, to consider related social and economic developments.[1] Demography has always been an invaluable approach to the past because it provides one way—often the only way—to study the overwhelming mass of people who are not members of the political or religious elite. From a demographic perspective, I contend that although this medieval age initially maintained a centuries-old stasis, a far-reaching transformation commenced from about 1280 and eventually gained momentum until it swept throughout the Japanese archipelago. (As defined here, the archipelago excludes Hokkaido and the Ryukyu chain, uncharted lands for which little or no data exist.) Crucial to the demographic breakthrough was the resolution of two central problems facing both the rulers and the ruled: how to supply a burgeoning population with sufficient food and how to keep the peace. The remedies worked out at this time laid the groundwork for further gains after 1600.

JAPAN'S DEMOGRAPHIC DARK AGES

Japan's medieval population—its size, fluctuations, regional variations, and vital statistics—has always presented historians and social scientists with a particularly perplexing riddle. Not only is it an impossibly complex puzzle, but it is also missing many pieces. To be sure, some gaps can be inferred from the context, but most of the puzzle remains scattered among thousands of enigmatic and none-too-reliable documents, a small number of laconic chronicles and diaries, and uncounted archaeological excavations. For these reasons, Japan's medieval era has been dubbed a demographic "Dark Ages."[2] The difficulty of piecing the puzzle together is matched only by its importance, for it is solely through a resolution to the mystery of medieval population, by giving scholars access to the everyday lives of commoner and servile people, that we can comprehend the whole of premodern Japanese history.

The fragmentary nature of the evidence has resulted in a piecemeal approach to the study of Japan's medieval population. By considering the earlier works of both historians and demographers, I have been able to identify three theories: one reflects prewar research; a second, the revisions of the early postwar era; and a third has been vaguely articulated in recent decades. The theories might be described, respectively, as "the hypothesis of continuous and sizable growth," "the theory of practically no growth," and "the assumption of growth starting in the middle." The estimates and arguments are sufficiently complex that some detailed historiographical discussion is necessary. Readers disinclined to follow the finer points of the evolution of scholarly opinion may move on to the next section of the introduction.

Yokoyama Yoshikiyo (1826–1879) established the first pillar of the prewar theory in a journal article published in the year of his death. Yokoyama, a legal and literary scholar, produced population estimates for the ninth, tenth, and eleventh centuries, as well as for the Kamakura era (1185–1333).[3] Working from a source named *Shūgai shō*, Yokoyama derived a figure of 9.75 million for Kamakura times. Since his totals for the ninth through eleventh centuries were much smaller (3.7–4.4 million), his work left an impression of substantial gain during the early medieval epoch.

Another influential figure was geographer and historian Yoshida Tōgo (1864–1918), who inferred a population number for the late sixteenth century.[4] In a series of lectures in 1911 on the epochal Meiji Restoration, Yoshida argued that because the amount necessary to feed one person for a year in the late 1500s averaged about one *koku* of rice (approximately five U.S. bushels), the population of the islands must have been equal to what he presumed was the total *koku* in rice, or 18.5 million. Like Yokoyama for the earlier era, Yoshida posited that the late medieval period was a time of substantial increase.

Despite many potential problems, the calculations of these two scholars and the assumptions lying behind them were remarkably long-lived, standing unchallenged for half a century and longer. Eventually, later scholars united Yokoyama and Yoshida's estimates into what I am calling "the hypothesis of continuous and sizable growth." Irene Taeuber, in her classic *The Population of Japan* (1958), referred favorably to Yokoyama's estimates and, using Yoshida's total for 1600, speculated that Japan's population had jumped from 4.4 million in 1100 to 18.5 million around 1600.[5] In 1975, William McNeill enhanced Yokoyama's credibility by basing his thesis about the impact of foreign-borne plagues partially on the Meiji scholar's numbers for the ancient and medieval epochs.[6]

Following a hiatus of some twenty years after World War II, research into Tokugawa-period population exploded during the 1960s and 1970s. Hayami Akira, under whose leadership the research revived, came to entertain serious doubts about Yoshida Tōgo's easy equation of one *koku* with one person, arguing instead that there was considerable regional disparity in the relationship in 1600. Moreover, Hayami noted that the *koku* figures for the late 1500s undoubtedly included grains other than rice, as well as other items such as silk that were calculated in terms of their rice value. He also argued that it required much more than one *koku* to sustain an individual at that time. Extrapolating backward from seventeenth- and eighteenth-century demographic data found in Kokura domain and later from data on villages from other parts of Japan, Hayami suggested that a more reasonable figure was about half Yoshida's estimate—9.8 million, to be exact.[7] In 1975, he proposed 12.3 million.[8]

The implications of Hayami's views for the pre-1600 era soon became clear, as Susan Hanley and Kozo Yamamura pointed out in their 1977 monograph on Tokugawa population and economy.[9] In addition to his low figure for 1600, Hayami supported Sawada Goichi's well-known estimate of about 6 or 7 million for the mid-eighth century. Sawada had utilized various methods in 1927 to calculate Nara Japan's population, and astoundingly enough, in 1980 lacquer-soaked documents uncovered in the Kanto (modern Tokyo and vicinity) seemed to corroborate Sawada's work.[10] By Hayami's reasoning, Japan's population around the year 750 would have been 6 million and only 10–12 million almost a millennium later, an anemic growth rate of .08–.1 percent per annum. Thus was born Hayami's "theory of practically no growth" for the Middle Ages.

TABLE I.1

Kitō's Population Estimates, Initial Jōmon Period to 1875

PERIOD	ESTIMATE
Initial Jōmon[a]	21,900
Early Jōmon[a]	106,000
Middle Jōmon[a]	262,500
Late Jōmon[a]	161,000
Yayoi[b]	601,500
750 CE	5,589,100
900	6,437,600
1150	6,916,900
1600	12,273,000
1721	31,277,000
1786	30,104,000
1792	29,869,700
1846	32,423,800
1875	36,527,600

Source: Kitō, *Nihon nisen nen*, pp. 12–13.
a. Kitō utilized Japanese archaeological periodization, which is based on the relative dating of ceramic styles.
b. Kitō's table simply says "Yayoi," but he seems to mean early in the era.

Meanwhile, beginning in the 1980s, Kitō Hiroshi, one of Hayami's students, began to extend his interest into the "Dark Ages." Surveying Japan's premodern history, he asserted that the entire era from the Jōmon epoch (10,500–400 BCE) to 1875 could be conveniently divided into three overarching cycles.[11] Each cycle consisted of a beginning, when population increased rapidly as new land was brought into cultivation or other innovations appeared, and an end, when the limits for that agricultural or economic system were reached and population came to a standstill or even began to decline. Kitō's three cycles were as follows: (1) the Jōmon age; (2) the Yayoi age (400 BCE–250 CE) until sometime in the medieval epoch (probably 1300–1500); and (3) the latter medieval era until the end of the early modern age. Although many scholars had long held the position that the fourteenth and fifteenth centuries encompassed a basic change in Japanese history, Kitō was among the first to give voice in demographic terms to the "assumption of growth starting in the middle."[12] As may be apparent from table I.1, however, Kitō was deliberately vague about when the transition from the second to the third cycle took place since he derived figures for only 1150 and 1600. The lack of solid analysis presented an enticing challenge and inspired my research.

"GROWTH STARTING IN THE MIDDLE"

In my view, Kitō's "assumption of growth starting in the middle" most reasonably explains what happened to the archipelago's population from 1150 to 1600. To state the increase more specifically, I shall argue that the population expanded on the order of 300 percent, from about 5.5–6.3 million in 1150 to 15–17 million in 1600, with almost all the growth coming after 1280. While demographic theory and mathematical computations appear to support the pace and scope of the growth, it is more concretely corroborated by a whole host of social and economic variables. During this time, Japan experienced a decline in mortality from pestilence and famine. Concurrently, there was a slow but sustained rise in farming yields and arable land through better agronomy and irrigation. Trade and industry too showed improvement, becoming more efficient and productive; cohesive social units such as the corporate village and stem family were created; and there was a sizable increase in urbanization. These changes in turn resulted in gradual but noticeable advances in the physical well-being of most of the populace, innovations that in turn resulted in lowered mortality and a heightened birthrate. Population change in medieval Japan, in other words, was synergistic, the action of multiple variables, which in turn led to a major transformation that none of the factors could have accomplished individually.

From a demographic perspective, I divide the 450 years of the medieval era into three subperiods: 1150–1280, 1280–1450, and 1450–1600. I further analyze each of these epochs according to elements that have either direct or indirect bearing on population trends. In general, factors that affect mortality, such as epidemics or war, fall into the first category, while background variables, such as agricultural technology, the labor market, and commerce, occupy the second. I utilize qualitative and quantitative information for each factor, although quantitative data tend to be more available for some than others (for example, agricultural productivity, famine, and cities). There is a dearth of quantifiable data on birthrates. This is unfortunate because most historical demographers acknowledge that fertility levels (including a limitation on the number of births through abortion, infanticide, or late marriage) have a greater impact on population than do mortality levels. In the absence of quantitative data on fertility, I present descriptive evidence on kinship, women, marriage, and the family, placing them in the category of indirect components in the demographic equation.

The first subperiod (1150–1280), as chapters 1 and 2 will show, represented both something new and something old. On the one hand, the demographic regime was novel in that the most deadly microparasites finally retreated to endemic status. At the same time, the population did not budge much from its former total of around 6 million. However, while the size of Japan's population may have differed little from 1150, a whole host of new "medieval" variables was at work, starting with rising immunities to especially lethal infections. Two other new factors appeared to keep mortality rates high: famine and war. The first was the more critical of the two. In three periods—1180–1182, 1229–1232, and 1257–1260—killer famines decimated the commoner population and turned Kamakura society upside down. In comparison to crop failure, war and the depredations of the military class were a minor nuisance. On the other hand, indirect factors such as agricultural techniques, industry, or trade suggest little change from bygone eras. The labor market remained tight. There appears to have been no marked improvement in the material circumstances of families and commoners more generally.

The second subperiod (1280–1450) was the beginning of a crucial transition to better times, delineated in chapters 3 and 4. During the "Muromachi Optimum" of 1370–1450, in particular, it seemed as though the former twin demons of famine and war might have been banished for good. According to the best estimates, by 1450 the archipelago had come to contain around 10 million inhabitants, marking the inception of a new wave of demographic growth. Direct, quantitative measures help to demonstrate the reasons behind this expansion: there was a noticeable decrease in both pestilential outbreaks and hunger after the near cessation of hostilities in the Wars between the Northern and Southern Dynasties in 1370. Of the three major mortality factors, only war claimed more victims than it had before, in battles notable for their duration and intensity. Among indirect variables too, almost all sectors showed substantial improvement. In agriculture, farmers spurred advances in three major areas: agronomy, engineering, and social organization. Industry witnessed one of its most innovative periods. The Muromachi era is known for the rise of a commercial economy, with Kyoto as its hub; markets sprang up and fee barriers were reduced all over western Japan. Although it is not possible to measure fertility, gradual changes in kinship, the family, and marriage suggest the appearance of a new demographic regime. Commoners also began taking advantage of improvements in all-important areas such as diet, clothing, sanitation, and housing.

The final subperiod (1450–1600) was a time of historical crosscurrents, with continued growth despite famine and war. The old issues of the first subperiod reappeared with a vengeance. Population increased, perhaps even sizably, from 10 to 15–17 million, but even with the expansion posited above, the growth was smaller in percentage terms than in that of the previous subperiod. It could be said that the Warring States and Unification eras comprised a time of unfulfilled potential.

This final subperiod may be further divided if we examine direct factors of mortality more closely. Chapter 5, for instance, reveals that outbreaks of well-known infections were more common until 1540, after which they dropped off precipitously. Moreover, early in the sixteenth century sailors introduced a new microbial threat, syphilis, that spread quickly and may have induced widespread death. Famine stalked the land as of old and was reported more frequently than during the late Kamakura and middle Muromachi epochs. By the late sixteenth century, however, demographic records hint that the medieval pattern of chronic malnutrition—known as the "spring hungers"—was being transformed into a more benign state. While quantitative measures suggest that disease and starvation played a bigger part in the demographic picture until about 1540, war among daimyo and local notables of various descriptions was a crucial factor, reducing growth rates and delaying dramatic progress throughout the subperiod. Deaths among combatants reached a new high, but even more deleterious for the general populace were the effects of scorched-earth tactics, wars of attrition, and military provisioning efforts.

Among indirect measures, examined in chapter 6, there is a mixed and nuanced picture. The Warring States daimyo appears to have been a Janus-faced figure, encouraging expansion within his domain while discouraging it abroad. Even though anecdotal evidence for agrarian improvements is spotty, trade and industry showed advances more readily, especially in formerly economically backward eastern Honshu.

Monetization and markets revealed progress all over Japan. The densely settled, well-organized village continued to form in areas farther from the Kinai (Kyoto-Osaka-Nara region). Many new stem families were created, even though a clear differentiation into main and branch households was slow to occur. In terms of physical well-being, the variety of foods was about the same, but commoners benefited from numerous other changes in clothing, sanitation, and even literacy and numeracy.

Before this story can be told, some description of the theoretical framework, patterned on anthropology, is necessary. Previously I have utilized the word "microparasitism," first coined by William McNeill, to indicate how seriously infectious diseases were depleting the pre-1150 population. McNeill also uses the related designation "macroparasitism" to refer to the way elites and the general populace interacted over history. The first human macroparasites were large carnivores, but when agriculture was invented, a class of primary producers came into being and along with it a new macroparasitic threat: other humans. The dominant strata of society stole all or part of a cultivator's meager harvest, often giving nothing in return. During the late twelfth and thirteenth centuries, peasants usually suffered from such an unbalanced relationship. Eventually, just as diseases withdrew into more modulated relationships with their human hosts (endemicity), rapacious elites learned to collect rents and taxes in a more or less regular way and markets appeared to recompense farmers for their surplus, as described in chapters 3 and 4. Despite the setbacks of the Warring States and Unification epochs, by 1600 rulers and the ruled worked out a new and more permanent "macroparasitic balance." The recurrence of two classic "macroparasitic" phenomena, famine and war, in Japan's medieval epoch suggests that these centuries were a time when a more reciprocal relationship was gradually and painfully coming into being.[13]

POPULATION BEFORE 1150

Before we embark on the detailed examination of the medieval period that is the focus of this study, a brief summary of the demographic picture before 1150 is in order. The two-thousand-year-long second cycle depicted by Kitō as commencing with the agricultural and metallurgical advances of the Yayoi age had reached its zenith by the eighth century. I have estimated elsewhere that by 730 the number of inhabitants of the archipelago had reached 5.8–6.4 million and remained at that approximate level until 1150. Around 950 the population may well have dipped to 4.4–5.6 million, and while it likely recovered to 5.5–6.3 million by 1150, stasis was the general trend from 730 through 1150.[14]

There were many reasons for this long period of stability. First, in the Yayoi and Tomb (250–650) eras Japan had benefited from substantial in-migration from Korea and China, but by 700 this had dropped to a trickle.[15] Contact with these areas did not entirely abate, however, and soon the Japanese archipelago entered the microbial orbit of the continent, where such lethal infections as smallpox, measles, mumps, and influenza thrived. The Japanese population may well have been exposed to these killers previously, but beginning around 730 repeated outbreaks of lethal epidemics cut deeply into a population that often had no previous experience with a particular pathogen. The result was massive die-offs—as high as 25–35 percent approximately every generation. This basic pattern—a population with little or no immunity decimated by a deadly virus or bacterium every generation—continued unabated until 1150 and drove up mortality for a populace already struggling to survive. To paraphrase William McNeill, this was Japan's age of microparasitism.[16] Effects were apparent in myriad aspects of the culture, even religion and art.

Frequent famines aided pestilence in driving up mortality and reducing fertility. According to figures for the well-documented eighth and ninth centuries, crop failure occurred on a widespread basis about once every three years, induced by drought until 1100 and excessive cold and precipitation between 1100 and 1150. Soil exhaustion, a shortage of adequate irrigation facilities, and a reduction in water-retaining woodland were also causes for food shortages. Malnutrition was common for many, especially during the early spring through early summer, when stored food supplies were exhausted. War and political instability played a much more minor role in the heightened mortality of the age, although the wars against the *emishi* ("barbarians") of northern Honshu in the late eighth and early ninth centuries, the revolts of Taira no Masakado and Fujiwara Sumitomo between 935 and 941, and the upheaval surrounding Taira no Tadatsune from 1028 to 1032 took their toll on specific regions.

In agriculture, the effects of heightened mortality were numerous. Land abandonment was common—perhaps as high as 40 percent of the arable in some regions. The desolate fate of the famous "early estates" *(shoki shōen)*, most of which had gone to wasteland by the 900s despite the best efforts of powerful religious institutions and the government, also bolsters the argument for a depopulated countryside. As a result of the dearth of farmhands and greater wide-open spaces for grazing, wealthy cultivators used draft animals in a new harness-and-plow system of tillage by 950. By the twelfth century, as the population expanded modestly owing to rising immunities, a bit more land came into cultivation, especially dry fields. Yet yields from rice paddies had hardly risen at all from the eighth century. Settlement tended to be dispersed or isolated, and most peasants moved frequently.

The labor market also presented a picture of demographic stasis because insofar as researchers can tell, wages rose while several major ceremonial and religious projects, such as Tōji and even the imperial capital itself at Heian, remained unfinished, both factors implying a shortage of workers. In industry, as with the plow in farming, the development of labor-saving devices became the watchword. For ironworks, operators shifted to a simpler furnace placed on a slope, where updrafts would substitute for a bellows. In salt making, workers changed from a labor-intensive method using a cauldron and seaweed to collecting dried crystals from salt fields cut into the beach. Even in ceramics, stoneware became simpler and less variegated by 1100.

In commerce, it is more difficult to draw conclusions, but there can be little doubt that people no longer generally used copper cash by the late tenth century and returned to barter. Perhaps a decline in trade can be inferred from the general shrinkage of the urban population. Certainly Heian was large, with a population of one hundred thousand, but Nara, Naniwa, and Dazaifu all suffered loss. Beginning in 1050, as the population recovered from the depths of the tenth-century decrease, trade and towns rebounded, as seen in the overseas trade with Sung China internationally and the growth of new ports such as Hakata and Hyōgo domestically.

The only quantifiable figures for fertility originate from the early eighth century and are very high: 45–50 births per thousand population. Infant mortality to age five was 50 or even 60 percent, leading to a life expectancy at birth of twenty-five at most. It is difficult to know how kinship, marriage, and the family fit into this story; scholars generally agree that kinship was bilateral, inheritance partible, and sexual liaisons loose and free. The frequent famines and epidemics undoubtedly acted to drive down the birthrate over long periods. The existence of a sizable slave class, at least until 900, may also have helped to reduce overall fertility.

Life was hard for peasants. The typical house was a pit dwelling with a dirt floor, prone to fire and cold in the winter; clothing was sewn from fibers of hemp or ramie and chilly and scratchy. As witnessed by the frequent famines, diet was just adequate in the best of times. Cities like Nara or Heian had poor sanitation, making them fertile breeding grounds for the microbes that killed so many.

By 1150, however, there were subtle signs of a transformation. In particular, the deadly pathogens that had taken such a heavy toll seemed to be less lethal for an adult population that had come to possess new immunities. Even the weather seemed to change, as the heat and drought of earlier times gave way to a cold, wet climate. The new era would see both continuity and change. It is to this early transitional stage that we next turn.

1

New Problems, Same Result

Mortality in Early Medieval Japan, 1150–1280

One characteristic of late Heian culture is its preoccupation with suffering and death. It was believed to be a degenerate age, the "Latter Days of the Buddhist Law," when even the most virtuous were destined for hell. The ruling elite manifested this gloomy outlook by commissioning art works that took some gruesome forms of death as a major theme; such works included *The Book of Sicknesses, The Hungry Ghosts Scroll,* and *The Picture Book of Hell.*[1] Judged by the pessimistic entries in aristocratic diaries, the late Heian and early Kamakura epochs were on the verge of the end of the world; death lurked at every turn.

In this chapter I propose to compute a total population for Japan in 1280 and examine three extraordinary causes of mortality: disease, famine, and war. While I conclude that Japan's inhabitants numbered about the same in 1280 as they did in 1150, the mortality factors relevant to that result differed from those of the great age of epidemics. First, I shall explore whether disease was still a major factor affecting death rates. Second, I shall describe and analyze another variable likely to produce elevated mortality: starvation. As noted in the introduction, three times during this epoch what may have been the worst famines in Japanese history struck the archipelago; by examining their causes, probable death rates, and the Kyoto-Kamakura dyarchy's attempts to handle these crises, scholars can come to some conclusions about their demographic impact. Third, I shall look at war and political instability. Conflict—including the epochal Civil War of 1180–1185, the Jōkyū War of 1221, and the Mongol Invasions of 1274 and 1281—was more common than before 1150. A consideration of both combatant mortality and "collateral damage" arising from battles and provisioning activities will shed more light on how demographic stasis was maintained.

During the Kamakura era, famous for its unintegrated polity, Kyoto and Kamakura jointly ruled over thousands of estates *(shōen)* and miscellaneous but substantial provincial lands *(kokugaryō)*. Although it is much more well documented than even the final century of the Heian period, the problem with the Kamakura epoch—as with the rest of the medieval age—is that there is nothing comparable to the province-by-province lists of rice loans found in *The Ordinances of Engi (Engi shiki*, 927) or paddy-land totals available in *Wamyō shō* (935) or *Shūgai shō* (1150).[2] In other words, a historical demographer lacks reliable archipelago-wide data from which to derive population.

Because of the lack of such data and his misinterpretation of *Shūgai shō*, Yokoyama's long-lived figure of 9.75 million for the Kamakura era is unlikely to be accurate. The Meiji scholar arrived at his number by assuming that *Shūgai shō* represented conditions of the thirteenth century, and then he simply multiplied the entry for administrative households (13,000) by the eighth-century standard for households per village (50) and the resulting figure by what he assumed was the average size of a household (15 persons). Problems with this calculation are legion. First, recent historical scholarship has revealed that *Shūgai shō* probably did not reflect conditions of the thirteenth century but rather those of the mid-twelfth.[3] Moreover, the administrative village listed in the famous compendium had dwindled considerably from its standard size of the eighth century. Finally, Yokoyama never stated the basis for his assumption that the mean household contained fifteen persons—a figure seemingly drawn from thin air. This century-old computation for the period 1185–1333 is thus of dubious reliability.

Having cast serious doubt on the assumptions behind Yokoyama's calculation, I searched for another, sounder basis for making a population estimate utilizing the fragmentary documents of the early to mid-Kamakura era. The most valid sources from which to estimate population for Japan in the late thirteenth century are the twenty-one Great Land Registers *(ōtabumi)*, which supply the total areas of rice fields in

TABLE 1.1
Extant Great Land Registers *(ōtabumi)*

PROVINCE	DATE	CONDITION	ARABLE S/O[a]
Hyūga*	1197	Complete	8,298/8,064
Satsuma*	1197	Complete	5,521/4,010
Ōsumi*	1197	Complete	4,907/3,017
Higo	1197	Partial	—
Hizen	1197	Partial	—
Chikugo	1197	Fragmentary	—
Bungo	1197	Fragmentary	—
Buzen*	1190–1199	Partial	13,221/13,300
Chikuzen	1190–1199	Fragmentary	—
Higo	1216	Fragmentary	—
Bungo	1216	Fragmentary	—
Noto*	1221	Complete	8,479/2,455[b]
Iwami*	1223	Complete	4,872/1,476
Awaji*	1223	Complete	2,870/2,283
Wakasa*	1265	Complete	3,139/2,218
Hitachi	1279	Mostly complete	42,038/9,005[c]
Bungo*	1285	Complete	7,570/6,964
Tajima*	1285	Complete	7,743/5,586
Tango*	1288?	Complete	5,537/4,667
Hizen*	1292	Complete	13,462/13,720
Hitachi*	1306	Complete	—

Note: Asterisks denote a Great Land Register used in this analysis.
[a]The acreage figures are given first for the *Shūgai shō* and then as recorded in the *ōtabumi.*
[b]When two numbers were listed, the higher one was used.
[c]Total follows Amino, *Nihon chūsei tochi seido,* pp. 476–477.

various provinces, ranging from southern Kyushu to the eastern Kanto and dating from 1197 to 1306.[4] (See table 1.1.) As with figures from Nara and Heian documents, these collections of data are subject to numerous qualifications and adjustments, but they probably constitute the only means to infer a defensible number for total population during the late thirteenth century.

Of the twenty-one extant land registers, only thirteen permit the two types of analysis undertaken with rice field figures from Heian sources.[5] I organized documents from these thirteen provinces by region: a Kyushu group (Hizen, Bungo, Buzen, Ōsumi, Satsuma, and Hyūga); a western Honshu/Kinai group (Iwami, Tango, Wakasa, Tajima, and Awaji), one from the Japan Sea littoral (Noto), and one from the Kanto (Hitachi).[6]

In subjecting these Great Land Registers to analysis, I confronted several problems similar to those faced for land totals in the Heian materials. The first difficulty is the accuracy of the field totals; in the case of earlier records, figures had to be taken merely on trust. Fortunately, supplementary data available from the Kamakura period, as well as the expert testimony of various Japanese scholars, allow for a more certain solution to this problem than do Heian sources. Many specialists have noted a tendency for the figures in the *ōtabumi* to become "frozen" over time.[7] In several cases, moreover, totals seem unbelievably low. Was the land being inclusively and precisely surveyed and recorded or not?

The short answer to this question is that insofar as Kamakura documents afford answers, ciphers in the *ōtabumi* seem to be reasonably accurate. Periodically, estate proprietors had their estate lands surveyed, and several of these Kamakura cadastres *(kenchū chō)* have survived.[8] The two most well-known cadastres from provinces that also have Great Land Registers originate from Tara Estate in Wakasa and Iriki in Satsuma. In the Wakasa case, the estate proprietor conducted surveys of Tara in 1254 and 1256; in the former year his men measured 21.7 *chō* of rice fields and in the latter, about 28.8. The *ōtabumi* for Wakasa reveals that officials in the provincial headquarters noted 25.8 *chō* in 1265. Given the vagaries of cultivation conditions, these figures suggest that the Wakasa Great Land Register was fairly accurate.[9]

Iriki presents a different story. The land register dated to 1197 lists 92.2 *chō*, of which about 75 were administered by the provincial headquarters. A 1250 survey, however, notes 164.3 *chō* of rice acreage—more than twice the area recorded in 1197. It would be natural to assume that the increase was the result of land clearance and conversion to paddy fields, an activity presumably occurring over the half century between the two surveys. A closer examination of the 1250 record, however, shows that only 76.8 *chō*—almost exactly the amount listed in the 1197 *ōtabumi*—were regularly yielding a harvest; surveyors described the other 87.5 units as *sonden* (damaged fields with little or no yield). In the absence of other records, it is difficult to determine how to

TABLE 1.2
Comparative Field Measurements from Great Land Registers and Estate Surveys *(chō)*

PROVINCE AND PROPERTY	GREAT LAND REGISTER	ESTATE SURVEY
Buzen, Ito	80	60
Buzen, Itoda	150	130
Buzen, Magusano	60	60
Buzen, Uhara	15	10+
Buzen, Hatabaru	15	16
Buzen, Shinozaki	80	80
Buzen, Tsubusa	80	80
Buzen, Ikejiri beppu	70	35
Buzen, Aratsu beppu	40	40
Buzen, Chūkanji	2	3
Bungo, Kamado	80	70
Bungo, Yasaka	200	130
Bungo, Matama	70	50
Bungo, Imi/Other	70	70
Bungo, Tokō	70	90
Bungo, Kusachi	25	25
Bungo, Kagachi	60	35
Bungo, Takedatsu	20	14
Hizen, Narata	125.7	100
Hizen, Ayabe	70	30
Hizen, Kamiyabu	27	20
Hyūga, Tomitaka	30	20
Hyūga, Funahiki	50	50
Hyūga, Shiomi	35	20
Awaji, Toshi	21.8	23
Ōsumi, Shimazu (new)	715	750
Ōsumi, Yose gun	750.8	750

Table 1.2 continues

Table 1.2 continued

PROVINCE AND PROPERTY	GREAT LAND REGISTER	ESTATE SURVEY
Ōsumi, Aira	121.7	145.5
Ōsumi, Yoshida	18.2	20.9
Ōsumi, Nine minamimata	40	41.5
Ōsumi, Gamō	110	142
Ōsumi, Kurino	64	74
Ōsumi, Chōsa (west)	271?	237
Ōsumi, Tsutsuwano	48.5	48.5
Ōsumi, Takarabe	100	100
Ōsumi, Yokogawa	39.5	39.5
Ōsumi, Kogawa Nagatoshi	12.6	12.6
Ōsumi, Ogawa	348.3	182
Ōsumi, Kuwa	345.6	353
Ōsumi, Tanegashima	500	500
Hitachi, Shida	826	890

Sources: Figures for Buzen, Bungo, Hizen, and Hyūga come from Document 432, "Mirokudera Kida in shoryō chūshin," in *Iwashimizu monjo,* 2, pp. 141–147; the document is generally believed to belong to the early Kamakura era. For Awaji, see Document 3, "Awaji no kuni Toshi gō Sō kenmyō yosechō an," in *HKS,* p. 459, dated to 1282. For Ōsumi, see *KI,* 16, pp. 318–325, dated to 1276. For Hitachi, see *KI,* 16, p. 261, also dated to 1276.

interpret these figures, but one possible view is that the provincial administrators knew that only about 75 *chō* regularly provided rice, and therefore, when it came time to record the "public domain" *(kōryō)* of Iriki, they listed the smaller, more realistic number.[10]

The Iriki case raises the nettlesome problem of whether and to what extent land figures in the Great Land Registers included abandoned fields. Before we take up that issue, however, it should be noted that there are several other independent corroborations for tallies recorded in the *ōtabumi,* all of which generally show that the Great Land Registers either overestimated or matched exactly the acreage listed in other surveys. (See table 1.2.) In addition to the data listed in table 1.2, it should be noted that paddy field numbers entered in the two Great Land Registers from Hitachi, dated to 1279 and 1306, show many similarities, although these may have arisen because provincial officials, too busy or lazy to survey the land themselves, merely copied the information from the earlier *ōtabumi* into the later one.[11] Finally, an analysis of the Iwami Great Land Register has shown that the list and area of properties was accurate to the date of compilation (1223).[12] Therefore, while historians will always entertain doubts about arable figures in the premodern era, it seems likely that those contained in the Great Land Registers of the Kamakura era survive the test of independent corroboration better than numbers in any earlier record.

Turning to the question of abandoned fields, I was surprised by how few references there were in the *ōtabumi* to lands out of cultivation. Only the Wakasa and Tajima documents include notations for land uncultivated *(fusaku)* or ruined by floods *(kawanari)*. Although I did not perform precise tabulations, the total for such wasted fields certainly amounts to less than 10 percent and probably less than 5 percent. Given what is known from estate surveys and other records, it seems apparent that agricultural units of the Kamakura era usually contained about 20–30 percent abandoned fields, even in the advanced Kinai.[13] As noted above, however, there is a possibility that provincial officials excluded irregularly farmed parcels when they drew up the *ōtabumi*. Therefore, for the sake of argument, let us assume that the acreage entered in the Great Land Registers encompassed only rice fields cropped fairly regularly. It should be noted that such an assumption may substantially overestimate the population supported by rice in the represented provinces, but it is less likely to produce an underestimate.

Having reasoned that the numbers in the land registers are an approximately accurate representation of the cultivation conditions for rice, I confronted another knotty problem: what was the average yield of a Kamakura paddy? Had productivity increased markedly from the eighth or even the mid-twelfth century? To begin with, a common notion is that a Kamakura rice paddy produced 1.08 *koku* of hulled rice per modern (seventeenth-century) *tan*, a figure purportedly based on Kamakura-era documents and a table contained in an early Meiji compilation.[14] Since the early Tokugawa *tan* was 20 percent smaller than the thirteenth-century version, a Kamakura *tan* would have produced about 1.3 *koku*. With a conversion of Nara and Kamakura figures to Tokugawa equivalents, it seems as though an answer to the problem of comparative productivity might be at hand. An average eighth-century rice paddy yielded a harvest of about .75 *koku* per *tan* in Tokugawa units of semi-polished grain.[15] A simple comparison with the figure of 1.08 *koku* per Tokugawa *tan* suggests that a rice harvest was 44 percent richer in the 1200s than in the 700s.

Unfortunately, this reasoning contains two critical errors. First, when I examined the Kamakura sources upon which the table was based to infer the estimate, I found that none offered data on yields. Instead, the various primary citations merely listed the amount of taxes (usually *shotō mai*) in Kamakura *koku* per unit of land. A typical entry might read as follows: (The fourth month of Jōō 2 [1223], Awaji Province,) "for Kamo Village *[gō]*, 6 *chō*, 2 *tan*, 20 *bu*: tax .3 *koku* per *tan*; for Yamada *ho* [administrative unit], 2 *chō*: tax .4 *koku* per *tan*; for East Kamiyo *ho, 2 chō, 8 tan, 350 bu*: tax .15 *koku* per *tan*."[16] The table, however, willy-nilly converts these tax rates into yields, apparently assuming that the tax rate was about 50 percent (the going rate when bureaucrats assembled the Meiji compilation). In any case, the figure of 1.3 *koku* per *tan* employed for this study is based on speculation and needs to be examined more closely.

The second mistake was the assumption that the Kamakura *koku* was equivalent to the Tokugawa *bakufu*'s (warrior government) seventeenth-century unit. During the Kamakura era there was no single, universally accepted capacity for the *koku*.[17] There was one unit for provincially administered lands *(kokugaryō)*, variously called the *hon to* or *koku to*. Although this measure derived from the Nara period (a Nara *koku* was only .406 of its Tokugawa-period namesake), some expansion or contraction had probably taken place between the eighth and twelfth or thirteenth centuries. Variation among provinces was also likely. Another measure, called the *shuden-ryō to,* also derived from an ancient precedent; unlike the units for provincially administered lands, it was considerably larger than the Nara volume. Then there was the *senshi to,* instituted by Emperor Go-Sanjō around 1070 and functioning on an archipelago-wide basis during the late Heian and Kamakura epochs. Its capacity was about 1.5 times greater than the Nara *koku* but still only 62.7 percent of the official Tokugawa unit. To make things even more complicated, most estates also had their own measures *(shō to).* In some cases, a proprietor might use the same unit for all his estates; in others, not. Different proprietors employed yet other varieties of measure *(ryōshu to)*; estate foremen developed still another *(gegyō to)* to allot food and seed to cultivators. Finally, according to cultivation conditions and other factors, estate administrators and proprietors could temporarily increase or decrease the volumes of rice they collected. Thus, by the thirteenth century, volume measures for rice and other grains were truly diverse and certainly not equivalent to the early Tokugawa unit.[18]

Having cast doubt upon these calculations, we must ask: Is there no way to determine the harvest from an "average" Kamakura rice paddy? Fortunately, materials to make a tentative estimate are available.[19] To understand how these data were obtained, it is important to know that estates often included some fields as the direct domain (demesne) of the proprietor; unlike farmers tilling other paddies and lands on an estate, cultivators traditionally paid the entire yield of the demesne to the proprietor. Historians believe that because the proprietor reserved these lands for himself, they were among the best in his estate. Nine examples of yields from such proprietor lands are extant: .4, .6, .8, .9, 1.0, 1.2, 1.4, and 1.6 *koku* of hulled rice per *tan* in estates concentrated in the productive Kinai but also found in Ise and even Tōtōmi. Officials recorded a yield of 2.0 *koku* per *tan* for Tara in 1243, a figure that was presumably about the highest possible at that time.[20]

The next question is: What mix (in *chō*) of field quality did the average farm contain? The mean of these harvests is 1.1 *koku* per *tan,* the median being nearly the same at 1 *koku.* Since I wanted to be even more precise, I reasoned by historical analogy. Lawgivers during the Nara and Heian periods applied a legal formula of 1:2:2:2 for high-grade *(jōden),* medium-grade *(chūden),* low-grade *(geden),* and very low-grade *(gegeden)* paddies respectively.[21] Assuming that some improvement in rice agriculture had occurred by 1280, as I shall propose in chapter 2, I inferred that high-grade paddies (1.6 and 2.0 *koku* yields) composed 25 percent of the total, middle-grade paddies (1.2 and 1.4 *koku* yields) about 40 percent, and low- and and very low-grade paddies around 35 percent. For the nine cases cited above, such a mix of yields computes to 1.23 *koku* per *tan.*

Then came the problem of what measure officials utilized to obtain these various volumes of grain. Clearly, there is no way of knowing for sure, especially since all the examples come from estate lands, where foremen probably employed differing measures. Of all the capacities listed, historians can be certain only about the *senshi to,* which was around 1.5 times greater than the Nara unit. It should also be noted that the editors of the Meiji compilation used the *senshi to* in their calculations. Therefore, assuming that tax collectors made their grain measurements in *senshi to*—a measure originating in the late Heian period, widely used in Kamakura times, and carrying the prestige of imperial endorsement—I computed an average yield in terms of Nara grain measures.[22] If the average harvest was 1.23 *koku* per *tan*, then in Nara units it would have been 1.85 *koku*. Since the usual yield of a Nara paddy was 1.57 *koku* per *tan*, the ratio of Nara to Kamakura yields computes to 1:1.18. In other words, there was an 18 percent improvement in yields from the 700s to the 1200s. Given the evidence I present on Kamakura agriculture in chapter 2, such an outcome seems a bit low but might be considered testimony to the exceedingly slow progress made in rice farming over those centuries.

Another computation also seems useful. The average rice yield computed by the editors of the Meiji source, 1.3 *koku* per *tan*, also happens to be the average of yields for medium-grade paddies cited above. Assuming that the *senshi to* was in force, I arrived at a 1:1.24 ratio between Nara and Kamakura harvests. Combining this figure with the tally above, I concluded that Kamakura rice paddies were *on the average* 1.21 times more productive than those of the eighth century. Given the agricultural conditions (to be elaborated in chapter 2), this figure appears to be about right, and therefore in converting into population the rice paddy areas contained in the Kamakura Great Land Registers, I deemed the multiplier 1.2 most appropriate.

The reader may well entertain doubts about this multiplier, especially given the confusing welter of Kamakura measurements. The *koku* could easily have been larger, it might be argued, in view of the fact that no one knows the volume of estate or proprietor measuring boxes *(masu)*. At the same time, the reader should be clear about two points. First, over the entire medieval period grain measures expanded about 2.5 times.[23] Assuming that the Kamakura volume was much larger than 1.5 of its Nara counterpart raises the danger of underestimating the degree of agricultural advancement in the latter half of the medieval period, when most experts agree that tillers made the greatest progress.

Second, many Kamakura measures were probably smaller than the *senshi to*. For instance, medieval tax assessors applied the *hon to* to provincially administered lands, and these officials derived that measure from the one ordained in eighth-century law. If tradition held any force, harvests on most Kamakura lands (provincially administered fields composed about 60 percent of the total rice acreage) were probably not too different from what they had been centuries earlier. If this were so, yields may actually have fallen in some places. To be clear, such a drop in harvests was probably not normal, but it is important to bring up the possibility merely to reinforce the validity of the 1.2 multiplier.

Now let us return to estimating population. A 20 percent improvement in wet-rice yields by the mid- to late-thirteenth century would mean that one person aged six and above required 1.81 *tan,* rather than the 2.17 *tan* of the eighth century, to sustain himself for a year.[24] To complete calculating the rural populace according to the first method, I accounted for infants by adding 16 percent to the total, the same proportion employed for the tenth and mid-twelfth centuries.[25] To finish computations for the second mode, I tried to enumerate the substantial proportion of the rural population who were not rice farmers, adjusting the first total upward by a factor of 1.4. This figure is considerably higher than the estimated 10 percent for 1600 and derives from the approximate percentage of dry fields and other data in the premodern and modern periods.[26]

The results of these computations for thirteen provinces, ranging from southern Kyushu to the Kanto, appear in table 1.3. From these numbers, the following generalizations seem to be in order, especially when comparisons are made to the computations for the mid-twelfth century. First, in Kyushu the population probably grew, especially in the north. Utilizing the calculations done according to the second method, I arrived at an increase of 35 percent over the thirteenth century. Second, in western Honshu and the near Kinai, contraction from the ninth to the thirteenth centuries seems to have been the rule, but the two sets of computations may lead to divergent outcomes. When I assumed that the ōtabumi figures embraced all provincial residents, the population of these five provinces fell by a whopping 43 percent; when I made allowance for the non-rice-farming populace, the region decreased by a mere 2 percent. I was particularly struck by the sharp drop in Iwami, a phenomenon responsible for much of the decline in this region. Third, along the Japan Sea littoral (Noto) and in the eastern Kanto (Hitachi), demographic collapse seems to have taken place: Noto's residents decreased by about two-thirds, continuing a long-term trend of population shrinkage dating back to the ninth century, while the number of Hitachi's inhabitants lessened by about three-quarters. Overall, the population of this random collection of thirteen provinces from the Kamakura era dropped by 14–59 percent, depending upon the method of calculation. Since the sample is random and subject to the vagaries of historical survival, I did not think it appropriate to place too great a weight on the precise sum.

TABLE 1.3
Populations for Thirteen Provinces during the Kamakura Period

PROVINCE	820[a]	Ca. 950[b]	1150	1280[c]
		YEAR		
A. Kyushu provinces				
Satsuma	17,400	28,500	34,048	25,700
		[26,942]		[35,980]
Ōsumi	17,400	18,400	29,028	19,336
		[26,942]		[27,070]
Hyūga	47,700	43,800	51,175	51,681
		[26,942]		[72,353]
Buzen	75,300	71,600	81,535	85,238
		[74,090]		[119,333]
Bungo	82,500	87,400	46,685	44,631
		[42,097]		[62,483]
Hizen	85,400	81,400	83,021	87,929
		[78,019]		[123,101]
Kyushu total	325,700	331,100	325,492	314,515
		[275,032]		[440,321]
B. West-central provinces				
Tango	49,200	50,700	34,147	29,910
		[26,695]		[41,874]
Wakasa	28,900	28,300	19,358	14,215
		[20,863]		[19,901]
Tajima	104,200	87,000	47,752	35,800
		[42,411]		[50,120]
Awaji	12,300	14,900	17,700	14,631
		[14,874]		[20,483]
Iwami	49,200	45,900	30,046	9,459
		[27,419]		[13,243]
West-central total	243,800	226,100	149,003	104,015
		[132,262]		[145,621]
C. Noto Province	62,200	45,300	52,291	15,734
		[46,059]		[22,028]

Table 1.3 continues

Table 1.3 continued

PROVINCE	YEAR			
	820[a]	Ca. 950[b]	1150	1280[c]
D. Hitachi Province	232,000[d]	216,900	259,252	57,712
		[225,038]		[80,797]
Grand total	863,700	829,400	786,038	491,976
		[678,391]		[688,766]

[a]The figures for 820 can be found in Sawada, *Nara chō jidai*, pp. 187–190.
[b]Upper figures in this column are for 927; lower ones are for 935.
[c]To compute the upper figure for 1280, I divided the total rice acreage found in the Great Land Registers by the amount necessary to sustain one adult (.181) and added 16 percent to account for children under age six. Thus for Satsuma, for example, 4,010 divided by .181 equals 22,155. Multiplying by 1.16 yields 25,700. The numbers in brackets assume that the *ōtabumi* do not compensate for non-rice-farming rural people and thus add 40 percent, as indicated in the text.
[d]Total computed by Kamata, "Kodai no jinkō," p. 141.

In general, the figures in table 1.3 seem plausible, but the populations inferred for three provinces—Iwami, Noto, and Hitachi—invite skepticism. It seems likely that surveyors completing the *ōtabumi* failed to record all the land under rice cultivation, thus leading to unreasonably low totals. For instance, the Hitachi land register may have recorded only the land the rice yields of which were used for the reconstruction of Ise Shrine; it could well be that assessors omitted noncontributing paddies.

In answer to this criticism, four points seem relevant. First, for both Iwami and Hitachi, other surveys provide independent corroboration for the tallies listed in the land registers. While it is impossible to know about what went unrecorded, the corroboration provides a measure of reassurance that the *ōtabumi* of these two provinces were fairly accurate.

Second, in the case of Noto and Iwami, the decline in the population was a long-term phenomenon dating back to the ninth century. To be sure, decreases were particularly sharp over the late twelfth and thirteenth centuries, but given the peripheral status of these two provinces at the time, a sharply declining trend may not be unthinkable. Third, it should be noted that Iwami, Noto, and Hitachi share certain geographical characteristics. Both Iwami and Noto border on the Japan Sea, while Noto and Hitachi are located in northern and eastern Honshu.

Fourth, in Hitachi, where demographic collapse appears to have

been the most dramatic, the *ōtabumi* reveals that the shift in political to-
pography was equally radical. In particular, northern Hitachi went from
a densely settled region in the mid- and late Heian period to a no-man's-
land by the late 1200s. During the heyday of Chinese-style institutions,
northern Hitachi contained three districts *(gun)*, fifty-one administrative
villages, and an estimated population of seventy-four thousand. By 1306,
administrators had combined the three districts into one (called Oku, or
"the hinterland"), and the recorded population had dropped to about
fifteen thousand. This shift alone accounts for about half the decrease
in Hitachi's inhabitants. Therefore, while the Hitachi Great Land Register undoubtedly is a less than perfect reflection of the province's cultivated rice fields, dramatic depopulation over the period 1150–1300
seems apparent.

Accepting that the figures derived from the thirteen *ōtabumi* represent a fair degree of demographic reality, I then needed to infer a population for the entire archipelago in the late thirteenth century. Of course,
this estimation entails a good deal of guesswork, given that data originate from only thirteen widely scattered provinces. However, noting
that with the striking exceptions of Iwami, Noto, and Hitachi, population seems to have held constant or even increased, I contend that the
total population of rural Japan in the late thirteenth century was only
marginally less than it had been 130 years earlier—that is, approximately 5.5–6 million.

To this range I added Japan's urban population, primarily represented by the two great political centers of Kyoto and Kamakura. Scholars have estimated that Kyoto in the late Heian period was home to one
hundred thousand people, and that figure seems likely to have remained
about the same in 1280. Historians have attempted various tabulations
for Kamakura, the usual range being between sixty and one hundred
thousand.[27] The latter figure seems large, given the mountainous terrain
within which the city is located; moreover, in digging Nara and Kyoto, archaeologists have remarked upon the high percentage of vacant lots and
considerable distance among residences.[28] Furthermore, Kamakura contained many sizable warrior mansions, further decreasing the space for
smaller commoner houses. If we apply such thinking to the warrior capital, sixty thousand would probably be a generous estimate. Finally, late-
thirteenth-century Japan had a few other small cities, such as Hakata,
Ōtsu, Yodo, and Hyōgo. Another forty thousand for these seems fair,
bringing the overall urban population to two hundred thousand—at least

until archaeologists are able to excavate the pertinent areas and provide more realistic numbers.[29]

To sum up, including an urban population of about 200,000, the archipelago's inhabitants probably numbered around 5.7–6.2 million in the late thirteenth century. As further support for this range, it should be noted that another recent study has concluded that Japan's population in 1250 was about 6.5 million, slightly larger than the estimate offered here.[30] Even if this higher total is more accurate, it confirms that the period from 1150 to 1280 represented the continuation, and probably the end, of Japan's long second cycle of demographic growth and stasis.

What factors kept Japan's population static and prevented it from commencing a third wave of growth earlier? The estimates from the Great Land Registers provide one hint since the overall trend suggests increase in Kyushu, stasis in most of central and western Honshu, and drastic decline in eastern and northern Honshu. A careful examination of Kamakura records shows how this state of affairs came into being.

MORTALITY FACTORS: DISEASE

Nearly thirty years ago in *Plagues and Peoples,* William McNeill proposed a diminishing role for pestilence in medieval Japan. In his view, the deadly foreign-borne epidemics of the 700s were naturally being transformed by the late 1100s into less lethal, endemic "childhood diseases." He cited original sources stating that measles and smallpox afflicted primarily infants beginning in 1224 and 1243 respectively.[31] The assumption behind McNeill's simple division of pathogenic outbreaks into "epidemic" and "endemic" types was that as various microbes become more common in society, immunities rise and the effect on population growth presumably lessens. Other scholars also write of declining mortality from infectious outbreaks during the Kamakura era.[32] Moreover, these plagues originated within the archipelago.

It is, however, too simplistic to assume that endemic "childhood diseases" by their very nature result in lessened mortality and greater population growth. In *The Natural History of Infectious Disease,* microbiologists criticize the simple division of infectious afflictions into epidemic—that is, many cases concentrated in time and space—versus endemic—that is, illnesses always present in the community—as "a very unsatisfactory dichotomy" not applicable to the real world. For example, in many cases it may be true that an endemic disease killing a fixed, low percentage of infants and young children every year or so could be even more devastating than an epidemic of the same disease that visited infrequently but carried off a high percentage of victims of all ages when it came. Remember also that a child who dies will never have the chance to reproduce, although his or her parents may choose to have another child to restore their loss. By contrast, adults dying in an epidemic may have already borne some young, but they take more years to replace. The problem for the historian is that plagues, which typically kill adults and may create great social, economic, and political turmoil, are tumultuous events usually noted in the records, while endemic diseases taking a constant toll on infants and young children rarely attract the chronicler's attention.[33]

Consider the case of smallpox in Japan. This affliction was endemic by at least the twelfth century, somewhat earlier than McNeill thought, as various pieces of anecdotal testimony attest.[34] By the Tokugawa period the virus was a constant drag on population growth, occasionally accounting for as much as 10 percent of all deaths or about one-fourth of the mortality among infants.[35] Lacking data of the sort available for the early modern age, scholars cannot be certain, but it seems almost certain that smallpox killed at least as many in the thirteenth century as it did later and was still a substantial damper on demographic growth even though the virus was fairly common in Japanese society by 1150.

To evaluate the effects of disease more precisely, it is necessary to examine the characteristics influencing the prevalence of infections. There are three factors that can be assessed for the medieval era: the qualities of the microorganism in question, the probability of contact between a susceptible host and a patient during the time the patient is infectious, and the extent to which the population is already immune to the disease under consideration.[36] For the period 1150–1280, my conclusion is that with one crucial exception, these three variables either remained constant or, more probably, improved somewhat since (1) sources mention only one new and rather benign disease (chicken pox) for one year; (2) transportation and other factors affecting the transmission of microorganisms remained unchanged from the previous epoch, as suggested in chapter 2; and (3) the population was probably more immune to pathogens present in Japan in the twelfth and thirteenth centuries than ever before.

Data relating to disease outbreaks would seem to confirm that infections were taking a lesser toll on the population. Smallpox continued to be the most frequently recorded illness in this epoch, breaking out in twelve years over this period. Only one outbreak seems to have been especially severe, however. Measles visited just five times; it, along with dysentery and chicken pox—all three diseases with only a minor impact on mortality—claimed victims in a handful of years. Chroniclers noted tuberculosis, malaria, and other sicknesses, but they had probably been present long before 1150, and the fragmentary nature of the sources makes it difficult to assess their demographic impact.[37] Hansen's disease was certainly more common, but it is not normally considered a fatal illness.[38] Generally speaking, therefore, the most deadly killers of ages past were notable for their rarity, again with the caveat that routine, endemic killers were just not recorded.

Yet one virus appeared with striking regularity and lethality: influenza *(gaibyō)*.[39] Elsewhere I have described the epidemic of 1134–1135, apparently related to unusually damp and cold weather.[40] Forty percent of all influenza plagues erupting before 1600 occurred between 1143 and 1365.[41] Three of the seven Heian-period influenza outbreaks took place after 1080, and eight widespread occurrences—or about 25 percent of the total for the Kamakura epoch—claimed their victims between 1240 and 1370. It seems likely that the influenza virus of this subperiod had mutated into a new and more deadly form, which, when combined with a colder and damper climate, claimed more victims than at any other time in premodern Japanese history.

Disease was still an important, if perhaps declining, component in mortality between 1150 and 1280. With the exception of influenza, outbreaks were rarer and less lethal than before 1150, but it is wise to remember that the death rate from common, endemic microbes cannot be measured. Just as we cannot be sure that the *ōtabumi* encompass all rice fields under cultivation, scholars cannot ascertain how many infants and children succumbed to smallpox, measles, or some other disease that historians of the period chose to ignore.

MORTALITY FACTORS: FAMINE

If we grant that microbial killers may have been subsiding somewhat after 1150, how is it possible that the number of the archipelago's residents did not grow significantly between 1150 and 1280? William McNeill, discussing the European population after 1700, is especially relevant here: "The result of such systematic lightening of the microparasitic drain . . . was, of course, to unleash the possibility of systematic growth. This was, however, only a possibility, since any substantial local growth quickly brought on new problems: in particular, problems of food supply, water supply, and intensification of other infections in cities that had outgrown older systems of waste disposal."[42] To be sure, a comparison of late Heian and Kamakura Japan with Western Europe after 1700 is inexact: Western Europe was much more highly developed economically, with a higher percentage of city dwellers. McNeill's essential point, however, remains applicable: two previously less significant causes of death unleashed a new lethality and combined to keep mortality at about the same level as before.

In the case of medieval Japan, food supply was the problem that came to prominence, although growing political instability and war also had a hand to play in the demographic game. As if to proclaim the dawn of a new era, ex-emperor Go-Shirakawa commissioned *The Hungry Ghosts Scroll* in the late twelfth century; its depictions of hungry specters are horrific even when viewed by the modern eye. (See frontispiece.) In fact, Go-Shirakawa's patronage of the painting might even be seen as an act of statesman-like foresight because the wily old politician had pinpointed the archipelago's main problem for the next several centuries.[43]

To be specific, just as the latter Tokugawa age has become famous for its three death-dealing famines of the Kyōhō, Tenmei, and Tenpō year-periods, so three less well-known famines—and probably far more lethal, if we compare death rates—ravaged the population in late Heian and Kamakura times. Like the early modern crises, the earlier catastrophes are known by their year-periods—Yōwa, Kangi, and Shōga—and their effects went beyond a temporary shortage of grain. Also as in the Tokugawa era, they signaled the end of one of Kitō's long cycles of demographic growth. These three famines, combined with the constant depletion of children by endemic disease and the depredations of war and the samurai, were the chief reasons that the archipelago's population remained essentially stable until about 1280.

The Yōwa Famine, 1180–1182

Of the three major famines, the Yōwa crisis is probably the least well documented and yet most widely known to the English-speaking world. Both phenomena stem from the same fact: the Yōwa year-period included the second and third years of the epochal struggle between the Taira and Minamoto lineages and their various allies and enemies. Historical materials are less apt to survive during periods of widespread conflict.[44] Because the Yōwa famine is relatively well known, I shall sketch it briefly.

Bad times dated from 1180, when little rain fell and the harvest was poor.[45] A monthly tabulation made from entries in aristocratic diaries reveals that from the first through the tenth months of 1180 on average there were only 7.2 days in which authors wrote of any moisture at all. For the ninth month, *A Record of the Rise and Fall of the Minamoto and Taira (Genpei jōsui ki)* used the word "famine," in which many had starved to death. The only way to survive was to leave home and migrate to the mountains and moors, abandoning family members to face almost certain death.

Without reserves of grain from the previous autumn, 1181 was even worse, it appears. The drought-induced famine is a constant refrain in Kujō Kanezane's diary: in the intercalary second month, he wrote that "the [Taira] Search-and-Punish Mission [aimed against the rebels] stationed in Mino has no provisions, and they are likely to starve to death." Four days later he made the same point. In the seventh month, he described the need to rebuild Kōfukuji and Tōdaiji, recently incinerated by Taira troops: "Even in a good year, we would become mired down completing these tasks; how much more so when people are starving to death?" Another aristocrat, Yoshida Tsunefusa writing in his diary, *Kikki,* added to the gloom by reporting that in the fourth month, as he was about to pass by Sanjō-Karasuma in Kyoto, he spied the corpses of eight starvation victims: "Therefore, I did not go there. Recently, we could almost say that the roads have been filled with dead bodies." The court annal *Hyakuren shō* provides a gruesome summary of the events of 1181 when it laconically states that "all under heaven suffered from famine; the number of those who have starved to death was unknown."

Historians will also forever remember 1181 as a famine year because Kamo no Chōmei wrote down his memories of the capital in that terrible year in his 1212 composition, *An Account of My Hut:*

> About 1181 . . . there was a famine that lasted two years, a most terrible thing. A drought persisted through the spring and summer. . . .
>
> Some of the people as a result abandoned their lands and crossed into other provinces; some forgot their homes and went to live in the mountains. . . .
>
> The capital had always depended on the countryside for its needs, and when supplies ceased to come it became quite impossible for people to

maintain their composure. They tried in desperation to barter for food one after another of their possessions, however cheaply, but no one desired them. The rare person who was willing to trade had contempt for money and set a high value on his grain. . . .

The lower classes and the wood-cutters were also at the end of their strength, and even as firewood grew scarce those without other resources broke up their own houses and took wood to sell in the market. . . .

In an attempt to determine how many had died, they made a count during the fourth and fifth months, and found within the boundaries of the capital over 42,300 corpses lying in the streets.[46]

This impressionistic narrative repeated many of the themes found in other sources; the figure 42,300 may have been inflated, but it has a precision suggesting intimate knowledge of the city's plight. After mid-1181 the war stopped for two years because of the lack of provisions owing to crop failure.[47]

Although sources are sparser, it is clear that the famine did not abate in 1182. A court history states that people were still starving in Kyoto, as robbery and arson flourished amid streets littered with abandoned children and rotting corpses. To add to the misery, an epidemic spread among the populace, although it is likely that the illness was really a debilitating diarrhea brought on during the last stages of starvation. In the tenth month, the court historian affirmed Kamo's account that since the summer of 1181 residents of Kyoto had been tearing down their homes and selling the lumber as firewood; the Investigators (*kebiishi chō*, Kyoto police) tried to stop this practice but apparently had little success. The disappearance of residences and people undoubtedly cast an eerie pall over the capital.

Drought was the immediate precipitating factor behind the Yōwa crisis, and in this sense it was a quintessential famine of the ancient age.[48] To elaborate, the middle and late Heian period appears to have been an epoch of unusual heat.[49] Data taken from Japanese sources, such as the dates noted in aristocratic diaries when cherry blossoms bloomed or when the ice on Lake Suwa melted, implied that the warming trend was equivalent to a rise in mean temperature of 2.6 degrees Centigrade as compared to the 1970s. More recent work by archaeologists and historians has corroborated this hypothesis.[50] Moreover, this inference asserting an especially warm Heian era meshes with evidence drawn from contemporary European and other sources.[51] The drought parching rice paddies and killing off wheat seedlings at this time was part of a world-wide climatic event taking place during the eighth through the twelfth centuries.

The impact of the famine on Kyoto is well documented in materials such as Kamo's *An Account of My Hut*. In fact, when scholars look for signs of the crisis in the provinces, results indicate that the brunt of the Yōwa famine was felt in western and central Japan, especially in the Kinai. The most detailed and poignant description originates with an 1181 petition written by the local foreman of Nagaizumi Estate in Izumi Province seeking tax relief for his cultivators: "In addition to the drought striking everywhere throughout the realm last year, because this year has been twice as bad, all crops throughout the province have been damaged or destroyed. . . . Because of this, peasants this year lack the strength to pay the rice tax *[onnengu mai]*. . . . Even last year they remitted only one-third the amount usually due. . . . I urge the authorities to encourage the people of the estate to give up their thoughts of running away, and to come up with a plan to settle them down."[52]

Also in 1181, the monk Kōun reported that his Kawachi estate would be unable to provide military provisions because of drought damage.[53] An 1182 record from Kongōji, a temple located near modern Osaka, mentions the famine as one cause for the turbulent state of society.[54] A prayer sent from the imperial house to the Shinto deities in the fourth month of 1182 begs for weather in which "wind and rain would follow harmoniously" and a bountiful harvest fill storehouses.[55] Finally, an 1183 order from the court to monks on Mt. Kōya mentions "anxiety about the drought" and that "those who had died young choked the roads."[56] Outside of these explicit references, there is little to suggest massive starvation in the provinces, although I was struck by the repeated appearance of documents dealing with dry fields and their crops, the nonpayment of taxes, and the inability to collect, or the remission of, labor dues.[57]

One thing seems certain: residents of Kyoto suffered the most, and in their case the dearth of grain was due at least somewhat to human, and not natural, causes.[58] During the height of the famine in 1182, a reliable source entitled *The Record of 1182 (Yōwa ninen ki)* stated that when Kiso no Yoshinaka rebelled in the provinces along the Japan Sea, "because roads were impassable, aristocrats and servants throughout the capital had little clothing or food." In an entry for late 1183, Kanezane wrote that "high and low in the central provinces *[chūgoku]* are bound to starve to death."[59] As a city dependent upon the surrounding countryside for provisions, Kyoto's plight was no mystery; the dual crises of drought and war multiplied the suffering manyfold.

The reaction of city dwellers and the court to such circumstances is fascinating and provides a contrast to the role that urban centers played during famines of the late medieval and Tokugawa epochs. Just prior to the famous imperial decree of the tenth month of 1183, when the court in effect granted Yoritomo the right to rule the Kanto, settle land disputes, and see that taxes flowed smoothly to Kyoto, Kanezane noted that "high and low alike mostly have fled to the countryside, because the city is blocked off on four sides."[60] To the west, there was the Taira stronghold, along the Japan Sea littoral reigned Kiso no Yoshinaka, and in the Kanto and the Tōkaidō Yoritomo held sway. Given the drought and devastation of war, Kyotoites could not survive on what the immediate vicinity could produce. Residents on the brink of starvation tore down their houses, sold what they could, and fled to the mountains and wilderness, where hunting, fishing, and gathering might see them through the crisis. The combination of the Yōwa famine and the Genpei Wars choked off Kyoto, leading both to the depopulation of the city and the broad grant of authority to Yoritomo, which was later to form one basis for the legitimacy of the Kamakura regime.

In sum, the Yōwa crisis was similar to most famines that struck the islands during the Nara and Heian periods: it was caused by drought, had its major impact in central and western Japan, and drove capital dwellers from their homes. To be sure, it is not clear which provinces were most harshly affected, nor can demographers come anywhere near to assessing overall mortality. Troops fighting in the Genpei Wars exacerbated the crisis by blocking off supply arteries and foraging for crops in the fields of hapless peasants, especially near Kyoto. In this sense the Yōwa famine was a true "macroparasitic event" and a fitting introduction to the medieval age.

The Kangi Famine, 1229–1232

Unlike its predecessor, the Kangi famine, possibly the most lethal in Japanese history, is well documented. Moreover, while the famine struck hardest over a period of four years, its social, economic, and political ramifications can be measured in decades. Finally, the origins of the Kangi famine were different from those of the Yōwa, and the Kangi famine probably killed more people in eastern Honshu than in western

Japan. All in all, it comprised one of the major turning points in Kama-kura history, certainly ranking with the Jōkyū War of 1221, the Mongol Invasions of 1274 and 1281, and Go-Daigo's revolt of 1331.

Beginning in the 1200s, reliable sources contain repeated references to heavy rains, strong winds, hail, and frost.[61] Drought punctuated these conditions, often leading to crop failure and regional famines, but from 1225, the unpredictably wet and windy weather seems to have become more troublesome. The year 1226 was particularly bad: the rain was so hard and continuous in the sixth and seventh months that the court sent out prayers for it to stop. The summer of 1227 was similarly wet, as noted by governments in both Kyoto and Kamakura, while the courtier Fujiwara Teika described the twelfth month as having a cold wind be-yond his expectation for winter. Once again in 1228, temple records and *Hyakuren shō* are filled with notations of long and heavy rains, such that the Kamo River flooded. Materials from the Tohoku (Aizu) and Kii also complain of too much moisture. Then, in the tenth month of 1228, a typhoon destroyed homes in Kamakura "beyond counting."

In 1229, most records are silent, but it seems as if a drought struck and the harvest failed, and by the third month three different writers state that a famine had set upon the land. Hōjō Yasutoki, the leader of the Kamakura shogunate, pressured the wealthy to lend money and rice to the poor to keep them alive. The drought continued into the eighth month, when suddenly *Mirror of the East (Azuma kagami)* began noting heavy rains and wind. There is some evidence that this condition also prevailed in Kyoto by the tenth month. Therefore, even in 1229, both governments were aware that many commoners were on the verge of starvation.

Perhaps good weather and a bountiful harvest in 1230 would have succored the peasantry and righted the dual ships of state, but instead there followed the most inclement, untoward conditions yet. On the elev-enth of the fifth month, Teika wrote in his splendid diary, *A Record of the Bright Moon (Meigetsu ki)*, that it rained all night. Then, almost as an afterthought, he mentioned that "until today this year has been cool," adding that the frigid temperatures meant that he had to wear more clothing. On the seventeenth it rained again in Kyoto.

Then on the ninth of the sixth month *Mirror of the East* noted a thunderstorm accompanied by strong winds; heavy rains and gusts re-sumed on the fourteenth in Kamakura. Rains also fell in Musashi about the same time; then on the sixteenth, officials of Makita Estate in Mino relayed to the shogunate the unheard-of news that snow had fallen. The *Mirror* goes on to note that the sixth month had been unusually wet and cold; there were no comparable conditions recorded as far back as the reign of Emperor Suiko in the early seventh century. Fears were expressed about the harvest, and then throughout the month more descriptions of snow filtered into both Kyoto and Kamakura from Shinano, Kōzuke, Mino (several times), and other provinces. At Namatsu Estate in Mino the snow was measured at two inches *(nisun)*; other locales in the province estimated the snowfall at three feet *(sanshaku)*. Yasutoki must have been heartened to know that the snow was not as deep in the provinces adjoining Mino.

Back in Kyoto, Fujiwara Teika wrote that "this morning [the sixteenth of the sixth month] was just like autumn." Complaints about the cold, wet weather fill Teika's diary for the sixth month; he repeatedly lamented his need to wear more clothing. It grew so cold that the blossoms on his Chinese scholar tree *(enju)* withered and fell off. Later in the month the court tried to restrict the skyrocketing price of rice to one string of cash for a *koku*. The seventh month—correlating to late summer in the solar calendar—witnessed more signs of cold, damp weather, this time in the form of frost in various provinces.

The eighth and ninth months delivered the knockout punch. Teika once again noted high winds and rain on the eighth of the eighth month and a "great rain *[ōame]* on the second of the ninth month." Since the ninth month coincided with the harvest, Teika, who lived off his share of the yield from various estates, began to report crop failures. On the third of the ninth month, he asserted that fields along the Japan Sea littoral north of Kyoto *(Hokuriku dō)* were damaged and destroyed "because of the cold." From a messenger he learned that his estates in Shikoku would provide nothing for him that year. On the tenth day, he described Kyushu as "destroyed," but reports of damaged and failed harvests came to Teika from various directions *(shohō)*. Weather in Teika's diary continued to be described as wet and windy throughout this time, even in the tenth month. There were days when the sun never appeared. On the twenty-first of the eleventh month, it may have turned unseasonably warm, as Teika wrote that in assorted provinces recent tiny sprouts of wheat plants were visible; he stated that it was just like the third month of any normal year. As cherry blossoms opened along Shirakawa, he witnessed persons eating bamboo shoots. On the twenty-fifth, he noted similar behavior in the Kanto; the *Mirror* also describes rainstorms and high winds during this time.

Previously, on the twenty-fifth of the ninth month, Teika had taken a concrete action to succor the starving. He had one of his servants dig up his gardens and plant wheat. He wrote: "Even though it is only a little bit, its purpose is to support the hungry during this awful year. One shouldn't insult the poor. Is there something else I can do?" Later, in the eleventh month, as he recorded more snow, Teika and his colleagues among the civil aristocracy met to decide how to deal with the crisis; conditions were "depressing." In one Harima estate, crop failure led to a protest of cultivators and low-ranking officials; Teika was of the opinion that this year little, if anything, would be available as his share of the harvest.

From the start of 1231, sources are unanimous in their assessment that a great famine was killing many. In *Hyakuren shō* it was noted that "from spring all under heaven have suffered from famine. This summer, corpses fill the streets; there has not been a famine like this since the Jishō era [1180]."[62] Soon pestilence joined famine; once again, since no disease was specified, it is likely that the epidemic was diarrhea occurring in the last stages of starvation. Statements about hunger, pestilence, and roads littered with the dead are so common for 1231 that they do not bear repeating.

Yet the weather and agricultural conditions did not improve. In the third month, Teika wrote of "typhoons and rain" violent enough to wreck houses and uproot trees. In the fourth month those who had imbibed from a dark pool in Kamakura were all found dead. Peasants in Iga protested to their proprietor Tōdaiji that while no area had escaped desolation, their estate exceeded even the worst case; since the cultivators had mostly starved to death or fled, they pleaded for a tax remittance. In the fifth month, rumors spread around Kyoto that mobs were breaking into the homes of the wealthy and after eating their fill, walking off with cash and rice. In the sixth month, a long rain resulted in a flood in Kyoto, where corpses lined the riverbanks. Prayers to halt the downpour were to no avail.

As the famine continued, civil order broke down, with reports of robber gangs and Kyoto shrines and temples providing their own security. In the seventh month, an interesting measure of the effects of the famine appears in aristocratic diaries. Palanquin bearers for the highborn were too weak from hunger to do their jobs and simply collapsed while bearing their esteemed riders. Eventually, it was revealed that over the last two years all but two or three of these menials had starved to death. The deceased seemed to be beyond number, recorded casually time and again by aristocrats sickened by the sight and smell of rotting flesh. On the seventeenth of the seventh month, Kyoto was the scene of another thunderstorm with heavy rains. By the eighth month, it was "cold just like winter."

After another all-day rain in Kyoto on the third of the ninth month, Kageyukōji Tsunemitsu, a minor noble and author of the diary *Minkei ki,* summed up the year so far:

> This year the entire realm was stricken with famine; the people have been wiped out. . . . From the third to the eighth months the gist of the realm *[tenka]* has been the same everywhere: a sad lamentation. . . . And a popular song goes: "Next year again there will be more famine." This year's area under cultivation amounts to only about half the usual; there are no people and no seed. Along with the uncropped portion, this year the wheat for the autumn has all withered and died. If some should happen to come forth, it is all eaten up and thus more wheat cannot be planted. In every case [the hungry] completely lay waste to the mounded rows *(guro)* with wheat on them. If a person searches out the price for wheat seed, it takes 1.2 *koku* of rice to buy just .3 *koku* of wheat seed. Thus next year there ought not to be any wheat. There is no doubt that next year people will be hungry.[63]

The year concluded with another downpour on the last day of the twelfth month in Kamakura.

Although written sources are sparser, 1232 did indeed witness a continuation of inclement weather and starvation. In the second month, Kyotoites were victims of an influenza epidemic, which they named the "barbarian sickness" *(ibyō);* on the twenty-sixth of that month, the court issued an order prohibiting the sale of wheat seedlings for cattle or horse fodder. In the fourth, fifth, and sixth months, once again it rained and rained until the court sent out prayers for the skies to close up; great winds blew through Kamakura. Yet the same conditions prevailed in the fall until it became colder, and once again the roads were filled with dying people. Indeed, for the next several years, the historian is struck by the repeated references to downpours, flooding, high winds, and snow in midsummer.

The proximate cause of the Kangi famine seems to have been wet, cold weather. Yet most Japanese climatologists are just beginning to address the thirteenth century directly, preferring to concentrate on the

warming trends apparent in the Heian era.[64] Recently, however, authors
of a local history have argued that the Kamakura era witnessed a shift
from the recurrent drought of the ancient age to cold, wet conditions.[65]
By their estimate, the "Little Ice Age" *on average* saw temperatures over
one degree Centigrade lower per annum than in preceding centuries. The
sudden fall in temperatures, it has been argued, was the result of volcanic
activity and the disappearance of large sunspots, which meant less solar
activity and a reduced amount of heat energy reaching the earth's surface. Other highly regarded medieval historians are beginning to second
this opinion.[66]

As an initial means to test this hypothesis, I collected and compared
weather references for selected centuries. (See table 1.4.) Although any
such compilation is admittedly subjective, in part because records do not
reveal regional or annual variations very clearly, table 1.4 supports the
view that conditions during 1000–1300 became progressively wetter and
colder, perhaps producing a "Little Ice Age" by the 1200s. The contrast
between the warm, drought-ridden eighth century and the cold, wet thirteenth is particularly striking.[67]

Instructive data on volcanism and climate in East Asia are available
for the epoch 1200–1699.[68] Ice core and tree ring studies help climatologists measure the prevalence of volcanism and its attendant climatic
effects, and "dust veil" and "volcanic explositivity" indices serve as indicators of colder, wetter weather on the affected areas of the earth's surface.
Most important, such information yields specific years when volcanism
played a major role in East Asian weather, and citations from Chinese,
Korean, and Japanese records corroborate the scientific data. The period
1225–1233 was apparently a time of unusual worldwide volcanic activity,
affecting not only East Asia, but also North America, Scandinavia, and
even north Africa.[69] The so-called "Northern Hemisphere Ice-Volcanic Index" reveals several spikes around 1230. It reinforces the descriptive
sources to indicate that the crop failures resulting in the Kangi famine
were in great part the result of unusually cold, damp weather that may
have been induced by volcanism.

Only when there are Japanese archaeological studies of the type and
range performed by European historians will scholars be certain
whether the idea of a "Little Ice Age" might be applicable to Kamakura
Japan. At present, however, we can only assume that the Kangi famine
was indeed caused by abnormally cold, wet weather, probably induced
by the dust and gases catapulted into the stratosphere when volcanoes

TABLE 1.4
Climatological Trends, 700–1300

PERIOD OF ENTRIES	WEIGHTED NUMBER OF ENTRIES				
	RAIN	COLD	HEAT	DRYNESS	TOTAL
697–791	59	10	67	103	239
Percentile	25%	4%	28%	43%	
	Drought index: 43		Wet, cold index: 29		
1000–1099	52	24	35	55	166
Percentile	31%	14%	21%	33%	
	Drought index: 33		Wet, cold index: 46		
1150–1200	133	10	42	72	257
Percentile	52%	4%	16%	28%	
	Drought index: 28		Wet, cold index: 57		
1200–1299	377	85	121	207	790
Percentile	48%	11%	15%	26%	
	Drought index: 26		Wet, cold index: 58		

Sources: For the eighth century, *Rikkoku shi sakuin* for the *Shoku Nihongi.* For the eleventh, twelfth, and thirteenth centuries, exclusively Sasaki Junnosuke, *Kikin to senso,* pp. 1–5.
Note: In weighting the various entries, I counted snow, frost, and hail as one point each for moisture and cold; drought counted as one point for both hot and dry; prayers for rain were entered as one point for dryness, and prayers to stop rain the opposite. Flood, great rain, violent rain, long rain, and even wind and rain all were considered to be one point for dampness. The drought index was arrived at by dividing the references to drought by the total number of entries; the wet, cold index was the result of dividing the references to wet and cold by the total number of entries.

erupted in East Asia, Siberia, and/or North America. Until 1230, the Kangi disaster was an unusual event in Japanese history, really the first recorded subsistence crisis of its magnitude caused by cold weather. Yet it was also a harbinger of death-dealing famines to come.

How many persons perished during the Kangi famine? Descriptive accounts suggest high mortality; repeated references to "roads littered with dead" and "abandoned children" and the countermeasures and long-term effects (to be noted momentarily) give the impression of an unparalleled death rate. Moreover, later sources usually put the proportion of victims at one-third of the population. That figure, however, is likely a set phrase used to describe any event that seemed to kill many people. Fortunately, other measures can be employed to gain a more precise idea of the famine's toll.

Two quantitative examples originate from central Japan, and while scholars will, as always, argue about exact percentages, it is clear that a sizable number of the archipelago's inhabitants died from the 1229–1232 crisis. The first case comes from Koazaka Estate *(mikuriya)* in Ise Province, a property belonging to Fujiwara Teika and about which he received frequent news. According to an entry in *Meigetsu ki* for 1231, probably the worst year of the famine, 62 persons died at Koazaka in the twenty-six days from the twentieth of the six month to the fifteenth of the seventh.[70] A reliable contemporary source places the total area of Koazaka at 43.8 *chō;* when we calculate according to the formula utilized for the *ōtabumi,* the total population of the estate would have been about 280 rice cultivators with householders, or about 392 if we assume that there was a substantial non-rice-farming populace attached to the estate.[71] In the first instance, mortality would have been 22 percent; in the second, it would have amounted to 15.8 percent. Without overemphasizing these figures, I should note that the computation assumes that all fields at Koazaka were cropped, a view not supported by most extant Kamakura estate records. And this death toll covered less than one month, even though the famine lasted for nearly four years.

The second instance also comes from the Kinai and tells a similar tale of high mortality, or at least massive depopulation. In 1189, long before the Kangi famine, officials made a detailed report on cultivation conditions at Esaka Village in Tarumi Nishimaki in Settsu Province.[72] According to this record, Esaka contained a bit more than 537.4 *chō* of paddy and dry fields, divided into 234 farming units.[73] Cultivators at Esaka fell mostly into one of two groups: 9 were responsible for more than 10 *chō,* while 122 cropped less than 1 *chō.*

Fortunately for historians, the proprietor, Kasuga Shrine, conducted two more surveys about fifty years later—after the famine—in 1239 and 1240.[74] These later documents did not encompass all of Esaka as the 1189 cadastre did, but instead registered lands cultivated in an area called Hozumi, a medium-sized part of the village. According to the historian who analyzed these records, in the half century between compilations, the number of farming units in Hozumi shrank from 113 to 71. Only 44 units listed in the 1189 material were also contained in the 1240 survey; 69 disappeared completely. At least as important, the way fields were farmed altered radically: large units all but disappeared, as did small ones. Instead of a wide range from 49 *chō* to less than one-hundredth of that area, the largest unit was now only 8.8 *chō,* and most cultivators tilled mid-sized parcels.

Because no one knows how many people actually comprised a farming unit, it is not fair to translate the 37.2 percent decline in listed cultivation units into mortality rates. But such a figure is suggestive. Moreover, it is notable that both tiny and huge farms disappeared, with a new concentration in the mid-ranges. If the Kangi famine was responsible for such changes, then it implies that farmers could no longer afford the labor to crop large units and that small units may not have provided enough sustenance to support a peasant and/or his/her family. This concentration in the mid-ranges suggests a parallel with paddy cultivation in the mid- to late Tokugawa era, when there was also an optimal size for farms as a result of a chronic labor shortage.[75]

Combining the results from Koazaka Estate and Esaka Village, we can see that once again, as in the Yōwa famine, mortality was high in central Honshu and the Kinai. Unfortunately, these are the only two quantifiable examples available. Still, there is good reason to believe that the death toll from the Kangi disaster was sizable in many parts of the islands. In 1231, for example, the governors of both Buzen and Settsu described their jurisdictions as "empty."[76] Moreover, although there is little direct evidence from the region, it is plausible that the Kangi famine killed even more people in eastern and northern Honshu than it did in the well-documented western archipelago. The primary basis for such an inference is that a subsistence crisis caused by cold and wet weather would have had its harshest effects in that region. Remember that Teika reported that his estates in the Japan Sea littoral north of Kyoto had all been damaged by the cold. In another famine induced by the same kind of weather in 1294, a Tōdaiji monk wrote that "the Eastern Provinces [Kanto] and the Northern Land Route *[Hokuriku dō]* have declined disastrously."

The tentative conclusion seems to be that the regional population trends evident in the Great Land Registers examined above represented the harsh realities of life during a century of unusually cold, wet weather. In northern Kyushu, where the climate would have been more benign, the population actually grew during the 1200s; in western Honshu and the near Kinai, the number of inhabitants probably held steady, except for Iwami, a snowy province facing the Japan Sea; in Noto and Hitachi, the cold, damp weather meant repeated crop failures and a striking loss of residents. To confirm this hypothesis, however, analysis of later famines is also necessary. To judge the impact of the Kangi famine, it is helpful to describe government policies and the long-term political, social, and economic ramifications.

As many as fifty-one responses to the crisis of 1229–1232 were undertaken by both the Kyoto court and the Kamakura shogunate.[77] For the most part, each resorted to tried-and-true palliatives employed by previous regimes. For example, Kyoto had religious institutions pray to the gods sixteen times over the years 1230–1232, a figure comprising well over half the initiatives known to have been taken by the court; Kamakura relied upon the deities' powers less often (only seven times). Another way to secure the blessings of heaven was to change the year-period, a court-monopolized rite invoked twice. Both administrations tried to reduce expenditures, encourage frugality, and enact sumptuary legislation, with Kyoto enunciating such policies four times and the *bakufu* twice. After the crop failure of 1230, warriors decided to eat less lavish meals, behavior that brings to mind the actions of Tokugawa samurai. In a similar vein, courtiers banned displays of expensive clothing in the summer of 1231. These old-fashioned remedies accounted for about two-thirds of the counterresponses made by both regimes.

Kyoto and Kamakura also attempted to enforce law and order and settle the myriad disputes arising during the famine. At court, one prohibition dealt with unruly monks and shrine people *(ji'nin)* in the summer of 1231; at the end of the year Kyoto issued a forty-two point list of "new institutes" *(shinsei)*, which required proper behavior from religious devotees, restricted the numbers of attendants *(bokujū)* at festivals, banned frivolous lawsuits, stringently admonished guards to make their appointed rounds, suppressed pirates in the Inland Sea and robbers in Kyoto, and proscribed the abandonment of the sick and orphaned. Capital residents were also warned to clean up the streets and bridges near their homes and to refrain from partying and gambling.[78]

Commanding most policing authority, the shogunate was more active in this sphere; about one-third of all policies drawn up by the warrior government fell under this rubric. Kamakura's first action to maintain the public safety came on the twenty-first of the fourth month in 1231, when it ordered its Rokuhara office in Kyoto to crack down on robbers, murderers, and violent unemployed persons appearing at the city's numerous festivals.[79] On the same day, the *bakufu* issued a five-article directive concerning the duties and incomes of its newest lieutenants on the land, the land stewards *(shinpo jitō)*, appointed after victory in the Jōkyū War, who obtained their rents mostly in western Japan and frequently quarreled with Kyoto proprietors.[80] Each of the five articles addressed conflicts between Kyoto lords or their officers and the land stewards. Most of the catalogue (1) stopped warriors from skimming their portion of the rice tax *(nengu)* off the top before allotting other officials their shares; (2) prevented land stewards from claiming peasant parcels *(myōden)* and denying proprietors their fair share of grain taxes and labor duties; and (3)–(5) told land stewards to keep their hands off peasant workers performing various duties *(zaike yaku)* for proprietors. Given the timing of the five-article law, it seems likely that warriors and proprietors, faced with revenue and labor shortages, were fighting among themselves for whatever surplus was available and that Kamakura was trying to keep its men in line.

Documents extant from this time suggest strongly that three phenomena—crop failure, tax nonpayment, and *jitō* (land steward) abuses—went hand in hand. Throughout the 1230s, peasants and estate officials were not shy about requesting tax relief. To cite a few examples, in 1231 peasants at Setaka Estate in Chikugo did not pay their rice dues, eventuating a conflict *(sōron)* between the proprietor and land steward.[81] At Fukui Estate in Harima, the *jitō* and his representative had not remitted the rice tax from 1229 to 1233, and they even had the temerity to quarrel over the allotment of cultivators' rations; the result was considered warrior abuse, and a judgment was handed down against the samurai by Rokuhara.[82]

Rice was not the only estate revenue that went unpaid; some records suggest that the high death toll from the famine induced a more severe labor shortage, and cultivators were as anxious to be freed of the burdensome corvée levy as land stewards were to enforce it. At Usa Shrine in Kyushu, a repair project was postponed for at least a decade: "Last 8/8/1230 [eighth day of eighth month of 1230] a violent wind suddenly blew, and when a 'spirit tree' *[reiboku]* fell over completely, the shrine halls and all the other buildings were knocked down. . . . On 7/26/1237 [twenty-sixth day of seventh month of 1237], an order *[migyōsho]* was once again handed down, but still construction has not met the schedule." This document, dated 1239, was written to prod officials into rebuilding the damaged shrine, and although it does not so state, the inability to raise sufficient labor may well have been one reason for the repeated delays.[83] Monks recorded a similar case for Mt. Kōya in 1239, when its Western Pagoda had weathered rains and snowfalls and the pillars were on the point of rotting away.[84]

It is clear that land stewards took seriously their jobs as rent collectors, whether the crop had failed or not. At Ōbe Estate in Harima, Tōdaiji protested against a land steward's representative who berated peasants with "all kinds of demands."[85] In Izumo in 1232, a murderous *jitō* went on such a rampage that he chased away all the cultivators.[86] There is a well-known case from Ōta Estate in Bingo, where the *jitō* was accused of bringing along too many assistants, stealing ripened wheat and taking the seeds, and collecting several unusual taxes.[87] A Kamakura order of 1240 cites a samurai in Aki in western Honshu who "injured and drove away cultivators"; the problems seem to have begun in the autumn of 1230, just when the famine was starting.[88]

Even though tax arrears and warrior abuses were very much on the minds of legislators in Kamakura, Hōjō Yasutoki and his administration addressed more problems affecting civil order in the summer of 1231.[89] One law directed constables *(shugo)* not to overstep the bounds of their authority; another reminded warriors to work through the Rokuhara office when disputes arose. Still a third piece of legislation cracked down on theft by setting penalties according to the amount of stolen goods: in bad cases, the offender could be incarcerated, but his family was to suffer no consequences. Fourth, the shogunate repeated the tired old ban against attacks at night *(youchi),* a particular threat because the identity of the attacker often remained unknown. On the twenty-second of the fifth month, Rokuhara punished the starving mobs that had stormed the homes of wealthy Kyotoites in search of food and valuables.

The shogunate wrote more laws trying to ensure order in 1232. On the seventh of the fourth month, it issued another directive to newly established land stewards exhorting them to extract only their due from peasants, whether it was rice, labor, or other items.[90] Two weeks later, the warrior council ordered its men to strengthen their enforcement of provisions against robbery and night attacks.[91] Three months later, members of the chief decision-making body, the *hyōjō shū,* signed an oath swearing to conduct administrative matters without taking personal advantage of the crisis *(watakushi naki no seidō).*[92]

The outlawry even spilled over into the realm of international affairs.[93] From 1223, Japanese pirates *(wakō)* from northern Kyushu had raided the Korean coast, quite probably in search of food. As the 1220s wore on, raids became more frequent and destructive, and the Koryŏ dy-

nasty requested that Kamakura take action to rein in its wayward inhabitants, many of whom turned out to be Kamakura housemen. Eventually
Yasutoki reprimanded the warrior in charge of Dazaifu, but the raids
worsened between 1229 and 1232, the height of the crisis. Only the end
to the Kangi famine brought a temporary respite for Korean residents.

While the court concentrated on rituals and the *bakufu* on crimes,
both governments devoted about equal energy to succoring victims. Documents from this era make it clear that agriculture of all types was se-
verely affected by the harsh weather. To cite a few instances, in Kuroda
New Estate in Iga, a priestly official wrote on the twenty-ninth of the
fourth month in 1231 that "the peasants' petition says that this year the
crops failed; even though it is the same throughout the realm, in this estate the damage is beyond other places."[94] The cultivators had "either
starved to death or fled, and they were nowhere to be found." According
to Imperial Prince Sonshō, the damage to farming was still readily apparent throughout the realm in the summer of 1233.[95]

One of Kyoto's economic proclamations to stem the tide has already
been noted—its attempt to place a ceiling on the price of rice on the
twenty-fourth of the sixth month in 1230. The court also doled out grain
relief *(shingō)*, a policy harking back to the eighth century, throughout
the summers of 1231 and 1232.[96] Facing another starvation year in
1232, aristocrats demanded on the twenty-sixth of the second month
that wheat no longer be provided to horses and cattle for fodder. In the
same forty-two article institute handed down on the third of the eleventh
month in 1232, Kyoto reissued an older law limiting the interest on loans
(suiko) to the amount of the principal.

If Kyoto provided more frequent economic aid to the hungry,
Kamakura made the most spectacular gesture. In fact, the first act taken
by Yasutoki, the de facto head of the *bakufu,* was to issue a call to "virtuous rule" *(tokusei rei).*[97] On the nineteenth of the third month in 1231
he had wealthier persons in charge of the warehouses in his home provinces of Izu and Suruga open their doors and lend rice to the peasantry.
The order he issued reads as follows:

> This year because of widespread famine, there are rumors that people are
> starving to death. This is most untoward. Moreover, those who usually
> lend out rice at interest in Izu and Suruga have not even begun to give it out.
> Increasingly people have no way to stay alive. Hereby I hand down an
> order to have the wealthy quickly give out their loan rice. Moreover, if

there is resistance to this order at a later date, deal with it as in the attached note.

Kangi 3/3/19 [1231] Yata Rokubeinojō[98]

Following this entry, *Mirror of the East* notes that the famine had caused farmers to give up cultivation and that Yasutoki's worries about the growing number of starving erstwhile farmers had led him to dole out to some of them thirty *koku* on his own. Initially, threats were made against peasants who failed to return the rice, but eventually Yata, an official of the administrative office *(kumonjo)* in Kamakura, oversaw the distribution of over nine thousand *koku,* and in the case of those who could not repay, he was ordered to collect lesser amounts or to "wait until next year."

There is another recent interpretation of the 1231 law and related ordinances.[99] As the translation above implies, the wealthy were afraid to make their customary loans of rice to peasants because they anticipated that borrowers might flee or die before they could make good on the interest-bearing loans. The effect of such refusals was merely to exacerbate the famine. By issuing the command to lend first of all in his own proprietary provinces of Suruga and Izu, Yasutoki was guaranteeing the wealthy there repayment with his own resources. Even the original thirty *koku* started out as a loan and not a gift, with Yasutoki's guarantee attached. Eventually the Hōjō leader enacted similar legislation aimed at "crisis management" for thirty provinces located all over the archipelago. By the end of the disaster, he was guaranteeing repayment of the interest and even the principal for the hard-pressed. Whatever their effects, this order and the policies that succeeded it were designed to speed recovery from the famine at the same time that they showed off Yasutoki's statesman-like qualities.

The various prayers and policies had swelled to a veritable flood by 1232, the final harsh year of famine, and yet the impact did not stop then. That year is well known among Kamakura historians as the time when Hōjō Yasutoki oversaw the compilation of the Jōei Formulary, the first in a long lineage of warrior law codes.[100] More and more scholars are coming to believe that this fifty-one article code itself was another product of the famine.[101] Conventionally, historians have tied the compilation of the Jōei Formulary to the *bakufu*'s victory in the Jōkyū War of 1221. That conflict, however, was eleven years old when the formulary appeared in 1232, and the idea for and compilation of the law code dated back only as far as 1232.[102]

Moreover, numerous articles in the Jōei Formulary reflect conditions of the day. To take just a few examples, the first two clauses called for the repair and construction of shrines and temples throughout the Kanto; they mirror similar laws in the court's forty-two article "new institute," also proclaimed in 1232. As a prelude to the articles, the court document described the difficulty of collecting labor dues and the laziness of officials "in recent years." If the mortality level was close to the statistics computed for Koazaka or Hozumi, there must have been a considerable labor shortfall, leading to construction problems. In any case, the famished would have been weak, bedridden, and busy surviving, unable or unwilling to tend to work. Articles 3 and 4 of the Jōei Formulary, directed to Kamakura's constables, repeat prohibitions issued during the famine, as did those aimed at wayward land stewards. Articles attempting to resolve conflicts among estate proprietors, their underlings, and the *bakufu*'s agents similarly remind one of the increased pressure placed on what little harvest there was during a hungry time.

Some argue that the Jōei Formulary was a product of many years of experience and that historians should not attribute too much influence to the Kangi famine. Two articles, however, seem especially to reflect the conditions of 1229–1232. Before we look at Article 41, consider the following evidence for a booming market in selling one's relatives and other dependents into servitude during the famine:

Point:
In Kangi 3 [1231] when people were starving to death, it was finally decided to the effect that a master *[shujin]* could plan [i.e., require] labors [in return] for the victim's sustenance. In general, the prohibition against buying and selling one's kin is extremely strong. During the years of the famine only, however, shall we permit it?

En'ō 1/5/1 [1239]
Point:
Buying and selling one's kin has been strictly proscribed by law. Yet during the famine, in some cases one sold one's wife, children, or attendants; in others, one allowed oneself to be placed at the home of the rich. . . . In general, hereafter one ought to stop this buying and selling without exception.[103]

In other words, the Kangi crisis was so severe that the shogunate reversed a policy, enunciated as early as 676 and as recently as 1226, and permitted starvation victims to sell themselves, their families, and/or their followers into slavery to sustain themselves or the "sale item."[104] And as a measure of the severity of the Kangi catastrophe, the law remained in force for eight years, throughout almost all of the 1230s. As if to underline the ineffectiveness of the 1239 prohibition, Kamakura reissued the law in 1240 and 1242 and then intermittently until 1255.[105]

Under such circumstances, it is hardly surprising that the Jōei Formulary included the next law as Article 41:

Point: About slaves and servants [nuhi; zōnin]:

Concerning the above, following the precedent of the shogun's house, if there is no assertion of rights for more than ten years, no matter whether right or wrong, a suit revising the current conditions will not be permitted.

As for sons and daughters of slaves, although there are details on this in the law, also following the precedent from [Yoritomo's] time, sons should adhere to their fathers and daughters to their mothers.[106]

This seemingly harmless statement is easy to overlook amid the colorful stipulations concerning monks and warriors in the formulary, but none is more revealing about an important social impact of the famine.

In essence, the Jōei Formulary altered the conditions of slavery and servitude in Japanese society.[107] According to the Taihō and Yōrō Codes, suits over the ownership of persons had been permitted at any time; the 1232 law ended all litigation after ten years, no matter how good a case might have been. One reason for the new time limit on litigation was presumably that Kamakura courts were choked with such cases during and following the famine. Starving persons who had sold their relatives into bondage during the famine wanted them back when conditions returned to normal and often demanded reduced sale prices such as had obtained during the crisis. The *bakufu* was not only placing a time limit on litigation, but also it eventually sided with the slaveholders by stipulating that the resale of kin in bondage must be at current prices and not those that had obtained in the hungry 1230s.[108]

Furthermore, Chinese-style statutes had stipulated that all slaves or servant children belonged to their mothers. In the Kamakura era, a new precedent required that children become the possession of the parent of the same sex. One way to interpret Jōei Article 41 is that when members of slave families were sold or transferred—as apparently was happening frequently in the 1230s—then servile families could be broken apart and had to live separately. Although we cannot be sure that the legal formulation that sons belonged to their fathers and daughters to their mothers actually meant that the family lived apart, most historians interpret it in that way.[109] The inclusion of this statute in the Jōei Formulary may well have indicated a great increase in the numbers of unfree persons and legitimated the disintegration of once intact families.

On the one hand, Article 41 implies that the legalization of a slave/servant market may have made demographic recovery from the famine even slower and more painful. As a rule, the full impact of a famine upon a population is seen not just because it kills people, but also because it lowers the birthrate. The *bakufu*'s policy of permitting parents to sell their children or a husband to sell his wife could well have made the increase in mortality greater and the drop in the birthrate sharper. As regards the death rate, if a family sold a child to a wealthy person, there was no guarantee that the child would find his/her way to the master's house or be treated well in service; the numerous references to abandoned children take on new light when this is considered. Concerning fertility, it is often assumed that servants produced fewer offspring because their living conditions—a small hut or lean-to on the master's property—were not conducive to a large family. Moreover, if a husband and wife dwelt apart under different masters, it probably restricted the number of offspring they could have. Of course, the wife may have taken a new mate (such as the master), but this is speculative.

On the other hand, the legitimization of the sale of kin into servitude may not have had so debilitating a demographic effect as it appears at first glance. As much as the authorities recoiled from breaking up families, such an act may have simply spread potential famine victims (especially children) around to the wealthy, who could provide them with food. In this respect, Article 41 and the other laws legalizing the sale of children and dependents may well have saved some lives. Heirs to a Confucian tradition, modern Japanese historians are often disgusted at the seeming immorality of these laws, but the distress caused by the Kangi famine may have called for extreme actions, another type of "crisis management." The debate over the impact of Article 41 relates to the nature of the Kamakura peasant family, a topic taken up more fully in chapter 2.

Article 42 suggests yet another aspect of the crisis:

Point: When peasants flee *[chōsan]*, he [i.e., the land steward] states that he has the right to confiscate or destroy the peasant's belongings and damages or takes them.

Concerning the above, when residents of the various provinces flee, the lord states that he has the right to their possessions, restrains the peasant's wife and children, and steals their valuables. The idea behind this behavior is a great betrayal of benevolent government. If even after having been invited back, the peasant is in arrears on his rice tax *[nengu shotō]*, then [the lord] ought to be able to make up the difference. If he is not in arrears, then the lord ought to return the damaged property immediately. However, in terms of [their] leaving or remaining at their parcels, the will of the people ought to be obeyed.[110]

This statute reflects the reality of samurai-peasant relations: fleeing cultivators left the land steward with empty fields and no rent; it is little wonder that warriors stole their possessions and restrained families of absconding farmers. And yet Article 42 is probably the most famous in the formulary because it appears to grant Kamakura peasants *(hyakusei)* legal freedom of movement as long as their taxes were paid. They do not seem to have been serfs, as the medieval European analogy would suggest, but instead constantly migrated, as rural people may often do in a labor-short economy. Famines such as that of Kangi make it easier to understand why movement would have been common; if the local samurai were too harsh in his demands during the crisis, the cultivator could leave to find a better deal. The consequent increase in the "floating populace" may not have had a positive effect on fertility, however, especially if the husband left his family behind. This article's relation to the labor supply in the 1200s will be examined in more detail in chapter 2.

Whether measured by the events, probable mortality, institutional remedies, or long-term effects, the Kangi crisis may well rank as the most horrific famine ever to strike the archipelago. Caused by cold, damp weather and unaffected by most government palliatives, this crisis was significant for Kamakura and Japanese history. In some regions the Tenpō famine of 1837–1838 resulted in the loss of population gains made over the previous ten years; it took about two decades for full recovery to become a reality.[111] Given the far more primitive state of Japanese agriculture and commerce in the 1230s, it seems only reasonable to think in even longer terms about the demographic impact of the Kangi crisis. The famine of 1229–1232 provides one piece of the puzzle as to why population remained static for most of the thirteenth century. And in less than thirty years, the islands would suffer another such visitation.

The Shōga Famine, 1257–1260

The Shōga famine shares many characteristics with the Kangi crisis: the causes were the same, mortality likely high, government actions only mildly helpful, and the long-term consequences severe. Unfortunately, the Shōga famine, like the Yōwa disaster, is poorly documented. There are no mortality estimates such as we can garner from estate records during the Kangi era. Still, the Shōga famine was surely a turning point; it marked the beginning of the end for the Kyoto-Kamakura system, as it gave rise to forces that eventually led to the collapse of the shogunate itself.

In some respects, it is difficult to be certain exactly when the Shōga crisis started because almost all the years between 1232 and 1257 seemed to witness troubles somewhere. As mentioned above, the Kangi famine continued to reverberate throughout the 1230s: in 1233–1234 drought and insects destroyed crops from Etchū to Tanba; during 1235–1239 cold, wet weather seemed to have been the main culprit again. In like fashion, the hot-dry/cold-wet cycles continued in the 1240s, and although harvests were probably less than optimal, the records do not tell of a famine stalking the islands during the decade.[112]

Then on the nineteenth of the fourth month in 1251, *Mirror of the East* devoted less than one line to an event that may have had immense repercussions: Mt. Akagi in Kōzuke erupted, spewing dust, debris, and gases into the atmosphere.[113] And in the intercalary third month of 1257, just before the Shōga famine, another source states that ashes fell on Kyoto, perhaps from a local forest fire, perhaps from another volcanic eruption. This volcanic activity added to the cold/wet tendency already described for the 1230s; for the period from 1251 to 1263, only 1252 and 1257 even contained mentions of drought. The litany of weather reports was typical of the "Little Ice Age": downpours, ice and snow, and violent thunderstorms. From 1251 to 1263, written sources reveal about twice as many references to excessively damp and cold conditions as to heat and dryness.

To cite some examples, on the twenty-third day of the fourth month in 1251, Kamakura witnessed torrential rains leading to floods that carried away rice seedlings. It rained in Kyoto heavily during the fifth month, and the *Mirror* notes that ice fell on Kamakura in the sixth month—"the cold was just like winter." Snow descended upon the warrior capital twice during the late summer in the seventh month. By the twelfth month the *bakufu* had rice-wine dealers stop production to free up more grain for aid. There are fewer data for 1253–1256, but the weather seems to have been wet and cold; for 1256 the *Mirror* notes great rains, floods, and frigid temperatures. It was dry in the spring and too rainy in the summer, and numerous provinces reported a "terribly bad harvest" *(dai akusaku)* for that year.

With no reserves to tide over a hungry populace in the spring of 1257, the Shōga famine began claiming its victims in earnest. In Kyoto, drought was noted at this time. An unnamed pestilence (possibly related to starvation) began afflicting the populace, and the number of persons who starved to death was "countless." Records show that northeastern Honshu was hit hard; in both Dewa and Aizu many died from "a great famine." In the fifth month it poured in Kyoto, but thereafter authors in both the ancient capital and Kamakura complained of drought. By the eighth month a late Kamakura source notes that "rains, floods, famine, and plagues" beset many provinces, where the stench of rotting corpses attracted vultures and dogs searching for an easy meal. The same annals later state that crops throughout the realm were damaged so that recovery the next year would be difficult.

If 1257 was bad, 1258 was even worse. Historical materials use the vague term "various provinces" to suggest the geographical extent of the famine. Among the areas noted specifically, we of course find Kyoto and also Yamato, where "everyone was frightened when the thunder and lightning shook and violent rain fell early [in the year]."[114] Noto, the lone province in northeastern Honshu discussed when I inferred thirteenth-century population from the Great Land Registers, is also listed as a province visited by starvation. As the populace suffered throughout the archipelago, suddenly it turned bitterly cold in midsummer. A Kyoto record states that during the sixth month the frigid temperatures were "just like the second or third month"; the *Mirror* also says that "it was just like winter." Floods and rains followed in the eighth month, and the harvest failed in Mutsu. The *Mirror* notes heavy winds and downpours that same month and writes that "the paddies and gardens in various provinces have all been damaged or destroyed." Both Ise and Kawachi reported widespread starvation in the autumn, and the year's catastrophic events in Kamakura were capped by heavy rains and floods, which washed away many homes and drowned the owners.

In 1259, another unknown pestilence added to the woes of a starving populace in Kyoto. The price of rice hit one hundred coins for three *shō* (.03 *koku*), presumably an exorbitant amount. The same conditions prevailed in both Dewa and Mutsu, where cannibalism was reported. In Iyo, Yugeshima Estate officials wrote that all the Shōga period was a time of famine: "the estate office is empty, and the peasants have either run away or died." As if to second the judgment of the Yugeshima officials, a Kyoto noble entered in his diary that "during the Shōga era, the realm has suffered from famine and pestilence and it has declined and become empty." In both Kyoto and Yamato, starvation and the accompanying diarrhea killed many, filling roads with corpses from spring to summer. In the old capital, "no household did not suffer" from the unnamed disease, and the streets and riverbanks were so littered with dead that they became impassable. Sources indicate that many outlying provinces also suffered mightily, especially Mutsu. All the court could manage was to change the year-period, intone sutras, and pray to the native deities. Apparently cannibalism was prevalent in Kyoto, and many fled the city for the mountains and moors, where roots, berries, game, and fish might diminish their hunger. Once again, the summer of 1259 was wet and cold, the harvest failed in many provinces, people died in great numbers, and law and order began to break down.

By 1260, people in Kyoto turned to a favorite custom: criticizing the administration by scrawling lampoons on the nearest wall. One read: "In the land [kokudo], there are disasters; in the provinces, there is famine; on the riverbanks, there are bleached bones." By spring of that year, even Kamakura was ordering temples to intone prayers, as it also proscribed the discarding of orphans' corpses along the roadside. Apparently the gods were not listening because in the sixth month strong winds, heavy rains, and eventually floods swept away homes, eroded a hillside, and drowned or buried city dwellers. For the rest of the year, similar conditions were noted not just for Kamakura, but also Kyoto and the provinces. Very little in the way of written materials has survived for the 1260s, although the weather continued to be unusually rainy and frigid, but the word "famine" disappears from the sources after 1260. Perhaps conditions improved and there were good harvests to stop the unremitting hunger and death, but we cannot really be sure.

Like the Kangi disaster, the Shōga subsistence crisis seems to have been caused primarily by excessive rain and frigid temperatures in the spring and summer, reinforcing the hypothesis about the "Little Ice Age" being a worldwide phenomenon applying to Japan as well as Europe in the thirteenth century. Tree ring and ice core data, as well as Chinese and Korean sources, confirm that the years 1256–1262 were a time of unusual volcanic activity and damp, cold temperatures throughout the Northern Hemisphere.[115] Sources appear to emphasize the damage done to eastern Honshu; Mutsu, Dewa, Noto, and Aizu are all mentioned as scenes of particular devastation. Data on the Shōga debacle lend credence to the idea that the great Kamakura famines reduced the population of eastern Japan at a greater rate than that of the rest of the archipelago, supporting the fragmentary information available from the Great Land Registers.

Unfortunately, there are no cases permitting the calculation of mortality for specific regions during 1257–1260. There is, however, one document indicating that depopulation was severe in some places. At Maeshima in Edo Village, located in Toyoshima District in Musashi, Taira Nagashige wrote the following in a letter of commendation *[kishin-jō]* dated the third day of the tenth month in 1261: "Because of the famine over the last two or three years, there is not a single peasant here. Based upon this, labor dues *[kuji]* have been resisted."[116] It is notable that this case originated from the Kanto, where conditions may well have been terrible.

Although the lack of demographic data is disappointing, there are plenty of indirect indications that the Shōga famine was disastrous; these often repeat the themes described for Kangi. Both the court and shogunate issued long orders immediately on the heels of the famine, Hōjō Nagatoki proclaiming a sixty-one article "new institute" early in 1261 and Emperor Kameyama announcing a court edict in the eighth month of 1263.[117] Each repeated time-honored remedies. Kamakura called for some positive policies, such as the staging of more Shinto rituals and the reconstruction of religious centers, but most articles were prohibitions trying to stop *jitō* abuses (such as excessive corvée levies and the employment of too many attendants); warrior ostentation in dress and weaponry; gambling and group drinking bouts; usury; slave trading (especially when the victims were kidnapped); and the abandonment in the streets of orphans, invalids, and the dead. Nagatoki also demanded the arrest of pirates and brigands and the timely feeding of imprisoned criminals lest they starve to death. Emperor Kameyama's edict reiterated notices of previous civilian administrations, focusing on sumptuary laws and religious sentiments while also banning slave trading and kidnapping, the growing of wheat for horse fodder, and bribery in officialdom.

Within documents preserved for the decade 1255–1265, three complaints surface time and again: the nonpayment of commodity taxes, the inability to raise sufficient labor, and warrior abuses of the peasantry. To be specific, in the eighth month of 1260, there was a notice of unremitted taxes for Ategawa Estate in Kii because the peasants had either died or fled. In the fourth month of 1262, a record from Tara Estate in Wakasa reads that "last year the rice tax was allowed to remain unpaid as desired."[118] Signs of a labor shortage are also evident in various ways. The best single instance appears in a record from Ategawa Estate, dated in the tenth month of 1259, stating that "because this year famine is spread equally over many provinces, all extraordinary labor levies have been stopped west of the Kanto" on orders from Kamakura. In the twelfth month of 1260, vassals were warned against demanding transportation work from "poor people."[119]

As might be expected, when taxes and labor dues were hard to collect, land stewards tended to abuse cultivators. Of course, Kamakura's lieutenants on the land had a history of improper behavior, but the Shōga crisis gave them more opportunities. In the seventh month of 1260, Shōni Sukeyoshi was reminded not to force peasants to do more labor than the law allowed. A long document dated in the third month of 1262 lists numerous violations occurring in Etchū, including land stewards' taking possession of cultivators' fields and not paying the rice tax. Disputes of all kinds were common, such that during the peak of the famine Kamakura placed limits on the length of paperwork coming out of the particularly contentious western provinces.[120]

The most famous and general prohibition of land steward misbehavior was also issued in the midst of the famine, on the ninth of the second month of 1259:

> Point: On stopping abuses of the mountains, moors, rivers, and seas and helping save the lives of vagrants [*rōnin*].
>
> Because of the famine in the provinces, hopeless people from near and far either enter the mountains and wilds to take various mountain roots and tubers, or they go to the rivers and seas, seeking fish and seaweed. They use these occupations to keep themselves alive. The local land steward, however, strictly prohibits them. We ought to lift the warrior ban immediately to save the lives of these vagrants.[121]

Two points about this order are interesting. First, it was originally handed down to officials in Mutsu, an undeveloped frontier in northeastern

Japan where the cold, wet weather had hit the hardest. Second, it suggests that there was a considerable "floating population" unable or unwilling to sustain itself by agriculture and turning to forager livelihoods such as gathering and fishing. Instead of going to large cities, as famine victims would do in the Tokugawa period, these poor folks knew the only place to save themselves was the woods, shores, and mountains.

Not all misbehavior originated with warriors. For example, the following was in the same 1259 record noting the Kamakura ban on extraordinary labors:

> In some places they open the proprietor's granary and give provisions to peasants, in others they have stopped both customary and extraordinary labor dues owed to the proprietor, and thus comfort the people.
>
> But the estate official here [*azukaridokoro*] since about the sixth month has not distributed even a grain of rice. Instead, he has turned loose ruffians who have taken several thousand boards from the peasants. Being unable to care for the lives of their wives and children, they have been caused to starve to death in countless numbers.[122]

These incidents took place in western Honshu at Ategawa Estate, located on the Kii peninsula.

Once again pirates residing along the northern Kyushu coastline raided Koryŏ.[123] After 1232 and the end of the Kangi famine, relations between the *bakufu* and Koryŏ court had been more friendly, as the Japanese elite sided with Koryŏ in its losing battle with the Mongols. From 1255 to 1265, however, Korean sources note repeated destructive forays by Kyushu pirates against its natives. Like Kangi, the immediate cause seems to have been food shortages and hard times in the islands.

As the revival of piracy suggests, perhaps the most important effect of the Shōga famine was the fatal blow it dealt to law enforcement. Not only did warriors take advantage of the crisis, but also the level of violence rose and remained high for the rest of the Kamakura period. By 1260, jails were so full that Kamakura issued a three-part order in which one article declared the following:

Point: On pardons [*hōmen*]:

Concerning the above, when it comes to murderers, recently over the last ten years we have pardoned them depending upon the gravity of their crime. But now, whether one speaks of the famine in the provinces or people dying from illness, when they have violated the law, no matter what their sentence, for those without extraordinary circumstances, based upon a special plan for those who have committed crimes up to this year, pardon them completely.[124]

There were several reasons to issue such a sweeping pardon. It was a Confucian sign of benevolent government and may have been carried out to curry favor with heaven. Or perhaps, as noted above, Kamakura could not feed all its criminals and did not want the starving inmates on its hands. Or, as alluded to in the order, maybe the jails were so full because of illegal acts committed during the Shōga famine that Kamakura just decided to empty them.

Be that as it may, the Shōga famine marked a new epoch for law and order and the *bakufu* because from approximately 1260 the word *akutō*, usually translated as "evil bands," becomes a constant refrain of shogunate administrators. The term was first used in a shogunate order dated on the twenty-first of the ninth month in 1258: "The evil bands *[akutō]* of various provinces have arisen, and we have heard to the effect that they plan to commit night attacks *[youchi]*, robbery, banditry *[sanzoku]*, and piracy *[kaizoku]*." The activities of the "evil bands" would become an increasing headache for the shogunate beginning with the Shōga crisis; in the fourteenth century they would help Emperor Go-Daigo topple Kamakura.[125] The Shōga famine was a crucial domestic factor behind the epochal changes of the late thirteenth and early fourteenth centuries.[126]

Contemporary literate persons also thought that the Shōga famine was the beginning of the end: in 1260 Nichiren submitted his *Discourse on Establishing Right and Pacifying the Country (Risshō ankoku ron)* to the shogunate's Hōjō Tokiyori. The advocate of the efficacy of the Lotus sutra wrote as follows:

A visitor came and lamented: "From recent years until just a few days ago, disturbances of Heaven and disasters of earth, famine and pestilence, filled the realm widely. . . . The rotting corpses and bones of cattle and horses fill the roads; those who have been summoned to death already exceed half the population. There is not one person who is a member of a family without sadness. . . . If one lamented for the people *[banmin hyakusei]*, then he ought to carry out the benevolent government *[tokusei]* of good administrators. Despite this, they simply invite honest behavior and are increasingly

TABLE 1.5
Famine Years, Extent, and Causes, 1150–1280

YEAR	EXTENT	CAUSE
1150	Widespread	Wet/cold
1151	Widespread	Wet/cold
1153	Local	Unknown
1155	Widespread	Unknown
1161	Widespread	Unknown
1174	Local	Wet/cold
1175	Local	Wet/cold
1180	Widespread	Drought
1181	Widespread	Drought
1182	Widespread	Drought
1183	Local	Unknown
1185	Widespread	Drought
1201	Local	Wet/cold
1206	Widespread	Unknown
1229	Widespread	Wet/cold
1230	Widespread	Wet/cold
1231	Widespread	Wet/cold
1232	Widespread	Wet/cold
1233	Local	Wet/cold
1252	Widespread	Wet/cold
1257	Widespread	Wet/cold
1258	Widespread	Wet/cold
1259	Widespread	Wet/cold
1260	Widespread	Wet/cold
1271	Widespread	Drought
1273	Widespread	Drought
1274	Widespread	Drought

Source: Sasaki Junnosuke, *Kikin to sensō,* pp. 10–55; Nishimura Makoto and Yoshikawa, *Nihon kyokō,* pp. 98–131.

beset by famine and pestilence. Beggars flood my eyes and the dead over-
flow them; outspread corpses make a sight and corpses lying side-by-side
form bridges."[127]

Like Kamo no Chōmei, Nichiren undoubtedly exaggerated what he saw,
but his graphic descriptions and dire predictions had a basis in reality.
Whether through the continuation of demographic stasis or the increasing breakdown in law and order as suggested by the appearance of the
akutō, the Shōga famine would haunt Kamakura for the rest of its days.

Other Famines

Between 1150 and 1280, there were at least 21 years of widespread famine, with another 6 years in which hunger was more localized.[128] (See
table 1.5.) Over the century from 1175 to 1274, there were 17 years in
which starvation was a common problem for many people; to be sure,
this was not as many years as during the well-documented eighth and
ninth centuries but still a sizable proportion. Despite incomplete and
vague sources, it seems certain that famine was a common occurrence
during these 130 years. Food supply was probably the critical life-or-
death issue for most of the archipelago's population at the start of Japan's medieval age. It dictated how many lived and died and helped to
determine, to some degree, what laws governments in Kyoto and Kamakura would issue and, more generally, how the society, economy, and
culture would be shaped.

WAR AND POLITICAL INSTABILITY

In the era before 1150, war contributed to mortality in a minor way, but
beginning in the last decades of the Heian period, it was a more common
experience as the political class slid toward the Civil War of 1180–1185.
While the period from 1150 to 1280 was not as stable or peaceful as most
of the Heian period, in general the Kyoto-Kamakura dyarchy functioned
well enough to make war an unusual experience, at least when compared
to the fourteenth, fifteenth, or sixteenth centuries. To be sure, there were
the Hōgen and Heiji Insurrections in 1156 and 1159 respectively. The
Civil War of 1180–1185, the most traumatic and protracted conflict
since Taira no Masakado's revolt during 935–940, was certainly Japan's
first archipelago-wide free-for-all. In addition, there were Yoritomo's

Northern Expedition of 1189, the Jōkyū War of 1221, and the Mongol Invasions of 1274 and 1281. Except for the Civil War, though, the length of these various hostilities, invasions, and counterinsurgencies was measured in weeks, sometimes even days.[129]

To gauge the impact of this violence in demographic terms, we need to ask two related questions. First, how sanguinary were these conflicts for combatants? Did many die, or were battles rare enough and combat casualties few enough to have had only a fleeting demographic impact? Second, how did war affect the commoner class? As noted for the Yōwa famine, war could serve as the handmaiden of hunger. Did these hostilities result in significant death and damage to people's livelihoods, especially food producers?

To answer the first question, it may be helpful to examine an especially well-documented conflict occurring at the very end of the Kamakura era. Most historians consider the Battle of Banbanoshuku in Ōmi, between the defeated and demoralized Hōjō and the supporters of Go-Daigo on the ninth of the fifth month in 1333, to have been possibly the bloodiest battle of the entire epoch. The Hōjō were determined to fight to the last man, and survivors committed suicide rather than falling into the hands of the enemy. A register *[kakochō]* tallies deaths on the Hōjō side: 430 men are named as expiring in the tragic demise of the Kamakura shogunate.[130]

To be sure, the record states that the monks who redacted this document listed only warriors whose names could be discovered, and the register does not seem to include attendants. Even so, by Kamakura standards, Hōjō casualties seem to have been unusually high; in the Jōkyū War of 1221, for example, the combined mortality from a single skirmish often did not reach fifty.[131] Yet even if we assume that substantial numbers of unnamed commoners were killed along with their masters at Banbanoshuku, the Hōjō death toll was, for example, less than half that of the court's army (1,061 soldiers) in the disastrous Battle of the Koromo River in 789. It was also undoubtedly far lower than the number of those who perished in Emperor Tenji's ill-starred expedition to revive the Korean kingdom of Paekche in 663. Combatant mortality was at most a tiny factor in population change during the era 1150–1280.[132]

Of course, the crucial point is that none of these battles took place in a vacuum. They happened after marches through particular locations, usually where peasants dwelt, and when armies or navies were organized, moved, and fought, they had to be provisioned and often caused what is today euphemistically called "collateral damage."[133] How did a samurai raise the food and other goods necessary to lead him to victory over his foes?

Historians know from documents relating to Taira no Masakado's and Taira no Tadatsune's rebellions in the mid-Heian era that combat could have dire repercussions for innocent bystanders. Similarly fragmentary evidence exists for the Civil War of 1180–1185.[134] (See figure below.) Shirakawa Estate occupied fertile lands in Echigo Province, and the Fujiwara Regents' House held the proprietorship *(ryōke)*. Around 1150, about 300 *chō* of rice fields were listed as under cultivation. On the eve of the Civil War in 1180, the number had decreased slightly to 287 *chō,* but in that same year Kiso Yoshinaka, a powerful Minamoto kinsman based in the Japan Sea littoral north of Kyoto, raised his banner of rebellion against the Taira. One of his first targets was Taira ally Jō Sukemoto, known as "the Lord of Shirakawa" *(Shirakawa no mitachi).* Yoshinaka arrived at Shirakawa before Sukemoto and immediately confiscated all of Shirakawa's tax rice to serve as supplies.

In 1181, estate officials seem to have found a way to submit some revenues to the Fujiwara, even though the area of rice fields under cultivation had dropped by half. In 1184, when the Taira and Yoshinaka were out of the way, Yoritomo took over the territory, but the amount of land yielding rice had fallen to less than 10 percent of the estate's holdings. The land

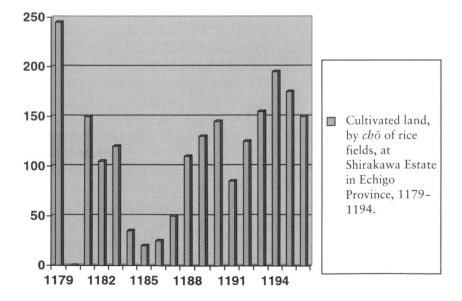

Cultivated land, by *chō* of rice fields, at Shirakawa Estate in Echigo Province, 1179–1194.

steward appointed by Yoritomo was probably responsible for the later woes of Shirakawa. Even in 1196, farmers at Shirakawa could maintain merely half its fields in production. To be sure, Shirakawa was subject to flooding and the effects of the Yōwa famine may have reached there as well, but warriors foraging from Shirakawa's fields caused the lion's share of damage. For the Shirakawa peasants, it did not much matter whether it was the weather, the river, or rampaging warriors: the result was no food.

Other evidence speaks to the brutal effects of war on ordinary folk. For example, in the fourth month of 1183, a variant of *The Tale of the Heike* states that the Taira robbed passersby of their valuables on the roads leading from the Kinai as they proceeded to do battle with Yoshinaka in Etchū and Echigo. Then when Yoshinaka defeated the Taira and invaded the capital region in the seventh month, "regardless of whether the lands belonged to Kamo or Hachiman Shrine, he had his soldiers cut down rice seedlings and feed them to his horses; his men broke into granaries and took the contents." Finally, in 1184 when Go-Shirakawa charged Yoritomo with restoring order in western Japan, Yoritomo wrote that "since punishment of the traitors [the Taira], the eastern [Kanto] and northern provinces are just as if there are no residents *[domin]*; from this spring, we ought to have the floating population *[rōnin]* come back and settle in their old villages." [135] There were even units of footsoldiers whose sole job it was to rob local cultivators of their crops for use as provisions. It is little wonder that peasants took to burying their valuables in shrine sanctuaries. [136]

Nor were samurai conflicts the only ones that destroyed property and killed bystanders. Religious institutions were sometimes to blame for damage and death. [137] In 1163, for example, monks from Onjōji killed those serving at Hiesha, and in retaliation Enryakuji burned Onjōji for the fourth time in less than a century. Ten years later, in 1173, three thousand Kōfukuji monks were responsible for burning many nearby farming residences. Similar cases fill chronicles for the late twelfth and thirteenth centuries.

Raising provisions for troops was intimately intertwined with the death and destruction arising from battle. Estates were a natural source of grain, men, and other items for the military, and there are examples as early as 1179, when Taira-led court forces first foraged at and then burned three estates belonging to the recalcitrant monks of Enryakuji. [138] The Taira established a short-lived institution for assembling provisions *[hyōrō mai]* in 1181, and Yoshinaka's actions have been noted above. [139]

As the Civil War proceeded, Yoritomo declared an end to the Taira system, but he still received resources from former Taira estates, often with the results evident in the Shirakawa case. For the rest of the war, there were three means by which Yoritomo's victorious armies garnered food: individual samurai raised it from their own lands; Yoritomo had it shipped from the Kanto; and fighters confiscated it at the battle site.

During the Kamakura era, the shogunate tried various means of provisioning, but in the end it usually came down to stealing cultivators' food en route and at the battle scene. During the Northern Expedition, Jōkyū War, and Mongol Invasions, special taxes or lands were assigned to feed fighters but often not until after the combat had ended. In other words, while the battle was on, warriors were on their own. Two documents apparently ordered provisioning at battle sites during the second Mongol Invasion of 1281.[140]

Ultimately, how soldiers provisioned themselves went right to the heart of Japanese society in the twelfth and thirteenth centuries. While means varied according to time and place, there was one overriding rule, summed up by the medieval concept *jiriki kyūsai*.[141] Literally translated as "aid by one's own power," it really meant that "might made right." The term *jiriki* by itself has been associated with Hōnen and Pure Land Buddhism; the devotee knew that he or she could not obtain entrance into paradise "on his/her own power" but surely needed the "help of another" *(tariki)*, a bodhisattva or buddha.[142] So in the religious context *jiriki* may be best translated as "self-help," but where provisioning warriors was concerned, a more apt rendering might be "help yourself." No wonder cultivators fled battlegrounds, hid their possessions, and generally detested samurai.

Warrior misbehavior was not simply a function of human nature, class antagonism, and military technology; Kamakura law aided and abetted wrongdoers, in line with the concept of *jiriki kyūsai*. Scholars note that Kamakura courts did not consider "the violent outrage of stealing someone else's crop" *(karita rōzeki)* a criminal act *(kendan sata)* until 1310.[143] Instead, it was a property issue *(shomu sata)*, and if a thieving warrior could generate the paperwork or witnesses necessary to sustain his or her claim to the harvest, then the handiwork became a fait accompli. All a warrior had to do was to prove that his antagonist owed back rent, and the theft was recognized as legitimate. And even if robbery could be proven, the owner or cultivator would have wasted time and effort going through the courts and would merely receive reimbursement for the value of the loss.

The same principle applied to "violent outrages along the road" *(roji rōzeki)*.[144] Until 1302, a warrior could seize the goods of a traveler, and his act was not considered criminal. As in the case of the confiscation of crops, this offense fell under the heading of property law, with all the accompanying disadvantages for illiterate peasants with less access to courts. If the warrior could produce evidence of indebtedness, then his seizure was viewed as lawful.

"Self-help" provisioning and other outrages inflicted untold burdens on a peasantry already living on the edge. It should come as no surprise that the problem was not confined to Japan and is nearly as old as civilization itself. The people of Mesopotamia faced the same issue under another conqueror, Sumerian king Sargon I of Akkad, around 2350 BCE:

> Sargon's household became a standing professional army. Yet there was a serious flaw in Sargon's power. He could not feed his army year in and year out. As a result, the great conqueror had always to be on the move, taking his troops to where plunder and food could be found. . . .
>
> From the point of view of the peasants and townsmen who had to support the king's soldiers . . . the arrival of Sargon's army was like a plague of locusts—unpredictable and all but ruinous.[145]

All we have to do is to substitute names such as Kiso Yoshinaka, the Taira, or even Yoritomo and his housemen throughout the late twelfth and thirteenth centuries to move the scene from the Fertile Crescent to Japan.

Yoritomo tried to correct, or at least stabilize, those unacceptable conditions. An underlying cause for the outbreak of war in 1180 was that samurai had no security of tenure and paltry incomes. When the Civil War broke out, soldiers on all sides—including Yoritomo's—"helped themselves" by collecting dues illegally; upset at its loss of revenues, the court charged the Minamoto leader with putting a halt to the rampant "violent outrages."[146] Yoritomo's solution to the related problems of military provisioning, rewarding his followers, and supplying the court with ample rents was simple: locate the samurai in an estate, guarantee his job, pay him some small but secure dues, and let him manage the land. If *Mirror of the East* is to be believed, Yoritomo brought his men under control by appropriating the positions of land steward and constable in 1185.[147] These posts, guaranteed by the *bakufu,* fed and paid for enforcers of law and order throughout the archipelago for the duration of the Kamakura era.[148] Yoritomo and his successors held the warrior accountable if he committed too many harmful acts against other officers or the cultivators themselves.

Unknown to Yoritomo, Sargon's successor and famous law giver, Hammurabi, king of Babylonia (ruled ca. 1700 BCE), had hit upon a similar solution three thousand years earlier. Like the Minamoto general, he stationed his men over his lands (Mesopotamia) and allowed them to collect rent from residents, according to records Hammurabi kept. The Babylonian king's system was far preferable to Sargon's: the soldiers were usually on the spot, and people became used to supporting them in a more or less predictable manner. Hammurabi may even have demanded more than Sargon, but "regular burdens were easier to bear and did less damage to ordinary civilian life and property."[149]

This political decision, whether made by Hammurabi or Yoritomo, had advantages and disadvantages. One attraction was its frugality; instead of a standing army being paid from shogunate or court coffers, each estate or provincial property provided the warrior with a customary income. A major drawback was that over time the loyalty of local warriors could be compromised; this, of course, is exactly what happened in Japan during the 1330s. Still another potential fault was that as the overseers of cultivators, troops could easily abuse their powers. It is unclear how Hammurabi dealt with this weakness, but as has been evident from the discussion of the great Kamakura famines, Yoritomo's men could and did abuse their positions. And they could be harsh and oppressive without regard to time or place, not just when crop failure meant that their incomes had diminished.[150]

Myriad indeed are records of warrior mistreatment of the peasantry during the thirteenth century, but there is one especially famous case showing just how far samurai were willing to go. In 1275, in the aftermath of a famine, residents of Ategawa Estate in Kii became so outraged at their land steward, Yuasa Munechika, that they wrote a thirteen-article protest in the Japanese syllabary *(kana)* explaining why they were abandoning the estate. Yuasa had doubled the land tax on hidden fields, used twenty underlings to take peasant hemp cloth, assembled labor gangs night and day, stolen the cultivators' millet, and used the cultivators to care for his horses. When the peasant men fled to the mountains and refused to return in time to sow wheat, Yuasa threatened to "capture [their] wives and children, slice off their ears, cut off their noses, shave their hair, make the females into nuns, and have them tied and lined up."[151] While custodial governors *(zuryō)* had been notorious for their greed in the Heian period, they do not seem to have gone as far.

Ategawa cultivators probably exaggerated their case for effect; nor were they entirely blameless. Indeed, Yuasa's actions took place as part of a larger dispute between the *jitō* and Jūren, a cleric responsible for the Sharakuji Temple's lands *(azukari dokoro)*.[152] The rational Ategawa peasants were not above playing one side off against the other to their advantage. Eventually, however, the argument between Yuasa and Jūren went to court at Rokuhara, and Yuasa won. No one doubts that Yuasa committed the atrocities listed in the protest, nor that warriors regularly wrecked peasant homes and stole their possessions when rents were insufficient.[153] Such behavior could not have been conducive to economic or demographic growth; from the cultivators' perspective, rural samurai could constitute a curse on the land.

Endemic and epidemic diseases, death-dealing famines, and hungry and abusive samurai raised mortality and lowered fertility for a populace just barely surviving. These factors were mainly responsible for the static population between 1150 and 1280. This explanation seems plausible, but by themselves these direct factors cannot "prove" the interpretation. Before we can feel more comfortable with this view of population stability, a whole range of background variables of a social and economic type needs to be analyzed.

2

Change within Basic Continuity

Agriculture, Labor, Commerce, and Family Life, 1150–1280

*I*n political terms, the late Heian and early to mid-Kamakura eras showed small changes within a bedrock continuity. While Yoritomo had established his warrior government in Kamakura after a bloody civil war, he could not oust the civilian and religious authorities living in Kyoto and Nara. In fact, rather than overthrow the land and tax systems that had throttled warriors for two centuries, he sought to confirm the old institutions based on the produce from provincially administered lands and estates *(shōen-kokugaryō)* and guarantee all the elites—warrior and otherwise—their rightful place in them. Yoritomo's reforms meant continued stability, albeit with a few emendations.

The economy and society of the era 1150–1280 reflect a similar theme, bolstering the picture of a stable population depicted in chapter 1. Here I will begin by examining the agrarian regime, suggesting that it was essentially the same as that of the tenth century. While there were technological improvements, they were just barely beginning by 1280, giving rise to the minor advance in per-unit rice yields computed above. The legal condition of workers also strongly implied a shortage of laborers, as did the record in construction. To the extent that evidence is available, it seems that most industries remained technologically unchanged from their state two centuries earlier. Although trade and cities had begun to grow, they too were just commencing by 1280. In the family, kinship was still bilateral, sex free and easy, and broken families and abandoned children prevalent. The overwhelming majority of commoners lived in material conditions that were little improved over those of the late Heian period.

The Annual Agrarian Cycle

Japanese historians have described certain unique rites and customs taking place during the annual agricultural cycle of the Kamakura period, most of which had their origins as far back as the tenth century.[1] On the first day of the new year according to the lunar calendar, peasants assembled at the estate or provincial lands for a ceremonial drink of sacred rice wine *(shōgatsu sechie)* proffered by the proprietor or local officials. Later in the month, cultivators and their families performed what was called "playing in the fields" *(ta asobi);* this ritual aimed at encouraging a rich bounty by soothing the spirits of the farmlands through dance and song.[2] Although by the Kamakura period one part of this rite had evolved into an attempt to chase off birds and insects *(torioi),* villagers originally intended it as a way for peasants to send an epidemic god *(shidara no kami)* away from their settlement and on to the next.

Not long after this ceremony, farmers and their families entered the fields and began *arata uchi,* a custom especially designed for ancient and Kamakura cultivation—breaking up the soil with hoes and shovels, in time to rhythmic songs and music.[3] The season for this back-wrenching activity could vary along with the location and type of field, as well as the intensity of the labor; *arata uchi* might take place any time from the end of the first month to the start of the fourth, with the second month being the most common.[4] *Arata uchi* was necessary because cultivators did not crop each plot every year; peasants carried out this practice regardless of the parcel's productivity in the previous growing season. In an era when there was almost no double-cropping, all arable lands required a thorough turning of the soil after the long winter. In the initial stages of soil breaking, unspecified rites took place for the "god of the fields" *(ta no kami matsuri).* The application of grasses and other fertilizers, the cleansing of irrigation channels, and the weeding of the rice seedling beds also occurred at this time.

While many country folk were busy with this critical preparatory labor, the estate proprietor sent his representative—or perhaps the land steward acted on the lord's behalf—to accomplish another crucial task known as *kannō* (lit., encourage agriculture).[5] Through this custom, the proprietor/managers assured themselves of an adequate labor force by assigning name fields *(myōden)* to cultivators in a process called *sanden,* not unlike the allotment system enforced in the Nara epoch.[6] Every effort was made to obtain tillers for vacant lands and achieve the proprietor's desired goal of "full cultivation" *(mansaku jōtai),* but records show that the area and location of parcels under cultivation shifted considerably from year to year.[7] Presumably, the proprietor and his underlings already had a good idea of the arable in the estate, and provincial officials knew the potential of their lands because they ordered cadastral surveys *(kenchū)* intermittently. Estate officials compiled a document known as a *kannō chō* when each cultivator received responsibility for his or her parcel.

During this process, residents and officials also decided which variety of rice or other crop to plant in each field; envisioned an appropriate tax rate; estimated which plots were the most liable to suffer from drought or flooding; and, most important, doled out seed and food to cultivators. Peasants might also obtain seed from relatives or wealthier residents of nearby lands, and even in the late Heian era they were knowledgeable enough to soak the grains to encourage early sprouting. It is clear that local officials, and especially warriors and land stewards, played a central role in securing adequate numbers of farmers and making other decisions.

Under the *kannō* regime, cultivators sharecropped—that is, they farmed their assigned parcels and paid rent in return for the remainder of the crop and the right to use other lands of all types. Two causes seem to lie behind the ubiquitous *kannō* system, which arose in the tenth century and remained commonplace until 1300. First, farming, and particularly wet-rice cropping, is hard work. It is back-breaking, down-on-your-knees labor; wet-rice cultivation is more akin to gardening than traditional American or European dry farming. Just as the working class did not immediately take to disciplined factory jobs in the nineteenth century, so residents of the archipelago were reluctant to expend the energy and care necessary to plant, tend, and harvest wet-rice in much of the premodern era. Great attention to detail and continuous work were necessary for successful rice cropping in regions like the Shōnai in the Tokugawa era; while rice cropping was less labor intensive and much less sophisticated in the Kamakura age, the same general principles held true then too.[8] Peasants who chose to cultivate wet-rice not only had to face the hard work and considerable risks of disease, weather, insects, and ultimately failure and starvation, but also, when successful, they had to hand over a tidy portion of their harvest to warriors, priests, and/ or civil aristocrats.

A recurring labor shortage was likely the other factor driving the widespread adoption of the *kannō* system. This point merits greater discussion when I examine the overall problem of labor below; suffice it to say that the practice would never have arisen had it been easy to secure willing workers. In fact it was not, as indicated by the numerous cases of peasant abuse, the countless orders to repair temples and shrines, and the constant remission of labor dues cited in chapter 1. In this sense, the static population of the era 730–1280 fed a vicious cycle in which agriculture could not improve much because labor was insufficient, and the population could not grow to provide labor because ecological factors (such as diseases and untoward climate), technological variables (such as unreliable irrigation facilities and the dearth of iron tools and fertilizers), and institutional/social problems (such as warriors on the land) discouraged growth.

As cultivators conducted *arata uchi* after being assigned parcels and receiving and soaking their seed, they sowed the sprouting rice grains in preparatory beds *(nawashiro),* eventually raising them during the second and third months to become seedlings ready for transplanting. After a brief ceremonial halt to all work on or about the eighteenth of the third month to mark the advent of summer, peasants returned to weeding and ground breaking. Once they had sufficiently broken up the soil through human and animal labors, peasants were in the habit of choosing a propitious day *(kichijitsu)* to introduce standing waters into their fields, and then they began a fine grading *(yokaki)* of the mud using a horse- or ox-drawn rake *(maguwa)*. This stage in soil preparation, as well as the tending of seedlings, lasted into the fourth month.

As the first peak in labor demand declined during the fourth month, peasants performed a ritual to their individual family gods *(ujikami)*. Little is known about this activity, but deutzia plants *(utsugi),* standing about 1.5–2 meters and arranged in rows around homes, had a prominent role. These flowering plants were hardy and dense and served to mark off boundaries and protect members from disasters. Since they also grew wild in the moors and mountains, where spirits of the deceased were thought to dwell, the ritual honored the last departure of a dead relative's soul from the family.

By the early summer, it was time for transplanting seedlings into flooded paddies in areas where that technique was used. Even in the Heian and Kamakura eras, transplanting was frequently done by young women, singing rhythmic songs dedicated to the "bird who encouraged agriculture" *(kannō no tori)*. From a demographic perspective, there are two issues: first, when pregnant women carried out the work, the chances of miscarriage and death increased; second, since planters were standing in pools of water for long periods, the possibility of parasitic infestations such as schistosomiasis increased greatly. The impact of neither can be assessed quantitatively, but the risks of this labor for both women and men were considerable.

The summer (the fourth, fifth, and sixth months) was a busy season, and both Kyoto and Kamakura strove to reduce the burden of other, nonessential labors during this critical time. In addition to chasing off birds and insects, cultivators would weed, harvest winter wheat from dry fields, and conduct by-employments such as raising silkworms. They would also plant barley, millet, buckwheat, soy beans, and other crops in nearby dry fields or garden parcels.

When the fall commenced (around the seventh month), it was time for the harvest. One critical task was the assessment of damage to crops from drought, floods, and insects, and if the harvest was poor—as it was about once every three years—cultivators wisely left the fields untouched and called for an examination *(kemi)* by responsible officials. Even then, protests frequently failed; payment was demanded; and peasants fled or went on strike by hiding in their homes, taking advantage of the scarce supply of agrarian labor to wreak havoc upon their overseers. If things went smoothly, the winter was given over to threshing with winnowing baskets and wooden mortars and pestles.

The annual agricultural cycle of the Kamakura era was not much different from what it had been in the tenth century. Highly ritualized, two practices seemed central to its smooth operation. The first was the relatively long period of soil breaking, aimed at bringing once barren paddies and fields back into cultivation. The second was the acquisition of sufficient laborers through the *kannō* process. The former implies the shifting nature of farmland, while the latter denotes the unstable and highly transient character of the labor force.

Technological Changes

Despite continuity in the annual rhythm of farming, by 1250, and especially by 1300, there were indications of small, incremental technological innovations. In some cases, they were clearly improvements over what had come before; in others, the result was mixed. One advance was the wider dispersion of iron tools; implements made of ferrous materials were more efficient for cutting into the earth and reaping the harvest. Archaeological evidence suggests that even in the 800s only about one in eight cultivators possessed hoes, shovels, or sickles with iron cutting edges, such tools being primarily the property of wealthy peasants and local notables who may have lent them to small cultivators.[9]

Several pieces of evidence point to the dispersion of basic iron tools to more peasants by the late 1200s. First, these implements appear more frequently in twelfth-century documents, literature, and paintings *(emakimono)*.[10] Second, police records from the period 1350–1450 show that even small cultivators had their own shovels and hand-axes by that time. Of course, the records do not mention *iron* in the tools, and it is mysterious that even wealthy farmers, who possessed plows and threshing equipment, did not own sickles. On the basis of these and other data, some have concluded that basic iron tools were more common by 1300, perhaps even among the servile class *(ge'nin)*.

Regional improvements in the iron industry comprise a third reason to believe that more peasants had iron tools by the end of the Kamakura era. Around 800, a half-submerged vertical shaft furnace *(han chika shiki tategata ro)* for heating and smelting iron sand or ore, built on hillsides to utilize up-drafting wind currents, had replaced the more sophisticated but labor-intensive box-shaped mechanism *(hakogata)*. The new vertical shaft furnace required neither blowpipes nor bellows. The amount and quality of iron so produced was inferior.[11]

Beginning in the late Heian epoch, iron-smelting techniques began to show some sign of advancement.[12] In place of the old furnaces, rectangular box ovens *(chōhō kei hakogata ro)*, standing 1.5–2 meters tall, made an appearance in the provinces bordering the Inland Sea. They developed right alongside the older vertical shaft furnaces and other varieties in northern Kyushu, the Japan Sea littoral, and the Kanto. While archaeologists have discovered only one bellows *(fuigo)* and no blowpipes *(haguchi)*, it is generally assumed that because of their structure, rectangular box ovens used both. The result was a gradual increase in the quantity and quality of smelted iron by the late Kamakura. Based upon these improvements, it seems reasonable that more and higher-grade iron was available for all sorts of tools.

Such technological innovations accomplished little without artisans to manufacture and sell the products. At first, iron-casters *(imoji)* and blacksmiths operated as peddlers, wandering over the countryside to sell their wares. Both Kyoto and Kamakura gave them freedom of movement through barriers and taxed them lightly. Eventually, iron-casters settled down in groups *(kugo'nin)*, developed their skills, and multiplied over the archipelago during the late twelfth and thirteenth centuries. By the end of the Kamakura period they were producing and selling in both western Japan and the Kanto; there is further evidence that settled iron workers were casting or forging blades for iron hoes and spades for local peasants. It is not clear that every villager recognized the utility of the new tools or could afford them, but the organization of a distribution network was a step toward more productive and efficient agriculture.[13]

A second change was a somewhat wider distribution of draft animals and their accoutrements.[14] The ox- or horse-drawn plow had likely become more common among wealthier farmers in the late Heian period as the population began to recover around 1050–1150.[15] The ownership of oxen in western Japan and horses in the eastern archipelago increased and may even have reached down as far as the middle levels of the cultivating class by 1280. *The Legend of the Gods of Matsuzaki (Matsuzaki tenjin engi)* and other paintings dating from the early fourteenth century display these beasts of burden prominently.

Moreover, greedy land stewards confiscated horses and cattle frequently for their own use or sale in the thirteenth century; peasants from Torikai Estate in Awaji complained of a *jitō*'s stealing two cattle and one horse in 1276 and a cow and four horses in 1277.[16] At Arakawa Estate in Kii in the late thirteenth century, "evil bands" *(akutō)* committed various crimes against peasants, burning over forty homes and roasting "several tens" of horses and cattle.[17] At Arakawa, about every other farmer may have had an ox or horse. Tales from the mid-Kamakura *A Collection of Sand and Pebbles (Shaseki shū)* suggest that peasants harnessed horses to carts carrying grasses, manure, and grains.[18]

A third gradual advance went hand-in-hand with the wider distribution of farm animals: more and better fertilizers.[19] Grasses (green manure) had always held a prominent place in agriculture, even in the Nara age; by the Kamakura epoch farmers applied animal waste more widely than ever before. A story in *A Collection of Sand and Pebbles* describes a "young monk . . . loading up a horse with manure to take to the fields, as is the custom in this [province of Hitachi]."[20] It seems a fair assumption that the fertilizer came from the horse.

One of the more common documents found among Kamakura

collections concerns quarrels among villages and between land stewards and groups of peasants over common lands. A major reason for an increased interest in common lands was that forest lands were a good source of fertilizer—brush, leaves, grasses, fibrils, and their ash. Nearly every settlement bordered on a mountain or moor where local farmers could collect products.[21]

A fourth technological change in the Kamakura era was the beginning of more efficient land use and therefore better yields. If the Great Land Registers are reliable, the area of rice lands declined in several provinces, particularly in eastern Honshu. To support the same number of people on a smaller area meant that land use had to improve. One aspect, the island dry field *(shimahata)*, has already been discussed elsewhere.[22] Agriculturalists would convert a previously drought-ridden rice field into a smaller but constantly productive rice field and a dry parcel by removing the topsoil from one half and piling it on top of the other. The *shimahata* first appears in documents from the early fourteenth century, but the practice probably predates 1300 somewhat.[23]

Double-cropping is the most well-known method of intensive land use; it developed and dispersed somewhat during 1150–1280. It is important to distinguish the double-cropping of dry fields and paddy land. The former entails rather little extra work—just more fertilizer; the latter involves much more labor to close off intake water or trench around an area in the field. Timing is trickier for the latter. Rent collectors may also be more likely to grab their share from double-cropped paddies.

The earliest evidence of the double-cropping of dry fields originates with Yugeshima Estate in Iyo in 1160. A commendation from Kii Province notes wheat planted in both the summer and autumn in 1296.[24] During the nearly 140-year interval, the practice had undoubtedly expanded, as estate lords were wont to tax dry fields twice.[25] The shogunate banned land stewards from exacting this "double taxation," probably because heavy taxation was enough to discourage farmers from reaping two harvests. In any case, the double-cropping of dry fields—to the extent that it existed—made more efficient and productive use of the land.

The double-cropping of rice paddies was another matter, and controversy surrounds this topic for the era under consideration. In 1264, the shogunate issued the following oft-cited order:

After peasants *[hyakusei]* of the various provinces have harvested rice from their paddies, they sow wheat at the site and call it "paddy wheat." Proprietors collect tax *[shotō]* from the aforementioned wheat. How can the land tax law be used this way? Hereafter do not take tax from paddy wheat. To the great joy of peasants *[nōmin]*, be aware of this point and notify the housemen *[goke'nin]* of both Bizen and Bingo.[26]

This law presumably proves that the practice of double-cropping had spread from the advanced Kinai as far as western Honshu by the mid-Kamakura era.[27]

The critical point about this order, however, is its date, 1264, just on the heels of the Shōga famine. The command may not have signified a booming agricultural sector but rather described the lengths to which desperate cultivators went to obtain grain in hungry years. In other words, the order was part of larger governmental efforts to return abandoned fields to production and relocate the "floating population" on their parcels. Peasants in Bizen and Bingo planted wheat in rice paddies not to supplement their food supply but to compensate for the failure of the first harvest. This law has more in common with decrees encouraging the planting of dry fields during drought and famine in the eighth century than with any growth of agricultural productivity in the thirteenth.[28]

At the same time, the 1264 law granted peasants freedom from taxation when they double-cropped. Such a policy may have helped to save lives and encourage the settling of erstwhile cultivators. Like the legalization of the sale of kin in 1231 and the opening of wildlands and the seashore to the floating populace in 1259, the 1264 legislation may have been another government action taken to manage the crisis arising from widespread starvation.[29]

Although the Shōga crisis looms large in any interpretation of the 1264 order, most scholars agree that double-cropping, even of paddy fields, existed on a small scale by the end of the Kamakura epoch. For example, a record from Yugeshima Estate shows that paddies uncultivated in 1188 were yielding rice and wheat by 1268.[30] A document from Naka District in Kii dated to 1276 lists both rice and wheat collected as tax from the same two *tan*, a practice implying double-cropping.[31]

The most concrete cases of double-cropping come from along the Ki River in Kii Province.[32] Peasants there began double-cropping wheat and buckwheat in paddy lands as early as the second half of the thirteenth century; the overwhelming majority of thirty-eight examples come from the fourteenth century, but it is clear that the practice had older roots. The double-cropping of rice paddies during the Kamakura era was inconsistent, and areas under cultivation varied by year; it may have started as a last resort to assist starving farmers.

Lest one become too sanguine about the initial development of paddy double-cropping in the 1200s, it is well to be aware of a few more facts. This technology requires the soil to dry out completely after the rice harvest; low-lying lands in river deltas and alluvial plains—Japan's best areas for constructing paddies—were poor candidates for a winter wheat crop. Valley paddies, where the runoff eventually trickled away and the soil dried, were better for double-cropping. Even as late as 1500 only about 20–30 percent of paddy fields in western Japan were double-cropped; the percentage was far lower in the Kanto and eastern Honshu.[33] One reason for this regional variation was that water-logged paddies were more common in eastern Japan in the Kamakura period and even as late as the 1950s.[34] Double-cropping at this initial stage could not come anywhere near to solving the problem of food shortage so necessary for propelling population into a growth cycle.

More construction of irrigation works and more attention to water supply constituted the fifth improvement commencing in this period.[35] As an example of the former, Hōryūji saw to the building of a "great valley pond" in 1275.[36] As a case of the latter, at Ito Estate in Chikuzen in 1294, when peasants threatened to strip a mountain of its trees, officials stopped the cultivators to save water runoff.[37] These examples are few, but like other improvements discussed above, they would become part of a greater story played out more fully in later centuries.

In addition to these five points, two other supposed innovations appear frequently in the literature. First, some argue that the Kamakura era witnessed a considerable increase in the number and varieties of crops, especially rice varieties.[38] These included the usual dry grains, such as wheat, barley, millet, buckwheat, and soy beans, planted in mountainous swidden fields, as well as in the more usual lowland and foothill dry parcels.[39] There are also references to many types of early-, middle-, and late-ripening rice. Because of historical and geographical variations in the names for plants, however, it is difficult to prove this point.

Second, historians often claim sizable expansion of the arable through land clearance for the Kamakura era. Much of the evidence for such development comes from entries early in *Mirror of the East:*

Awa, Kazusa, and Shimōsa have lots of uninhabited moors *[kōya]*. But since the people do not cultivate them, there is no gain for either the state or

private concerns. Thus we ought to invite the floating population *[rōnin]* and have them open [these lands] and prepare rice taxes.[40]
[Second month, 1189]

[The shogunate] ordered land stewards in the eastern provinces *[tōgoku]* to open water resources for wastelands. . . . In general, no matter whether it is called abandoned land or uncultivated, for land where the taxes have declined, hereafter do not permit proprietorship.[41]
[Fourth month, 1199]

It was ordered to the effect that land stewards in Musashi should clear open lands and moors.[42]
[Third month, 1207]

The shogunate issued similar commands for other lands in Musashi in 1230 and 1239.[43] Finally, in 1232, the shogunate requested that peasants be drafted to repair a dam that had burst at Suginuma in Musashi, while in 1241 there was a long debate before the *bakufu* moved to have workers divert the waters of the Tama River to flood planned new fields at Musashino.[44]

As with official orders promoting land clearance in the Nara era, these commands each have their own context, and as with the eighth-century proclamations, mere words should not be equated with results. The 1189 order was issued just before Yoritomo prepared to chastise the Northern Fujiwara, and it was probably intended to raise provisions. Moreover, this law was part of the plan to revive the provinces ravaged first in Tadatsune's revolt of 1028–1032 and then during the Yōwa famine and Civil War of 1180–1185.[45] The 1199 command made specific reference to the reopening of abandoned fields in Musashi, and the 1207 law followed years of bad harvests in the Kanto. Kamakura promulgated all the other legislation in the 1230s and early 1240s, the era of the harsh Kangi famine, and it was undoubtedly viewed as another way to revive agriculture—especially tribute-producing wet-rice—after the near-decade of inclement weather and failed crops. As in the ancient period, land clearance, abandonment, and reopening appear to have been part of an endless agricultural cycle.

None of this should be taken to mean that cultivators never brought new fields into production in the Kamakura period—far from it. For example, tillers constructed irrigation works and opened new paddy fields at Hineno Estate just after the Kangi famine.[46] Reclamation from the sea was also apparently more common, led by wealthy peasants *(myōshu)*, people with access to tools and labor.[47] Extant Kamakura documents occasionally record cases of small amounts of land clearance; my impression is that the number of such activities grew somewhat over the course of the 1200s.[48]

To sum up, Kamakura agriculture probably represented a small improvement over the same sector of the mid-twelfth century.[49] The advances, however, tended to make more intensive use of the land rather than expanding the arable. In this sense, Kamakura farming was a prelude to bigger breakthroughs beginning in the fourteenth and fifteenth centuries and coming to fruition during the 150 years from the age of Nobunaga to Tsunayoshi.

Settlement and Migration

An examination of documents, estate plans, and old maps has revealed that the type of settlement that historical geographers know as the compact village *(shūson)* did not begin to form in Japan until the thirteenth and fourteenth centuries.[50] To be sure, there may have been clustered habitations as early as the twelfth century in some provinces in the Kinai, but these seem to be exceptional and are open to dispute. Examples at Ikeda, Otogi, and Wakatsuki support the view that nucleated settlements were mostly created after 1250.[51]

The main factors promoting the rise of compact villages were a more efficient and intensive use of the land; both characteristics were evident in the preceding discussion of Kamakura agriculture. It is thus probably best to think of this period as a transitional time, especially in the Kinai after about 1250, when more large, moated, clustered settlements were coming into existence. It is interesting that the development of compact villages initially had little to do with increased warfare, as was once thought. The surge in crime by "evil bands" in the late thirteenth century may have played some role, however.

Finally, all the data presented so far suggest that residents of the archipelago moved about frequently, a factor that affected population in complex and diverse ways. Migration might have served to spread pathogens, separate spouses during the wife's child-bearing years, encourage trade, and/or facilitate tax evasion, for example. During the great famines, people deserted Kyoto and their estates to forage in the mountains and moors. When warriors from Yoritomo down to the lowliest land steward wanted to clear or reopen fields, the stock phrase in *Mirror of the East* and Kamakura documents was to "invite the floating population"—that is, badger or entice them—to do the work and then settle them on the parcels so created. Constant movement was not just a reaction to institutional factors but was ingrained in the social structure of the Kamakura countryside.[52]

LABOR AND INDUSTRY

In this section I shall begin by examining free peasants and servants in an attempt to understand how the rural labor market functioned and, by implication, the effect of a substantial servile class on demographic growth. Then, I shall focus on the most famous construction project of Kamakura times and its snail-like pace of completion. Finally, I shall briefly describe industrial developments. The thrust of these remarks will be to bolster the picture of a static population, as commoner peasants moved frequently from one estate to another, indicating a shortage of agricultural labor, while more and more persons fell into classes of servitude where fertility may have been lower. The construction project stalled, and industries advanced only modestly from the previous epoch.

Freedom and Servitude

On the face of it, the key to understanding agrarian labor in the Kamakura period appears to be the final line of Article 42 in the Jōei Formulary (also cited in chapter 1): *"In terms of [the peasants] leaving or remaining at their parcels, the will of the people ought to be obeyed."* Even though this sentence would appear to grant freedom of movement to cultivators, not everyone agrees.[53]

As with many debates in Japanese history, there are numerous interpretations of Article 42. One group of scholars reads the statute as a guarantee to absconding commoners that they would not be unreasonably or forcibly returned to their homes—that is, they see it essentially as a preventive measure against cruel land stewards. Another sees the main emphasis of the law as prohibiting local lords from using unpaid taxes or other debts as a pretext to turn commoners into servants. Still a third envisions the legal formulation as an attempt to stop land stewards and other local officials from using physical restraint on commoners.[54]

No matter what the statutory niceties may be, even a casual perusal of Kamakura records shows that cultivators frequently resorted to "fleeing and scattering" *(chōsan)*. If land stewards or the local foreman became too abusive, for instance, then peasants could essentially go on strike. In these circumstances, the men of the estate or provincial lands met, declared a collective oath, and then went into hiding, leaving their wives and children behind. The women would then draw down the shades of their homes and take care of the remaining members of the family, being careful not to exit too often.[55] The timing of such an action was also important—always in the late winter or early spring, just when estate officers were getting ready to assemble workmen.

The tactic of fleeing and scattering easily drew the ire of *jitō* and others, who responded, as at Ategawa, by rounding up women and children and injuring or tying them up. Another warrior maneuver, *chōki* (lit., fleeing and wrecking) was legal. If an estate official could prove that an absent man was behind in his tax payments, he might confiscate an appropriate amount of property or even destroy the peasant's house, in accord with provisions of Article 42. He had to be able to prove, however, that the family in question was indeed in arrears.

Given that absconding was such a favorite tactic of cultivators in distress, most Japanese historians lean toward the position that commoner farmers *(hyakusei)* possessed freedom of movement. In other words, many cultivators could come and go as they pleased, changing employers in the process. Farmers may have based the decision to stay or leave most commonly on crop failure or damage from natural disasters or on misbehavior by the *jitō* or other estate officials. What would such freedom of movement mean for the rural labor market?

Even thirty years ago the conventional view was that the most natural system in a labor-short agrarian economy was binding workers to the land using slavery or serfdom.[56] Why was Article 42 applied in the demographically static Kamakura period? The answer seems to lie in the degree of unity of the ruling elite: when the propertied class was unified—such as in the antebellum South, premodern Russia, or ancient Rome—then slavery or serfdom was indeed the likely outcome. When the ruling class was fragmented, however, as it certainly was in Japan from the tenth century on, competition to draw cultivators away from one employer and to another could occur more easily. This same circumstance was also true for medieval Europe after the Black Death during 1351–1500, when the labor shortage actually led to the collapse of serfdom. The second half of the Tokugawa era also presents a similar condition. Article 42 gave cultivators the legal right to move because proprietors could not unite to stop them.

There was a significant limitation to this customary right, however: it applied to commoner farmers only. If a person had sold a family member or himself into bondage as a servant *(ge'nin; shojū)*, then he was at the beck and call of his master. The late Heian-Kamakura labor market was legally only half free—I can envision wealthier cultivators moving independently from estate to estate, bringing their servants along with them. The literature on these unfree persons is voluminous; a brief examination of the evidence and a summary of findings will have to suffice here.[57] (I shall also address this topic under family and kinship.)

Historians have uncovered numerous examples of *ge'nin* living in various circumstances. The Nejime, a warrior family of Ōsumi, held servants, ninety-four of whom were transferred to sixteen offspring between 1275 and 1278. The structure of these servant families is of interest: generally they constituted nuclear units or groups of mothers with their children. Why the husband was no longer present in the latter case is unclear. *Ge'nin* debt seems to have been the primary means of accumulating servants, and the main reason for assembling great numbers of these persons was to fulfill labor needs.[58]

A 1289 record relates to the Tadokoro, a warrior-official family of Aki in western Honshu.[59] This document shows that on a little less than thirty *chō* of farmland, divided into seventy-two parcels, at least fifty-six male servants were ensconced; the record notes females only sporadically, but if their number equaled their male counterparts, then the Tadokoro possessed over one hundred such *ge'nin*. Of the fifty-six, only four (7.1 percent) had been slaves *(nuhi)* for several generations; most had been in that status for only their own lifetimes. About half for whom there were clear records had become servants during and immediately after the Kangi famine. In addition, falling into debt had proven to have been the proximate cause for about half. The Tadokoro case suggests that there was a large populace of unfree persons but that movement in and out of that status was relatively common.

Information on such servants and slaves also survives in records composed on the back of Nichiren's scrawlings (late Kamakura period).[60] In one case from Chiba property in Shimōsa, a wealthy neighbor charged a commoner observing funeral rites for his grandparents with nonpayment of his labor duties and forced him into servitude. In another instance, the *ge'nin* and his master became embroiled in a lawsuit over whether the servant's family was in bondage for just the time it took him to repay his debt (a rice loan) or for myriad generations. In yet a third, an unfree person who dwelt a good distance from his master was able to enter into an arrangement with the local shrine to escape his overlord's clutches.

Medieval scroll paintings suggest that there need not have been any reason at all for turning an unsuspecting person into a servant. These paintings show what have been called *fukuro mochi,* or persons bearing large gunny sacks.[61] They appear in both the famous *Pictorial Traditions of Saint Hōnen (Hōnen shōnin eden)* and another lesser known scroll; in both cases the sack seems to contain a squirming person, probably kidnapped and about to become someone's (probably a warrior's) underling. Amid a labor-short market in a society known for its ties of dependency, a person used whatever methods he or she could.

As we might imagine, the condition of the medieval unfree is hotly debated among Japanese scholars; despite the natural differences of opinion, there are several points of agreement. First, three factors might lead a person to become a *ge'nin:* famine, debt, or war.[62] The first has already been discussed in detail, especially for the Kangi crisis; undoubtedly hundreds of former peasants could not find food and sold their kin or themselves into servitude.[63] Debt, especially nonpayment of taxes, was another common route into bondage. Finally, later in the medieval era, when warfare became endemic, samurai converted captives into *ge'nin.*

Second, a review of transfers *(yuzuri-jō)* of *ge'nin* on an archipelago-wide basis shows that servants lived all over the islands, from northeastern Honshu to southern Kyushu, but particularly in the hinterlands. Usually they numbered only a few per family; warriors, especially land stewards, were the most common owners and also had the most numerous holdings, but *ge'nin* could be found at all levels of society. Owners frequently listed these unfree persons as possessions, similar to livestock.[64]

Third, the degrees and types of servitude varied considerably.[65] There were personal slaves *(nuhi),* field hands in bondage *(ge'nin),* grooms for warrior horses *(shojū),* and various other categories and statuses *(zō-nin).*[66] Moreover, a person might be sold into service for a set number of years, a lifetime, or several generations. So perhaps making too many sweeping statements about the servile class is unwise.

Within these boundaries of general agreement, Japanese scholars tend to be either optimists or pessimists, with the optimists being more numerous and vociferous lately. Optimists stress that servants often seem to have had their own families and land and that exit from the status was frequent. Pessimists emphasize the severe conditions under which *ge'nin* entered bondage—as a result of debt, imminent starvation, or war; that shogunate law held that sons were to live with their fathers and daughters with their mothers in the case of slaves *(nuhi, zōnin)*; and that archaeological remains suggest that *ge'nin* lived in small lean-tos and additions to their masters' houses.[67]

The demographic impact of the existence of a large group of servants and slaves would seem to have been negative, as family units were often broken up and living conditions may have been unsatisfactory. Yet this assumption is certainly debatable; I will handle the topic more fully when addressing family structure. In terms of the labor market, however, these classes of servants and slaves seem to have arisen from the general scarcity of workers or from hardships arising during the twelfth and thirteenth centuries.

Construction

Monumental building offers another perspective that buttresses the argument for a Kamakura labor shortage. For example, in 1269 the monk Dōgyo wanted to reconstruct Mibudera in Kyoto, which had burned in 1257; unable to employ commoners for the job of laying the foundation, he gathered the poor, famine victims, and outcasts *(hi'nin)* to accomplish the task in return for food. The monk would probably not have resorted to such tactics if his funds had been generous or workmen plentiful.[68]

The most famous temple building of the Kamakura era was the raising of a new Tōdaiji, the Nara version having been put to the torch by Taira no Shigehira in 1180.[69] The reconstruction of Tōdaiji was a project of the highest priority for the Kyoto elite; the temple represented and protected the welfare of the realm. The powerful noble Kujō Kanezane remarked in his diary that when he learned that his family's temple, Kōfukuji, had been burned at the same time as Tōdaiji, "my sadness was just like losing my mother and father." Although the Fujiwara family was able to rebuild Kōfukuji rather quickly, Tōdaiji was another story.

The monk Chōgen is famous for his devotion to rebuilding the great temple, and indeed, in 1185 the statue of the Buddha for the temple was rededicated by a leading supporter, retired emperor Go-Shirakawa. Yet almost from the beginning Kyoto aristocrats complained that the new

Buddha was not the equal of its Nara predecessor; the same was soon also said of the various religious gates and halls, done in a style borrowed from India and adopted because it saved on labor and lumber. Workers hauled timber posts in from far-off Suō Province, and few were the equal of Nara posts. Labor problems in the form of land steward and peasant resistance dogged the project throughout. When Chōgen died in 1206, the project was still a long way from completion, not reaching that state until 1289. In other words, the raising of the Kamakura Tōdaiji, inferior in important ways to its Nara ancestor, took 109 years. Given the urgency placed upon the project, that duration alone speaks most directly to the fiscal hardships of the court, the problem of obtaining fine lumber, and the difficulty of maintaining an adequate labor force.

Industry

Because information on the industrial sector has been slow to come to light for the late Heian and Kamakura epochs, it is difficult to ascertain how manufacturing developed during these eras. I have examined several significant and diverse industries, including iron, silk, transportation, salt, and ceramics, arguing that all of them betrayed signs of retrogression or the application of labor-saving techniques between 900 and 1100.[70] In essence, most industries remained the same through 1280, with the adoption of new technologies rare and the differentiation between production and marketing uncommon. Slow, incremental change may well have gathered momentum after 1250, however.

With regard to iron, it will be recalled, a new type of furnace featuring bellows and blowpipes appeared in the region along the Inland Sea in the late Heian period, and the new device was also evident there during the Kamakura period. Marketing of ferrous products probably improved, as shown by more cultivators possessing iron tools. The construction of "salt fields" had begun in the middle Heian and continued during the Kamakura period because it saved labor in comparison to earlier techniques. Salt was produced not by professionals but by peasants attached to estates for which saline products were a tax item. In pottery, the medieval period is known for its many glazed stonewares, such as Bizen and Seto ware, but the general consensus is that glazes were not in widespread use until after 1300. Silk production stayed as it had been during the Nara and early Heian epochs, handled by peasant households according to methods of the tenth century; regions specializing in fine silk fell from twelve to nine during 900–1300, with Chinese brocades imported to suit the tastes of the late Heian and Kamakura elites. Travel was time consuming and there was little investment in infrastructure, affecting everything from the spread of pathogens to the payment of taxes. In a word, prior technologies may have dispersed slowly, but dramatic new developments were unusual.[71]

COMMERCE AND URBANIZATION

If there was marked growth in the thirteenth century, it took place in commerce after 1250. The Kamakura period falls into two phases: until 1250 estate lords relied upon their lands to provide them with an appropriate mix of goods, but after the midcentury trade became more prominent.[72] Whereas only six records indicated a commutation of commodity taxes before 1250, from 1251 to 1300 there were 38, and then 126 from 1301 to 1350.[73] Moreover, negotiators conducted only 21 percent of known land sales in cash between 1186 and 1219; the figure rose to 42 percent from 1220 to 1283 and to 66 percent from 1284 to 1333. In addition, local markets proliferated after 1250, while the rise of various merchant specialists and moneylenders and the use of bills of exchange began about 1279. It seems fair to conclude that commerce was on the upswing by the second half of the Kamakura era.

Two points about commerce seem relevant to any discussion of demography. The first regards the nature of the trade. Much of it was in luxury goods and involved the warrior, monastic, and civil elites only, at least until the late thirteenth century: "Even in the second half of the Kamakura period, market activities, monetization, and commutation affected the lives of cultivators only to a limited extent. Market days were still few; commutation was far from universal; many cultivators were still paying all or part of their dues in kind; and the paddies of most cultivators did not yield large or reliable surpluses that could be sold. Most of the cultivators' lives were still dictated more by the rhythms of nature than by the widening ripples of the cash nexus."[74] The effects of the Sung monetization or regional commerce were merely a potential beginning, just like the improvements in agriculture or some industries.

Second, the expansion of trade could indicate modest population growth, but it might still occur under static conditions. In theory, scholars argue that commerce surges as the number of persons increases and craft and regional specialization takes place. Yet history also presents plenty of cases where trade grew despite a static or even falling population, such as Western Europe during the late fourteenth and fifteenth centuries and the second half of the Tokugawa era. In the case of twelfth- and thirteenth-century Japan, expanded commercialization seems to have occurred without significant differentiation between production and marketing, possibly suggesting little or no population growth.

Urbanization may well have increased over the course of the 1200s. As estimated in chapter 1, there were two hundred thousand city dwellers, but given recent discoveries by archaeologists and more careful perusal of records by historians, the total may have been higher. In addition to the cities of Kyoto, Kamakura, and Hakata (mentioned above), there were ports such as Tosa in northern Honshu; Mutsura near Kamakura; Obama and Tsuruga along the Japan Sea littoral; Kusado Sengen, Anotsu, Mihonoseki, and Onsennotsu in western Honshu; and Honotsu in southern Kyushu.[75] Moreover, former provincial capitals often provided a headquarters for Kamakura officials such as constables and may have comprised a nucleus for urban development.[76]

It is prudent, however, not to push urban totals too high. Unlike Kyoto or Kamakura, the nine ports or provincial capitals mentioned above may not have had enough inhabitants to merit the designation "town," here defined as including five thousand residents or more. It should be further noted that many large centers, such as Kamakura and Hakata, did not reach their maximum size until 1300 or later, and of course Hiraizumi was put to the torch in 1189.[77] Even with sundry other towns such as Ōtsu, Hyōgo, Yodo, or some of the ports and provincial capitals suggested above, it is unlikely that the number of people living in urban centers came to three hundred thousand (about 5 percent of the inferred total population). The overwhelming majority continued to live in the countryside.[78]

KINSHIP, FAMILY, AND WOMEN

Sources provide no quantifiable data on the birthrate, a shortcoming also true for the Heian era prior to 1150; thus kinship, family, and women are classified as indirect factors and may merely be described. Basic questions such as average family size upon completion or age intervals between offspring must go begging for lack of documentation. In this section I shall attempt to summarize information and interpretations as they now exist, with an eye toward social trends that may have affected fertility and infant mortality. First I shall examine kinship, marriage, and the family; then describe motherhood and children; and finally discuss the servile population.[79]

The most well-documented and persuasive interpretation of kinship, marriage, and the family during the early medieval era (through the first few decades of the 1300s) derives from analysis of two rare case studies from Tanba and Ōmi.[80] In these two areas, individual rural families tended to be nuclear and highly unstable; they still basically retained all the characteristics of matrilocal or neolocal marriage. This pattern of marriage revealed the continued vitality of bilateral kinship at the commoner level; there was no such thing as the stem family *(ie)*, in which the father's headship was passed down generation after generation to the appropriate son. This familial pattern went hand in hand with the lack of stable villages; most small peasant families of the type described above had only loose connections to a given area.

If kinship was still bilateral and there was no stem family or village community in the Kamakura era, then what held kinship groups together? In Ōmi and Tanba, lineage units known as *uji* comprised most settlements. At Yamakuni Estate in Tanba, there were only five surnames, all of which harkened back to ancient times. Although no statistics are available, each *uji* seemed to have been quite large. These lineage groups performed several functions, including religious duties in local shrines, especially during the agricultural cycle noted above (rites of the fourth month and for the lineage gods). They also served as mutual aid societies during cultivation and at other times when familial needs arose. Finally, village *uji* held landed property, both as fields and *shiki,* which might be loaned out to individual nuclear families. Every lineage unit had a few elders *(korō)* who had survived long enough to gain the experience necessary to make decisions for the group.[81] The nuclear families of which the elders were a part were the most stable.

Within these larger groups, nuclear families came and went rapidly. Both husband and wife kept their original surnames and held separate property. There was no familial patrimony since the individual nuclear families often broke up without an heir. Divorce and remarriage were common. In support of this newer view, a prominent female scholar has asserted that (1) Kamakura women often kept their own names; (2) a man frequently went to live with the wife's family; (3) mothers had greater power over the children than fathers did; (4) women commonly held property, even among the peasant classes, where women's rights were equal to those of men; and (5) both adoption and remarriage were widespread.[82] In sum, the Kamakura peasant family was not too different from its Nara and Heian predecessors.[83]

As tempting as it might be, it is still too early to designate the two cases from Tanba and Ōmi as representative of the entire archipelago. For one thing, it is unclear where the ancient *uji* could have come from since the surnames were limited to the aristocracy at first.[84] Several authors maintain that peasant couples held property together and that they may have already formed stem families.[85] Despite the doubts, however, it seems prudent to assert that peasant families led difficult lives, that units were inherently unstable, and that variant arrangements existed concurrently.[86]

If we assume that this overall description applied most commonly to thirteenth-century peasants, what implications does it have for fertility? In recent years, medieval mothers and children have garnered growing attention. Commoner women in the child-bearing years apparently had ample opportunity for sexual liaisons; single women may have been *muen,* or without entanglement, and travel was an especially easy way to meet men, even for married women.[87]

The life cycle of commoner medieval women reveals several interesting points. First, babies may have been breast-fed until age three, according to pictorial evidence in scroll paintings. Second, the concept of virginity did not exist, and women engaged in sex easily and freely from an early age. Third, marriage in the commoner class was unstable, with divorce and remarriage frequent, and mature women not only took care of the home, but also worked in the fields and at trades. Paintings of medieval villages are complete with parturition huts, where a midwife often assisted.[88]

There may have been a trend toward "respect for motherhood" *(bosei sonchō)* beginning at this time.[89] This idea, however, had a negative aspect, as mothers were expected to care for their children under all circumstances. Because care of children involved the killing of living things for food, the mother became guilty of grievous Buddhist sins, often leading to her demotion to hell in the next life as a hungry ghost. Eventually, the increased emphasis on motherhood and the mortal sins associated therewith led to inflexible mother-child relationships, in which the mother was actually seen as an extension of the child. Such a concept may have helped pave the way for a narrowing of women's social and economic opportunities and the rise of patriarchal elements in the late medieval age.

Despite the possible increased importance attached to motherhood, pregnancy and birth were dangerous times for both mother and infant. Little care was given to pregnant women, and as many worked in the fields in the summer and fall, the preferred season to give birth was the winter, when there were fewer tasks to bother with. Unsurprisingly, miscarriages, premature births, and stillborn babies were quite common.[90] Parturition huts and midwives were available in almost every peasant settlement, but the times surrounding labor and birth were considered moments of pollution for the mother and child. Birthing was doubtless a primitive procedure. Above it was stated that nursing continued for three years after birth, just as in the Tokugawa period, but the basis for this inference is scroll paintings, and we should be skeptical that the later practice reached back as far as the Kamakura era.[91] With the high rate of infant mortality, adoption remained a popular alternative, a hallmark of bilateral kinship.[92]

Like single women, young children were considered "unattached," or *muen*. In the well-known phrase, until the age of seven children "belonged to the realm of the gods" *(nanatsu made wa kami no uchi)*— undoubtedly a reflection of the frightening infant mortality rate. Yet frequently their labor was needed around the farm and home, children being employed in myriad ways—fetching, watching, holding, and even looking after livestock.[93] Given a labor-short economy, it should not be surprising that there was a market in buying and selling children, as well as renting, borrowing, and sharing them. The market in purchase and sale has already been noted for the great famine periods; scholars differ on just how vigorous they think it was.

Demographically speaking, the market in young children probably could have cut two ways. On the one hand, it may have improved some children's chances of survival if the desperate could sell them to someone who could make use of them in return for food and shelter. Much undoubtedly depended on the largesse of the master. On the other hand, children made easy kidnap victims, in which case the master may have been none too kind. The market also included the sale and abduction of unwanted young girls for prostitution.[94] Moreover, if a child were expected to find the road to the master's house, then he or she could easily have become lost and been abandoned. Finally, as will be adumbrated below, servants often had no rooms or quarters of their own; they were crowded into unhealthful lean-tos or even the kitchen of a larger home. For these reasons, the condition of youthful servants was probably less than what might have obtained had their original families been able to remain intact and support them; the market in children may well have been a net drag on population.[95]

At the same time, references to orphans in laws issued at both Kyoto and Kamakura are frequent. In Kyoto, the court had erected orphanages (*hiden'in*) from the ninth century, and they became increasingly important in the eleventh and twelfth centuries.[96] Especially during the great famines, the number of orphans increased, either because of the death or departure of parents or the sale or donation of a child. Documents do not enumerate services available in the orphanages, and one historian believes that they were just places where young children with no alternative went to die. Orphans may also have been common because parents did not yet widely practice basic methods of birth control, such as abortion and infanticide. The apparent rise in orphans therefore may have reflected improved chances of surviving infancy, although it could just as easily measure the growth of broken families.[97]

Finally, sources reveal a large number of households headed by women; numerous females who chose not to have children, especially those who entered convents; and frequent references to abandoned elderly and children.[98] In a word, if the household in the Nara and Heian periods was highly diverse in structure, during the era 1150–1280 it became even more so. In addition to these various broken families, there were also the giant composite households containing dependents and servants.

Concerning slaves and servants, it is uncertain how the existence of a growing servile class would have affected fertility in the Kamakura era. The standard generalization, based upon Kamakura law and noted in chapter 1, has been that *ge'nin* unions were even more unstable and produced fewer children than those of commoners because spouses could be sold to different owners at any time.[99] Analysis of the Tadokoro and Nejime documents mentioned above seems to suggest that some servants formed families but that broken families were more common, especially units containing only mothers and daughters.[100]

Still, such a generalization may stem from an anachronistic concept of marital fidelity. If women of both commoner and servile status had ample opportunities to form sexual liaisons, it is uncertain if sale of a husband and wife to different masters would have been an impediment to further reproduction. Female *ge'nin* may have been at the beck and call of their masters or formed other unions, with frequent requests for sexual relations (and presumably some offspring). It is possible to conclude that there was no great hindrance to servants forming their own families or producing many children from different spouses.[101]

In sum, the evidence presented above may be read in many different ways, as household records that might admit of quantification are simply not available. On the one hand, scholars may stress the ease of sexual relations within a kinship system similar to the ancient age, the new-found respect for motherhood, the construction of orphanages, and the market in children and famine victims as promoting survival. In that case, fertility would have remained high and a few more children may have lived beyond infancy; the population total may have been somewhat higher than the spectrum of figures calculated for 1280.

On the other hand, historians may emphasize the ephemeral nature of peasant nuclear families, the numerous broken homes, the high infant mortality rate as seen in the frequency of miscarriages and still- or premature births, the recurrence of famines, and the harsh lives of the servile population, especially young children. Under such circumstances, the birthrate may have been curtailed while overall mortality—especially for infants and young children—would have remained frightening. These factors would constitute another reason that the archipelago's population did not expand markedly as late as the last decades of the thirteenth century. In the event, the picture portrayed here for kinship, the family, marriage, children, and the unfree need not be greatly at odds with a conclusion stressing an essentially static population.

COMMONER MATERIAL WELL-BEING

For the great mass of the population, the period under consideration saw few improvements. Peasants continued to weave pieces of clothing similar to those worn in the ancient age from hemp or ramie fibers. Regular bathing was not yet a well-established custom and would not become so for several centuries. Several toilets have been uncovered from the twelfth and thirteenth centuries, but they were simply holes in the ground, above which the user squatted on a pair of boards and excreted. When the hole became too full or repulsive, it was covered over with dirt.[102]

Given the numerous references to corpses in the streets and the sanitary provisions of the day, both Kyoto and Kamakura were probably filthy centers of disease. A report on an excavation at Yuigahama beach in Kamakura notes a mass grave filled with refuse and human and animal remains.[103] The same area seems to have contained a market. With regard to Kyoto, archaeologists suspect that relatives and friends merely abandoned the sick and deceased on the banks of rivers. Hakata too betrays no signs of cemeteries for this era. It is little wonder that the few cities and towns that existed required constant replenishment of their populations from the surrounding countryside.

Diet may present a somewhat more positive aspect.[104] While evidence is scanty, the mainstays of peasant nutrition seem to have remained brown rice and gruel, barley, millet, wheat, buckwheat, various vegetables, bean paste, and rice wine. There is some suggestion that the number and kinds of side dishes multiplied—including more meat, salted fish, bean curd, noodles, and tea—but most of these foods were limited to the warrior and priestly (especially Zen) classes. Perhaps diet improved some, but the repeated famines would imply that the rural population suffered from chronic malnutrition. In the big cities, commerce afforded residents with a dietary variety lacking in the countryside.

Housing between 1150 and 1280 seems to have stayed the same as it had been previously for much of the archipelago. Most peasants thatched their three- or four-meter square dwellings with grasses and carried on daily life on an earthen floor. A house had perhaps one window with a blind, making it dark, dank, and with an unregulated temperature. By the Kamakura period, peasants in western Japan possessed boilers *(kamado),* but if there was no proper hole for the smoke to escape, the house soon became blackened with soot on the inside. In eastern Honshu, the sunken fireplace *(irori)* began to replace simple campfires *(ro),* with consequent gains in warmth and safety.[105] At night, residents slept on straw, probably in their daytime clothing.

There is one other issue regarding housing: the conditions under which the numerous *ge'nin* and other servile peoples lived. According to Japan's leading expert on medieval peasant residences, many *ge'nin* had no homes of their own; they slept in the kitchen, sharing space with the food and fuel.[106] This custom was prevalent among servants in southern Kyushu as late as 1930. Undoubtedly, some were better off, and diagrams of warrior villas typically have assorted small additions and lean-tos, where their *ge'nin* probably carried out the indoor portion of their daily lives. One thing seems certain, however: these living conditions would not have promoted stable or large families and would have encouraged servants to sell or give away extra children.

The legacy of the era 1150–1280 is mixed, linking it both back to the Heian period before 1150 and ahead to the later medieval epoch. The connections back included the size of the population, the nature of the agrarian regime, settlement and migration, the labor market, industry and construction, kinship and the family, and the material well-being of most of the populace. The forward-looking aspects encompassed the enlarged role of famine and the increasing abuses by warriors, nascent improvements in agricultural technology, the development of more broken families and a large servile class, and the growing commercialization of the economy. As of 1280, however, the latter were harbingers of the future, but from two of these components—the intensification of the agrarian regime and the rise of a booming commercial economy—would come hope for better times.

3

The Dawn of a New Era
Lowered Mortality and the "Muromachi Optimum," 1280–1450

*J*apanese historians have long looked upon the fourteenth century as a turning point. Arai Hakuseki, the Tokugawa philosopher and political adviser, may have been the first to express this view in his *Historical Essays (Tokushi yoron),* revised for the last time in 1724. While Arai saw the change as primarily political, with the warrior class overtaking the Heian aristocracy, others have claimed that the fourteenth century was a social and cultural watershed too. These latter scholars have variously defined the change as the decline of multilayered ancient social organization *(shiki),* the rise of feudal ties, the appearance of a commoner class, and the assertion of greater local autonomy. The portrayal of the fourteenth century as the beginning of "Japan's medieval world" is merely the most recent assertion of this view.[1]

In demography too, myriad factors—from famine and disease to agricultural technology and settlement patterns to industry and commerce to family structure—suggest that the epoch from 1280 to 1450 witnessed a turning point from stasis to growth. This chapter will consider the beginning of Japan's third wave of population increase, seeking to infer a defensible archipelago-wide total for 1450 and then explain why that figure is the most reasonable given the social, economic, and political conditions existing during those 170 years. Various calculations suggest that the archipelago contained about 9.6–10.5 million by 1450, or about 4–5 million more people than in 1280.

The calculated population range is an outcome of the complex interaction of many social and economic factors. Here I shall address mortality, termed a direct variable because scholars can quantify it to a certain degree. Disease, especially endemic die-offs, posed an age-old threat to a population with growing immunities, but the era from about 1370 to 1450 seems to have been relatively free of infectious outbreaks. The central difficulty of the age—how to obtain an adequate food supply—subsided notably, and the government and populace began to react to famine in different and more sophisticated ways than had been the case during the Kangi or Shōga crises. Moreover, a local death register *(kakochō)* covering most of this time allows more nuanced insights into hunger. Only the problems of war and political instability produced greater mortality, as the Wars between the Northern and Southern Dynasties lasted from 1333 to 1392. Combatants may not have died in significant numbers, but the wars inflicted untold casualties on farmers and merchants through warrior "self-help" provisioning and scorched-earth tactics.

As Kitō predicted in a general way, the era from 1280 to 1450 was the start of a brand-new demographic cycle, with a growth spurt lasting for the rest of the medieval epoch. In particular, for the half century from the cessation of widespread hostilities in 1368 until the famine of 1420, residents entered an age appropriately termed "the Muromachi Optimum," when the new shogunate was at its height and social and economic expansion most vigorous.

A POPULATION ESTIMATE FOR THE MID-FIFTEENTH CENTURY

The 170 years from 1280 until 1450 were a time of great political instability. By the late thirteenth century, the dominant partner in the Kamakura dyarchy, the *bakufu,* was experiencing growing difficulty in governing, mostly through the increasingly violent and bothersome activities of the "evil bands" *(akutō),* described repeatedly in documents of the time. Then, between 1331 and 1368, most of the archipelago was ripped apart in sweeping warfare among those who sided with Go-Daigo or his various opponents, a Japanese version of Europe's destructive Thirty Years' War of 1618–1648. After a brief respite of fifty years or so, the specter of famine again haunted the land, first in the 1420s and then again in the late 1440s.

Because of these conditions, the Muromachi shogunate never succeeded in administering the entire archipelago effectively. And because its reach usually exceeded its grasp, historians have very little in the way of quantifiable materials that might provide a clue to Japan's total population in the fourteenth or fifteenth centuries. There are certainly no census data, and nothing even approaches reliable acreage records such as the Great Land Registers of the Kamakura era, from which I was able to infer, however dubiously, the islands' total number of inhabitants. How can scholars possibly arrive at an acceptable estimate grounded in the primary sources?

One method, based upon Muromachi-period military records, yields what seems to be a fairly plausible total.[2] To be sure, this computation is speculative, even more so than those already employed, but it reveals that Japan's population in 1450, at the end of the Ashikaga heyday before the maelstrom of civil war, may have already achieved an important milestone. And another scholar has provided corroboration for this figure by an independent means.

According to the highly reliable diary of the monk Mansai *(Mansai jūgo nikki)*, in the eleventh month of 1433 the Muromachi shogunate decided to punish the frequently unruly monks of Enryakuji, a major temple located northeast of Kyoto. According to Mansai, the Yamana, a daimyo family who ruled several provinces, were particularly enthusiastic about the expedition and were able to provide numerous troops for the venture: 300 mounted warriors and about 2,000–3,000 common footsoldiers called *nobushi*.[3] Another powerful daimyo family, the Doki of Mino, was less motivated, but still furnished 20–30 horse riders and 1,000–2,000 infantry.[4] Forty-four years later, in the ninth month of 1477, the shogunate engaged the Hatakeyama family in a fight for its life. According to another highly reliable source, a diary kept by monks at Kōfukuji *(Daijōin jisha zōjiki)*, the Hatakeyama assembled 350 mounted fighters and 2,000 armored footsoldiers.[5] These are only three examples of the numbers of soldiers at the disposal of the Muromachi lords *(shugo daimyō)*, but they seem to represent fairly accurately the maximum size of fighting forces committed to campaigns. It is especially noteworthy that both events occurred in the autumn, after the harvest had been gathered, allowing the various warlords to draft a large number of peasants or peasant-samurai to serve as infantry.

Leaving aside the Doki as exceptional, owing to their lack of commitment to battle, I arrived at an average number of horse riders (325) and footsoldiers (2,500) for the Yamana and Hatakeyama. I then proceeded to calculate an approximate size for all the expeditionary military forces within the archipelago around 1450, performing the operation in two ways to obtain a range of results. First, I simply counted the number of Muromachi daimyo (37) and multiplied that figure by 2,825 (horse riders plus footsoldiers) to derive a sum of 104,525; to this subtotal I added the troops of the Muromachi shogunate itself, probably equivalent to about ten daimyo armies (28,250).[6] The grand total of Muromachi soldiers calculated in this way is 132,775.

Several Muromachi daimyo administered more than one province, and so it may be argued that many daimyo could outfit 2,825 men *per province*. For example, the Doki ruled only Mino, but had they wished, they could probably have provided 3,000 or more troops in 1433. Therefore I made another calculation based not on the number of daimyo but on the provinces that could provide troops. Omitting tiny jurisdictions such as Shima, Aki, Oki, and Awa (where the number of troops would have been very small) and assuming that the total number of provinces that could produce around 3,000 soldiers was sixty, I obtained a figure for all provinces of 169,500. Adding to that a *bakufu* presence of 28,250, one derives a total of 197,750.

So far the calculations have yielded a minimum drawn from a tally for daimyo and a maximum based on the number of provinces likely to produce troops. Both have been founded on various assumptions, not the least of which is the idea that a clear demarcation existed between samurai and peasants. Setting aside that problem for the moment, I required a method to convert these soldierly numbers into archipelago-wide population estimates. For this operation, one choice is to turn to the eighth century, when both the maximum number of soldiers and the total population are known. Under the Nara system, it has been proposed that a population deemed to range from 5.8 to 6.4 million could support 100,000–120,000 troops *at the most*.[7]

Utilizing the average of 110,000 troops for the early eighth century, I then obtained multipliers for 1450. If the 1450 military numbered 132,775, as implied by the number of daimyo, then the multiplier is 1.21. If we use 197,750, tabulated from provincial totals, then the multiplier is 1.8. If we multiply the average early *ritsuryō* population of 6.1 million by a factor of 1.21, the estimate for 1450 equals 7.4 million. If we employ the higher multiplier of 1.8, then the total population is equivalent to 11 million. Averaging these two figures results in a population of 9.2 million for Japan in 1450.

This number, however, does not represent the whole population because urbanites have been omitted. For the late Kamakura era, Japan's

urbanized population was computed at about 3 percent; by 1450, all indications are that despite the demise of Kamakura, urbanization had expanded fairly rapidly. Assuming that the figure for 1450 was around 4
percent, I found that the total archipelago-wide population would have
been about 9.6 million.

Given the numerous assumptions behind this number, the reader
may easily entertain doubts; three suspicions seem particularly telling.
First, it is uncertain whether the ratio of maximal military forces to total
population was the same in the eighth as in the mid-fifteenth century.
After all, few would doubt that the Japanese economy in 1450 was far
more advanced than it had been in 730. If the economy was more specialized and commercialized, with improvements in agricultural production,
then fewer, more productive persons could have supported a larger number of troops in the field. If this were the case, then the 9.6 million estimate would have to be decreased by some appropriate amount. This
reasoning would lead to the conclusion that the islands had fewer—
perhaps even considerably fewer—than 9.6 million people by 1450.[8]

A second doubt cuts the other way. The figures adduced for the
Yamana and Hatakeyama represent only those warriors going on expedition. Presumably, both daimyo would have left some warriors at home
to keep the peace. Historians have no way of knowing what percentage
of troops would have been left behind, but it is important to note that any
calculation would serve to increase the maximum number of fighting
forces and the multiplier, thus leading to an even higher population.

The third doubt raises the question of how well-defined the status of
samurai was in 1450. It is not clear from entries in diaries that fighters
listed therein were all specialized warriors. *Nobushi* were typically estate
residents, and the only other notation merely calls footsoldiers "shields."
Traditionally, scholars have thought of warriors after 1333 as not being
a clear-cut status and the samurai class as difficult to define. Under these
circumstances, provinces may have contained many more or fewer peasant-
samurai, and the Muromachi military could have been much larger or
smaller than the diary entries suggest. A firm estimate of Japan's population in 1450 would seem to be problematic.

It has been almost a truism among historians of Japan that the line
between warrior and peasant was vague from the appearance of the "evil
bands" in the late 1200s until Hideyoshi's artificial demarcation in the
late sixteenth century. Recently, however, some have come to question
this assumption and to assert that the status of warrior/samurai was

quite separate from the rest of society even during the tumultuous era of the Warring States (1467–1568). In a path-finding book, the leading Japanese authority on that age contends that even in the late fifteenth and sixteenth centuries, warriors were a specialized class and status.[9] Rural folk did not care for samurai, resented their interference in village affairs, and participated in battle mostly as porters and manual laborers. In this view, the line between fighting experts and most peasants was much clearer than heretofore imagined.

If samurai and peasants were sharply differentiated as late as 1450, the figures drawn from the two diaries noted above could well represent the maximum forces available to the *shugo daimyō* for campaigns, and the method employed above to estimate Japan's population would be more reliable. It is critical to note, however, that if the line between fighters and commoners was blurred, then it would become much more difficult to use the above method to compute Japan's population in 1450 with any degree of certainty.

I have raised and admitted these suspicions so as not to make the figure seem more reliable than it is. Fortunately, tentative corroboration for the 9.6 million figure has come from an expert source. Japanese demographers studying the Tokugawa period have recently begun to take an interest in the period before 1600; Saitō Osamu has also made an estimate for the year 1450, arguing that the archipelago was home to 10.5 million in that year.[10]

Because Saitō's research is still in a preliminary and unpublished stage, he has not laid out his argument in detail, but in effect he worked backward from the widely known census figures of 1721, making modifications according to his knowledge of Tokugawa-period population. The Malthusian demographer conducted extensive studies of the demographic effects of famine and disease during the era 1600–1868 and concluded that even under optimal conditions it was doubtful that the rate of demographic increase could have exceeded .4 percent per year for very long. Given this assumption and based upon his knowledge of subsistence crises before 1600, Saitō then proceeded to make population estimates for 1000 (6 million), 1250 (6.5 million), and 1450 (10.5 million).[11]

Because Saitō's work is based upon data from the Tokugawa period and is intimately bound up with the controversial question of Japan's population in 1600, it is inappropriate to deal with it in detail at this time. (See chapter 5.) Suffice it to say that the estimate of 10.5 million is reasonably close to the earlier result; it is probably most prudent to suggest a

range from 9.6 to 10.5 million for the mid-fifteenth century. Most important, this research, derived according to more conventional demographic
methods, provides crucial support for my figure.

In chapter 1, I calculated that Japan's population in 1280 was about
5.7–6.2 million. If the above figures are reliable for 1450, then clearly the
archipelago had begun a wave of growth sometime between those two
dates. Just to make the calculation simpler, assume that the population
was 6 million in 1280 and 10 million in 1450. While not spectacular, the
rate of increase would have amounted to .23 percent per annum, an altogether reasonable figure given what is known about premodern populations in general and Tokugawa-era demography in particular. With the
estimates of 6.5 million for 1250 and 10.5 million for 1450, the rate of
growth would have been a slightly less impressive .2 percent per year. In
either case, figures demographers can now produce tend to support the
contention that a new growth cycle began not long after 1280. Numbers
are handy, but now the overriding question becomes the following: why
did Japan's population begin a slow but steady ascent in the late thirteenth century? To answer this query, once again scholars must examine
all the relevant social and economic factors, beginning with death rates.

MORTALITY FACTORS: DISEASE

For the period 1280–1450, the historical record identifies three major illnesses: smallpox, measles, and influenza.[12] Smallpox, the virus that traditionally had the greatest demographic impact, struck in 1314, 1342,
1361, 1365, and 1374; the epidemic of 1365 seems to have been the
harshest. Measles afflicted the populace in 1306–1307, 1320, 1362,
1380, 1405, and 1441, killing mostly children in the first outbreak. It
may never have become endemic in Japan and killed relatively few
people.[13] In particular, the three-day measles, a less virulent disease from
which survival rates may well have been high, is commonly noted, especially for Kyoto. Influenza visited in 1329, 1345, 1365, 1371, 1378,
1407–1408, and 1428. This repetition of influenza outbreaks may have
foretold a shift in Japanese disease patterns toward respiratory ailments,
but from what is known of Tokugawa epidemics, this proposition seems
unfounded.[14] There are no notices of dysentery or chickenpox, and other
common ailments, such as malaria and tuberculosis, remained active but
do not admit of quantification, as in previous periods.

Viewed in this way, the large majority of epidemic outbreaks was concentrated before 1380, suggesting two points. First, the years from 1331 until 1380 witnessed most of the fighting in the Wars between the Northern and Southern Dynasties; it seems appropriate to posit a relationship between the social dislocation accompanying war and an increased incidence of microbial afflictions. Second, beginning around 1380, the number of epidemics dropped off markedly, with none being noted for smallpox and only two apiece for measles and influenza.

The microparasitic drain upon the population therefore likely decreased as the epoch progressed. In chapter 1, I noted three factors that affected the number and virulence of disease outbreaks: the qualities of the microorganism under consideration, the likelihood of contact between a susceptible host and a patient during the time the patient is infectious, and the extent to which the population is already immune to the disease in question. Of these three factors, only the increased likelihood of contact would have served to expand the role of disease, as trade and transportation improved, a point noted in chapter 4. Yet there were no new notable microorganisms, and it is likely that the immunity of the populace continued to rise. This analysis indicates a lessened role for disease in the epoch 1280–1450.

Furthermore, in at least ten years, all occurring during 1368–1450, plagues were associated with famine. This tie could mean that hungry peasants were more susceptible to the unnamed affliction or that disease outbreak hindered harvest work. It was more likely, however, that famine was the root cause, the recorded epidemic being a reference to maladies induced during the death throes of starvation. In sum, the written record implies that disease was a declining cause of mortality over the course of these 170 years, leading me to posit the existence of a "Muromachi Optimum" from about 1370 to 1450 and to place the beginning of Japan's "medieval" growth cycle at that time.

Lest one become too complacent about epidemics, however, it is wise to remember that archaeological, artistic, and ethnographic sources, as well as laconic historical entries, still suggest that the populace feared disease outbreaks. To take one example, from the fourth to the seventh months of 1421, an unknown infection struck Kyoto, claiming victims of all ranks. While the capital was especially hard hit, "the fear of illness among all under heaven was without limit." Civil aristocrats afflicted with the malady took the tonsure one day and died the next. When the shogun Yoshimochi made a pilgrimage to Kiyomizudera, the sick poured into the temple precincts, and he fled for his life. Prayers were intoned and the *nenbutsu* recited to succor the dying. Even the ancient Heian custom of performing court rituals to chase the epidemic god *(ekishin)* out of the city took place at major thoroughfares. Eventually a message was sent to Ise Shrine in hopes of soothing the gods' anger, and by the end of the month, the situation was indeed calmer.[15]

While the written record only hints at the deadliness of epidemics, archaeologists have come upon concrete evidence of the fear provoked by "ordinary" endemic sicknesses. At famous excavations such as the port town of Kusado Sengen near Hiroshima, they have uncovered pictures of the bull-headed king of the *devas,* associated with disease, and numerous wooden tablets *(jufu)* written to ward off illness. Other relics from medieval excavations, just now coming to light, suggest that rural folk as well as their citified neighbors envisioned disease as a curse *(tatari)* that only the proper ritual could lift.[16] And ethnographic studies of Tokugawa and later sources show a rich tradition of family rituals dealing with infectious disease, including tying garlic cloves to the doorway to prevent entry of an infectious agent, chasing the smallpox or other god into the next village through prayer and various other means, singing and dancing the smallpox god's favorite songs to calm him down, performing an annual ritual every new year to protect the family, and utilizing shamans to exorcise disease demons.[17] While no one knows how far back these and other superstitions harken, it would not be surprising to find that some of them are quite old. They stand as vivid testimony to the anxiety still provoked by these once universally fatal microbes.

MORTALITY FACTORS: FAMINE

Although there were no crises of the magnitude of the Kangi or Shōga eras, the 1280–1450 period continued to suffer frequent hungry years. And as in the late twelfth century, the interrelated problems of food supply and violence combined to prevent the population from achieving a high rate of growth. Unlike warfare, which claimed more lives than ever before because of the drawn-out hostilities between the Northern and Southern Dynasties, however, famine over the fourteenth and first half of the fifteenth centuries appears to have receded as a major cause of mortality. Combined with the gradually lessening impact of plagues, this decline played a crucial role in the spurt of demographic increase beginning in the late thirteenth century.

Several factors suggest a diminished role for famine. To start with,

TABLE 3.1
Climatological Trends, 1280–1450

PERIOD OF ENTRIES	WEIGHTED NUMBER OF ENTRIES				
	RAIN	COLD	HEAT	DRYNESS	TOTAL
1280–1350	198	14	41	73	326
Percentile	61%	4%	13%	22%	
	Drought index: 22		Wet, cold index: 65		
1351–1399	139	34	52	74	299
Percentile	47%	11%	17%	25%	
	Drought index: 25		Wet, cold index: 58		
1400–1450	301	41	71	128	541
Percentile	56%	8%	13%	24%	
	Drought index: 24		Wet, cold index: 63		

Sources: Sasaki Junnosuke, *Kikin to sensō*. Entries weighted as in table 1.4.
Note: The drought index was arrived at by dividing the references to drought by the total number of entries; the wet, cold index was the result of dividing the references to wet and cold by the total number of entries.

the archipelago's weather, which was mainly responsible for the three great crises of Yōwa, Kangi, and Shōga, may have become more benign for most of the period, at least according to some indicators. Written sources for climate data revealed that in general it was warmer and damper, especially during the early 1300s, than it had been in the 1200s. After 1350, however, conditions seem to have turned much colder until 1400, when it became warmer and wetter again.[18] (See table 3.1.)

Viewed in the aggregate, however, these data can be misleading. For example, nearly one-third of the references to frigid temperatures over the period 1400–1450 occur for the single year 1415. In particular, these long-term statistics do not show how weather conditions tended to gyrate back and forth from drought to excessive precipitation, inducing many famines during this era. Moreover, because of the disproportionate number of diaries and other sources compiled by the literate few residing in Kyoto, the figures probably exaggerate the role of that region's climate and the city's constant struggle with its waterways, especially the justly famous floods of the Kamo River. It is probably wise to conclude that the epoch under consideration was somewhat drier and warmer than table 3.1 would lead the reader to believe.

Japan's leading experts in climatology have looked at various sets of data and have come to somewhat differing conclusions. Japan's first and most well-known climate historian, Yamamoto Takeo, suggested in an article published in 1967 that the fifteenth century, most particularly the decades from 1400 to 1450, represented a "Little Ice Age," not only in Japan, but also throughout the world. Utilizing worldwide data on ocean levels and Japanese descriptions of the freezing of Lake Suwa, the timing of Kyoto's cherry blossoms in the spring, and the number of snowy days in the capital, Yamamoto concluded that the average temperature in Japan declined precipitously beginning around 1400, bottoming out around 1450, only to rebound and then plummet once again in the first half of the sixteenth century.[19] This opinion has become the conventional wisdom.

Recently, however, another historian, Isogai Fujio, has reexamined these older findings, combining them with new scientific data regarding the pollen of the creeping pine *(haimatsu),* a tree normally growing high in the mountains of the Kanto and Tohoku.[20] This plant flourishes in cold weather; an archaeologist who conducted the pollen analyses found that his data fit the conventional view relatively well. This general correspondence still left scholars in the dark as to specific, absolute dates for the hypothesized "Little Ice Age," in particular because the information on ocean levels and pollen analyses yields only relative dates.[21] In the newer view, the cold, wet spell of the early and mid-Kamakura epoch continued throughout the fourteenth century, reaching its harshest extent around 1400 and then warming until the turn of the sixteenth century. This conclusion conforms more closely to the data presented in table 3.1 than does the conventional interpretation.

Analyses of tree rings and ice core samples (mentioned in chapter 1) combined with records from throughout East Asia yield more insight.[22] In particular, the period from 1444 to 1465 was fraught with volcanism in the Indo-Pacific area, and another wet, cold trend characterized world climate. There is especially strong evidence for Europe, but also China, Korea, and Japan. This information would contradict that gathered in table 3.1 and tend to verify the older theory that the mid-fifteenth century witnessed the harshest cold of the period.

Given the variety, sparseness, and inconsistencies in these statistics, it is probably wise to wait for the results of future research. Some scholars admit as much, indicating that historians need to integrate their more recent documentary findings about the relationship between famine and climate with facts presented by researchers in other disciplines.[23] Although convincing evidence is elusive, it should be noted that the conventional theory holds that the period from 1370 to 1420 comprised a "little optimum" *(shōkō ki)*, an interpretation dovetailing nicely with the findings on volcanism and the record on mortality from pestilence, famine, and war.[24] Drawing on this same information, another scholar has expanded the "little optimum" to include the century from 1350 to 1450, when the weather was warm and damp, agrarian production more stable, and famine less frequent.[25]

Turning more specifically to statistics on food shortages, we find that they were not as widespread nor as severe as they had been in the 1200s. One characteristic was the somewhat lessened frequency of generalized starvation years as compared to the previous era (1150–1280).[26] (See table 3.2.) Over the 130 years ranging from 1150 to 1280, hunger was a serious problem about once every 6.2 years, whereas from 1280 to 1450 the incidence of such subsistence crises was around once per 7.4 years, even when major regional events are included. When I calculated strictly on the basis of years when general famine could be proven to have struck, the ratio declines even further, to about once every ten years. This difference is sizable enough to allow for several decades for which no widespread lean seasons were recorded at all. Considering that none of the famines occurring between 1280 and 1450 resulted in the severe social and economic repercussions of the Kangi or Shōga eras, I came to the conclusion that mortality from hunger declined in the late Kamakura and first half of the Muromachi periods.

The dramatic increase in written sources between 1250 and 1450 renders this historical comparison all the more persuasive. Scholars can know the causes, effects, and regional impact of famines for the 1280–1450 era in a way that is just not possible for late Heian and early Kamakura Japan. Despite this bountiful documentation, materials from the epoch under consideration do not tend to show a greater frequency of far-flung famines.

Of course, the forty-one local crises between 1280 and 1450 far outnumber the mere six noted for the preceding epoch. One conclusion could be that local famines were undoubtedly far more common in the late Heian and Kamakura periods than the data show; the seeming dramatic increase in regional hungry years for 1280–1450 was likely due to the aforementioned greater numbers of surviving records in various areas. Another explanation might be that the more advanced agricultural and

TABLE 3.2

Famine Years, Extent, and Causes, 1280–1450

YEAR	EXTENT	CAUSE
1283	Local	Unknown
1287	Local	Unknown
1294	Local	Cold, rainy weather
1298	Local	Drought
1310	Local	Unknown
1314	Widespread	Cold, rainy weather
1320	Widespread	Cold, rainy weather
1321	Widespread	Drought
1322	Widespread	Drought
1323	Local	Drought
1330	Widespread	Unknown
1334	Local	Drought
1335	Local	Unknown
1336	Local	Unknown
1337	Local	Unknown
1338	Local	Unknown
1339	Local	Drought
1340	Local	Drought
1344	Local	Cold, rainy weather
1345	Local	Cold, rainy weather
1349	Widespread	Drought
1352	Local	Unknown
1353	Local	Drought; cold, rainy weather
1356	Widespread	Cold, rainy weather
1357	Local	Cold, rainy weather
1360	Widespread	Drought
1362	Widespread	Drought
1363	Local	Drought
1366	Local	Unknown
1369	Widespread	Drought
1370	Widespread	Drought
1377	Local	Drought

Table 3.2 continues

Table 3.2 continued

YEAR	EXTENT	CAUSE
1379	Widespread	Unknown
1390	Widespread	Cold, rainy weather
1391	Widespread	Unknown
1393	Local	Drought
1401	Local	Drought
1402	Local	Unknown
1403	Local	Cold, rainy weather
1404	Local	Unknown
1405	Local	Cold, rainy weather
1406	Widespread	Cold, rainy weather
1407	Widespread	Drought
1408	Local	Unknown
1409	Local	Unknown
1411	Local	Unknown
1412	Local	Unknown
1419	Local	Drought
1420	Widespread	Drought
1421	Widespread	Drought
1423	Local	Cold, rainy weather
1424	Local	Unknown
1427	Local	Cold, rainy weather
1428	Widespread	Cold, rainy weather
1429	Local	Drought
1430	Local	Unknown
1431	Local	Merchants
1434	Local	Drought
1437	Widespread	Cold, rainy weather
1438	Widespread	Cold, rainy weather
1441	Local	Unknown
1443	Local	Unknown
1448	Widespread	Cold, rainy weather
1449	Widespread	Cold, rainy weather

Source: Sasaki Junnosuke, *Kikin to sensō*, pp. 63–117.

commercial sectors of the Muromachi epoch prevented some potentially major famines from spiraling out of control and limited their effects to local regions.

A Brief Narrative of Hunger, 1280–1450

To press the argument further, I will describe several notable famines in more detail. Surveying the data from 1280 to 1450, we can discern four sequences of bad years: those few at the end of the Kamakura age, the ones associated with the Wars between the Northern and Southern Dynasties, a small number during the "Muromachi Optimum," and the more well-documented crises during 1420–1450. Most important, the narrative of crop failure and starvation for the fourth subperiod suggests significant changes in the way people reacted to famine, as the rising commercial sector and institutional policies of food relief made their dual impacts felt.

The late Kamakura era, in contrast to preceding decades, was blessed with relatively good harvests.[27] The longest and most general famine of the late Kamakura era took place over the years 1320–1322, with hungry people still common in Kyoto until the harvest of 1323.[28] Written sources are brief, but the immediate cause of the crisis seems to have been the abnormally cold winters of 1319–1320 and 1320–1321, followed in each case by drought in the summer. Two points come across clearly: first, in Kyoto the price of barley hit 300 coins per measure *(to)*, causing Emperor Go-Daigo to delegate the Investigators to oversee merchant sales of the grain to starving residents in the six month of 1320.[29] To one historian, this description is reminiscent of conditions during the Yōwa famine, when routes to the capital were closed and desperately needed grain shipments shut out.[30] Second, as in previous bouts with hunger, the populace fled Kyoto, preferring to tear down their homes, sell or barter the materials, and head for the hills in search of sustenance. For the rest of the Kamakura era, famines were primarily local in character.[31]

In 1333, a conflict erupted between two claimants to the throne and survival for all may have been greatly imperiled. Yet few sources concerning food shortages are extant for the second subperiod, and the tie between war and famine can usually be only inferred.[32] The first notable crisis came in the winter of 1338 and during 1339–1340, when "an unknown number" of Kyotoites starved to death, while the city's temples announced that they had tried to help many by "leading them . . . to the countryside."[33] The same source also notes that many would-be movers were too exhausted to make the trip. Even in the mid-fourteenth century, starving city dwellers were still resigned to leaving their homes to find food in the countryside, just as they had done earlier. Despite a bountiful harvest in the autumn of 1340, temples continued to care for the needy at that time.[34]

The next bad year was 1349, but again the sources are so brief that one cannot be certain of the famine's extent or the number of deaths. It is clear that drought was a factor; moreover, this hungry time came when the Wars between the Northern and Southern Dynasties raged from Kamakura to Kyushu. This coincidence makes it tempting to posit a relationship between the fighting and bad harvests, but sources make no such direct link. In the sixth month of 1351, the Northern Dynasty discussed changing its year-period to ward off starvation because the previous year had been lean, but there is no mention of famine in Kyoto until the spring of 1352.[35] To repeat, forces on each side of the military conflict were trading turns occupying the capital; given Kyoto's history of isolation and starvation during war, the instability in the capital may have been the real cause behind the shortages.

Regional famines of the mid-1350s became a general crisis in 1360 and again in 1362. Drought was the major cause in both years, and roads between Kyoto and the countryside were filled with corpses. Crops were damaged in Wakasa in 1361, but outside of the excessive snow in the winter of 1361–1362, nothing else indicated that 1362 would see a repeat of widespread hunger. In the summer of 1362, severe drought again occurred, so harsh that the level of Lake Biwa reportedly fell thirty-six feet *(sanjō rokushaku)*. Crops failed and those who starved to death were beyond counting.[36] As earlier, fighting around the capital region had flared up during these years, lending further credence to the suspicion that war played a role in the incidence of famine, at least around Kyoto.

The last general famine for this subperiod occurred in 1369, as crops failed and uncounted hundreds died. Again the sources are too sparse to allow more than a glimpse of the event, but it is notable that in the next year (1370) hunger stalked Honshu east of Suruga, probably induced by unusually damp, cold weather. The Muromachi *bakufu* reacted to the crisis by prohibiting excessive displays of wealth.[37] Ultimately, the sparseness of written sources, undoubtedly arising from the destruction of war, frustrates any attempt to do more than infer a causal relationship between famine and war.

The third subperiod of lean harvests from 1370, which nearly coincided with the end of archipelago-wide hostilities, until 1420, was the so-called "Muromachi Optimum." Multi-year or widespread famines occurred only thrice: during 1379, 1390–1391, and 1406–1407. Little is known about the famine of 1379 except that regions as far apart as Tsushima, Buzen, Kii, Kyoto, Kōzuke, Aizu, and Mutsu announced heavy death tolls and the spiking of grain prices (at 280 *monme* per unit of rice and 230 *monme* per unit of wheat). Climate again had a hand in the problem, as it was unusually damp and cold that year.

From 1379 to 1390, harvests seem to have been adequate, and even the famine of 1390–1391 is noted at first only in the most general terms in historical materials from Kyoto as applying to "all under heaven." As during similar crises, the court altered the year-period, but as 1390 wore on, the situation became more critical. Crops failed in Kōzuke in the fall of that year, but written records do not become more specific until 1391, when officials in Tanba, Kyoto, Mino, Kōzuke, and Mutsu noted crop failure owing to excessive rain and cold, skyrocketing prices for rice and soy beans, and far-flung famine. These conditions lingered in Kyoto and other unnamed provinces through the sixth month of 1393, in part because of drought. From 1393 until 1406, local famines were the rule, almost all in eastern Honshu.[38]

Regional shortages in 1405 multiplied into bad years for the entire archipelago during 1406–1407. Responsible officers in the assorted provinces of Buzen, Tanba, Yamashiro (Kyoto), Mino, Etchū, and Mutsu announced that their people faced crop failure owing to excessive rains and winds. Even Kasuga Shrine complained of a shortage of supplies.[39] The crisis deepened in 1407, when the Kinai region (Kyoto and Harima) and Mutsu indicated widespread hunger. Despite evidence of cold, wet weather for the next few years, however, starvation does not appear as a problem in the sources. This brief respite from hunger lasted through 1418.

From 1419, a regional shortage in the food supply spread to become perhaps the worst famine of the entire period, lasting from 1420 to 1421.[40] It effectively brought the "Muromachi Optimum" to a close and ushered in the fourth subperiod. The crisis began in the Kanto, especially Shimotsuke, with heavy rains and floods described as the primary cause. Then in the summer of 1420, a hot sun beat down across the islands, and harvests failed throughout the Kinai and western Japan. The water level in the Yodo River became too low for boat traffic, and Lake Biwa dipped far below its usual shorelines. Gion Shrine and the shogunate canceled rituals because of the weather and sundry shortages. In addition to officials throughout western Japan, those in Etchū, southern Dewa, Aizu, and various unnamed provinces also described far-flung famine, suggesting the general thrust of the crisis. By year's end, a measure of rice cost 1,000 coins in the capital and one *shō* went for 100 coins in some rural areas, but the next year was no better. Tanba, Kyoto and its vicinity, Etchū, Echigo, Noto, and the entire Tohoku were the hardest hit, but other unnamed provinces were victimized as well. In Kyoto, prayers were sent to nearby shrines to relieve the suffering from the deadly combination of drought and starvation.

The famine of 1420–1421 was harsh, but it was also notable for other reasons that suggest an important change in the reactions of both the government and the populace to the problem of food supply.[41] As usual, sources tell horrific tales of body counts in Kyoto, with carts piled high with corpses. And as in the late twelfth and thirteenth centuries, many of the city's residents fled the capital and "filled the mountains, moors, and estuaries." At the same time, however, for the first time in history, the poor and hungry were noted as streaming *into* Kyoto in record numbers to find food relief. The number of migrants was so great that they may have triggered a secondary famine within the city.[42] Victims begged throughout the city and assembled at wealthy Zen temples such as Tenryūji and Shōkokuji, where handouts might be had. Moreover, the *bakufu* itself, as well as several resident daimyo, doled out grain to the poor along the riverbanks near Fifth Rank Avenue *(gojō kawara)*.[43]

These trends were significant because they suggest fundamental changes in the islands' society and economy. Instead of exiting a city cut off from food—a death trap for those caught therein—starving people for the first time went *into* Kyoto en masse looking for grain. They did so for two crucial reasons: first, the commercial system had become developed enough to move food into the city, attracting hungry hordes from rural areas; and second, secular and religious institutions had begun to provide food relief to these migrants as never before. For these two reasons, the famine of 1420–1421 may not have taken so many lives as the sources implied. This famine looked more like crises of the Tokugawa period, when folks with empty bellies regularly left the countryside for Edo, Kyoto, Osaka, or other towns. Somewhere between 1280 and 1420, the archipelago's social structure and economy had made a fundamental transition toward a more developed commercialization.

From 1421 to 1427, bad years came in fits and starts. The year 1428 seems to have been a time of major famine. Most places reporting starvation—Kyoto, Ise, Shimotsuke, Kai, Kamakura, and Aizu—were located in the central and eastern portion of Honshu. One source states that twenty thousand died in Kamakura—undoubtedly a great exaggeration. The wheat crop withered in Musashi too. Yet there is mention of suffering among "all under heaven." Crop failures were probably tied to the excessive rains of the previous growing season.

It should come as no surprise that in 1428 the first in a long line of local riots *(do* or *tsuchi ikki)* began in Kyoto and elsewhere.[44] (See chapter 4.) Angry mobs with empty stomachs flooded into Kyoto from nearby Ōmi and Yamashiro, seeking food handouts while also demanding and receiving relief from their debts *(tokusei;* lit., virtuous administration). In the process they committed various violent outrages, including arson and theft from granaries. They destroyed the buildings of moneylenders *(dosō; sakaya),* stole their property, and ripped up debt contracts. Even daimyo and their warriors were powerless to stem the tide of the angry mob; in fact these troops seem to have often joined with the rioters. With hungry poor people congregating in Kyoto, grain was in short supply in the spring of 1429. Local protests then took place in Harima (Yano Estate) and Etchū. Rioters at Yano were so determined that they broke through samurai lines of the *shugo daimyō* Akamatsu family.

One of the reasons for the riots was the weakness of the ruling elite. The emperor had just died, and the position of Muromachi shogun was vacant, rendering the government impotent to direct relief activities. Just as important as the vacuum at the top, however, was the increased commercialization of the local economy, which entangled farmers in cash contracts. When crops failed, cultivators were not only beset by hunger, but they also could not make good on their contractual obligations. They then flooded into the capital seeking food and revenge against their creditors.[45] Because of the violence it provoked in and around Kyoto, the famine of 1428–1429 served as the first in a series of escalating steps toward the Ōnin War of 1467–1477. In a different way from the events of 1420–1421, this debacle also showed the new-found power of the market to provide food to debtors, who then had the stamina to protest against loan agents. The market was at the root cause of the violence, giving rioters both the strength and the reason to act.

In 1431, as if to give further testimony to the growing effect of the cash nexus and merchants, Kinai traders created a subsistence crisis for their own benefit. As many starved in Kyoto in the seventh month, the Muromachi shogunate got wind of the deed, arrested and bound up six rice merchants, and interrogated them in the Office of Warriors *(samurai dokoro).* At another location near Kyoto, residents of Yamashina attacked Sen'yūji and burned local homes. At last the *bakufu* stepped in, obtained confessions from the merchants (one of whom had once been a beggar!), and sold the hoarded grain to the hungry citizens of Kyoto. Most famines are "artificial" to some degree, but the plot uncovered in 1431 shows just how low merchants would stoop for profit and just how far the improved systems of transport and commerce allowed them to manipulate the market.

Until 1436, harvests appear to have been adequate. A drought in 1436, followed by excessive rains the next year, caused the crop to wither around Kyoto and eastern Honshu; the Kanto, Etchū, and Aizu were singled out for specific mention. At Shogun Yoshiaki's request, monks at Shōkokuji gathered and doled out grain to Kyoto's suffering poor, some of whom may have entered the city to find such relief. The hungry times continued into 1438, but outside of the descriptions of corpses piling up in Kyoto, the roads in and out of the city being choked with wanderers, and vague references to "all under heaven" and "various provinces," it is impossible to discern the extent of the emergency.

One last harsh famine struck in 1448, ranging from Buzen, Kii, and Kyoto in the west to Kōzuke, Musashi, Noto, Aizu, and Mutsu in the east.[46] A summer that simultaneously saw too much rain, then a typhoon, and finally drought was the chief cause, especially in eastern Honshu. Poor cultivators displaced from the region around Kyoto flooded into the city, crying out for food and debt relief and smashing and burning pawnshops.[47] The famine continued to haunt some areas, especially Kyoto, in 1449, when the year-period was changed to invite better fortune.

Described in such detail, the period 1280–1450 appears to have witnessed frequent food shortages, even though there was no Kangi or Shōga famine. Yet both the late Kamakura and middle Muromachi were times of relative plenty. Moreover, for the first time the commercial and social systems gave signs of ameliorating the deadly conditions of hunger, although the cash nexus could also bring down the ire of poor cultivators on loan agents and the rich. Yet the impression of one hungry season following upon another is not mistaken because even in the best of times medieval peasants were not too far removed from malnutrition and eventual starvation. Fortunately, demographic records extant from this period help scholars to examine the role of famine from a different, quantitative perspective.

The Yūgyōji Death Register

It is a truism of the Japanese historical profession that there are no demographic records for the so-called "medieval" age (usually taken to mean 1185–1600). Like many truisms, it points to a basic verity: the difficulty of finding raw data to measure population change during these centuries. Also like many truisms, however, it is not exactly correct. For many years, Japanese scholars have known of the existence of death registers, almost all of them recounting local mortality in the Tokugawa period. The surprise is that there are also death registers for the medieval period and that their contents have a direct bearing on the discussion of famine mortality.[48] In particular, these registers provide a greater depth of understanding and some corroboration, albeit limited, for the above narrative.

All together, there are many death registers for the premodern and even middle ages, but because they belong to temples whose members do not wish the contents to become public, only five from the medieval epoch have been widely used or published. The most famous is the mammoth Hondoji Death Register from Shimōsa.[49] In addition, there are the Akahama Myōhōji register from Hitachi, the Tōji register from Kyoto, the Ichirenji register from Kai, and the Yūgyōji register from Sagami.[50] In the discussion of mortality for the late Kamakura through mid-Muromachi periods, the Yūgyōji register has the most direct bearing. (See table 3.3. For the other registers, see relevant tables in chapter 5.)

Before leaping to conclusions from these documents, however, we need to consider three cautionary notes. First, because they record the deaths of temple members, we should not assume that the registers represent only one village or even one region. Members may have been scattered over a wide area. Second, because we never know the population at risk, we cannot employ statistics to construct a death rate. The numbers may serve merely as general indicators of mortality, and causes are not usually noted. Finally, as should be clear from table 3.3, the sex ratios are skewed toward males, and infants were normally not recorded, probably because young children's mortality rates were so appalling that their deaths were a common event not even drawing unusual attention.[51]

In regard to the data in table 3.3, two other points should be kept in mind. First, Yūgyōji belonged to the "Sect of Timely Teaching" (Jishū),

TABLE 3.3
Yūgyōji Death Register, 1276–1405

ANNUAL MORTALITY, 1276–1404			
YEARS	MALES	FEMALES	TOTAL
1276–1285	24	23	47
1286–1295	57	53	110
1296–1305	69	58	127
1306–1315	49	62	111
1316–1325	41	39	80
1326–1335	57	35	92
1336–1345	40	79	119
1346–1355	108	85	193
1356–1365	120	62	182
1366–1375	79	59	138
1376–1385	119	61	180
1386–1395	67	26	93
1396–1405	43	11	54
Total	873	653	1,526
Average per year	67.2	50.2	117.4

SEASONALITY OF DEATH			
MONTH	MALES	FEMALES	TOTAL
1	113	65	178
2	87	62	149
3	67	63	130
4	81	60	141
5	57	58	115
6	91	60	151
7	47	42	89
8	66	42	108
9	60	53	113
10	63	50	113
11	46	49	95
12	79	35	114
Total	857	639	1,496
Average per year	71.4	53.3	124.7

known for its popular appeal through ecstatic dancing and recitation of Amida's name *(nenbutsu)*. One characteristic of this group was a devotion to "gender equality"—that is, the belief that both men and women could obtain salvation. Therefore the sex ratios from the Yūgyōji data are more balanced than those derived from records kept by other Buddhist sects. Second, it is important to note that for a majority of the persons whose deaths were entered in the Yūgyōji register, the dates of demise were not included, thus limiting the applicability of the record and raising questions about the quality of the sample.

Still, if we are to credit the Yūgyōji register as having some value as a measure of mortality, the following observations seem to be in order. First, during the period covered by the register (1276–1405), the years from 1346 to 1385 stand out as a time of greater death for members of this temple. This generalization may in fact merely be an accident of the enthusiasm with which deaths were noted, as we can easily see that the Yūgyōji register begins and ends with small totals. Nonetheless, we can posit several other reasons for the greater numbers of deaths in the mid- to late fourteenth century. Even a cursory examination of the Wars between the Northern and Southern Dynasties shows that battles took place in the Kanto, especially over the period 1339–1363—first between Takauji and Kitabatake Chikafusa, then between the brothers Takauji and Tadayoshi, and finally between the Ashikaga and remnants of the Southern Dynasty.[52] By 1368, however, most of the fighting had died down, at least in the Kanto, as Yoshimitsu became the third Muromachi shogun.

Consequently, the reason for the clustering of deaths among the adherents of Yūgyōji between 1346 and 1385 must lie in other factors too. Since famine has already been described as a major cause of death, we might search for confirmation of this idea. Referring again to table 3.3, the reader will note an unusual concentration of mortality in the first six months of the year. This so-called "season of death" highlights the problem of food shortages: more people—both males and females—tended to die in the spring and early summer, presumably when supplies of grain from the previous year had been exhausted.[53] This pattern confirms the general impression gained from the chronological discussion of famines above that even in relatively good times, medieval peasants were never too far from malnutrition or even starvation.

Consider also the early years listed in the death registers appearing in chapter 5. When we examine the Hondoji, Akahama Myōhōji, and Ichirenji records, we note that more deaths were entered for the years 1430–

1450, the final years under consideration in this chapter. The data in these three registers correlate fairly well with the narration of the crises presented above, as well as with the conventional view of climate and crop failure in Japan and East Asia. Moreover, they reinforce the observation concerning the significance of "spring hungers." Of course, especially in the case of Hondoji and Akahama Myōhōji, it may have been that monks were not as thorough in recording mortality among their parishioners when they were just beginning to chronicle deaths.[54] Then too since the death registers all come from the Kanto, they may simply be describing local conditions not corresponding with general trends. To the extent that we can place trust in all four registers (Yūgyōji, Hondoji, Akahama Myōhōji, and Ichirenji), however, they support the related ideas of famine as a major cause of medieval mortality and a brief respite—a "Muromachi Optimum"—in this case falling between 1385 and about 1430.

The problem of food supply was the crucial issue facing most residents of the archipelago in the era 1280–1450, and although merchants and institutions ameliorated the problem in this transitional era, they did not solve it. Starvation still claimed lives most commonly among the three extraordinary causes of mortality. But insofar as the available data and historical narratives can be trusted, they suggest that famine was less frequent and harsh than during the preceding 130 years, with the late Kamakura and middle Muromachi eras being times of relative freedom from hunger. This somewhat improved condition was based on advances in agriculture and commerce and goes a long way toward explaining why a cycle of population growth started after 1280.

MORTALITY FACTORS: WAR

Among the causes of death for the era 1280–1450, only war and political instability resulted in significantly heightened tolls when compared with the preceding epoch. I draw this conclusion simply by referring to the long Wars between the Northern and Southern Dynasties, fought most intensely from 1331 to around 1363. By comparison, the late Heian and early to mid-Kamakura eras were peaceful, with the only lengthy all-out combat occurring during the Civil War of 1180–1185. That war too was marked by a halt in hostilities during 1181–1182.

Even when the wars had calmed to a great degree as Yoshimitsu took his long-awaited post as the third Muromachi shogun in 1367, there were still significant battles, as when the Yamana and Doki rebelled between 1390 and 1391 and the Ōuchi in 1399. As has been noted above for the riots of 1420–1448, sporadic violence plagued the first half of the fifteenth century as well. War seems to have been the rule somewhere in the archipelago almost all the time, but the important point is that sustained fighting was concentrated in the second third of the fourteenth century, suggesting that mortality was highest then. The data from war fit those for epidemic disease and famine in that death rates declined markedly in the late fourteenth and early fifteenth centuries.

Violence in the Late Kamakura Period

Warriors on the land continued to be unabashed abusers of rural folk even when "peace" was the rule. They were not the only ones, however, as other groups, from estate officials to peasants themselves, were frequently violent. The following narrative describes some of the most outrageous and brutal misbehavior of the last decades of the Kamakura era—for warriors first, then other estate officials, then *akutō*, and finally peasants themselves.

Regarding warriors, in 1287, for instance, the land steward of Wakasa's Tara Estate was accused of various misdeeds, including taking over provincial rice and dry fields to steal grains, hemp, and mulberry products.[55] Unable to bear the warrior's abuses, the farmers absconded in the autumn.[56] In that same year in Awaji, the *jitō* made excessive demands upon peasant laborers and their packhorses, stole the wheat harvest, and commandeered cultivators' paddy and dry fields.[57] In 1298, housemen and others *(kō otsunin)* were accused of entering the precincts of Saidaiji, overworking the people, and pillaging their lands.[58]

As the fourteenth century began, law and order seemed to be failing everywhere. In 1315 in Hizen, a local military man cut down and confiscated the rice crop at Kawazoe Estate.[59] Also in 1315, the land stewards and housemen living around Yano Estate in Harima fought among themselves, in the process robbing, murdering, and then burning parts of the settlement.[60] In 1320, the representative *(daikan)* of the constable of Bingo forced his way into Ōta Estate and along with several hundred other men killed, maimed, and robbed residents while incinerating several houses.[61] Later that same year warriors in an Ōmi estate murdered inhabitants, committed outrages, and stole the rice crop.[62] In 1322, quarreling samurai brothers burned down farmers' homes and robbed and pillaged in Satsuma.[63]

Nor were warriors the only ones to blame. Among estate officials, a district magistrate-cum-houseman in Yamada in Satsuma was cited for murdering his follower *(ge'nin)* and stealing the rice harvest *(karita)* in 1287.[64] Months later a low-level manager *(zasshō)* at Kumazaka Estate in Kaga was accused of entering shrine lands forcibly and taking the rice and dry crops for his own uses *(sakumō o karitoriowannu)*.[65] In 1314, the estate official *(azukari dokoro)* at Yugeshima Estate in Iyo carried out a reign of terror so harsh that farmers fled.[66] In 1321, a constable's man *(shugo-dai)* in an Echizen estate was guilty of absconding with the rice crop.[67]

Perhaps the most frequent persecutors were the famed "evil bands," and their violent activities were so widespread and common that it would be impossible to list them all.[68] Selecting the years 1283, 1287, 1294, 1298, 1310, 1314–1318, 1320–1324, and 1330 arbitrarily, for example, I found that these bands of armed peasants, lapsed housemen, thugs, and other misfits were implicated in about 40–50 incidents of disorderly, criminal behavior. They murdered, robbed, resisted taxation, mounted night raids, cut down and appropriated farmers' crops, harvested mountain timbers and built fortifications, and resorted to various other unspecified misdeeds. Moreover, it is clear that over the last fifty years of the Kamakura era, the "evil bands" became ever more daring; during the random years listed above, only nine incidents occurred before 1300.[69]

Although warriors and "evil bands" seem to have comprised the most common hindrances to peaceful, productive agrarian activities, peasants could and did fight among themselves. To cite just three examples, in 1294, peasants living in Yamato's Hiranodono Estate and Anmyōji's Yoshida Estate went to war; according to the complaint from the Hiranodono cultivators, their adversaries "led a large force, donned armor, took up bows and arrows, entered the estate, and stole timbers and grasses as they pleased."[70] In a border dispute in 1310, residents at Zenjōji in Yamashiro forced entry into Sozuka Estate and cut down trees, wrecked their neighbors' charcoal braziers, and robbed and injured their fellow commoners.[71] And starting in 1317, a famous and long-running dispute erupted between locals at Ikagodachi and Katsuragawa Estates in Ōmi, where murders and the devastation of forest lands continued until at least 1318.[72]

Yoritomo had placed his men in estates and provincial lands to keep the peace and see to it that a regular flow of tribute items continued to Kyoto and elsewhere. By the 1280s, warriors and other officials were no longer part of the solution; they were part of the problem. The last decades of the Kamakura epoch saw "advancing chaos" as the land system itself was undermined everywhere.[73] Given this backdrop, the drawn-out wars of the fourteenth century should come as no surprise.

The Wars between the Northern and Southern Dynasties

As with the demographic impact of war and violence during 1150–1280, it is best to divide the analysis here into two parts: combatant mortality and the death and destruction wrought against the rest of the populace. On a basic question affecting all mortality, the duration and extent of the conflict commencing in 1331, there is general agreement.[74] While the evidence is difficult to read because combatants often applied variant names to the same battle, war was endemic in the 1330s—between 1336 and 1338 battles took place on almost every day of the year. From 1339 through 1350, hostilities became regionalized in eastern Honshu, Kyushu, and Yamato. Then widespread violence erupted again between 1350 and 1355 in the Kannō disturbance pitting Takauji against his brother Tadayoshi. After 1355, encounters among forces were mostly restricted to western Honshu, Kyushu, and Yamato. The intensity of hostilities dropped off noticeably after 1363, gradually ebbing away by 1394.[75]

There are also specific death tallies for soldiers. As with battles in the Civil War of 1180–1185, mortality seems to have been low. To be sure, there are doubts about the accuracy of the military loyalty reports *(gunchū-jō)* and battle wound lists *(kassen teoi chūmon),* but apparently few warriors died in battle, with the largest casualty figure being 300 out of 1,633 fighters.[76] The highest ratio of deaths was 57 percent—a horrifying 210 out of 370—but usually the death rate was much lower, only about 10 percent or so. The average was merely nineteen dead per report.[77] Only 30 percent of wounds occurred to the head or torso, with the rest coming to the limbs, especially the legs.[78] These documents suggest that casualties among combatants were generally low and wounds not life-threatening.

Yet there is uncertainty about how far these military reports actually reflect battle conditions.[79] If famines were fewer and agriculture was becoming more productive while population was growing and commercial networks were spreading rapidly and widely, then would it not make sense for armies to have been larger?[80] And if martial forces were larger, then would not combatant mortality and casualties also have been higher? Even if warrior deaths were greater than these documents state, however, if the population and enlistments were growing, then it is still possible that combatant mortality as a percentage of troops in the field remained about the same. Higher enlistments probably did not raise the overall death rate much at all. The most judicious conclusion seems to be that soldierly casualties had only a fleeting effect on population trends.

As in the case of earlier hostilities, however, merely assessing samurai mortality does not fully account for the wars' demographic impact. For example, consider the following scene from *Taihei ki*. The battle pitted Kamakura's proudest against the loyalist Kusunoki Masashige at the opening of Go-Daigo's revolt. Kanto warriors were laying siege to Kusunoki's stockade; after meeting stiff resistance, they are reported to have said the following to each other: "Let us remain awhile in this place, so that led by men acquainted with the Home Provinces we may cut down trees on the mountains, burn houses, and guard thereby against warriors waiting in reserve to fall upon us. Then we can attack the castle with tranquil spirits."[81]

In essence, this brief passage conveys the character of a typical battle of the late thirteenth and fourteenth centuries: two relatively small armies squared off, with the loser of the initial skirmish or the weaker of the two quickly retiring to a hastily built wooden fortress. Thereafter, siege warfare ensued, in which the stronger force laid waste to the entire region around the stockade to deprive its enemy of supplies and water. Even Kusunoki was said to have resorted to the same tactic, burning "commoners' houses" at the beginning of the war.[82] Moreover, enemies were not above blocking roads to starve out their foes or impressing peasants for battle service.[83] Under such circumstances, having a battle take place near a village may have had disastrous consequences.

Scholars might dismiss this description if it appeared only in *Taihei ki*, but in fact documentary collections repeat the same sad tale over and over. Table 3.4 lists misdeeds over the period 1333–1392. A few of the more colorful examples are as follows: in 1336 a samurai from Chikuzen wrote that "the people and estate officials are afraid of the upheaval *(dō-ran)*; when they heard about this they fled *(chikuden)*. We ought to hurry and get them to return to their original homes." In Suō in 1351, peasants wrote a protest in which they stated that "several myriads of soldiers broke into your [the proprietor's] estate. Without knowing their status, we allotted rice provisions *(hyōrō mai)*, but our generosity could not bear up under their demands. In some cases, they bound us, while in others

TABLE 3.4
Commoner Suffering, 1333–1392

NUMBER	DATE	PLACE	MISDEED	SOURCE
1	1335	Echizen	Provisions stolen	*DNS*, VI, 2, 255–256
2	1335	Settsu	Arson	*DNS*, VI, 2, 739
3	1335	Sanuki	Arson/theft	*NBCICS*, 1, 110–111
4	1336	Bingo	"Outrages"	*NBCICS*, 1, 153, 194
5	1336	Aki	Village burned	*NBCICS*, 1, 205
6	1336	Chikuzen	Farmers flee	*NBCIK*, 1, 153
7	1336	Izumi	Village burned	*DNS*, VI, 3, 716
8	1337	Kawachi	Villages burned	*DNS*, VI, 4, 5
9	1337	Kii	Roads blocked	*DNS*, VI, 4, 30
10	1337	Ōmi	Arson	*DNS*, VI, 4, 48
11	1337	Hitachi	Homes burned	*DNS*, VI, 4, 84
12	1337	Izumi	Villages burned	*DNS*, VI, 4, 195–198
13	1337	Kawachi	Provisioning	*DNS*, VI, 4, 247
14	1337	Kawachi	Villages burned	*DNS*, VI, 4, 273
15	1337	Izumo	Villages burned	*DNS*, VI, 4, 277–278
16	1337	Izumi	Village burned	*DNS*, VI, 4, 283
17	1337	Iwami	Villages burned	*NBCICS*, 1, 228–229
18	1338	Kawachi	Village burned	*DNS*, VI, 4, 745–746
19	1338	Kii	Provisioning	*DNS*, VI, 4, 754–755
20	1338	Settsu	Villages burned	*DNS*, VI, 4, 779
21	1338	Ōmi	Village burned	*DNS*, VI, 4, 788–789
22	1338	Izumi	Village burned	*DNS*, VI, 4, 814–815
23	1338	Kawachi	Homes burned	*DNS*, VI, 4, 817
24	1338	Mutsu	Homes burned	*DNS*, VI, 4, 844
25	1338	Kawachi	Homes burned	*DNS*, VI, 4, 849
26	1338	Kawachi	Village burned	*DNS*, VI, 4, 856–858
27	1339	Hitachi	Provisioning	*DNS*, VI, 5, 442–443
28	1339	Tōtōmi	Homes burned	*DNS*, VI, 5, 614–615
29	1339	Chikuzen	Harvest stolen	*NBCIK*, 2, 36
30	1340	Higo	Village burned	*NBCIK*, 2, 36
31	1340	Satsuma	Crop stealing	*NBCIK*, 2, 182
32	1340	Iyo	Provisioning	*NBCICS*, 1, 326
33	1340	Echizen	Villages burned	*DNS*, VI, 6, 267
34	1340	Kawachi	Provisioning	*DNS*, VI, 6, 328–329

Table 3.4 continues

Table 3.4 continued

NUMBER	DATE	PLACE	MISDEED	SOURCE
35	1341	Echizen	Villages burned	*DNS*, VI, 6, 643
36	1341	Satsuma	Village burned	*NBCIK*, 2, 121
37	1343	Hitachi	Roads blocked	*DNS*, VI, 7, 598
38	1345	Bingo	Crop stealing	*NBCICS*, 2, 178–179
39	1346	Inaba	Forest stripped	*NBCICS*, 2, 200
40	1346	Yamato	Provisioning	*DNS*, VI, 9, 883
41	1347	Bingo	Robbery	*NBCICS*, 2, 233
42	1347	Kii	Provisions/laborers	*DNS*, VI, 11, 67
43	1348	Bizen	Arson/crop stealing	*NBCICS*, 2, 286
44	1348	Higo	Village burned	*NBCIK*, 3, 34
45	1350	Iwami	Arson	*NBCICS*, 2, 339–340
46	1350	Aki	Arson	*NBCICS*, 2, 342–348
47	1350	Kawachi	Arson	*DNS*, VI, 14, 158
48	1351	Suō	Robbery	*NBCICS*, 3, 44
49	1352	Kaga	Provisioning	*DNS*, VI, 16, 87–88
50	1352	Bingo	Villages burned	*NBCICS*, 3, 106
51	1352	Yamato	Provisioning	*DNS*, VI, 16, 401
52	1352	Yamato	Provisioning	*DNS*, VI, 16, 432
53	1352	Suō	Villages burned	*NBCICS*, 3, 140
54	1352	Kawachi	Provisioning	*DNS*, VI, 17, 38
55	1353	Capital	Arson	*DNS*, VI, 18, 113
56	1354	Suō	Roads blocked	*NBCICS*, 3, 206
57	1354	Hitachi	Provisioning	*DNS*, VI, 19, 71
58	1355	Harima	Provisioning	*DNS*, VI, 20, 34
59	1356	Bungo	Village burned	*NBCIK*, 4, 57
60	1359	Buzen	Arson/Crop stealing	*NBCIK*, 4, 140
61	1361	Harima	Provisioning	*DNS*, VI, 23, 744–745
62	1363	Harima	Provisioning	*NBCICS*, 4, 54–57
63	1373	Aki	Arson	*NBCICS*, 4, 357–358
64	1373	Bizen	Crop stealing	*NBCICS*, 4, 381–382
65	1374	Hizen	Village burned	*NBCIK*, 5, 112
66	1374	All Kyushu	Villages damaged	*NBCIK*, 5, 113
67	1375	Chikuzen	Village burned	*NBCIK*, 5, 125
68	1381	Bungo	Crop stealing	*NBCIK*, 5, 321
69	1382	Ōsumi	Arson/Crop stealing	*NBCIK*, 5, 292–293
70	1385	Chikuzen	Village burned	*NBCIK*, 6, 8
71	1386	Ōuchi	Crop stealing	*NBCICS*, 6, 86

they hunted out valuables from within our homes. When we reported the exhaustion of this property, was that an exaggeration?" In a letter in 1374, Imagawa Ryōshun stated that one of his chief duties as the Muromachi shogunate's representative in Kyushu was to "see to it first of all that the local areas were not further damaged."

In battles in both *Taihei ki* and documentary sources, it is clear that the most deadly weapon that a samurai army possessed was neither the sword nor archery equipment. It was fire. In the countryside, where everything was built of wood or straw, and amber fields blew in the wind, a few well-placed torches could finish an enemy and his economic base faster and more completely than all the swords in the islands could flourish in one gigantic, slashing swoop. The effectiveness of fire as a weapon had been recognized for centuries, but only during the wars of the fourteenth century, for which there are repeated references to incineration, do we see scorched-earth tactics applied across the length of the archipelago on such a systematic basis.[84]

Of course, the cases listed in table 3.4 are merely the most egregious examples taken from a cache of documents that is admittedly fragmentary. In particular, since the handiest collection for the period of the wars has been completed only for Kyushu and western Japan, it is difficult to evaluate how harsh war conditions were in the central and eastern half of the archipelago.

East of the war-torn Kinai, however, the story was probably much the same: wherever battles were fought or soldiers marched, the residents and the local economy suffered. It falls to future historians to narrate and quantify the story across the rest of the archipelago, as documents are not printed for some areas (especially the Kinai), and those published for eastern Honshu are found primarily in prefectural and municipal collections. Two further examples, however, may suffice. In the first, the Ōtomo were reporting on the failure of cultivators to pay taxes at Miiri Estate in Mino in 1340 when they noted that "the previous governor of Mutsu (Kitabatake Akiie) along with [other] bandits attacked residences, stole the rice and other grain laid aside as seed, so the peasants fled and there is no cultivation going on."[85]

An even more telling description originates from Mino's Akanabe Estate in 1337:

> From the early winter of the year before last, the world *[sejō]* has been in upheaval. Since markets and fords have remained unestablished, we could

not sell our grain, and it was difficult to find a use for it. While we were waiting for a quiet period, increasingly by the day, the forces on both sides were trying to get to the capital morning and night.

They forced their way into our estate and made us carry off our cattle, horses, and possessions beyond counting; the same was true of our rice and soybeans. Even though we berated them repeatedly, because we had no place to hide these items, they were taken without recompense. It was clear that we would all starve to death [if this kept up]. Thereafter, we met them in one place, and setting aside our lives, we discussed this problem with the troops, to the effect that they ought to be protecting us. Then, uniting our power with one heart, we kept a lookout for consecutive days. Even though the extreme violence stopped, our expenses are beyond calculation.

Thereafter, when the constable and staff of the provincial governor learned that things seem to have quieted down, in some cases they ordered us to produce soldiers; in others they demanded provisions, horses, and other items. If we did not do [as ordered], they would claim that we were their enemies, take us into custody, and burn our residences *[zaike]*.[86]

There can be no more evocative example of how war fought on one's home territory induces starvation, economic dislocation, and population loss.

Of course, battles did not occur everywhere all at once, and therefore it is possible that the impact of warfare on commoner mortality was minimal. Before we endorse such a conclusion, however, we must remember that armies needed food and other supplies every day. Especially when they were on the march, there was a chance for warriors to "help themselves" *(jiriki kyūsai)*. In an effort to supply its troops during the wars, the soon-to-be Muromachi shogunate designated certain territories as "provision lands" *(hyōrō sho)*. References to these lands are common in the documents regarding the Wars between the Northern and Southern Dynasties, and a careful reading discloses two interesting practices.

First, regions could be named as "provision lands" temporarily for a year at a time *(azukeoku)*. Usually this occurred when an enemy's fields had been seized and even after they had been cut down by the victorious side. Instances of this practice come from rice paddies in Ōsumi in 1353 and 1359 and Aki in 1373.[87] This custom had been handed down from the Kamakura era and essentially legalized "self-help" by another name.

Second, numerous times the *bakufu* berated its underlings for declaring fields, especially paddies, to be "provision lands" and plundering their products when no such arrangement prevailed. To cite just a few cases, warriors at Iyo's Yugeshima Estate commandeered "huge quantities of rice" *(bakudai hyōrō)* and the boats to move it in an act of "self-help" *(jiriki sata)* in 1349.[88] In 1352, Nagato samurai used the designation "provision land" as an excuse to commit violent outrages *(ranbō).*[89] In Buzen in 1354, warriors called local dry fields "provision lands" and provoked upheaval *(iran).*[90] In 1364, the shogunate tried several times to put a halt to designating "provision rice lands" in Suō but to no avail.[91]

As numerous scholars have noted, the institutionalization of the "half-tax," or *hanzei,* in 1352 by the Muromachi shogunate gradually stemmed the tide of these abuses.[92] The cases listed above show that warrior mistreatment of commoners did not halt overnight; "provision lands" continued to be granted well after 1352. The half-tax solution to the provisioning of military men, however, helped to regularize procedures, and for peasants this represented a true gain over the unpredictable vicissitudes of war.

In a sense, the Muromachi government was rediscovering and solving all over again the problem that Yoritomo (and Sargon of Akkad and Hammurabi in Babylon) had first understood so well: that armies had to be paid and fed in some way, and since the central government (Kyoto or Kamakura) was neither able nor willing to pay warriors' expenses out of its own treasuries, the only solution was to let the local peasants pick up the tab. Moreover, because both the Kamakura and Muromachi regimes had been created during wartime, leaders knew that irregular and unpredictable levies such as had occurred during the Civil War of 1180–1185 or the Wars between the Northern and Southern Dynasties were ultimately unacceptable to everyone—except perhaps samurai themselves. Yoritomo's creation of the position of land steward and the Ashikaga's adoption of the half-tax were both attempts to sustain the peace, revive and maintain prosperity, and satisfy the regime's warriors by locating soldiers at various farms and stations throughout the realm and regularize provisioning.

There were only two problems with "Hammurabi's (or Yoritomo's or the Ashikaga) solution." First, it required accurate record keeping and strong central authority. In both Kamakura and Muromachi Japan, records were kept at the local level, which meant that troops might become more loyal to a region than to the supreme, central commander. Rebellion was ever a possibility, and with the outbreak of warfare once again, provisioning became a matter of "self-help." This was the fate that ultimately befell both the Minamoto and Ashikaga regimes.

Second, even in peacetime when military men collected grain, products, and labor from commoners in their region, abuses could easily take place. These have already been documented for the Kamakura period, and they also occurred under the Ashikaga.[93] When rent producers were ill-used, they not only could fail to perform for that year, but they might also flee and never come back. Disruption of the local economy and a rise in mortality often resulted. The ultimate solution was to move the warriors off the land, out of the way of the peasantry and other producers, and pay them out of a central fisc, but as late as 1450, the problems with "Hammurabi's solution" were not severe enough to warrant such drastic action.

The costs associated with the old policy were rising, however. From 1280, Japan entered a period of increasing political instability and warfare, and the toll in lives was growing. Although disease and famine probably accounted for fewer deaths than ever before over the era 1280–1450, the wars of the mid-fourteenth century made survival more precarious for many. Fortunately, like the former two extraordinary causes of mortality, warfare diminished enough from 1363 to 1450 to open the way for the "Muromachi Optimum," when the economy grew by leaps and bounds and the third cycle of demographic increase gained momentum.

Evidence presented for disease, famine, and war has suggested that the time from the recovery from the Shōga famine around 1280 until the seventeen years before the outbreak of the Ōnin-Bunmei disturbance (1467–1477) represented the beginning of a new demographic growth cycle for the archipelago. Population almost doubled, to around 10 million, and famine and disease were less lethal. Much of the gain undoubtedly came during the "Muromachi Optimum," after the Wars between the Northern and Southern Dynasties and until about 1420. To corroborate these generalizations, however, we need to examine many other background factors, from agriculture and commerce to family and marriage.

4
The Best of Times
Agriculture, Commerce, and Fertility, 1280–1450

*I*n chapter 3, I argued that the era from 1280 to 1450 constituted a demographic turning point, as a population that had been static at around 6 million during the early medieval age entered a period of slow, uneven growth, culminating in a 67 percent increase to about 10 million by 1450. Declines in two mortality factors, disease and famine, seem to have more than compensated for the death and destruction resulting from the Wars between the Northern and Southern Dynasties. Lowered death rates, however, were only one side of the demographic equation; before ascribing a pivotal role to this epoch, we need to examine indirect factors affecting the society and economy.

In this chapter I attempt to deal with such variables, starting with agriculture and settlement. Records from these 170 years show important incremental improvements in three crucial areas: agronomy, engineering, and the village. Expansion and innovation in trade, industry, and cities are other background economic components helping to explain the beginning of a growth spurt in population. With advances in farming, trade, and industry, it is little wonder that commoners' physical well-being improved markedly for the first time in the medieval age. Innovation overtook clothing, diet, sanitation, and housing. Advances in material culture were also closely intertwined with the slow transformation of family, settlement, and class, although exactly how these structures affected fertility remains uncertain. Almost every factor tends to support the proposition that population was beginning another long growth cycle, and in 1450 the tide was apparently just beginning to turn.

AGRICULTURE AND SETTLEMENT

Since agriculture had commenced in earnest during the first millennium BCE, cultivators had been tinkering with techniques constantly, making small improvements over generations. These advances first became noticeable after 1000 CE, and, as suggested in chapter 2, the application of more fertilizer, the invention of double-cropping, the spread of iron tools and livestock, and better care of irrigation works were leading to more efficient and productive agriculture in a few regions by the mid-Kamakura era. Unfortunately for Japanese peasants and the archipelago's economy, these various new technologies could not disperse more widely until after 1280 because the population remained sparse, owing to a variety of causes, most especially the high mortality induced first by epidemics and then by great famines.

Michael Postan has written the following for Europe: "The real problem of medieval technology is not why new technological knowledge was not forthcoming, but why the methods, or even the implements, known to medieval man were not employed, or not employed earlier or more widely, than they in fact were."[1] This was precisely the quandary that residents of the islands had faced for over a thousand years. After 1280, and especially after 1363, mortality from disease, famine, and war drifted lower, and as the population increased, the methods known to Kamakura-era cultivators began to spread more rapidly. Demographic and agricultural growth reinforced each other in complex ways, starting in the Kinai and gradually fanning out to other regions, especially western Japan. As noted, advances were of three types: agronomic, engineering, and social.

Agronomy

The five improvements described in chapter 3 did not become widespread in the Kinai and western Japan until the fourteenth century. Among them I noted, first, that an inventory of peasant tools between 1350 and 1450 showed many more implements in the hands of small cultivators by the latter date. Second, the use of livestock continued to spread during these centuries, as supported by the repeated issuance of documents protecting peasants' draft animals from theft. Third, the use of more and better fertilizer dispersed farther afield. Ashes were critical for a good crop on lands belonging to the temple Kokawadera along the Ki River by at least 1408, if not earlier. Moreover, records from Upper Kuze Estate in Yamashiro state that farmers placed ashes into rice paddies there by the 1440s. Laws prohibiting the free harvesting of grasses and leaves used for green manure also multiplied during the fourteenth and fifteenth centuries.[2]

More and better tools; wider use of livestock; and the application of ash, manure, and other fertilizers made a further, even more critical advance possible: expanded double-cropping, especially in dry fields. This practice existed as early as 1160, and by the 1300s, double-cropping in dry fields was common, particularly in the rich lands around Kyoto and in western Japan. For example, in Upper and Lower Kuze Estate, cultivators were planting two crops of wheat, one to be harvested in the summer and one in the fall. The practice of double-cropping such grains as wheat, buckwheat, soybeans, and barley on properties belonging to Tōji, Katsuodera, and Katori Shrine in the fourteenth century is another example.[3] Cultivators at the famous Tara Estate in Wakasa were harvesting two crops of wheat, soybeans, or buckwheat by the time the wars erupted in 1331, and estate officials reacted to the rise in yields by charging added rent *(kajishi)*.[4]

Another well-known example is Yano Estate in Harima. From 1341 to 1392, documents make repeated references to both "autumnal wheat" *(akimugi)* and "summer wheat" *(natsumugi)*, with the latter presumably denoting a second harvest to tide peasants over the hungry months of spring and early summer.[5] In addition, the estate produced buckwheat, soybeans, and barley, so it became a popular target for "evil bands" and constable lords throughout the time of turmoil for both its laborers and its rich yields. Records also make it clear that estate officials marketed *(washi)* surplus grains when war did not prevent their traveling with produce.

What is more, double-cropping in paddy fields became increasingly prevalent in the Kinai and throughout western Japan.[6] An examination of land commendations to the Mikage Hall of Mt. Kōya reveals thirty-eight incontrovertible examples of paddy double-cropping for the period 1221–1441, only nine of which fell on or before 1280. Three findings are especially noteworthy. First, throughout the thirteenth century double-cropping was a hit-or-miss endeavor, used primarily as an emergency means to succor victims of starvation. Second, as peasants learned to plant an autumnal wheat crop more widely and certainly after 1300, Mt. Kōya began to tax the harvest as "added rent," soaking up some of the surplus to support its religious projects.

Third, by plotting what types of land cultivators sowed with wheat in the Ki valley, scholars have been able to calculate over time the percentage of paddy acreage given over to double-cropping. In 1275, only about 13 percent of paddies produced two crops; by 1300 the figure had increased to 20 percent. By the mid-fourteenth century, about 30 percent of the valley yielded two crops, with some areas yielding as much as 50–60 percent and others as little as 10. In particular, cultivators of valley paddies— where drainage was optimal—could regularly plant twice a year.

Other documents also indicate a rising trend toward paddy double-cropping. At Takashi Estate in Yamashiro, peasants harvested summer wheat from rice paddies in the early 1400s.[7] Evidence also suggests cultivators became skilled in the use of early- and late-ripening rice strains— for instance, in Settsu by 1415.[8] Farther west in Aki in 1433, paddies yielding rice in the autumn then produced wheat and soybeans the next spring. On Mt. Kōya's lands, winter wheat followed the autumnal rice harvest.[9] When Chosŏn dynasty ambassador Sŏng Hi-kyŏng toured Japan in 1420, he wrote in Settsu that "Japanese farm families cultivate rice paddies in the fall, planting wheat or barley, and during the early summer of the next year they harvest it. Then they sow seeds and reap rice in the early autumn. Planting wheat thereafter, in the early winter they bring in that crop, and start all over planting wheat or barley again. In one year they sow three times."[10]

By 1450 evidence suggests that paddy double-cropping was a fairly common practice on well-drained lands in farms around Kyoto and into western Honshu. In other regions, however, the custom seems to have been much less widespread, mostly for topographical and climatological reasons.[11] Farmers in the Kanto, for example, could employ double-cropping on no more than about 10 percent of their paddies. At lands under the control of Tsurugaoka Hachiman Shrine in Kamakura, the harvesting of two crops was fairly common for dry fields, but farmers did not conduct double-cropping of rice fields until the 1390s and never on the same scale as at comparable institutions in the Kinai.[12]

One major reason for the low percentages in the Kanto was that much land in the flat plain there was water-logged *(tsumida)*, rendering it unsuitable for double-cropping. North of the Kanto, the growing season became progressively shorter, and it was more difficult to fit two crops in. So the double-cropping advances of the fourteenth and fifteenth centuries affected the archipelago differentially, making western Japan, and especially the area around Kyoto, richer and more productive relative to eastern Honshu.

Wherever it was practiced, the double- and triple-cropping of rice paddies helped to accelerate population growth in at least two ways. First, a second or third harvest often meant the difference between starvation or plenty during the spring and summer months. Second, since tillers probably sowed wheat, barley, and soybeans most usually, the assortment enhanced a peasant's ability to produce a greater variety of foods, raising the standard of living for rural folk in general. In addition, farmers could raise beans of different kinds, oil-producing seeds, melons, buckwheat, sesame seeds, tubers, and other edible plants in the family garden plot. It seems safe to assume that along with a more variegated diet went a healthier populace.

Double-cropping was an extension of an older custom, but farmers made a crucial addition to their repertoire during this era: Champa rice (*Oryza sativa indica* var. *spontanea* or *perennis;* in Japanese, *akagome; daitōmai; tōboshi).* Probably introduced into the islands between 1100 and 1300 from Sung China, this Indian or Southeast Asian grain had three main advantages: it was blight- and insect-resistant, withstood drought and flood better than native rice, and produced higher yields.[13] The only drawback was that Japan's original rice variant, *Oryza sativa japonica,* tasted better and therefore brought a higher return at market.

Scholars debate exactly how and when Champa rice first made its appearance in Japan. The earliest attested example comes from Sanuki in 1397, but monks or other travelers visiting Sung China probably introduced the grain in or near Kyoto much earlier. Realizing its numerous advantages, religious centers came to encourage its nurturing upon their scattered lands, most of which were located adjacent to Kyoto or in western Japan. Assuming that peasants in the Kinai would have been the first to sow the red-awned rice, it had probably been producing plentiful harvests for at least a century by 1397.

Other materials support the idea of the Kinai as the entrepôt for Champa rice. The strain may have been mentioned in planting songs in the Kinai as early as the twelfth century.[14] Records for Yano Estate in Harima show that peasants grew Champa rice there in the early 1400s, further enhancing the argument for initial entry into the Kinai and then a gradual dispersion westward. On the other hand, northern Kyushu is another likely source for the grain.[15]

By 1300 or perhaps a little earlier, peasants recognized the value of Champa rice. Farmers could grow it in low-lying soggy fields and sow directly to produce a substantial yield. Champa rice thrived on the alluvial plains, where, when transplanted, it bore plentiful harvests even on poorly watered lands. Given these advantages, it is little wonder that the early-ripening rice was popular from the start. In Sanuki it produced 30 percent of one estate's revenue by 1300, and at Yano farmers planted it at a ratio of 1:6 to native rice. Yano documents also suggest that residents frequently took Champa rice to markets, where it fetched about 90 percent of the sale price of other brands.[16]

Champa rice played a significant role in developing flood-prone alluvial plains and deltas.[17] To explain more fully, peasants commenced ancient wet-rice agriculture in the generally less fertile, small, flat stretches of the archipelago's innumerable mountain valleys, and the creation of paddies proceeded slowly over the centuries. Development did not reach the rich broad river plains until the latter stages of Japanese history, between 1300 and 1700. The conversion of fertile alluvial plains and deltas to wet-rice cultivation did not begin in Hizen until the fourteenth century.[18]

Between about 1300 and 1450 Champa rice became prevalent in the Kinai and western Japan as farmers there began to develop the fertile river plains more intensively. *Akagome*'s various advantages—its resistance to blight, insects, drought, and especially flood—made the new strain perfect for farmers who wanted to open the area's river bottoms to more routine cultivation. Champa rice became an indispensable instrument, leading the way to the conquest of Japan's richest areas. Once superior irrigation facilities were in place in the Tokugawa period, peasants could then safely convert lands formerly given over to Champa rice to more tasty native strains, as occurred in the Kinai in the 1700s. In eastern Honshu, by contrast, development lagged, and only Echigo and a few areas along the Pacific as far north as Sendai became major centers for the cultivation of Champa rice by 1450.[19]

The "island dry field" *(shimahata)* was another agronomic factor behind the gradual conversion of alluvial fans and deltas to wet-rice and dry farming.[20] Like Champa rice, the island dry field had a brief history before 1280 but became widespread from about 1300. There are examples in the lowlands of the Katsura River near Kyoto, along the Tenryū in Shinano, at Ōi Estate in the Nobi plain, and the Yao fan in Kawachi. Champa rice and the island dry field were crucial in developing the Takada plain in Echigo.[21]

The dispersion of these improvements taken together, especially throughout western Japan, made a fundamental difference by 1450. To be sure, many regions, particularly eastern Honshu, remained less developed and probably less densely populated than the booming western half of the archipelago. Cultivators had taken steps toward a healthier, more prosperous lifestyle, however. In agronomic terms, a corner had been turned, and better farming techniques went along with gradual advances in irrigation techniques and village organization.

Engineering

More and better irrigation facilities were also an important component in the slow conversion of alluvial plains to farming. Once again, the Kinai led the way. In Izumi, for example, land clearance for Hineno Estate had begun in the early 1200s; by 1234, in the wake of the great famine, records indicate that a mere twelve *chō* were available for cropping. By 1316, however, the total had nearly trebled, to thirty-three *chō;* in 1417, almost fifty-four *chō* were producing. A major reason for the increase was the construction of four new irrigation ponds by the early fourteenth century, most probably at the same time that cultivators had brought formerly abandoned fields into cultivation around 1308. Moreover, these ponds drew their waters not from valley runoff, but from the nearby Kashii River.[22] Dramatic village growth, the redevelopment of formerly abandoned lands, and the final phase in the surveying of field arrangements *(jōri sei)* all followed in the 1300s.[23]

This story is repeated time and again throughout the provinces adjacent to Kyoto. The Katsura River, for instance, was one of the most badly behaved rivers in the Kinai; in the fifteenth century it caused mighty floods about twenty times, wiping out paddies nearly once every five years.[24] In response to these crises, peasants built dams and sluices at ten sites, ranging over several kilometers, from Hōrinji to Katsura Bridge, enabling them to control excessive runoff and provide for dry years as well. They also employed river-driven waterwheels to dampen paddies at appropriate times.

Ōyama Estate in Tanba is one of the most well-known medieval properties in western Japan.[25] In the early 1400s, the proprietor (Tōji) and cultivators of Ōyama were confronted with an emergency as nearby Miyata Estate devoured all the water from the saucer pond between the two farms. In response, peasants built a new pond and channels leading from the Miyata River; by 1444, lands yielding tax rice had increased by 30 percent. Shortages of water would continue into the 1600s, but the efforts of peasants in the early 1400s staved off a serious crisis. Two other points about the Ōyama case are worth noting: bosses paid in cash for the labor for constructing the new irrigation channels, suggesting market penetration into the estate's economy; and by the 1400s peasants were planting early-ripening rice strains, perhaps to conserve water or harvest more than one crop.

Harima presents another feat of engineering skill. Hiroyama, Ikaruga, and Ōyake Estates were ranged along the lower reaches of the Ibo River, and early on they competed for water.[26] According to a map of the 1300s, however, the three estates had begun to work out their conflicts by constructing several channels leading away from the Ibo; each estate received its share of water from at least two sources in the irrigation system. Essentially, these facilities remained in place until the seventeenth century, when residents expanded and improved them to prevent occasional problems with drought.

To the south was Kii Province, famous for its double-cropping, and it is no accident that it was also renowned for advanced irrigation. On the lands of Kokawadera along the Ki River, farmers constructed several ponds between 1296 and the late 1400s. Cultivators divided the rights into 305 shares. It is not surprising that Eastern Village, where most of the agriculturalists lived, eventually became a communal entity *(sōson)*.[27] At Arakawa Estate, also in Kii, the problem of insufficient water was ameliorated when farmers assembled to expand a ditch *(ōimizo)* in 1413.[28]

Other examples lie farther afield. In Ōmi, peasants of Kashiwagi Village first tapped into the Yasu River in 1448.[29] Beginning in the 1300s along the Inland Sea, peasants rebuilt and improved irrigation facilities that had deteriorated during the Heian period, reducing the chances of flooding and raising overall productivity.[30] Even in northern Kyushu, at Tokō Estate in Bungo, cultivators constructed irrigation channels with sluices, beginning in the 1300s; they set aside funds for maintenance, and new paddies came into production. A similar pattern may well have prevailed at Tajiri Estate, also in Bungo.[31]

The increasingly widespread employment of the waterwheel was another key to the improved watering technology.[32] Beginning in the 1300s, references to this machine appear repeatedly—in tales, picture scrolls, and even random lampoons scrawled on walls. Perhaps the most famous reference to the device comes from the annals of the Chosŏn dynasty. In

1428–1429, Ambassador Pak Sŏ-saeng attended the funeral of Ashikaga shogun Yoshimochi, bringing greetings to his successor, Yoshiaki. According to Chosŏn annals, Pak later said: "Japanese farmers set up waterwheels, which pour water and flood paddies. When the student Kim Sin investigated how these machines were made, [he learned that] they had a place where the water could ascend, automatically turning themselves. Then pumping the water, they poured it into [the paddies]. . . . Yet this machine could be set up only where there were rapids and not where the water pooled. . . . When your subject secretly studied this point, [he saw that] where waters pooled, the farmers had people use their feet [on a similar machine] to raise up and pump the water."[33] Because Pak's journey took him to northern Kyushu, up the Inland Sea and only as far as Kyoto, it is certain that he was describing peasants he had seen in western Japan.

Finally, scholars know that irrigation engineering became much more sophisticated in the archipelago between 1300 and 1450 because as never before villagers began to regulate access to river waters and the repair of dams, channels, and sluices. References to such regulation mostly began in the middle and late 1200s.[34] Communities charged fees for upkeep and permitted the flow of water to each peasant for a set period of time. It was not unusual for the village to hire an overseer.

Until 1450, the management of irrigation facilities was most common in the Kinai and vicinity, the same region where Champa rice, double-cropping, and the waterwheel were making a multiple impact by enticing peasants to open alluvial plains. On lands held by Saidaiji and Hōryūji, cultivators opened alluvial fans; beginning in the late 1300s, peasants demanded additional support from the proprietor Tōji to maintain facilities at Upper and Lower Kuze Estates. While aristocratic lords and warriors played a role in formulating rules at Kuze, so did the cultivators, who stood to lose the most by misguided policies.

The multiplication of water regulations also naturally meant that the rural landscape was becoming more crowded. Population increase heightened pressure on precious resources such as water, timber, and grasslands. As of 1450, however, the expansion of cultivation to new areas such as the alluvial fans and the intensification of techniques were still in their early stages. Yet agronomic and engineering improvements helped along the trend, first seen in the Kinai, toward more compact settlements and village communities capable of handling their own affairs and confronting violent warriors or greedy merchants when the need arose.

Villages

In a discussion of technological developments, it is easy to lose sight of human agency. Cultivators applied more fertilizers; raised more livestock; built bigger and more sophisticated irrigation works; and planted, tended, and harvested multiple crops. Therefore it should come as no surprise that they also began to settle in different arrangements and organize and manage the affairs of their communities as never before. This trend began in the Kinai, where peasants were already making so many other innovations, and it gradually spread to other central and western regions by 1450.

Let us look at settlement patterns first. At Wakatsuki Estate in Yamato, the construction of a moated, clustered residential area probably dated from the mid-fourteenth century.[35] The layouts of Miyata Estate (in Tanba, mentioned above) and Tomita Estate show compact settlements, in Tomita's case complete with an encircling rectangular moat twenty-two meters on one side.[36] A clustered pattern is evident at Esaka Village in Settsu from about 1343.[37]

Compact settlements were first and foremost a phenomenon of central and western Honshu, with other areas revealing a greater variety. Iriki Estate in southern Kyushu seems to have always been dispersed.[38] Similarly in the Kanto, villages ranged from those in the mountains to others on alluvial plains to still others built on natural levees.[39] In eastern Honshu, warrior residences and stockades usually dominated peasant dwellings.[40]

Compact villages developed mostly adjacent to Kyoto, and scholars ponder the reasons for such a transformation. The conventional explanation links population growth to agrarian improvements, suggesting that it was more efficient to group dwellings in one area and fields in another. There may be something to this line of thinking, but at least two other interpretations need to be examined. First, as villages acquired more oxen, pigs, and horses, it made sense to locate stables in an area away from residences and to protect human habitats with a wall or moat.[41] Second was the impact of the "evil bands" and the long Wars between the Northern and Southern Dynasties; the moated settlements of the Yayoi period probably arose from the constant threat of depredations from neighboring villagers.[42] It would not be the first time in history that cultivators banded together to protect themselves from marauders.

The physical landscape was not the only remarkable change in the way that peasants lived from the late 1200s, however. As never before, rural folks engaged in various occupations began to form corporate villages *(sō)* to regulate their own affairs. At Imabori in Ōmi, residents wrote regulations for themselves from at least 1383.[43] Organized around the shrine association *(miyaza),* Imabori elders were charged with handling and paying for rituals and holidays and administered special shrine lands just for those purposes. They made decisions about irrigation works—when and where to build and where to send the waters first. They kept records on lands and crops, husbanded their forests and grasslands, and policed themselves. And they made distinctions among themselves based upon age and status and between their members and outsiders.

While Imabori is the most famous example, there are numerous case studies of corporate villages in the Kinai region.[44] At a mountain village along the Katsura River, also in Ōmi, elders made the rules and drew strict distinctions between residents and outsiders.[45] Cultivators in Upper and Lower Kuze Estates in Yamashiro formed their own village organization, also based around irrigation rights and duties.[46] From the late 1200s, Esaka Village in Settsu organized itself as a corporate community, with a sophisticated internal status system.[47] At Kata Estate in Kii, a hamlet combining fishing and farming, fourteenth-century residents formed a shrine association with rituals for each type of occupation; wealthier peasants with longer lineages maintained the greatest power in the community.[48] At other corporate villages in Kii, the maintenance and operation of irrigation facilities were major functions. Like Imabori and Kata, Kii's Eastern Village (noted above for its advanced watering technology) had its own shrine association and distinguished among its high- and low-status residents and between locals and outsiders.[49]

As in the case of settlement patterns, historians ask why corporate communities came into existence at this time. Of course, population growth and improved farming techniques played a crucial indirect role, but the raison d'être for communal villages near the Kinai was likely the control and management of common property, such as irrigation works, forests, rivers, and grasslands. Each of these resources could become scarce, so individuals faced risk if use was determined on a personal, ad hoc basis. Therefore, peasants united to make rules governing water, timber, and grasslands to guarantee that each person minimized risk and maximized access.[50]

A requirement for the rise of self-regulating peasant communities was that at least a few cultivators could grasp the essentials of reading, writing, and arithmetic.[51] Village temples played a significant role in educating rural folk. Authors usually brushed their regulations in syllabary *(katakana)*, a simple form easy to master. The advance of literacy and numeracy at least to the level of local notables and some wealthy peasants seems to have begun after 1300, coinciding with the economic and demographic changes outlined above.

Finally, as rural folk settled in compact villages with their own identity and rules, the percentage of "floating population" began to decrease. It was not that peasants did not migrate or travel, but they gradually established a sense of "connectedness" with a certain region or hamlet. Migration and travel continued and may even have expanded, but they were different in character from the era before 1280 because origins and destinations were more often fixed.[52]

To be sure, not every village in the islands was a compact settlement housing a corporate community by 1450. Corporate communities probably did not comprise a majority, even in central and western Japan. In southern Kyushu and eastern Honshu, where the social and economic changes discussed so far had yet to take hold, the older regime of scattered dwellings with little sense of local identity probably prevailed. To the extent that these rural areas had a sense of self-awareness, it originated from the local notables-cum-warriors, whose moated residences and stockades dominated the landscape. A stronger sense of peasant identity was a trend of the future, however, and farmers committed to their fields and villages contributed substantially to the overall growth of agricultural productivity.

An Estimate for Per-Unit Rice Yields

The diffusion of better agronomic practices, more efficient and sophisticated irrigation facilities, and more cohesive and economically motivated peasant communities improved agricultural productivity and accelerated population increase. But by how much did yields improve? Is there any way to obtain an estimate, however crude? No one can ever be certain of the answers to these weighty queries, but enough data have survived to provide an interesting possible answer for wet-rice cultivation.

In Hizen in northern Kyushu, per-unit rice yields in the later medieval era varied widely according to such factors as weather, soil, and amount and temperature of the water, but generally they ranged from .5–.6 to

1.7–1.9 *koku* per *tan,* in units of that time.[53] It is unlikely, however, that Hizen was as developed as the Kinai; for example, there was probably neither double-cropping nor "added rent," although Champa rice thrived in northern Kyushu. Drought was common and the use of natural irrigation was widespread in Hizen, circumstances that contributed to a failed harvest about once every three years and malnutrition among a large sector of the rural populace.

The figures quoted above may well be applicable throughout much of the archipelago in the fourteenth or early fifteenth centuries, but in the advanced Kinai, per-unit rice yields were likely higher. At Kuze Estate in Yamashiro, the average amount of "added rent" taken by Tōji was around .6 *koku* per *tan;* on the assumption that the temple was siphoning off most of the added surplus, high yields in some parts of the advanced Kinai may have been 2.3–2.6 *koku* per *tan.*[54] Positing that poor (.5 or .6 *koku* per *tan*) and middle-grade (1.7–1.9 *koku* per *tan*) paddies amounted to 45 percent each and high-grade rice fields producing "added rent" composed the remaining 10 percent, I arrived at an average figure of about 1.3 *koku* per *tan.*[55]

The historian next confronts the all but insoluble problem of what measure cultivators were most likely using. By 1450 the *senshi to* was no longer widely in use; the *koku* must have been larger by then, although local variation was undoubtedly still the rule.[56] In fact, no one knows what unit of measurement held sway, except to say that the *koku* was 1.5 times larger than the Nara unit and could not have been more than 2.5 times that measure. For example, when I utilized a conservative multiplier of 1.75 instead of 1.5 *(senshi to)*, then the *tan* described above would have produced 2.28 eighth-century *koku*. Since the average yield of a *tan* planted in rice around 700 was 1.57 *koku*, this meant that the average paddy of 1450 was 1.45 times more productive than the same unit of the early eighth century, or 1.21 times better than a typical Kamakura rice field. Or put in different terms, while it took about 2.17 *tan* to support a person in 700, by 1450 only 1.50 *tan* was required.

A comparison with the productivity figure calculated for 1280 is even more instructive. While a rice cultivator could on average expect 20 percent more grain in 1280 than he could in 700, by 1450 his descendants were reaping a 45 percent better crop. Or, again expressed in area, while it required 1.81 *tan* to sustain an individual in 1280, as little as 1.50 *tan* may have been sufficient 170 years later. The decrease from 1280 to 1450 may seem small, but when the reader recalls that it is an archipelago-wide average and considered over time, the acceleration in the growth of rice harvests is striking. Finally, the improvement from Nara to late Kamakura times was almost imperceptible when viewed on an annual basis; the precise figure is .05 percent per year. In contrast, from 1280 to 1450, growth was almost five times faster, at .24 percent per year, if we use the 2.28 *koku* per *tan* figure.

Another piece of evidence suggests that there was an acceleration in rice farming productivity. In institutional terms, the late Kamakura through mid-Muromachi periods purportedly marked the dissolution of the *myō* (tax units composed of numerous interdependent cultivators, their homes, and fields) and the rise of independent small producers.[57] Rich peasants acquired their own slices of the produce, and a new group *(bantō)* emerged. To be sure, books and articles published over the last forty years give the feeling that the small producer was always "rising," in much the same way that the European middle class ascended to its rightful place in society anywhere from the 1100s to 1800s, depending upon the historian. More concretely, at Tara Estate individual cultivators had many more possessions in 1450 than they did in 1347.[58] Better cultivation techniques were giving smallholders a chance to survive on their own and making more people well off.[59]

To be sure, readers may wish to use different numbers to arrive at an average per-unit yield other than 2.28 *koku* per *tan*. No one can be sure about the usual mix of paddy land or the size of unit volumes—was the *koku* of 1450 only 1.75 times greater than that of 700? This unit increased by 2.5 over the medieval era, and although the year 1600 was still a long way off in 1450, the 1.75 multiplier may be too small.[60] If the *koku* was larger, however, then the yield would have been correspondingly greater, thus making the case for the rise in wet-rice productivity even more dramatic.

In the event, the statistics above are meant merely to be suggestive of the changes that the archipelago was starting to undergo by 1450. Population was growing steadily, in many areas farming productivity had reached heights never hit before, and Champa rice and better irrigation facilities enabled peasants to begin opening fertile alluvial plains previously closed to them. Peasants were converting dry tillage to wet-rice, and more "floating people" in the countryside were settling down. And as of 1450, the changes had yet to reach most of Japan, especially eastern Honshu and southern Kyushu. Much of this initial transformation has been documented; unfortunately, lots must also be inferred from scraps of evidence. The random survival of written records rarely leaves the historian with a sure path to the past.

With sizable increases in population and farming productivity, it should come as no surprise that the era from 1280 to 1450 witnessed the birth of a full-fledged commercial economy in Japan, centered on the Kinai. It is a general rule of thumb that when these demographic and agrarian changes occur, people and regions become free to specialize in products favored by their factor endowments—that is, they do what they can do best. This in turn results in a greater volume of trade.[61] The trend was visible in Japan not simply in the economy, but also in the increasing size of armies and greater number of urban dwellers. If social division of labor is to be equated with the advent of "civilization," as Amino asserts, then there might be more than a kernel of truth to his belief that this was the time when Japan moved from a primitive to a civilized society.[62]

Commerce

The major developments during this epoch were the following: the archipelago-wide creation of new markets and towns; an increase in trade in and around Kyoto, served by improved transportation; monetization and the consequent commutation of more product and labor taxes; and the penetration of the market into rural society, as shown most strikingly by the appearance and spread of riots led by indebted commoners, especially farmers.[63] Because it was an important factor in the demographic expansion inferred in chapter 3, the birth (or perhaps rebirth) of Japan's commercial economy will receive a brief description and analysis here, addressing topics in the order listed above.

In the period from 1280 through 1450, former markets came back to life and new ones sprang up like kudzu. Many provincial headquarters served as market towns even in the eighth century; this was a natural result of good location, a unified transportation system maintained by the Nara court, and a resident consumer class of maybe six hundred or more officials.[64] Four examples from medieval times are Hitachi, Owari, Wakasa, and Aki.[65]

In Hitachi by 1350, there was a *rokusai ichi* (market) six times a month, frequented by officials, monks, and shrine attendants. Served by the Kiso River, Shimotsu Itsuka Market in Owari was in business by at least 1314, if not earlier; it opened its gates on land near the provincial headquarters and specialized in converting tax goods to cash. In Wakasa, peasants from Tara Estate took their grain to sell at O'nyū Market, also near what had been the provincial headquarters. Vendors at O'nyū, which opened on the seventh of every month, sold hemp cloth, silk, and swords, mostly for cash. The Wakasa headquarters was also close to Obama, a port leading to Echizen and northern Honshu. The market at Aki dated from at least the early fourteenth century, with older ties to traffic to and from Itsukushima Shrine. Many provincial headquarters had moved offices since the 700s, and as economic and demographic revival accelerated after 1280, the new offices took on a commercial function.

The new markets created after 1280 were even more impressive than the holdovers from a bygone age. Commerce grew during the Wars between the Northern and Southern Dynasties, when even military encampments served as markets. There are 113 known centers scattered across the islands and dating from about 1200 to the late fifteenth century. Although the earliest was open by the first years of the thirteenth century, only seventeen operated prior to 1280 and only seven before 1250. The geographical distribution is also notable: 41 (36 percent) did business in the Kinai or adjacent provinces of Tanba, Harima, Wakasa, Kii, and Ōmi; 63 (56 percent) opened their gates in provinces stretching from Ōmi to northern Kyushu. There were only thirteen (11.5 percent) in the Kanto and northeastern Honshu.[66]

Mt. Kōya oversaw eight markets in one of Japan's most advanced areas, Kii Province.[67] Established in the late Kamakura era, these markets were home to two types of merchants—long-distance specialists distinct from the agrarian society and peasant-artisans, such as those called *himono ya* at Ategawa Estate. Even during the insurgencies of the "evil bands" in the late Kamakura era, these traders were willing to take risks for sizable profits. They bargained for the rich products of Kii's many estates, converting commodities into cash for the temple complex at "ad hoc markets" *(toki no washi)*. Monks and local peasants also bought and sold at these centers.

Beginning in the Muromachi era, Kyoto and the various regions around it became home to merchant stalls containing agricultural products of every description—grains, vegetables, and processed foods. The populace of the old capital became dependent upon rice merchants who, as has already been noted in chapter 3, did not always put the welfare of their customers ahead of profits. The budget of a unit of Daitokuji, the famous Rinzai Zen institution of Kyoto, shows that over 13 percent of cash expenditures went to acquire rice, with another 10.6 percent going for vegetables and other food products such as gingerroot, radishes, and mountain tubers *(yamaimo)*. Another major market was located in Hyōgo, where in 1390 agents *(toimaru)* purchased the tax rice of Tō-daiji's Ōta Estate for cash; other rice merchants operated out of Tennōji in what would later be called Osaka.[68] Yodo was also a critical commercial center, where merchants and consumers could buy and sell fish and sea products. Still other traders bought up tax rice and used the grain to ferment rice wine, especially in Ōtsu, Sakamoto, and Kawachi.

By 1400 or even earlier, processed agricultural goods available in the Kinai included all sorts of items. Both silk and hemp thread and cloth were for sale in Kyoto, with most silk coming from the northern littoral of the Japan Sea, especially Echigo. Workers produced hemp in north-western and central Honshu, transshipped it at Sakamoto, and sold it at Kyoto and Tennōji through "guilds" *(za)* of merchants, who limited their membership and obtained monopoly rights backed by political authorities, such as the aristocratic Sanjōnishi family. Red *(akane)*, purple *(murasaki)*, and blue-green *(ai)* dyes also appeared at Kyoto markets by 1400, all controlled by specialized *za*. Perilla oil *(egoma)*, used for lighting lamps, was another processed good, handled in Kyoto by the famous Ōyamazaki guild and in Nara by Kōfukuji.[69] By the 1400s, these organizations had expanded their activities into Settsu, Sakamoto, and Yoshida. In addition, the capital attracted traveling merchants and their wares from even farther afield.[70]

The Kyoto dynamo engendered the formation of local markets specializing in goods for the capital, such as the silk of Mino and Kaga; the hemp of Echigo and Etchū; paper from Harima, Mino, and Echizen; knives and swords also from Mino; pots from Chikuzen; and rice wine from Ōmi, Kawachi, Settsu, and Nara. Population increase stimulated regional specialization, in turn creating a vibrant commercial network throughout central and western Japan.

There could be no doubt that Kyoto was the commercial hub of the islands by 1400, home to forty guilds and over 350 moneylenders *(dosō-sakaya)*.[71] With an urban population of about two hundred thousand, Kyoto probably contained half the city dwellers in the islands, including a large consumer class composed of the shogun's government, various samurai officials, shrine-temple complexes, and the old aristocratic/imperial class.[72] Many merchant and artisan outfits were small, but large moneylenders wielded considerable influence, charging as much as 60 percent interest and paying the shogunate to guarantee enforcement of their contracts.[73]

The guilds, dating from the end of the Heian period but not coming into their own until the 1300s, contributed to commercial development by limiting competition—even though it was still in its initial stages—and providing for greater specialization by reducing risks and improving incentives while at the same time lowering information and transaction costs. The most famous *za*—the Ōyamazaki oil producers, Kitano malt brewers, Kōfukuji salt marketers, and Gion silk weavers—wielded considerable economic and political power.[74]

Improvements in transportation assisted in the development of trade. While land conveyance remained essentially the same as earlier—reliant upon pack animals and humans traversing dirt roads occasionally covered with sand or stones—sailing technology underwent significant changes during the fourteenth and fifteenth centuries. Until the late Kamakura period, Japanese boats were nothing more than hollowed-out logs, sometimes with planks (called strakes) attached to the sides to promote seaworthiness.[75] Although simple to construct, these ships had many disadvantages: the hold was limited to the diameter of the log, they were wasteful of timbers, and vessels were usually not seaworthy enough to cross from Kyushu directly to China.

Scroll paintings and other documents tell a different story by the early 1400s. Gone was the primitive hull design; the boats had two bamboo sails and elegant structures on deck, including a house shingled with Japanese cypress bark. From top to bottom the ships measured three or four stories and had a capacity three to seven times that of Heian or Kamakura vessels. This transformation was possible because shipwrights had learned to construct the hull completely from planks sometime in the early fourteenth century, if not before. Crossbeams served to reinforce the hull structure. Larger hulls not only meant greater seaworthiness and room for more cargo, but by 1400 larger decks also had more space for masts and large sails. When oars were employed, as many as forty men pulled in synchronization—more than quadruple the number in the 1200s. It is also likely that sailors had adopted the compass from the Chinese by 1450.

What is more, this new technology became widely dispersed during the 1300s among merchant families dwelling in northern Kyushu and along the Inland Sea. The famous trade missions sent by the Muromachi shogunate to the Ming dynasty, beginning in 1401, were all composed of ships chartered from Japanese mercantile houses. The waters in western Japan became so crowded that traders observed *Regulations for Cargo Vessels (kaisen shikimoku),* covering such diverse topics as collision, rescue, and salvage operations.

The technology of land transport may not have gained much over the era 1280 to 1450, but other developments helped lower costs. First, as the economy became more highly monetized, shippers and tax agents stopped sending commodities to their Kyoto consumers and began offering cash. This arrangement was superior for Kyotoites not only because coins are fungible, but also because the shipping cost was extraordinarily lower. Given the same value, the price of ferrying cash was about one-fortieth that of ferrying rice.[76]

Second, in its heyday, the Muromachi shogunate reduced to a minimum barriers *(sekisho)* where fees were collected.[77] During the early 1300s, all sorts of institutions erected many such obstructions in the hopes of raising money, at rates varying from 1 to 10 percent of the value of the shipment. Such rates may not seem prohibitive, but when we consider that there were eighteen barriers between Nara and Mino, it becomes apparent that costs mounted quickly.[78] Religious centers were particularly eager for such income to pay for the repair and construction of new buildings, and they dealt a harsh blow to merchants seeking to market their wares. Emperor Go-Daigo tried to outlaw barriers, especially during famines.[79] During its first years, the Muromachi government countermanded Go-Daigo's directives and once again permitted the establishment of some barriers, especially to earn income with which to help rebuild damaged and dilapidated shrine-temple complexes. The only notable exception was during times of starvation. The Southern Dynasty, a loser on the battlefield with few sources of income, allowed the obstructions wherever possible.

After the unification of the two courts in 1392, however, the third shogun, Yoshimitsu, wisely turned to other sources of revenue to support religious construction, such as land *(tansen)* and property *(munabechi sen)* taxes paid in coins. From the 1390s, the Muromachi government abolished innumerable barriers and enforced this policy until the 1430s, at which time it reinstated many barriers. The lowest transaction costs for traders occurred precisely during the "Muromachi Optimum," coinciding with a time of lower mortality from war, disease, and famine.

The conversion of commodity and labor taxes into cash and the disestablishment of barriers emphasize another critical aspect of the commercial boom: monetization.[80] For instance, none of the documents at Mt. Kōya referred to cash before 1200, and only 24.6 percent did so prior to 1250. Between 1251 and 1300, almost 51 percent made notations in cash, while 86 percent of transactions took place in cash between 1301 and 1350. Almost all purchases were carried out in coins after 1351.

A visitor to the islands summarized the new emphasis on cash forcefully. On a tour of western Japan in 1429, Chosŏn ambassador Pak wrote the following:

> In Japan, when we traveled from the capital along the coast [of the Inland Sea], the use of money exceeded even that of hemp cloth or rice. Thus even travelers who journeyed a thousand leagues [J., *ri*; K., *i*; Ch., *li*] wrapped money belts [around them] and did not carry provisions. Each of those who dwelt on the side of the road established a travelers' lodge, and if a sojourner arrived they fought among themselves to serve him. They counted and received cash from their visitors to supply them with porters and horses. At barriers and bridges—that is, at great rivers—they set up ferries; over valleys they built bridges. Those who lived nearby were in charge of the fee to cross the bridge and let the traveler pass. They collected five or ten coins, having built small or large bridges, using the proceeds to make repairs later. When it came to land, . . . boat, and cart fees, we had to use cash. Thus cash payments were widely accepted.[81]

Among the other items Pak listed as available for purchase with coins were rice, beans, fish, and even a hot bath.

While the network of markets and money did not reach everywhere and was especially slow to develop in eastern Honshu, there can be no doubt that it had its most direct effects upon the local populace in western Japan.[82] For example, with the establishment of O'nyū Market near Tara Estate by 1243, even small cultivators began to bring their hemp, dyes, and other products to sell for cash. Some abandoned agriculture altogether and became artisans or merchants dealing in silk. By the 1330s, wealthier peasants, artisans, middle and even small cultivators, along with rural lenders, comprised a class of "small merchant farmers"; in 1334, there were at least fifty-nine such individuals resident at Tara. They took advantage of the opportunities presented by the market, but they could also entangle other locals in a web of loans from which they could not always extricate themselves.

Yano Estate in Harima is another example of the market in action. As noted previously, Yano was one of the earliest attested cases of Champa rice cultivation, and records suggest that peasants sold the grain at market in the 1400s. Moreover, Yano's arable was difficult to irrigate, making it a prime candidate not only for the Southeast Asian product, but also for wheat. Records indicate that from 1300 to 1450 Yano peasants sold their wheat at markets to pay their taxes in cash, despite the proprietor's (Tōji) preference for goods-in-kind.[83] Kuze Estate in Yamashiro, the home province of Kyoto, also exemplified the effects of the market.[84]

The market was a double-edged sword. It provided more and a greater variety of goods, as well as sales opportunities to many cultivators, helping to offset the "macroparasitic drain" from rents and taxes. Because of these growing advantages, it seems likely that the birth of commerce would have served as a stimulus to fertility and improved longevity, at least in the areas near markets, especially in the Kinai and environs. In less developed areas, such as eastern Honshu or southern Kyushu, where centripetal economic forces were not nearly so strong, samurai, civil aristocrats, and temple complexes initiated, oversaw, and benefited from commerce. Peasants there were less directly involved or affected by the market, at least until 1450.[85]

At the same time, debts contracted in deflationary times had the potential to bankrupt peasants whose crops failed, and flight or resistance then became the order of the day.[86] As noted in chapter 3, commoners began to demand food and debt relief and to riot, often in groups of a thousand or more. In an early uprising among teamsters and cultivators in Ōmi Province in 1428, the dispossessed broke into pawnbrokers' shops, tore up their loan contracts, and walked off with their collateral. There were twenty-six similar large-scale riots, including debt relief riots *(tokusei ikki),* between 1428 and 1500.[87] Peasant behavior during these events was similar to that of the Kamakura "evil bands" because both peasants and the bands "cut off traffic on roads, raised stakes *[sakamogi],* built palisades, and refused to pay their taxes."[88] As in Western European history, the advent of the first true riots in Japan after 1400 coincided with the penetration of the market to local agrarian society.[89]

Industry and Labor

The period from 1280 to 1450 was one of the most innovative in Japanese manufacturing. I have already described one example—the invention of larger and more seaworthy boats. Almost all occupations benefited from growing commercialization, as the demand for products increased and the distinction between artisans and marketers became sharper. In this context, I shall discuss only a few representative sectors.[90]

As with so many products, lumber became even more highly sought in Muromachi times.[91] Already during the eighth century, timber stands in the Kinai were insufficient to sustain construction in the vicinity, and with the massive expansion of the old capital's population and religious and government building during Yoshimitsu's era, it is not surprising to find merchants going farther and farther afield to locate adequate supplies. Hida, Mino, and Shikoku were especially popular, with the timbers of Hida and Mino floated down the Kiso River. For example, when workers erected a pagoda at Tōfukuji in 1442, two hundred rafts and six thousand packhorses bore the lumber from Mino. Or again, a freight report from Hyōgo *(Hyōgo kitaseki nyūsen nōchō)*, dated to 1445, stated that ships loaded with timber from Awaji, Tosa, and Awa carried 1,910 measures *(koku)* in their holds *in one month.* This evidence of a construction boom lends further credence to the hypothesis of sizable population expansion at this time.

Moreover, advances in tools and techniques aided the boom. New measuring instruments for marking off angles and lengths, such as the *magarikane* and *urame,* were invented, eventually making Japanese carpentry into the fine art that it was to become by the Tokugawa era. Two new cutting tools, a great saw *(ōnokogiri)* and plane *(taihō),* made work faster, more efficient, and more precise. As in so many other societies, population growth coincided with technological innovation, in this case in the lumbering business.

Salt production expanded and changed as well.[92] Ancient residents of the archipelago used the labor-intensive "seaweed method" to boil down ocean water into brine and then crystals.[93] By the late ninth or early tenth century, this method was no longer used as the number of laborers had decreased, and the well-known technology involving "salt-fields" constructed on beaches became the norm. There were two variants of the latter technology, one in which seawater was trapped in ridged sandlots as the tide flowed and ebbed, and then allowed to evaporate in the sun. Laborers then collected the salt-laden sand and boiled it in more seawater, and the crystals and sand separated.

In the second method, workers actually carried the liquid in buckets to a destination farther up the beach, dried it in lots, collected it, and boiled it down in kettles. The second variation was more labor intensive since it required workers to transport the brine away from the ocean before further treatment. This second system became increasingly common during the Muromachi period and was the direct ancestor of the Tokugawa-period technique known as *irihama*.

Fishing also underwent technological and organizational transformations in the late thirteenth and fourteenth centuries.[94] Although the basic equipment for this occupation had been available since Jōmon times and important developments had also occurred in the late Heian and early Kamakura eras, two critical, interrelated changes came in the Muromachi epoch. First, nets became specialized according to the catch (e.g., *katsuo ami* for bonito), expanded in size, and fixed in place. Second, while fishing had previously been a mobile occupation, specialists now claimed inlets and rivers, set up their nets and equipment, and formed villages where none had existed before. Roaming bands of anglers still existed, but growing commercialization and specialization affected fishing like they did nearly every other industry. The former "floating population" of rural areas shrank, and settled artisans and marketers multiplied with the growing economy.

Ceramics was yet another sector to grow dramatically in the mid-Muromachi era.[95] Even in the late Kamakura period, the technology of glazing stoneware to produce the highly esteemed Bizen ware was limited to the Inland Sea. The fifteenth century, however, witnessed a great increase in production and a change in labor organization. Whereas previously kilns had been scattered here and there, by 1400 villages began to specialize in the production of ceramics, as shown by the three and four kilns found at certain medieval sites. According to the Hyōgo freight report cited above, on average about one hundred pieces passed through the port per month; the busiest season was summer, when peasants manufactured pots as a by-employment. Potters settled from northern Kyushu to the eastern edges of the Kinai. The technology was not new, but it had dispersed as demand rose and commercial routes and opportunities opened up. Seto ware also came into its own in the 1400s.

In sum, agriculture, forestry, salt making, fishing, and ceramics—all basic premodern Japanese industries—began to mature at this time, both technologically and organizationally. Other sectors, such as water control, weaving, and metallurgy, also underwent considerable development and expansion. The era from 1280 to 1450 laid the foundation for early modern industries.

Cities

With population growing, agricultural production rising, transportation improving, and commerce and industry booming, it should come as no surprise that urbanization took place as never before. No one can be certain how many new cities and towns—here defined as having a population of at least five thousand—sprang up during these 170 years, but a 1942 source notes twenty new centers, including three temple/shrine municipalities, six ports, three hostelries, five former provincial capitals, and three market cities. From the late twelfth to the end of the fourteenth century, about forty towns sprang up in the archipelago; over the course of the 1400s another forty-five developed.[96] While the lion's share of those municipalities were formed after 1450, even a conservative tabulation would place the number at about 50–55 in the mid-fifteenth century, far in excess of urbanization before 1280.

Moreover, many centers were sizable.[97] Kyoto had perhaps 200,000; Hakata, 40,000; Tennōji, 30,000; Kashiwazaki in Echigo and Ōtsu, 20,000 each; Yamada in Ise, Naoetsu (also in Echigo), and Anotsu in Ise, 15,000 each; Nara, 9,000; and Zuisenji (Etchū), Ishidera (Ōmi), and Fuchū (Suruga), 5,000 apiece. The total was about 379,000 city dwellers —just under 4 percent of an archipelago-wide population hypothesized at about 10 million; in both percentage and absolute terms, Japan was much more urbanized than during the previous epoch. And the list does not include Kamakura, which, although incinerated in the demise of the Hōjō in 1333, continued in an administrative function under the Ashikaga.[98] In fact, other sites with smaller populations or those yet to be discovered may easily push the sum higher.

Scholars have studied a few of these communities. Of course, we know much about Muromachi-age Kyoto, with maps showing the locations of major shrines and temples and even those of pawnbrokers, rice wine brewers, and oil dealers.[99] Moreover, in recent years archaeologists have confirmed the existence of roads and sewer ditches for much of what once comprised the eastern half of ancient Heian, including areas north of Emperor Kanmu's capital. The east-west thoroughfares seem to have developed right on top of the old grid layout. Dwellings were concentrated in the lots lying between Ume no kōji and Nijō, north to south, and Higashi Kyōgoku and Ōmiya, east to west. With more than twice the tenth-century population squeezed into a much smaller space, the city must have been far more crowded and possibly suffered from even greater sanitation problems.[100]

Nara was the other old capital to survive the ancient period, although much diminished from its past splendor. It was reorganized as seven "villages" *(shichigō)* in the late Heian period, and Kōfukuji, Tōdaiji, and Gangōji saw to the city's administration throughout the medieval epoch. Practically no written materials are extant from the Kamakura era, but by the Muromachi period records suggest substantial building, with many references to laborers during the reign of Yoshimitsu. Temples and merchants carried on a booming loan business, but the city had its underside too, as documents frequently note disposal of the sick and dying in the streets.[101]

Archaeologists have also turned their attention to Hakata, Japan's major port for traffic with the rest of Asia. Large quantities of Chinese porcelain shards have come to light, and merchants from Hakata trans-shipped ceramics as far away as northeastern Honshu. The greatest period of Hakata's growth may have begun in 1050 and lasted through 1300, yet workers did not dig the main street connecting Hakata to the ocean or the ditches that formed the borders of the city until the late 1200s. The center of population moved to Okinohama after 1350, with both the old and new town located in low-lying swamps surrounded by dry fields.[102]

Today Kyoto, Nara, and Hakata are all vibrant cities, but some medieval municipalities simply disappeared. One such town was Anotsu in Ise, once numbering perhaps twenty thousand but destroyed in 1498, when a mammoth earthquake struck in the ocean floor just offshore from the port, giving rise to a giant tsunami inundating residences. Little excavation has taken place, but at a few small sites fine pottery has been recovered. Some experts even perceive the remains of a street layout.[103]

Of all the ghost towns of the medieval era, however, the most famous is undoubtedly Kusado Sengen, located near modern Hiroshima.[104] Established in the late thirteenth century and reaching its apogee between 1350 and 1400, this port on the Inland Sea was a booming market until the end of the sixteenth century, when the Ashida River changed course and obliterated the town. Served by a network of roads and canals, in the late 1400s Kusado Sengen was composed of two blocks, one about 70 meters square and the second over 110 meters to a side. Archaeologists have recovered a wealth of sites—house and shop foundations, graves, temple remains—and artifacts, including wooden tablets *(mokkan)*, cloth, sandals, bone jewelry, pottery shards, knives, lacquer ware, coins, and tools.

Wooden tablets are especially valuable for piecing together daily town life. Numerous slips suggest market activity, such as those listing the name and quantity of a commodity and its price in coins. Many tags indicate that loaning cash was a thriving business, and Kusado Sengen even had its own pawnshop *(dosō)*.[105] Right along with written materials showing a "rational" economic consciousness, however, archaeologists have found dozens of wooden strips appealing to magic and superstition to ward off disease and other disasters. Apparently the residents' good fortune had dissipated around 1600, when the town was inundated; but the trend toward urbanization that Kusado Sengen symbolized was only starting when these unfortunate urbanites lost their homes and property.

FERTILITY: FAMILY, WOMEN, AND CLASS

As is true for the rest of the medieval age, there is no direct evidence bearing on the birthrate, perhaps the most critical component in the demographic equation. It is impossible to know the average size of the family upon completion or the age intervals between offspring, much less compute anything resembling a birthrate from nonexistent census data. In this section I therefore examine structures, such as family and class, that may have made a difference in fertility. First, I shall address family, then women and marriage, then children, and finally the lot of the servile class.

Prior to 1280, the fundamental pattern of kinship among rural folk and other commoners was bilateral, and persons could trace descent through either their father's or mother's line. The status of women was relatively high; both bilateral kinship and the lofty position of women likely came about because of the lack of labor.[106] Individual peasant families were nuclear and highly unstable; residence was either neolocal or matrilocal. Young people engaged frequently in sexual relations from puberty, and marriage was a vague arrangement. Divorce and remarriage were common, and it was not unusual for a family to disintegrate before it could designate an heir. Infant mortality was appallingly high—up to 50 or 60 percent to age five.[107]

Information on the family, women, and social class in the late Kamakura and first half of the Muromachi eras suggests that a transformation was starting but that it was hardly fully formed by 1450. After all, as sizable as the beginning of this cycle of demographic and economic growth was, it was still just under way in 1450 and was to last for another 270 years. By the time the expansion was finished in 1720, it had deep-seated repercussions throughout the archipelago, but in 1450 it was limited mostly to the Kinai and certain regions in western Japan.

The sparse evidence on family comes first of all from Yamakuni Estate in Tanba.[108] For one thing, wealthy cultivators and even ordinary peasants were no longer sharing names *(ujina)* associated with the extensive pre-1280 lineages *(uji)*, such as Wake, Saeki, Ki, or Minamoto, but had begun applying individual names *(myōji)* to their households. Typical cognomens included Mizoguchi, Torii, Fujino, Kohata, and Arai. According to materials from Yamakuni, this trend could be found among all classes of peasants throughout the nine villages within the estate. This change started about 1340 in Yamakuni but did not become commonplace until after 1450. By the 1500s, the old lineage names had all but disappeared and the new family cognomens were nearly universal.

What lay behind the gradual transformation? Most new appellations referred to locales or topographical features within Yamakuni. The appearance of new surnames seems to be related to the settlement of cultivators at established places; in other words, after 1340, peasants had a set lot where they expected their homes to remain for generations. The macroeconomic growth trends in agriculture and commerce had resulted in greater wealth and possessions among the peasantry, in turn fostering stability and a need to pass along a patrimony. At Yamakuni, more than fifty family names were passed down over the next 400–500 years.

Data are also available for Suganoura in Ōmi, a famous corporate community of the medieval age. They show that of 709 current household names, only 3.8 percent came into existence before 1400. Only a little over 14 percent of households applied those names in the 1400s; the overwhelming majority (77 percent) were not in use until the 1500s. In the period from 1280 to 1450, only about 8 percent of families utilized these surnames, indicating that development of the new family units at Suganoura was just in its initial stages even in 1450. We can therefore infer a lag time between the economic and demographic expansion commencing about 1280 and the creation of new, more stable families among the peasantry at Suganoura.[109]

Although a scholarly consensus by no means obtains, many argue that the cases of Yamakuni and Suganoura indicate that some peasants were forming incipient stem families *(ie)*, ubiquitous in the Tokugawa era (1600–1868).[110] Among cultivators, the stem family not only placed great value on lineage, managed and passed along family property and business, and cared for the elderly and ancestors' tablets, but was also responsible for tax payment and had membership in evolving village communities through such institutions as the shrine association.[111] These corporate units were comprised of the conjugal pair—with the husband as head—their offspring, and unrelated persons such as servants or other underlings. While the heir was almost always a male (but not necessarily the eldest), he might be adopted into the family by marriage to a daughter.

Other features of this familial organization began to appear by 1450. Fathers (presumably household heads) named their sons with Chinese characters borrowed from their own personal appellations; positions within the shrine association accompanied designation as heir. Most important, families assembled their own patrimony; separate estates for wife and husband started to disappear. Corporate villages made rules mandating that each family delegate a son as sole heir to ensure the continuation of the family, even when the former head was guilty of a capital crime. They also expelled from the shrine association heads who did not pay their taxes *(zaike yaku)*. The creation of corporate communities required changes in the household, and the development of more cohesive families in turn reinforced the new village organization.[112]

Even the treatment of death began to change. From the 1400s, the word for graveyard shifted from *tsukahara* to *hakahara*, as stupas replaced stone markers.[113] Corporate villages had their own common cemeteries, where cremation was the rule; funerals became events in which numerous relatives participated through notification of death, gift giving, sutra reading, grave digging, the making of various ritual implements, the washing and placement of the remains in a coffin, and participation in the funeral ritual itself. Furthermore, the time of burial altered from night to day, and interment became a community-wide happening. This transformation indicates both the penetration of popular Buddhism into rural society and the development of social units capable of considerable organization.

The gradual creation of the *ie* coincided with a major shift in marriage. Conventionally, the fourteenth century is known as the period when virolocal institutions *(yometori kon)* became common, as evident in the delivery of dowries and a new term for divorce (*oidasu*, "to chase out [the wife]").[114] Moreover, the wife increasingly came to be viewed as the husband's possession, as indicated by (1) women either keeping their childhood personal names throughout their lives or adopting their husband's given appellation plus a female indicator (either *ko* or *me*), and (2) female adultery necessitating the death penalty at the hands of the husband for both the wife and her lover. In elite society, women had almost completely lost the right of inheritance by 1400.[115]

There was a gradual deterioration in women's status over the fourteenth and fifteenth centuries. At Eastern Village in Kokawa Estate in Kii, a 1365 regulation stated that daughters who left their local families would no longer be allowed membership in the village shrine association; this rule may have indicated the growing popularity of virolocal marriage and a consequent loss of female privilege. There was also an increase in the number of widows who could not remarry, a phenomenon that would not have occurred in earlier periods.[116]

Women still held many occupations—in trade, in manufacture, and as always, in agriculture.[117] Increasingly, however, as a female brought a dowry into a husband's home, stress was placed upon the wife as heir-producer and child-bearer. In rural areas, birthing took place in a parturition hut with a midwife in attendance. The floor was earthen, and infant mortality remained high.[118] Either not bearing or losing an infant meant a sentence of eternity in hell for a woman, with no possibility of attaining Buddhahood. And even though maternity was required of a woman, it was also considered polluting *(kegare)*.

For some medieval women, it is possible that these incipient changes—loss of inheritance and property rights, life in a household overseen by a male head, the creation of a separate vocabulary and pattern of speech for women, along with a duty to bear and care for children while working in the fields—were just too much.[119] Note, for example, that temples established only about 15 percent of convents before 1280; sixty (61 percent) began between 1270 and 1470.[120] Was this an attempt by women to escape from the new familial system? To be sure, Buddhist nuns may have already had children, so perhaps the formation of these new convents had relatively little impact on fertility. In such an institution, however, mature women could manage their own property, run their own lives, and avoid adult males and the duty of repeated childbirth. Buddhist nuns—along with some outcasts, servants, and prostitutes—comprised one type of "woman who did not form a family."

It is difficult to know what all these changes in family and marriage would have meant for the birthrate. In the Nara and Heian epochs, when these structures were looser and less stable and women had higher status, quantitative and descriptive data imply that both fertility and infant mortality were exceedingly high. The growing farm and commercial surpluses between 1280 and 1450 could have encouraged couples to have more children, although it is hard to imagine how the birthrate could have climbed much higher. Alternatively, as noted above, there may have been a larger share of women who preferred not to reproduce. Finally, as diet and other aspects of material welfare improved a bit, more children could well have survived infancy. The formation of some stem families and the concentration on maintaining the lineage may have translated into better care for offspring. At this stage, convincing evidence supporting one or more of these generalizations is not available.

There are, however, several assertions that can safely be made about children's lives in the late Kamakura and first half of the Muromachi periods.[121] Most important, infant mortality remained high; until age seven, children's deaths were so unsurprising that their parents did not even give them a proper funeral—they merely placed the corpse in a sack and abandoned it in the wild. At the same time, however, it seems likely that infant mortality was lower than in the late Heian period, at least if medical texts are a guide. To be sure, the famous Heian medical encyclopedia *Ishin pō* contains sections on obstetrics and pediatrics, but since it was modeled on a Tang work, it is difficult to tell how well it reflected Japanese reality. Moreover, it was written in Chinese characters and listed only three maladies for pregnant women.[122] By contrast, in the early fourteenth century, there were more medical texts, some of them written in *kana* syllabary and others specializing in obstetrics, suggesting that more care was being given to a growing number of infants surviving childbirth.[123] On the other hand, it is unclear how long mothers suckled their infants, with weaning perhaps taking place at age one or two, earlier than in Tokugawa times.

As children matured, they were given considerable latitude for play but were also expected to work, doing such tasks as driving livestock or rowing a boat. Parents laboring elsewhere often left the elderly (but not older siblings, as in the Tokugawa period) to watch children. Progeny of commoners received little in the way of education, except for what they could obtain from wandering monks and musicians. And of course, despite silence in legal sources, literary works and some documents imply that there was a sizable market in buying and selling children, even after 1300. On the one hand, merchants specializing in these transactions probably did a booming business during famines and epidemics, possibly saving some lives in the process.[124] On the other, the prevalence of kidnapping and the occasional harsh master were the main hazards of the market.

Orphanages established in the early Heian period continued to operate, suggesting a large pool of unattached children.[125] During the Kamakura epoch, they flourished in both capitals, but with the demise of the warrior city, the orphanages there faded from history. Those located in Kyoto, however, functioned into the Tokugawa period, and one even added a hospital in the tumultuous 1300s. It would be misleading to suggest that the evidence for abandoned children and orphanages was as plentiful as it had been prior to 1280; the effects of the Wars between the Northern and Southern Dynasties (and later the Ōnin conflict) may well have been devastating for youth, but hostilities also destroyed the orphanages and the records about them.

What happened to all those unattached children decried in Kamakura law? Two alternatives seem plausible. First, they were still there, but as in the case of servants and slaves (to be discussed below), the new *bakufu* simply turned a blind eye to their plight. References in Muromachi songs and *kana zōshi* (popular stories) support this argument. Second, there were not as many unwanted children in society after 1300. This hypothesis would correlate with the booming economy and the slow establishment of stem families and corporate communities, both rural and urban.[126] Women were still bearing lots of children, but because of various economic opportunities, offspring became an asset within a society containing more whole families and caring villagers.

When the term "unwanted children" is mentioned, it calls to mind practices of the Tokugawa era—abortion and infanticide. Medical know-how for such procedures was available at least from the Heian period, as the classic *Ishin pō* treats the topic of birth control. The customs do not seem to have become common, however, until the sixteenth century, when Jesuit monks such as Luis Frois condemned them. Current data suggest that both the Jesuits and the Edo government overestimated the ubiquity of these primitive methods of birth control, and it would have required common reliance on these techniques to have made much of a dent in the rate of infant survival. What is more, in a world where as many as half of the babies may never have reached age five, why would abortion or infanticide be deemed necessary? Still, one fact suggests caution in dealing with another topic that sources do not describe much. It is known that Kumano *bikuni*, the wandering female storytellers and entertainers, sold abortion-inducing drugs. No one knows how frequent their sales were, but the very fact of commodification implies that there was some demand.[127] The use of these birth control methods may also imply that infants stood a greater chance of survival naturally than before.

In the case of servants *(ge'nin, shojū)* and slaves *(nuhi, zōnin),* as with orphans, Muromachi legal sources convey little but a deafening silence. During the late Heian and Kamakura periods, as we may recall from chapters 1 and 2, this class greatly expanded, laws were written, and the sale of human beings—one major source of *ge'nin*—was condemned by the *bakufu* time and again. Suddenly in the Muromachi period, the government stopped issuing those laws altogether, and while there are documents indicating the sale of children and adults into servitude, especially during famines, they are relatively few.[128]

As with orphans, there are two plausible conclusions: (1) the number of *ge'nin* was decreasing, or (2) they existed widely but the government ignored them and few sale records survived. Evidence supporting the first contention comes in the form of records (few though they may be) showing servants buying their freedom.[129] Furthermore, if the population grew greatly and famines and epidemics were less frequent and severe between 1280 and 1450, then there would have been both less need for servant labor and fewer opportunities for such transactions. Following the logic of this argument, we might assert that by 1450 there was only a small number of *ge'nin*.[130]

Once again, however, literary sources and travelers' accounts come down on the side of the second proposition.[131] Slave merchants and their "products" make regular appearances in Muromachi *kana zōshi* and *kyōgen* (comic sketches), poetry, popular songs, and even Buddhist sermons, proving that the class had hardly disappeared. Chosŏn ambassador Pak noted the following with disapproval during 1429: "In Japan, where there are many people and little to eat, they sell lots of slaves. In some cases in secret they sell children."[132] Cheap and easy to abuse, children aged twelve or under made the best servants. This may be one reason that *ge'nin* are frequently portrayed as infantile, and most could not maintain their own families, representing a drag on fertility.[133]

Given the dearth of testimony and the difficulty of proving a negative proposition, I believe that the *ge'nin* class either shrank or remained constant between 1280 and 1450.[134] This tentative conclusion seems to fit best with other data presented on the population and economy. Any effect on fertility would probably have been minimal, perhaps canceling out the lowered reproduction of nuns and prostitutes, who chose not to bear children.

In sum, it is difficult to ascertain what the effect of all these changes would have been on the high birth and infant mortality rates from the previous era. For instance, did the creation of some stem families serve to lower the possibilities for sexual liaisons and also fertility? Or did stable families with more to eat encourage couples to have children, more of whom survived in a world less beset with famine? Did the market in children save the lives of those destined to die prematurely or lead to precisely the opposite result? Did the seeming reduction in the numbers of *ge'nin* portend a better life for more people, with more intact families and offspring? No one can answer these questions for sure, but on balance it seems likely that fertility remained high, with infant mortality dropping as the general physical well-being of the populace improved somewhat.

MATERIAL LIFE

With a sizable increase in agricultural productivity and the birth of a commercial economy, there were numerous signs that the standard of living for some of the population was beginning to rise. These improvements took place slowly and unevenly and were limited mostly to western Japan. In this section I shall describe briefly only the most important aspects.

Traditional peasant garb throughout the ancient and early medieval eras had always been made of hemp or ramie, products that were chilly and rough on the skin. Beginning in the mid-fifteenth century, an alternative appeared—cotton. Native to India, the cotton plant had entered first China and then Korea sometime prior to 1400. Initially, the elite of the archipelago discovered the advantages of cotton clothing and imported it from the continent. The first verifiable record of cotton growing in the islands, however, turns up for Kaita Estate in Chikuzen in 1429. The production of cotton probably spread from the continent (especially Korea) to Kyushu and then diffused slowly throughout the western archipelago. While it is doubtful that many commoners wore cotton clothing by 1450, eventually its use would increase greatly and create a whole new industry. Like so many other developments portrayed in this chapter, what would later become a significant transformation was just commencing at this time.[135]

Diet presents an even more positive picture. With the spread of double-cropping and Champa rice, more peasants escaped scarcity in the springtime and the constant state of malnutrition characteristic of earlier periods. Of course, this advance was by no means universal, as even under optimal conditions only a small portion of Japan's arable could produce more than one harvest, but at least for those areas mentioned above—especially the Kinai and environs—the chances of starving to death were somewhat diminished. Moreover, as the market developed, it delivered more and better side dishes, such as meat, salted fish, bean curd, noodles, and tea—not just to warriors and priests, but even to wealthier peasants. An overview of the grains, vegetables, and fruits available during this era reinforces this conclusion.[136] It is also important to recall that fishing had begun to emerge as an important commercial venture, delivering more protein for the average diet.

Sanitation and cleanliness also seem to have been undergoing modest improvement. On the one hand, there are relatively few toilets excavated for this era, and those that have been uncovered (for early Sakai) were still primitive. They were either jars or holes in the ground lined on four sides with wooden planks.[137] While the jars were undoubtedly emptied regularly, the holes were simply buried under piles of dirt when they had fulfilled their function. Paintings also depict this old-fashioned method.[138]

The jars hint at the start of another early modern custom (or business): the collection and sale of human excrement as fertilizer.[139] It may have gone together with double-cropping, as the famous "Lampoons at Nijō kawara" *(Nijō kawara rakugaki)* of the 1330s mention "excrement buckets" *(koe oke)*. Other Muromachi literary accounts also describe the utility of these containers; it seems likely that the night soil business dated back to the early fourteenth century. *Seiryō ki,* the first agricultural handbook *(nōsho)* in Japanese history, reflecting conditions of the Warring States era and later, however, emphasizes grass and ash as the major fertilizers, barely even referring to night soil. While farmers occasionally used human waste as fertilizer, it was not the all-pervasive enterprise that it would later become.

If excrement found little practical use, then was it being cleaned up? In this instance, as in the other cases cited above, the Muromachi government never issued laws about cleaning the streets of Kyoto.[140] The aforementioned reference from the "Lampoons" merely indicated that urbanites urinated in the streets, not that there was a booming business in night soil. The cleaning of Kyoto streets until 1450 took place at the hands of outcasts *(hi'nin, inu ji'nin)* associated with big temples and shrines such as Gion. Muromachi Kyoto was still one of the filthiest and smelliest places in Japan, reminiscent of the shantytowns in the industrializing Third World today. In sanitation, anyway, there seems to have been only a small advance.

The same cannot be said for bathing. As noted above, by the Muromachi era even a keen-eyed Korean ambassador visiting western Japan noticed the public baths: "They [the residents of the archipelago] like bathing and cleaning their bodies. Thus each large house has a bathhouse. At the gate of every village, they build them all over the place. The management of these facilities is clever and convenient. When the water is hot, they blow a horn, and those who hear strive to pay cash for a bath. Even in welfare agencies, inns, saunas, bridges, and hospitals, where there are many people, they erect bathhouses."[141] Not only did wealthy individuals and shrine-temple complexes have their own bathhouses, but also the city bathhouse *(machi no furo)* was a thriving center as early as the 1360s in Kyoto.[142] Most references do not appear until the seventeenth century, so it is prudent not to make too much of the evidence, but like the initiation of the night soil business, the maintenance of public baths probably reflected a modest improvement and, more important, a symbol of a major trend in the future.

Housing also reflects a similar improvement and symbolic trend.[143] On the one hand, it is clear that the Muromachi period represented a great advance for some peasants dwelling in western Japan. There are a few farmhouses *(nōka)* partially preserved from these times; along with documents and paintings, their materials suggest that these dwellings could be impressive structures. Residents constructed the walls of boards plastered with mud, with a ridgepole supporting a thatched roof. They planted pillars in the earth at regular intervals; the floor was at ground level and partially covered by boards and/or straw. The main residence *(yashiki)* might have measured 6–12 *tsubo,* or about 20–40 square meters, depending upon the wealth of the owner, and could include a kitchen, bathroom, living space, and storage area. Various small buildings and lean-tos (called *kadoya*), where servants and others lived, complemented the residence. The average city home *(machiya)* was similar, except that it was much smaller and used wooden shingles.

This description fit the homes of only a portion of the peasantry, however, and probably a small percentage at that. Over the past fifteen years, archaeologists have begun to excavate medieval villages, and the few examples available indicate that the luxurious dwellings portrayed above were exceptional, especially in eastern Honshu. For example, at Shimo Furudate in Tochigi Prefecture, the most common residence was still the pit dwelling—104 such houses have been found, averaging 3–6 square meters.[144] A large posthole *(hottate bashira)* structure, most likely belonging to a warrior, dominated the village. The differential development of the eastern and western archipelago was apparent even in housing.

Overall, Japan in 1450 had experienced a reversal of fortune from just two hundred years earlier, moving from stasis to expansion. This trend was similar to those that had already taken place in China and Western Europe and was about to start in Korea.[145] Unfortunately, the upswing did not solve the two most pressing problems confronting residents of the archipelago in the medieval age: the assurance of a constant food supply for all and a more stable and less damaging way of paying for the military. The last 150 years of the medieval epoch, from 1450 to 1600, eventually helped to produce a temporary resolution of the food issue and an end to the depredations of premodern warfare. But the cost was dear: riots, military conflicts, severe famines, and epidemics of new diseases lasted for over a century. In the period of the Warring States (1467–1568) and Unification (1568–1600) social and economic growth continued; the chronic warfare served in some ways as a stimulus, but, more important, it retarded expansion, postponing a complete breakthrough until after 1600.

5
Return of the Demons of Yore
Mortality during the Warring States and Unification Eras, 1450–1600

*B*etween 1280 and 1450, Japanese population and economy entered a period of expansion, a marked contrast to the near stasis of the prior five and one-half centuries. It is wise, however, not to be too sanguine about this growth. Most was restricted to the central and western archipelago during the last fifty years of the Kamakura period and the "Muromachi Optimum." Notably, when the Wars between the Northern and Southern Dynasties erupted in 1331, demographic and economic expansion slowed, in the form of soldierly harassment of the peasantry and blockages in the transportation network. In essence, the civil strife of the mid-fourteenth century showed that Japanese society had not overcome the two critical, interrelated problems of the medieval age: how to feed a burgeoning population and how to provision the military without harming the rest of the populace. After 1450, the specters of disease, hunger, and war would come again to haunt the islands, and the key to fulfilling the promise of the preceding period was to tackle the two problems that cut right to the core of medieval Japanese society.

This chapter deals with the archipelago's population over the years 1450–1600. The first—and perhaps most daunting—task will be to infer archipelago-wide figures for the year 1600. The conventional estimate is 12.3 million, but recently widespread criticism has surfaced. Most demographers now believe that Japan was considerably more populous in 1600, containing as many as 15–19 million inhabitants.

Whatever the number, it was the result of a complex interaction of many social and economic factors. In considering mortality, I shall first look at disease, which may have experienced a renewed lethality thanks to near-constant warfare and the appearance of a new microbe. Second, I shall review the data on food shortages, which seemingly occurred more frequently than ever before. Death registers can help us assess the effects of famine both generally and locally. Third, I shall analyze the wars pounding the populace incessantly during these years. Overall, death rates were higher during the Warring States and Unification periods than they had been during the "Muromachi Optimum," perhaps higher than at any time since 1280. The remarkable feature of these 150 years was that despite the scourges of disease, famine, and war, the population continued to grow, probably significantly.

JAPAN'S POPULATION IN 1600

The issue of Japan's population in 1600 is both one of the most daunting and one of the most seminal questions in all premodern Japanese history. Most would say that the issue is compounded by a dearth of information, but given the lacunae already encountered, especially for 1450, making a reasonable estimate for 1600 may seem relatively simple. Certainly part of the difficulty is that the greatest quantity of high-quality data—figures for total agricultural output, along with fragmentary demographic data for selected villages—originates from the 1600s and later. Moreover, there is the first reliable census in 1721: 26 million commoners, or about 31.3 million persons overall.[1] In contrast, only a few death registers and other (mostly descriptive) sources enlighten discussion of population in the last century and one-half of the medieval epoch. While lack of numbers is a true hardship, there is another reason for caution in dealing with this question.

In essence, 1600 is a pivotal year, the dividing line between "medieval" and "early modern" Japan. Any estimate affects scholarly assessment of both periods. For instance, the higher the proposed population figure for 1600, the greater becomes the contribution of earlier periods to Japan's later demographic and economic growth; the seventeenth century turns out to be a smaller watershed, leading up to the 1721 census. On the other hand, a smaller number in 1600 suggests slow development in the medieval epoch and grants a much larger role to an epoch-making seventeenth century, when the population purportedly doubled or even trebled. Did the medieval period witness sizable expansion, or was Japan truly a so-called "late developer"? These questions involve experts on both sides of the 1600 divide and can provoke considerable controversy.

As indicated in the introduction, the first estimate for 1600 was 18.5 million. This prewar figure was based on the number of *koku* supposedly being produced around 1600 and the faulty assumption that it required one *koku* to support a person for a year. The reasoning, if not the conclusion, has been universally rejected by subsequent scholars.[2] In 1966, Hayami Akira tried a new method. Extrapolating growth rates for several villages backward from the seventeenth and eighteenth centuries, he arrived at a mere 6.2–9.8 million for 1600.[3] This estimate came under immediate criticism as being too low. Admitting that his first result may have been biased because he had used information from several villages, especially in Kyushu (Kokura) with known high growth rates, Hayami recalculated in 1975. He again projected backward from the eighteenth century, this time using numbers from the Tokugawa shogunate. Dividing Japan into three regions, Hayami assumed that the population of each region tripled over the course of the mid-sixteenth to early eighteenth centuries, beginning with the economically advanced Kinai. The new total was 12.3 million, or a growth rate of almost 1 percent per annum over the 1600s. He bolstered his contention by citing the Suwa region as a location where 1 percent annual growth could obtain for as long as one hundred years.[4]

Currently, scholars usually cite Hayami's second estimate when they raise the question of Japan's population in 1600.[5] It is interesting to note, however, that some expressed reservations as early as 1977:

> Hayami offers little supporting evidence to help fill the void created by the lack of data to show why the population as a whole should have grown so rapidly during this century, or century and a half, and then have leveled off. Another major difficulty in accepting Hayami's backward extrapolation is that it means that the population of Japan, estimated by Sawada Goichi to have been from 5 to 6 million during the eighth century, either completely failed to grow or grew extremely slowly during the nine centuries prior to the Tokugawa period, despite the known growth of the economy from the thirteenth century.[6]

Noting that "no other data exist at present, except for scattered years or brief periods during the late seventeenth century," Hanley and Yamamura wisely concluded that "all sources do indicate a rising population in the seventeenth century, the magnitude of which is yet unknown."[7]

TABLE 5.1

Hayami's Estimates for Population, Arable, and Product, 1600–1720

YEAR	POPULA-TION (N) (MILLIONS)	ARABLE (R) (THOUSANDS OF *CHŌ*)	*KOKUDAKA* (Y) (THOUSANDS OF *KOKU*)	R/N *(TAN)*	Y/N	Y/R
1600	12	2,065	19,731	1.721	1.644	0.955
1650	17.2	2,354	23,133	1.37	1.346	0.983
1700	27.7	2,841	30,630	1.026	1.106	1.078
1720	31.3	2,927	32,034	0.936	1.024	1.094

Source: Hayami and Miyamoto, *Keizai shakai no seiritsu,* p. 44.
Note: All figures are Tokugawa-era units.

TABLE 5.2

Hayami's Estimates for Various Growth Rates, 1600–1720

	(PERCENT PER ANNUM)		
YEARS	POPULATION	ARABLE	KOKUDAKA
1600–1650	0.72	0.26	0.32
1651–1700	0.96	0.38	0.56
1701–1720	0.61	0.15	0.22

Source: Same as for table 5.1.

As the quotation above suggested, several of Hayami's assumptions seem problematic, particularly when we look at them with the experience of thirty years of additional research on both sides of the medieval-early modern divide. Two interpretations seem especially open to doubt. First, in extrapolating backward from the early 1700s, why did Hayami surmise that dramatic growth began in 1550? Given the evidence presented so far, does it not make more sense to commence the cycle of growth much earlier, in the thirteenth century as proposed above, and then lower the improbable 1 percent annual growth rate for the 1600s as warranted? Hayami believed that "economic society" in Japan did not emerge until 1550; most evidence points to a much earlier start. (For Hayami's estimates, see tables 5.1 and 5.2.)

Hayami made the mid-sixteenth century his origin for a dramatic spurt of population based on the role that he believed Hideyoshi's surveys played in Japanese history.[8] He thought that the cadastral surveys had the effect of freeing servants *(ge'nin),* slaves *(nuhi),* and others to receive their own land and form their own families, thus stimulating fertility. At the same time, the seemingly never-ending carnage of the Warring States era (1467–1568) was drawing to a close, significantly lowering mortality. The result was a surge in population. New economic opportunities—whether in newly opened arable or in the construction of numerous castle towns—also engendered demographic expansion. Under those circumstances, Hayami's mode of calculation fit to a tee his view of social and economic trends.

A second doubt resides in Hayami's premise that population tripled between 1550 and 1721—he seemed to be assuming what he was trying to prove. To be sure, the Kokura and Suwa data lent some validity to his view, and most scholars agreed that the 1600s witnessed sizable population expansion, but was a 300 percent increase possible? Could the economy, just coming out of a long civil war, have borne such mammoth growth? Where would the food have come from? All these questions require careful thought.

Despite the ease with which scholars might criticize Hayami's views, he is deserving of high praise for even attempting such a difficult feat. Privately, Hayami has always been self-effacing; he notes that no one can be sure what Japan's population was in 1600. By laying out one possible line of argument and the calculations and reasoning behind it, however, he did the academic world the great service of providing a baseline from which others might make further progress. Recently several Japanese historical demographers, Hayami's own students among them, have begun to entertain new ideas about the number of inhabitants in the Japanese archipelago around 1600.

More recent estimates have basically utilized many elements of Hayami's method but changed his assumptions to suit the opinions of the scholar at work. As early as 1988, the premises behind Hayami's numbers became objects of doubt. First, it was difficult to find Hayami's purported change in family structure over the sixteenth and seventeenth centuries. Second, numerous advances in research on the medieval period challenged Hayami's beliefs about the dismal state of commoner and servant life before Hideyoshi and argued that the much ballyhooed "independence of the small cultivator" supposedly occurring during the transition from medieval to Tokugawa times was doubtful. While there were no numbers yet, these questions began to undermine the thinking upon which Hayami's calculations lay.[9]

In 1999, a Tokugawa-period specialist, Fujino Shōsaburō, not only called Hayami's theory into question, but he also utilized different data and arrived at a much higher total.[10] Pointing out numerous inconsistencies in Hayami's figures (such as the higher output per person in 1600 than in 1871), Fujino proceeded to select sixteen domains, ranging from Morioka and Sendai in the northeast to Kumamoto and Kagoshima in the southwest. These domains all possessed fragmentary population data for a few years between 1665 and 1734, and Fujino's calculations showed that the growth rate using these data was only about .4 percent per year—less than half Hayami's proposed explosive growth. Then, extrapolating backward from the estimated population in 1721, he arrived at 19.4 million in 1600 and 23.65 million in 1650. Compared to Fujino's figures, the original estimate for 1600 (18.5 million) looked pessimistic.

Fujino's research, however, immediately drew fire. Kitō Hiroshi, who had helped Hayami compute the 12.3 million figure, noted that Fujino, like Hayami before him, had used only data that supported his case. More specifically, Fujino's domains included several places where data were available for only a short time span—thus easily introducing the possibility of bias. Moreover, many of the domains were located in northeastern Honshu and southern Kyushu, the more backward areas of the archipelago. Finally, Fujino's cases all dated after 1650, when the highest growth may have already come to an end.[11]

If the figure of 12.3 million was too low and 19.4 million was too high, was the answer more likely to have lain in between? Kitō Hiroshi and Saitō Osamu began to point to this probability as Fujino was publishing his research. In 2000, Kitō revised his earlier pathfinding book and openly criticized his teacher's view that population could have grown at 1 percent per annum for a century. Reasserting his belief that his "third cycle" began in the fourteenth or fifteenth centuries, Kitō recalculated on the assumption that growth had started twenty or thirty years earlier than Hayami had proposed. His new figures for 1600 ranged from 14.3 to 15.5 million, with growth rates over the seventeenth century shrinking to .65 or even .58 percent per year. Now a well-known Hayami student was at odds with his teacher.[12]

Soon another student followed. Saitō Osamu evaluated the problem in his own way, focusing on the incidence of famine in the Tokugawa period.[13] Examining population data from 1721 to 1885, he showed that the highest documented growth rate over a sustained period was indeed about what Fujino had estimated: .4 percent per year. Even that occurred during 1840–1885, when the recovery from the Tenpō famine of the

1830s and the early Meiji reforms were under way. While Saitō stated his conclusions carefully, readers could have taken his work to mean that annual growth rates markedly exceeding .4 percent prior to 1721 were unlikely. Hayami's view lost even more support. In criticism of Saitō, scholars may wonder how applicable demographic data from the eighteenth and nineteenth centuries could be to the seventeenth, when evidence is scarce and most have assumed high rates of expansion.

At the same time as he was writing his article, Saitō was engaged in estimating the *world's* population at intervals since the year 1000.[14] In the course of this work, he repeated Hayami's (and Kitō's and Fujino's) curve-fitting exercise, retaining most of the major premises but adjusting some assumptions, in particular the one about when the "medieval cycle" commenced. Saitō's new number for Japan in 1600 was 17 million. Not only did it fit the mathematical exercise, but it also came out midway between Fujino's 19.4 million and Kitō's revised calculation of 15 million. If Saitō's figure is used, then growth from 1450 to 1600 was .3 percent per year, still considerably less than the highest known for the Tokugawa period, yet high if we take into account that the era from 1450 to 1550 saw continuous warfare, upheaval, and famine. Saitō's number left room for a growth rate of .51 percent per year between 1550 and 1721, much lower than Hayami's but higher than any previously known era.[15]

A few points are clear from this discussion. First, Hayami's figure of 12.3 million for 1600 is on the verge of rejection by the Japanese scholarly community today. Second, the various alternatives propose that population did not grow nearly as fast in the early Tokugawa period as once assumed but expanded notably between 1300 and 1600. Third, although the reasoning was invalid, many would assert that the prewar figure of 18.5 million was not far wrong.

To repeat, no one knows for sure what the archipelago's population was in 1600, and all the estimates put forward here have their own strengths and weaknesses. Moreover, the existence of large regional variations makes it easy to criticize any archipelago-wide figure. One way to approach the problem is to take the range of 12–19 million and merely choose a middle path. Because of the repeated wars, disease, and famines of the late fifteenth and early sixteenth centuries and the peace and relative plenty of the era 1550–1721, it seems appropriate to assign a range of 15–17 million to 1600. This appraisal has many advantages, including both a recognition of the early origin of the medieval growth cycle and the acknowledgment that the seventeenth century was a time of sizable (about 80–100 percent) overall expansion.

In any event, it seems plausible that sizable demographic growth continued between 1450 and 1600. Now the task becomes one of fitting these estimates not just to the early Tokugawa data on agriculture and other factors, but also enmeshing them within the social and economic trends of the late medieval era. In carrying out this work, we shall find that the weight assigned to each factor leads to a differing numerical preference.

MORTALITY FACTORS: DISEASE

In evaluating the effects of pathogens on the populace, I have adopted a three-factor formula that is more precise than the usual endemic-epidemic dichotomy. During the last 150 years of the medieval era, two of these three factors trended higher. First, at least one new microorganism (syphilis) appeared, and although evidence is sparse, it may have had a considerable demographic impact for a short time. Second, contacts among susceptible persons during the time the afflicted were infectious undoubtedly multiplied as the commercial boom and improvements in transportation (to be discussed in chapter 6) continued unabated. Third and more positively, immunities for common diseases such as smallpox, measles, and influenza probably grew.

There is a recognizable pattern to the incidence of plagues between 1450 and 1600: repeated outbreaks early on, followed by a period of lessened frequency.[16] Smallpox was especially active, visiting in 1452–1453, 1477, 1495, 1523, 1525, 1531–1532, and 1537. Except for 1495 and 1525, however, the disease seems to have claimed mainly children, perhaps accounting for Jesuit Luis Frois' observation that nearly all inhabitants of the islands bore pockmarks from bouts with the virus. Measles appeared more often as well, menacing the populace in 1471, 1484, 1489, 1506, 1513, 1520, and 1529. The illness ravaged many people of all ages in 1471, 1484, and 1513, but in 1520 and 1529 the milder, three-day strain was most common. Influenza struck only in 1520 and 1535, perhaps suggesting moderation of the cold, damp climate of the early medieval centuries.

From 1540 to 1600, these diseases became more benign forces. Smallpox, the most terrible minister of death, was recorded in 1550, 1557, and 1571; measles, in 1557, 1578, and 1587; and influenza, in 1556. An unknown plague of 1593–1594 was probably related to Hideyoshi's invasion of Korea. Historians recorded neither dysentery nor chicken pox at any time, and although maladies such as malaria and tuberculosis receive mention, it is impossible to determine how widespread or lethal they were.

Consequently, after ninety years of increased epidemics, the last portion of the sixteenth century was less disease-ravaged. The evidence on infections suggests that Hayami was correct in seeing the mid-sixteenth century as a turning point, although perhaps less important than he believed. The parallel with the fourteenth century is clear, and in both cases warfare seems to have exacerbated the scourge of disease.

Essentially, war prepared the way for an increased incidence of plagues in two ways. First, war promoted social dislocation for a sizable portion of innocent bystanders as armies marched and countermarched and did battle. For example, in Tsuru District of Kai Province, an attendant of Katsuyama Fuji Asama Shrine wrote the following for 1477: "This year prices *[urikai]* are high and there is famine without limit. Over half the infants suffer from smallpox *[mo]*; among newborns, only one in a thousand lives. Musashi Nagao Shiroemon has been doing battle with his uncle the Governor of Owari."[17] By roaming over the countryside, spreading their viruses, and then blocking up roads, armies made everyone more vulnerable. Sieges often trapped a large number of susceptibles in the path of infection.[18]

Second, soldiers themselves were easy victims. Usually living together when on campaign and often coming from the same village, a group of fighters provided a fertile breeding ground for a foreign microbe. Again, the Katsuyama attendant wrote in 1550: "This spring, infants are sick with smallpox; many have died. The situation is beyond words. Even in Shimo Yoshida fifty persons have died."[19] Later in the text, it is apparent that Shimo Yoshida was a village unit of peasant-samurai, with a total population of just over one hundred.[20] In this case, the pathogenic enemy was far more deadly than the human one.

In addition, war opened the way for the spread of the potentially deadly new microorganism: syphilis. Possibly originating in the New World, it was noted in Western Europe by the 1490s; writers observed horrible and distressing symptoms, often ending in early death.[21] In Western Europe, the microbe was responsible for the demise of the Valois royalty in France and the Ottomans in Turkey.[22] By 1498, the new disease had appeared in India and by 1505 in China.

By 1512, syphilis had arrived in Japan and was immediately dubbed the "Chinese pox" *(tōgasa)* because of its supposed origins in the Central

Kingdom. Sailors were undoubtedly responsible for its spread, as ports like Noto in 1515 and Osaka and environs in 1522 reported the disease. Other than these brief mentions, however, no other data are available on syphilis in Japan during the medieval era, but three points suggest a considerable role for syphilis in dampening fertility and raising mortality, at least in the short run.

First, there is the history of syphilis in Western Europe. A French scientist noted that in its initial stage, between 1494 and 1516, "as the disease spread through the victim's body, palate, uvula, jaw, and tonsils were often destroyed. General physical deterioration followed and often culminated in early death."[23] During 1516–1526, two more symptoms appeared, and the disease continued its previous deadliness. A general abatement began only after 1526, lasting until 1610, when its virulence declined to what we know today: dangerous, to be sure, but not so "explosive" as earlier.

Second, as in Western Europe in the late fifteenth and sixteenth centuries, war prevailed in Japan, a condition leading to "such chaos that sexual morality broke down."[24] Soldiers had no women, and women often had no food; the resulting prostitution spread the infection rapidly among those engaged in battle, and when they returned home, they carried the disease to new groups of susceptibles. Moreover, some victims became sterile, and infected women transmitted syphilis directly to their babies.[25] It is not hard to imagine a rapid spread of the scourge throughout the islands under such conditions.

Third, a study from the Tokugawa epoch suggests a widespread dispersion and possibly considerable impact of syphilis on the population. Scientific examination of skeletal remains from that era indicates bone lesions (a sign of syphilis) on 54.5 percent of the adult population. The disease was "rampant" among commoners.[26] Given the experience in Western Europe, it is tempting to conclude that in its early stages, before it was endemic, between 1512 and the early 1600s, the disease manifested particularly horrific symptoms and killed a sizable portion of the population. It is important to emphasize, however, that without more records from the period 1512–1600, any estimate of mortality or the general demographic impact of syphilis is guesswork.

In sum, disease apparently claimed more victims during these 150 years than at any time since the late Kamakura epoch. Moreover, it is wise to remember that many endemic infections went unrecorded, making pathogens even more deadly than they appear. Quieting the angry spirits of illness continued to occupy a prominent place in superstition and family ritual. At the least, disease acted as it had throughout the medieval period—a chronic drag on population growth that drove up infant mortality and occasionally killed weakened adults. At the most, the lethality and dispersion of new and old pathogens in a war-torn archipelago had a more significant demographic impact and would tend to favor lower estimates for Japan's population in 1600.

MORTALITY FACTORS: FAMINE

Between 1450 and 1600, there were twenty-eight widespread famines and forty-three of local impact, computing to one major subsistence crisis about every 5.4 years.[27] Compared to either the relatively poorly documented era 1150–1280 (one major crisis every 6.2 years) or particularly 1280–1450 (one every 7.4 years), the end of the medieval period appears to have been more often characterized by general starvation. Some of the increase may arise from a continuing improvement in the number and kinds of historical sources, however.

Unlike the data on epidemics, those on famine for 1450–1600 fall into three distinct phases. (See table 5.3.) From 1450 through 1497, starvation reappeared as a common scourge for many islanders. Eight widespread and twelve local outbreaks took place over those forty-seven years; the famous Kanshō famine of 1459–1461 is often assumed to have claimed many lives. From 1498 through 1540, the crisis deepened as crop failure recurred almost every other year—seventeen times for the populace as a whole and eleven times regionally. Put in statistical terms, between 1450 and 1540, there was *on average* a major famine every 3.7 years, just under twice the rate of the "Muromachi Optimum."[28]

Beginning in 1541, the problem abated. Until 1600, there were only three years of major famine, although there were twenty local crises.[29] Even those regional bouts were often restricted to one or just a few provinces. On average, the era 1541–1600 saw a serious famine only once every two decades. And almost every one of the eleven famines extending into multiple years occurred in the 1540s and 1550s.

The return of inclement weather may have been one reason for the increased frequency of famine during the last 150 years of the medieval age. Tabulation from written sources suggests that it was gradually becoming cooler and damper over these years. (See table 5.4.) These climatological trends may have represented a continuation from the late fourteenth and

TABLE 5.3
Famine Years, Extent, and Causes, 1450–1600

YEAR	EXTENT	CAUSE
1455	Widespread	Wet, cold summer
1456	Local	Wet, cold summer
1459	Widespread	Drought
1460	Widespread	Drought
1461	Widespread	Drought
1466	Widespread	Unknown
1472	Widespread	Drought
1473	Local	Drought
1475	Local	Drought
1476	Local	Wet, cold summer
1477	Widespread	Wet, cold summer
1482	Local	Wet, cold summer
1484	Local	Unknown
1489	Local	Drought
1490	Local	Drought
1492	Widespread	Unknown
1494	Local	Drought
1495	Local	Unknown
1496	Local	Drought
1497	Local	Unknown
1498	Widespread	Drought
1499	Widespread	Unknown
1500	Local	Drought
1501	Widespread	Drought
1502	Widespread	Drought
1503	Widespread	Drought
1504	Widespread	Drought
1505	Widespread	Drought
1506	Widespread	Drought
1510	Local	Unknown
1511	Widespread	Unknown
1512	Widespread	Unknown
1513	Widespread	Unknown
1514	Local	Drought
1515	Local	Wet, cold summer

Table 5.3. continues

Table 5.3 continued

YEAR	EXTENT	CAUSE
1516	Local	Wet, cold summer
1517	Widespread	Unknown
1518	Widespread	Unknown
1519	Widespread	Unknown
1523	Local	Unknown
1525	Widespread	Unknown
1528	Local	Drought
1532	Local	Unknown
1534	Local	Unknown
1535	Widespread	Drought
1536	Local	Wet, cold summer
1538	Local	Unknown
1540	Widespread	Unknown
1541	Local	Unknown
1542	Local	Unknown
1544	Local	Unknown
1545	Local	Unknown
1546	Local	Unknown
1547	Local	Unknown
1550	Local	Unknown
1551	Local	Unknown
1552	Local	Unknown
1556	Local	Unknown
1557	Widespread	Wet, cold summer
1558	Local	Drought
1562	Local	Unknown
1563	Local	Wet, cold summer
1565	Local	Unknown
1566	Local	Wet, cold summer
1567	Local	Drought
1573	Widespread	Drought
1582	Local	Wet, cold summer
1585	Widespread	Unknown
1594	Local	Unknown
1598	Local	Unknown
1599	Local	Unknown

Source: Sasaki Junnosuke, *Kikin to sensō*, pp. 109–200.

TABLE 5.4
Climatological Trends, 1451–1600

| PERIOD OF ENTRIES | WEIGHTED NUMBER OF ENTRIES | | | | |
	RAIN	COLD	HEAT	DRYNESS	TOTAL
1451–1500	362	22	154	215	753
Percentile	48%	3%	20%	29%	
	Drought index: 29		Wet, cold index: 51		
1501–1550	304	68	114	133	619
Percentile	49%	11%	18%	22%	
	Drought index: 22		Wet, cold index: 60		
1551–1600	345	76	91	121	633
Percentile	55%	12%	14%	19%	
	Drought index: 19		Wet, cold index: 66.5		

Sources: Sasaki Junnosuke, *Kikin to senso*. Entries weighted as in table 1.4.
Note: The drought index was arrived at by dividing the references to drought by the total number of entries; the wet, cold index was the result of dividing the references to wet and cold by the total number of entries.

fifteenth centuries. (See table 3.1.) When data in table 5.4 are compared with those of table 1.4, the years 1450–1600 seem not to have been so drought-stricken as the eighth or eleventh centuries. The period 1150–1200 appears to have been slightly drier too. In statistical terms, the sixteenth century appears to have been about as cold and damp *on average* as the thirteenth, which witnessed the horrific Kangi and Shōga famines. This appearance may be real, but perhaps the cold and dampness were spread more evenly over the years, thus having milder results. Alternatively, the cold and damp trend could also have arisen from the random survival of a greater number of documents, or it might indicate that such entries as "great rain" or "cold" are too inexact and subjective to be instructive.

As noted in chapters 1 and 3, historical climatologists are engaged in a lively debate about the weather during the medieval age. There are essentially two views regarding the epoch 1450–1600. The conventional one, based on diaries kept in Kyoto and at Lake Suwa, holds that temperatures dropped throughout the first half of the fifteenth century, reached a nadir around 1450, and then began an ascent. During the sixteenth century, temperatures gradually grew much warmer, except for a trough around 1550.[30] A more recent variant argues that a "Little Ice Age" took place from 1200 to 1400 but then agrees that the temperature may have begun to warm in the sixteenth century.[31] Scientific data about world-wide volcanic activity through 1699 give little support for the idea of a cold and damp sixteenth century.[32] There have also been attempts to correlate these findings with worldwide trends such as eustatic changes in sea levels, for which only relative dates can be surmised.[33]

In the second view, several other authors have taken the opposite interpretation—that is, that the late fifteenth and sixteenth centuries were cool and wet. Two Japanese experts used tree ring data on Yakushima in the southern archipelago to support this opinion.[34] A senior Japanese historian has also asserted that the late fifteenth and sixteenth centuries were cold and wet, basing his view upon his reading of the causes for famine and the slow growth of agricultural productivity.[35] This research supports the evidence that I drew from written sources—that is, that the period 1450–1600 was somewhat cooler and damper than preceding or later times.

As with many issues of the Warring States period, agreement on climatic trends is hard to come by. The reader may side with the older view of a warm and wet sixteenth century, tie the good weather to the conversion of large tracts of land to tillage, and argue that the population boomed. Or he may prefer to believe that the years covered in this chapter were on average characterized by an overabundance of rainfall and cool temperatures, conditions that may have been harmful to agriculture, notably in eastern Honshu. In either case, there is no denying that the literate few regularly noted crop failure.

Even during the harsh years of the late fifteenth and early sixteenth centuries, however, historians may entertain suspicions about the degree to which famines boosted mortality and lowered fertility. The dual safety nets—trade and welfare—had begun to operate by at least the early fifteenth century and continued to reduce suffering, particularly during the late fifteenth century. While the lack of food undoubtedly killed many, the results would have been much worse without the intervention of merchants and religious and governmental institutions. Nowhere is this more evident than in the Kanshō crisis of 1459–1461. While it was likened to Western Europe's Black Death, it was in fact far more benign.[36]

A Brief Chronology of Hunger

In this section, I shall discuss some notable famines during the three sequences of lean years: the crises of 1450–1497, the depths of misery from

1498 to 1540, and the measure of relief bestowed upon the populace between 1541 and 1600.[37] During the first stage, the Kanshō famine has
come to symbolize the return to hard times. It marked the longest siege of
starvation in the second half of the fifteenth century, and descriptive
sources leave an impression of widespread distress.

In 1457, Kyoto was beset by an influx of neighboring malnourished
farmers seeking food and debt relief because of a poor harvest arising
from drought, although conditions were not severe enough to apply the
word "famine" to that year.[38] Then, beginning in 1458, it is clear that
grain was in short supply because in the second month of 1459 the cleric
Gan'ami asked shogun Ashikaga Yoshimasa for one hundred strings of
cash to buy the makings of gruel and vegetables to feed hungry people
looking for a handout in Kyoto.[39] Apparently monks succored a thousand people in eight days. Despite the aid, the only certain way to solve
the problem of hunger was to harvest a bumper crop, but the weather did
not cooperate. Officials in far-away Hyūga stated that no rain had fallen
for forty days during the monsoon season of 1459, and monks intoned
prayers for precipitation in Kyushu and Kyoto. Rain fell in fits and starts,
but it was not enough, and in the middle of the sixth month peasants in
nearby Yamato said that "because of the drought this year, there will not
be even one grain [to eat]." These conditions continued throughout the
summer, and when it was time to harvest in the tenth month, it rained
and the wind blew, causing floods in the capital. In the Kanto, the constable
of Shinano, Ogasawara Mitsuyasu, rebelled in 1458, and sources note
ominously at the end of 1459 that "the rebel was not defeated. Thus the
roads are all blocked and bands of merchants cannot get through."

The year 1460 was no better. One source, undoubtedly in exaggeration, wrote that two-thirds of the populace had died. It is clear that the crisis was widespread: in addition to Yamashiro, Yamato, Kii, and Tanba
(surrounding Kyoto), drought, disease, and starvation were reported in
Shikoku and western Honshu (Sanuki, Bizen, Bitchū, Bingo, Mimasaka,
and Hōki); the Japan Sea littoral (Echizen, Etchū, Noto, and Dewa); the
Kanto (Musashi); and northeastern Honshu (Mutsu and Aizu). Peasants
stole water from each other to irrigate their fields in Yamashiro and Kii;
cannibalism occurred. The Zen monk Taikyoku told the story of a
woman holding a dead child, whom she had carried from Kawachi,
where crops had failed for three years running. She had come to Kyoto
hoping for relief, but her child had died. Taikyoku promised to conduct a
memorial service for the child and gave her money for the burial.[40] At the

end of the year, the court changed the reign period, but fields in unnamed regions were afflicted with an insect infestation and people said, "Next winter, spring, and summer there will be one great famine."

And indeed there was. Officials in provinces from Echigo and Mutsu in the northeast to Kii and Yamato in western Honshu announced that their residents were dropping dead. In Kii corpses jammed an irrigation ditch, while they filled thoroughfares in Kyoto. Prices of food skyrocketed, and Yoshimasa apparently had the temerity to choose this time to refurbish his Palace of Flowers, "with no pity for starvation in the provinces." Meanwhile, great masses of hungry folks poured into Kyoto, begging for food and money and seeking debt relief. Finally, the shogunate decided on fifty coins per person as a satisfactory donation, at an overall cost of 500 strings of cash. Buddhist prelates also doled out gruel and disposed of the multitude of corpses, said to number "a thousand myriads" (lit., 10 million). Diarists were shocked to see fifty or a hundred dead at a time when they left their homes and monasteries on business. Throughout the spring of 1461, monks performed ceremonies for the dead and buried them in mass graves beneath and near the bridges at the Fourth and Fifth Great Avenues *(shijō, gojō)*. In the end, chroniclers estimated the tally of dead in Kyoto at eighty-two thousand, based upon the number of stupas raised. Every day 300–700 succumbed, and the smell of rotting flesh permeated the city. Everyone in Kyoto agreed that there had never been anything like it. The summer of 1461 continued dry; relief did not come until the next year.

Three points about the Kanshō crisis are significant. First, like the Yōwa and other famines, war exacerbated the effects. Not only did the conflict with the Ogasawara keep merchants out of the Kanto so that they were unable to market food there, but also in 1461 the Hatakeyama fought among themselves in Kawachi and Kyoto, while the Shiba did the same in Echizen.[41] Armies trampled fields, destroyed and consumed crops, and killed villagers. The Kanshō crisis may have begun as a natural event, induced by drought, but war quickly added a human dimension. A local revolt *(tsuchi ikki)* of residents in Nara and Kyoto in 1462 was both cause and effect for further peasant misery, as many were on the verge of losing their land through debt to big moneylenders. Rioters resisted shogunate troops so effectively that for a while they cut Kyoto off from the surrounding countryside, preventing grain from getting through and provoking a secondary famine in the capital.[42]

Second, despite the sporadic warfare and horrible descriptions of death and desperation in Kyoto, mortality may have been far lower in the rest of the country than is usually assumed. For example, data for Yamashiro and Yamato Provinces, regions specifically noted as hard hit by starvation, hint that few died.[43] In Yamashiro, Upper Kuze Estate produced 70 percent of its usual crop in 1460 and 1461, with a mere 15 percent listed as lost to weather damage. Moreover, rain fell regularly in Yamato in 1460, and ponds and rivers supplied water to needy farmers, so that officials permitted no tax reductions for Yumoto Estate. While Wakatsuki, Niiki, and other estates had heavy crop damage in 1461, it was less than in other nonfamine years.

At least one other quantifiable statistic is available for the Kanshō famine. According to the Kōfukuji monk Jinson's diary for the twentieth day of the seventh month of 1461, 9,268 people *or* coins' worth of production—the text is garbled—were lost to famine at Kawaguchi Estate in Echizen.[44] Given that the area of the farm was 600 *chō,* even if it required a mere one *tan* to feed an individual, the figure 9,268 cannot possibly refer to starvation victims. Rather, it must mean coins, in which case inferring a death rate becomes a subjective enterprise.

Assuming, however, that each *tan* produced about 100 coins' worth of grain or goods—a standard measure for the Muromachi period—then only about 93 persons, or 2.3 percent of the residents of Kawaguchi, perished.[45] More important, Jinson also noted that 757 persons fled Kawaguchi; at an average of 1.5 *tan* to support an individual, it would mean an exodus of about 15–20 percent of the cultivators in one year. It would not be surprising if many headed for Kyoto. At Suganoura in Ōmi, however, the devastation and social consequences were much more severe.[46]

Third, efforts on the part of the shogunate, wealthy Kyotoites, and religious institutions to feed and shelter the hungry, bury the dead, and placate the angry spirits of starvation victims *(segaki-e)* saved many.[47] At the height of the crisis in Kyoto, the *bakufu* tried to distribute fifty coins to rural immigrants and also doled out six coins to beggars. Yoshimasa may have been encouraged in his efforts by a nightmare that chided him for his many excesses. He then ordered the construction of temporary shelters, the cooking of gruel, and the delivery of 1,500 units *(hiki)* of cloth to keep the homeless warm in the first month of 1461. One of Yoshimasa's biographers also argues that the shogun coordinated religious efforts to succor the hungry. Wealthy merchants and other urbanites initiated construction projects, such as temple refurbishing and bridge building, to employ the hungry and thereby feed them.[48] Viewed from this perspective, Yoshimasa's order for work on his Palace of Flowers may have been an attempt to save the weak and famished.

Yet religious devotees, especially Gan'ami and his followers, belonging to the Timely (Jishū) sect, were mostly responsible for dealing with victims. They built shelters, made gruel, and prayed for the souls of the departed. In front of Rokkaku, they organized volunteers to give out cash; they may have served food to as many as eight thousand daily. Just as important as caring for the weak and indigent, Gan'ami and his disciples disposed of corpses, reducing the possibility of pestilential outbreaks. In contrast, Zen temples of the Five Mountains *(Gozan)* restricted themselves to organizing six rituals for the souls of starvation victims in the late spring and early summer of 1461, when death was most widespread in the capital.

The Kanshō crisis fits into the pattern already established for famines of the early fifteenth century and later. The disaster was undoubtedly serious enough to induce peasants to flood the capital (and possibly other cities) in search of sustenance available through relief agencies and the commercial network. Such assistance may well have kept mortality lower and fertility higher than the many sad anecdotes indicate. Along with Japanese society as a whole, the nature of famine had undergone a fundamental transformation from earlier centuries. A comparative quantitative view of the Kanshō famine's impact on selected populations is available in tables A.1–A.13 in the appendix to this chapter.

After 1461, the next spate of lean times began in 1466 and was likely related to the outbreak of the Ōnin War.[49] Debt riots during 1465–1467 drew lowly troops *(zōhyō)* into Kyoto, where they threw in their lot with hungry local farmers. As the conflict proceeded, a drought-induced major famine occurred in 1472, attacking the residents of Kyoto, its surrounding province of Yamashiro and Izumi in the Kinai, Kōzuke and Shimōsa in the Kanto, and Aizu in northeastern Honshu.[50] Kai, the Japan Sea littoral, and Aizu experienced starvation in 1477. Exactly how the war in the capital contributed to these poor harvests is unclear.

Other than some local food shortages, harvests seem to have been adequate until 1491–1492, when a "great famine" struck Kai, and elders in Kyoto said that "conditions were just like Kanshō," when corpses had littered the streets.[51] The remaining crop failures through 1497 were local. Despite the reputation of the late fifteenth century for famine and upheaval, the overall effect on population was probably not as drastic as is often surmised. Moreover, for about a decade after the Ōnin War, there were no famines at all. Worse times lay ahead, however.

During the second sequence, from 1498 through 1540, there was an unparalleled stretch of bad harvests and hardship, as general famine enveloped the land during fourteen of the next twenty-three years. Possibly because distress was so widespread, there are few details about most of these famines. This section will highlight the times for which there is the most information and attempt to show a connection between the fluctuations in the food supply and domain formation among daimyo.

Between 1498 and 1506, drought-induced, far-flung famines were the rule.[52] While bits and pieces of evidence for this period name random provinces or refer to untoward cold or ice storms, 1504 seems to have been the harshest season of all. Provincial functionaries from many parts of Japan noted hardship: in western Honshu, Kyoto, Izumi, Yamato, and Kii; Noto along the Japan Sea littoral; on the Tōkaidō, Suruga and Musashi; in central and northeastern Honshu, Kai, Aizu, and Mutsu. Early in the year, a source from Kyoto wrote that from place to place throughout the archipelago several myriads of people had died; many had traveled to Kyoto and its outskirts only to breathe their last. In Musashi, the famine was complicated by the Battle of Kawagoe, as factions of the Yamauchi family aligned with the Go-Hōjō, Uesugi, and Imagawa while battling among themselves.[53] In Suruga, snow fell five times amid the drought, and a pestilence spread. In Aizu, one *shō* of rice cost 100 coins, apparently an exorbitant amount. In Kai, snow also fell five times in the sixth and seventh months, while grain prices were unusually high. At Hineno Estate in Izumi, peasants buried their remaining grain and other valuables to keep them from predatory samurai. All in all, the tragedy was "beyond words" *(gongo dodan)*. While 1504 was the worst year, officials in Aizu, Noto, Musashi, and Kyoto claimed their people were starving all during the following two agricultural cycles.[54]

The cause for these terrible harvests at the turn of the sixteenth century seems to have been a lack of rain.[55] A study of tree rings and written sources for Kyoto and at Hineno Estate in Izumi for the period 1501–1504 suggests that it was not merely the lack of rain, but also the dryness of the monsoon months—especially the fourth through seventh—that doomed the harvests of the early 1500s. At Hineno, even irrigation ponds and rivers turned to dust. As the famine proceeded in 1504, a plague broke out. (See tables A.4 and A.5.)

The period 1511–1513 presents a textbook case of how human and natural causes combined to produce suffering. During 1511, battles raged around Kyoto, with the Hosokawa coming out the victors—but not before shutting down the Yodo River and other transportation arteries in the third month. Unsurprisingly, by the sixth and seventh months of 1512, a "great famine" had killed many in the capital. In Kai and Echigo, harvest rice was difficult to buy at 80 coins for one *shō;* there were scenes of protracted battle and starvation.[56] Later in Kai, snow fell and blocked the roads, and the price of dried rice (used for provisions) hit 100 coins a measure, while rice wine went for 10 coins a bottle. Nara and Awa in western Honshu were also objects of dislocation and famine. In 1513, a Kyoto source announced several thousand people had died from lack of food at many places throughout various provinces.

Bad times continued through 1519. In 1514, a famine afflicted most of the Kinai, and Settsu officials made gruel to succor the hungry gathered there. Late in the year, the literate noted rain filled with ash, with the origin unknown; heavy snowfall in Kai in the next year led to another collapse of the food system. The cold and snowy weather hit Aizu as well, leading to further crop failure and starvation late in 1516. The year 1517 was the beginning of a major time of massive hunger owing to cold, damp weather. In both 1518 and 1519 there were numerous reports of starving persons: in Kyoto, Kai, Kōzuke, Musashi, Izu, Hitachi, Aizu, and eventually "various provinces throughout the realm." Notations of frost, great snows, and food shortages fill records for these two years. Chronicles in areas as isolated from each other as Kai and Kyoto repeatedly complained of high grain prices and numerous starvation victims throughout many provinces.

By the end of 1519, the islanders had come through the worst of times, and it is interesting to note that this two-decade-long spate of poor harvests coincided with the first stage of domain formation for many Warring States daimyo. This initial phase lasted from 1491 until 1527, when the Go-Hōjō and Imagawa combined to destroy the Muromachi's Kanto deputy; the Uesugi began their rise in Etchū; Takeda Nobutora solidified his control of Kai; and the Matsudaira and Oda started their careers in Mikawa and Owari respectively. In the Kinai, the aftershocks of the Ōnin War still lingered, exacerbated by the internecine struggle among the Hosokawa for the post of shogunal deputy *(kanrei).* Beyond the reach of the shogun in western Japan, the Mōri began their road to rule in Aki, as did the Ōtomo in northern Kyushu.[57]

From one end of the islands to the other, new samurai families were coming to power and solidifying their hold, as the old Muromachi *bakufu* and its coterie of *shugo daimyō* collapsed and political fragmentation was the order of the day. While the connection between famine and war cannot be made explicitly in most cases, it seems likely, given past patterns of samurai provisioning. Moreover, with battles raging and political authority hotly contested, commercial routes easily became blocked and governmental relief agencies were unable to operate. The connection between hostilities and widespread, continuous hunger will be addressed in more detail when I discuss the issue of war mortality below. Here suffice it to say that the recurrent food shortages of 1498–1519 coincided with battles destroying the Muromachi government and catapulting various local families to power.[58]

The 1520s were a quieter decade. Even an eruption of Mt. Asama in 1527 and a terrible drought in the late 1520s seems to have had little effect, except for Kai, where the roads became blocked and grain prices spiraled. Only in the Kinai, where the Hosokawa continued to battle for supremacy within the tottering shogunate, did crops fail. The 1530s were harsher. Notably, in 1539 people starved to death from Ōmi to Hyūga, as unusually cold weather and an insect infestation made bad conditions worse.[59] To cap off four decades of the most severe misery, in 1540 a last general famine struck "various provinces of the realm," noted in Kyoto and environs, all of northeastern Honshu, and Kōzuke. Diverse records equated it with the Kanshō disaster. Cold, damp weather seems to have been the main cause in the north, while another insect infestation ruined the Kinai harvest. Those whose crops failed fled for Kyoto once again.

In sum, the years from 1498 through 1540 included some of the most severe famine conditions ever recorded for Japan. Exacerbated by internecine warfare, hunger seemingly beset people somewhere on the islands almost every season. Unlike during the crises of 1450–1497, there are few signs that either the commercial network or governmental or religious institutions acted to save lives. The crises of this era surely slowed or negated demographic expansion, preventing growth from reaching its full potential. Depending on how heavily we weigh these events, a lower estimate for Japan's population in 1600 may be preferable.

In the remaining sixty years of the sixteenth century, hunger was still present, but fragmentary sources suggest that it was primarily local in character. The lack of widespread famines may have been a result of many factors, including milder weather, the rehabilitation of various relief agencies, increasingly open travel arteries for merchants selling grain, and more powerful daimyo overseeing stable domains and eager to expand production at home to carry on battle. While the number and extent of crop failures diminished significantly, records suggest that warfare continued to play a critical role in the lean years that did occur.

During the 1540s, starvation was limited mostly to individual provinces.[60] In 1550, a great earthquake and typhoon were responsible for famine conditions in isolated areas from the Kinai to Kanto, and hunger lingered in Kai into 1551.[61] In 1556 hunger was prevalent in Mutsu, and this seemed to be the prelude for famine in 1557, the first season of widespread starvation since 1540. The weather was particularly cold and damp in the north, and it is little wonder that eastern Honshu felt the brunt of the crisis. Officials in Mutsu, Kai, and Shimōsa announced starvation conditions, and the next year (1558) Hitachi followed. Meanwhile, people living in the capital complained of parching heat, crop failure in "various provinces," empty fields containing nothing but red dust, and an "incomparable great famine." As usual, the hungry streamed into Kyoto.

While the crop failures and misery of the 1540s and 1550s were nothing like those of half a century earlier, it is interesting that these two decades witnessed the further consolidation of daimyo domains.[62] In particular, the period 1531–1534 was generally quiet, and it is little wonder that there was merely one local famine in those years. Beginning in 1541, however, the war heated up, along with the weather. In western Honshu, the Mōri began to oust the Ōuchi; in the east, as Takeda Shingen took over from his father and advanced into Shinano, the Oda, Go-Hōjō, and Imagawa engaged in a three-way battle. The Tohoku entered its first sustained period of conflict during 1542–1548, and it is interesting that most famine records for this era come from domains in that region. In northern Kyushu the Ōtomo defeated the Ōuchi, while in Shikoku the Chōsokabe advanced. In a word, the creation of the new order must have been related to some of the local food crises of the 1540s and 1550s.

The 1560s were another decade of local famines, with cold, damp weather and military expeditions the main causes. Taken together, food shortages of the 1560s have a distinctly eastern tilt and may best be regarded as localized to that large region.[63]

In the last quarter of the sixteenth century, there were six periods of starvation, only two widespread. First, crops were damaged in Mikawa and Tōtōmi in 1570, but in 1573, the Kinai and eastern Honshu had a bumper crop while all of western Japan suffered from drought and starvation. The dead littered the roads, and hungry farmers dug for roots in Iyo. Second, parching heat and lack of rainfall for 1583–1585 resulted in a general famine, noted only briefly in Kyoto and Mutsu sources. The crises of the 1590s were all local. In general, however, as domains stabilized and political unity came to the islands, the immediate payoff was a diminution in deaths from chronic hunger.[64] Overall, the period from 1541 through 1600 brought a measure of relief to a populace living on the edge of subsistence.

Evidence from Death Registers

Narrative sources of necessity relate a highly subjective view of late medieval famines. Fortunately, four death registers have data for this period: the Akahama Myōhōji register from Hitachi, the Tōji register from Kyoto and environs, the Ichirenji register from Kai and the western Kanto, and the lengthy Hondoji register from Shimōsa. Taken together, these records can give a somewhat more nuanced view of mortality for selected regions between 1400 and 1700.

Before analyzing these registers, I should remind the reader of their shortcomings. First, because clerics recorded deaths for temple members, the statistics in tables A.1–A.11 are not representative of a single village or even area. Second, since the population at risk is unknown, the numbers cannot be equated with a death rate but serve merely as relative indicators of mortality. Finally, as is clear from a comparison with the Tokugawa-period death registers from Kokubunji and Ōgenji (tables A.12 and A.13), the medieval records are appallingly biased: the sex ratios are highly unbalanced, and children, who accounted for around 40–50 percent of deaths in the late eighteenth, nineteenth, and twentieth centuries, were nearly missing from the medieval documents.

Still, if these four death registers have something to contribute to the debate over mortality from famine in the late medieval age, two overarching generalizations seem to be apparent. First, they confirm the previous narrative that deaths spiked beginning as early as the 1430s, lasting until at least 1460, and the spikes were particularly noticeable between 1490 and about 1520. Second, with the exception of the Tōji register, until 1600 the most common months for death were those in the first half of the year, especially in the case of the Akahama Myōhōji and Hondoji registers. As with the Yūgyōji register (analyzed in chapter 3), this clustering in the first half of the year, a "seasonality of death," most likely came about because grain from the previous year's harvest had been exhausted.

Each register has its peculiarities. At Akahama Myōhōji (a temple founded in 1303 belonging to the Lotus sect), the late fifteenth century was somewhat less deadly than either the periods preceding or following, and both the eras 1556–1565 and 1596–1605 show more deaths among the community of believers. The season of death for men and women varied considerably, with women not following any discernible pattern. A preliminary analysis of one area encompassed in this register shows it to have been a "typical" farming community, with some artisans in residence. Measles was responsible for several deaths.[65]

The Tōji register from the Shingon sect is important because it is the only example from western Japan and also because it records an urban death pattern. As noted above, the era 1490–1520 was particularly harsh. In the seasonality of death, however, there is a different pattern in the Tōji register from the other registers: a disproportionate number of deaths occurred during the late spring and summer. This inverted V-pattern can be attributed to the prevalence of epidemics, most active in the summer months in an urban setting.[66]

In some respects, it is hard to know what to make of the Ichirenji register. Ichirenji was a member of the Timely sect, and thus the balance between the genders is much better than at either Akahama Myōhōji or Hondoji. Exhibiting an extreme clustering of deaths in some decades, it nevertheless confirms the overall picture of high mortality during the late fifteenth and early sixteenth centuries. More interesting are the figures on spring hunger, which exhibit a classic N-shape for the first four months of the year. This N-pattern is found widely in premodern agricultural societies in which the populace suffers from chronic malnutrition.[67] It should be noted that neither the Yūgyōji nor the Akahama Myōhōji register conformed precisely to the N-shape, but both still showed a pattern consistent with "spring hungers."

The register from Hondoji, also a member of the Lotus sect, contains the best and most data of any published medieval death register.[68] Like the others, it confirms the hypothesis from narrative sources that the mid-fifteenth through early sixteenth centuries were years when starvation was rife in the Kanto. The late sixteenth century also seems to have been unusually deadly. In regard to "spring hungers," there is a pattern similar to that of the Akahama Myōhōji register, with deaths peaking in the first, third, fourth, and sixth months. While not exactly conforming to an N-shape, the pattern should probably be construed as that of a society suffering from spring and early summer starvation.

At the same time, however, there was a sign of a transformation in mortality for commoners, especially as stable daimyo domains formed after 1540. In addition to the death registers listed above, we can observe the seasonality of death in the Kōfukuji diary, *Daijōin jisha zōjiki,* and the listing of bureaucratic appointments, *Kugyō bunin.*[69] Unlike the death registers, these two records listed deaths of well-to-do monks and aristocrats dwelling in the city—that is, persons unlikely to starve. And unlike the pattern of mortality revealed in the death registers, a W-shape, marked by high death rates in the winter and summer, is apparent. These wealthier persons died not from starvation in the first half of the year, but rather from respiratory illnesses in the winter and digestive tract maladies (food poisoning) and epidemics in the summer. The W-shape is symbolic of a society that no longer suffered from severe food shortages in the spring and summer, as medieval peasants did, but rather had what we might term an early-modern death pattern.

Now consider the minimal data from after 1600 for the Akahama Myōhōji, Ichirenji, and Hondoji registers. Both the Akahama Myōhōji and Ichirenji data conform fairly closely to the early modern W-pattern; deaths spike in the winter months and summer, just as we would expect for a populace leaving behind chronic starvation and moving toward a new pattern of death. Only the Hondoji case is unusual, with few deaths in the winter and most in the summer. Similar W-patterns seem clear for four late Tokugawa villages.[70]

Apparently, by the late sixteenth and seventeenth centuries peasants in many parts of Japan had begun to overcome the problem of chronic hunger and advance to a period of greater plenty. I have mentioned factors in this improvement throughout the last two chapters—more productive agriculture, more highly developed commerce, and the advent of food relief campaigns aimed at helping the starving. At least temporarily, the central problem of the medieval age—the misery and death caused by famines—had been ameliorated. It is particularly notable that this new pattern of death was registered for two areas in eastern Japan, less developed than the western archipelago. Of course hunger would reappear from time to time, especially later in the Tokugawa era; Japan did not permanently leave behind the demon of periodic starvation.

To summarize, the evidence on famine—both narrative and statistical —seems to read as follows. Certainly such factors as the possibly cold and damp weather, the heightened incidence of lean years, the numerous lurid anecdotal stories, and the role of warfare in inducing starvation indicate that famine increased mortality and reduced fertility significantly for

these 150 years, especially when compared with the preceding late Kamakura and mid-Muromachi epochs. At the same time, however, the low
death rates inferred for the supposedly severe Kanshō crisis; the localized
nature of famines after 1540; the enterprise of food merchants bringing
grain to hungry residents; and the operation of relief agencies run by the
wealthy, the government, and religious institutions allayed the harshest
effects of the "spring hungers," especially during 1450–1497 and 1541–
1600. Most important, by the late 1500s, the seasonal pattern of death
seems to have shifted to a more benign pattern, where chronic malnutrition was rarer. While there is latitude to view population growth differently, depending upon which of these various factors we grant the most
weight, it seems prudent to conclude that famine was prevalent and took
a significant, if progressively diminishing, toll on Warring States society.

One final characteristic of the Akahama Myōhōji and Ichirenji registers is interesting: in both cases, deaths spiked in the tenth month, especially for males. Why should this be so? The tenth month was when the
harvest was to be gathered, and we would expect bountiful times. Yet
deaths ranged above average. These figures could be a statistical aberration, but the occurrence in more than one death register suggests that
such was not the case. Rather, the trend was due to another cause, related
to the harvest but more especially to those who would steal it by violent
means.

MORTALITY FACTORS: WAR

The period from the Ōnin War in Kyoto in 1467 until Oda Nobunaga
entered the city in 1568 conventionally encompasses the era known as
the Warring States, the most protracted and brutal time of disorder in Japan's premodern history. Moreover, the century so demarcated does not
include all the violence; until Toyotomi Hideyoshi destroyed the Go-
Hōjō at Odawara in 1590, warfare among ever-expanding armies was
persistent. Even after 1590, Hideyoshi turned his warriors loose on the
Chosŏn dynasty in Korea. Then followed the epochal Battle of Sekigahara in 1600, Tokugawa Ieyasu's Winter Campaign against Hideyoshi's
survivors in Osaka in 1615, and various executions of suspected Chris-
tians, which lasted until the Shimabara Rebellion in 1639.

Warfare would seem to have been a significant cause of mortality and
a brake on population growth. It is difficult to confirm this hypothesis,
however, because unlike the reports on military loyalty from the Wars be-

tween the Northern and Southern Dynasties, quantifiable data for the Warring States era are scarcer. Mortality figures for battles are rare; when they do exist, they often originate with Tokugawa-period sources. As of yet, no one even knows how often armies went to war in the late fifteenth and sixteenth centuries. While it is undoubtedly true that war was a more significant cause of death than ever before, scholars have made real progress in this area only recently.[71]

Combatant Mortality

We should view the topic of combatant mortality within a context of changing tactics and the ever-increasing size of armies. During the Civil War of 1180–1185, the number of warriors for each battle usually totaled no more than several dozen horsemen, each with two or three foot-soldiers, and mounted archers usually engaged in single combat. During the Wars between the Northern and Southern Dynasties in the fourteenth century, it is doubtful that armies numbered more than several hundred to perhaps a few thousand per battle. Mounted troopers were still important, and the major weapons included the bow and arrow, the sword, and possibly the pike. In the early stages of the Warring States era, forces may have counted only a few thousand in their ranks, as *shugo daimyō* and local notables, known as "men of the province" *(kokujin)*, engaged each other, but by the 1550s, strong Warring States daimyo could put together sizable hosts. In eastern Honshu, for example, the Go-Hōjō began with a few hundred troops in 1495 and about a century later could field over fifty thousand.[72] The Takeda also raised as many as fifty thousand warriors to join their major expeditions.[73] The Mōri commanded sixty-five thousand men in 1578, when they battled Hideyoshi, whose troops reportedly numbered one hundred and fifty thousand.[74] In 1579, the Chōsokabe of Tosa led a force of twelve thousand into Sanuki; when they attacked Awa and Iyo in the early 1580s, the army purportedly had thirty-six thousand.[75] Hideyoshi's invasion of Korea included at least two hundred thousand men, a federation of western daimyo forces.

These numbers may be testimony to population expansion in the sixteenth century, but they are also characteristic of a new way of fighting. Instead of the single combat of the late twelfth century or the small-scale siege warfare of the fourteenth, massed armies fought in open fields using coordinated movements. Moreover, in 1543 the Portuguese introduced the blunderbuss to Japan; it was in use in battles by at least 1575, to

TABLE 5.5
Battle Deaths among Mōri Opponents, 1540–1600

DATE (YEAR/ MONTH/DAY)	NUMBER OF HEADS COLLECTED	LOCATION/ENEMY
1540/6/16	33	Aki
1540/9/4–12/26	10	Ft. Kōriyama, Aki
1540/11/22	70	Ft. Kōriyama, Aki
1541/1/13	63	Izumo; Amako family
1552/7/23	7 dead; 163 wounded[a]	Bitchū
1570/4/17	164	Izumo
1575/1/1	304	Bitchū
1600/8/25	172	Ise
1600/9/9–10	247	Owari

Source: MKM, 1, pp. 250–462.
[a]Mōri casualties.

deadly effect. In a word, Japan's Warring States military fits into the global trend toward larger and more lethal armies.[76]

The increase in the size of armies, along with the importation of the musket and cannon, would lead most to believe that combatant casualties were high by the end of the sixteenth century, and yet statistics are few and do not necessarily support such a conclusion. The most certain and exact tallies originate with the Mōri, the famous daimyo of far western Honshu.[77] (See table 5.5.)

These numbers should not be taken at face value; they undoubtedly do not include all those killed in battle but rather refer to mounted samurai, whose heads opponents especially prized as trophies and sources of income. Compilers probably omitted from these documents the deaths of common peasant infantry known as *zōhyō* or *ashigaru.*

There are, however, ways of estimating the ratio of mounted warriors to their footsoldier underlings. In the case of a Chōsokabe enemy, the Yamamoto, the proportion was about one to three, a seemingly low figure.[78] In the case of the Takeda from Kai, the number varied from five to fifteen footsoldiers for every horse rider, although one author has his doubts about the accuracy of these counts.[79] Given that the ratio was 1:2 in the Kamakura age and as high as 1:10 for 1450, a proportion of about 1:12, yielding a multiplier of thirteen, would be liberal.

After the addition of presumed footsoldier deaths, casualties inflicted by and against the Mōri between 1540 and 1600 range from modest to sizable and increase as the sixteenth century wears on. During the early battles with the Amako in Aki and Izumo, the Mōri probably killed at most between 130 and 1,000 of the enemy (that is, $10 \times 13 = 130$; $70 \times 13 = 921$). In 1552, the Mōri suffered only seven dead, but a disproportionately high number of wounded (163). Many undoubtedly died, but even with the addition of presumptive deaths among unrecorded footsoldiers, mortality seems low. As the Age of the Country at War proceeded, armies expanded along with casualty figures. In 1575, Mōri troops probably killed several thousand; during the decisive Battle of Sekigahara, they may have murdered about three thousand of their enemies ($247 \times 13 = 3,211$).

In addition to those of the Mōri, there are other scattered notices of mortality. When the Chōsokabe were unifying Tosa in 1562, their armies always numbered a few thousand; at one battle, on the eighteenth of the ninth month, they lost 511 men while inflicting 343 deaths.[80] Moving to eastern Honshu, we note somewhat higher counts among the big warlords. When Takeda Shingen began his rise by conquering Shinano in the early 1540s, his armies consisted of a few hundred mounted warriors and about a thousand infantry.[81] In the conquest of Ogasawara castles in Shinano, losses on either side ranged from three hundred to over three thousand.[82] When Tokugawa Ieyasu engaged Takeda Shingen at Ft. Yoshida in Tōtōmi in the spring of 1571, Ieyasu's army may have killed about two thousand.[83]

When the Warring States daimyo were implacable personal enemies, casualties seem to have risen. One of the fiercest rivalries was that between Shingen and Echigo's Uesugi Kenshin. If later figures are credible, at the bitterly contested Five Battles of Kawanakajima, beginning in 1553, armies numbered about 10,000 on each side, and mortality reportedly amounted to half or more of those participating.[84] In the last duel, in 1564, sources record Kenshin as losing 3,400 and Shingen 4,600, not including wounded, tabulated at almost 20,000. I must reiterate, however, that all these figures are suspect, coming from after the wars, when veterans could gather and reminisce about "the good old days." Consequently, it is probably safe to assert that mortality per battle was low to start with and increased considerably as the age progressed and the size of armies grew. Although combatant deaths for each battle numbered more than ever before in Japanese history, reliable figures are not particularly high, especially when compared to the toll that famine or disease may have been taking. Armies were more likely to take defeated soldiers prisoner and sell them than to kill them.[85]

There is, however, another question to ask before reaching a conclusion about combatant mortality: how often did battles take place? A perusal of any survey history makes it seem as though generals were calling their men to arms almost all the time, yet such was not the case. Moreover, this question is exceedingly difficult to answer because many records remain unpublished or undated. Fortunately, it is possible to convey some sense of battle frequency for the opposing daimyo at Kawanakajima, Kenshin (1530–1578) and Shingen (1521–1573). (See tables 5.6 and 5.7.)

The first conclusion apparent from tables 5.6 and 5.7 is that both Kenshin and Shingen campaigned almost every year. From 1541, when he was twenty, until 1569 Shingen stayed at home in Kōfu during only five years. Kenshin missed only four years over a twenty-three year span. Moreover, armies were often gone for months at a time, especially in Kenshin's case, when an expedition of six months was not unusual. Of course, the months away from home were not always spent in battle; it would be surprising if armies fought even half the time. Still, the frequency of campaigns is striking.

To be sure, these tables record the activities of strong Warring States daimyo; during the earlier phase of domain formation, between 1490 and 1520, it was unlikely that the lord ventured out of his unstable province at all, especially if local samurai challenged him, as they did Shingen's father Nobutora. Between the end of the Ōnin War in 1477 and 1520, violence seems to have been more sporadic and localized, as the Muromachi shogunate writhed in its death throes. Still, plenty of small battles with forces of several hundred took place then too.

Studied carefully, this pair of tables yields three more points relevant to population trends. First, if daimyo armies were away on expedition, that meant that spouses might be kept apart. Certainly prostitutes followed these armies, and soldiers had other outlets as well. Yet campaigning had the same effect as long-distance commuting *(dekasegi)* does today and probably did in the latter half of the Tokugawa period. Both footsoldiers and mounted samurai were away from their spouses for several months at a time, and therefore fertility was likely lowered.[86]

Second, the data supplied by the two tables help clear up the small mystery noted at the end of the last section. Both the Akahama Myōhōji and Ichirenji registers showed higher mortality for men in the tenth month. Given the deadliness of the spring months, this finding was totally unexpected. If we examine the timing of many of Kenshin's and Shingen's expeditions, however, we see that armies were in the field during the tenth

TABLE 5.6
Frequency of Military Expeditions: Uesugi Kenshin, 1555–1576

DATE (YEAR/MONTH)	NUMBER OF MONTHS	LOCATION
1555/7–Int. 10[a]	3	Shinano
1557/4–5?	2	Shinano
1560/3	1	Japan Sea littoral
1560/8–1561/6	10	Kanto
1561/8–9?	2	Shinano
1561/11–1562/3	4	Kanto
1562/11–1563/6	8	Kanto
1563/12–1564/4	5	Kanto
1564/7–9?	3	Shinano
1564/11–12	2	Kanto
1565/7–10	4	Shinano
1565/11–1566/3	4	Kanto
1566/6–7	2	Japan Sea littoral
1566/12–1567/5	6	Kanto
1568/3–?	?	Japan Sea littoral
1569/8–10	3	Japan Sea littoral
1569/11–1570/4	6	Kanto
1570/9–11?	3	Kanto
1571/3–4	2	Japan Sea littoral
1571/11–1572/4	6	Kanto
1572/8–1573/4	9	Japan Sea littoral
1573/7–8	2	Kanto
1574/1–5	5	Kanto
1574/9–12	4	Kanto
1576/3–4	2	Japan Sea littoral
1576/9–1577/3	7	Japan Sea littoral

Source: Fujiki, Zōhyōtachi, p. 95.
[a]Int. 10 refers to intercalary tenth month.

TABLE 5.7
Frequency of Military Expeditions: Takeda Shingen, 1541–1569

DATE (YEAR/MONTH)	NUMBER OF MONTHS	LOCATION
1541/5–6	2	Shinano
1542/4–7	4	Shinano
1542/9–10	2	Shinano
1543/9–10	2	Shinano
1544/10–11	2	Shinano
1545/4–6	3	Shinano
1546/5–6	2	Shinano
1547/7–8	2	Shinano
1548/2–3	2	Shinano
1548/7–10	3	Shinano
1549/7–9	3	Shinano
1550/7–10	4	Shinano
1551/7	1	Shinano
1551/8–9	2	Shinano
1551/10–11	2	Shinano
1552/8	1	Shinano
1553/3–5	3	Shinano
1553/7–10	5	Shinano, Kawanakajima
1554/7?	1?	Shinano
1555/4–Int. 10	7	Shinano, Kawanakajima
1557/4	1	Shinano, Kawanakajima
1561/8–9	2	Shinano, Kawanakajima
1561/11–?	?	Kōzuke
1563/9–?	?	Kōzuke
1564/11–1565/2	4	Musashi
1564/3–?	?	Shinano
1564/5–?	?	Kōzuke
1564/8–10	3	Shinano, Kawanakajima
1565/5–?	?	Kōzuke
1566/Int. 8–?	?	Kōzuke
1568/5–?	?	Shinano
1569/8–10	3	Sagami; Go-Hōjō

Source: Shibatsuji, "Sengoku daimyō no gaisei to zaikoku," p. 24.

month. For Kenshin, five campaigns lasted into that month, while Shingen had eleven such conflicts. Although there is no direct substantiating evidence, one possible reason that males died more frequently in the tenth month was that they were being killed in battle. To support this inference, it should be noted that both death registers pertained to Kanto residents, where some of the heaviest fighting took place.

Third, "spring hungers" played a role in determining the timing and destination of campaigns. Since Echigo's growing season was too short to sustain double-cropping, everything depended upon the autumnal harvest. For Kenshin, long expeditions all headed for the Kanto in the late fall, suggesting that that time was the easiest to conscript troops. Moreover, if the year had been good, provisions would have been plentiful, at least for a while. Battles in nearby Shinano and the Japan Sea littoral were generally much shorter and frequently took place in the spring. In other words, when the harvest was good, Kenshin might march on the distant Kanto, but if reserves were low, a shorter agenda was in order. And part of that agenda was undoubtedly to steal food, just as Kenshin's Yayoi forebears had done many centuries earlier.

A deeper examination of the sources also reveals that in four years—1560, 1561, 1566, and 1574—there was widespread distress, if not outright famine, in Echigo. By directing his troops outside of the home province during those years, Kenshin accomplished two goals: he stole grain at the same that he reduced the population's suffering back home. This process of campaigning is termed *kuchiberashi* and means "to provide for unwanted family members by shipping them elsewhere."

If this pattern is visible in the Uesugi case, it is even more noticeable for Shingen. Of the thirty-two campaigns listed in table 5.7, twelve took place in the spring, the season when death was most frequent. No wonder Shingen called the fourth month "the time when we have no provisions."[87] Moreover, records for Tsuru District in Kai are so good *(Katsuyama ki)* that we can correlate Takeda expeditions with hungry years. Famine wracked Kai nine times during the campaign years listed in table 5.7, including 1544, 1550, 1551, 1554, and 1563, dates when Shingen marched his men after crops had failed. Until recently, researchers have not realized how much the conflicts of the Warring States era were a result of humans' most basic instinct to fill their bellies. The age-old practice of "self-help" still seems to have been the most common form of provisioning during the fifteenth and most of the sixteenth centuries.

To sum up, there can be no doubt that war accounted for greater mortality among combatants between 1450 and 1600 than ever before. Casualties may have been small for the first half of this period, but by 1550 it was not unusual for a few thousand men to lose their lives in a battle. Undoubtedly the wider dispersion of the pike *(yari)* and the introduction of the blunderbuss encouraged the increasingly sanguinary nature of hostilities. Furthermore, by the sixteenth century, stable Warring States daimyo were going on campaign nearly every year, sometimes for months on end. They did not fight every day while on expedition, but the crescendo of battles and campaigns must have elevated overall mortality (and reduced fertility) to some degree.

Still, it is wise to keep battle mortality in historical perspective. During the U.S. Civil War, the bloodiest conflict in American history, when soldiers used the Minié ball rifle, the death rate from war was a terrifying 18.2 per 1,000 population.[88] Combatant mortality during the Warring States period certainly did not approach that figure, although it was moving in that direction. No one knows for sure by how many points Warring States battles raised overall mortality. The one certainty is that Japan was following the global pattern of increasingly lethal battles and armies.

How did the rest of the population fare? Examination of the Civil War of 1180–1185 and the Wars between the Northern and Southern Dynasties emphasized that war dealt its cruelest blows to the innocent peasantry through whose paddies soldiers trudged and whose homes and fields the "hounds of war" incinerated. Can the same assertion be made for the Warring States period? Did daimyo still "help themselves" when it came time to look for provisions? Was Yoritomo's answer to this problem, so obvious in 1185 but gone awry by 1300, still the most common? Or did warlords and soldiers of the late fifteenth and sixteenth centuries find another solution to the dilemma? To answer these questions, I offer three well-documented cases: that of the Mōri in western Honshu, Hineno Estate in the Kinai, and the Takeda of Kai, bordering on the Kanto. In the present state of research, these individual studies, drawn from western, central, and eastern Japan respectively, seem to present the best way to analyze the problem.

The Mōri

The daimyo regime of the Mōri was one of the most famous and powerful of the Warring States period.[89] The family of local magnates, most well known for helping to oust the Tokugawa shogunate three hundred years later in 1868, began as one of a large number of "men of the province" in Aki in western Honshu. When the Mōri first appear in records in 1497, the Amako and the heralded Ōuchi were bitter rivals throughout the region; in their rise to power the Mōri had to destroy both, a classic case of "the inferior overthrowing the superior" *(gekoku jō)*. By 1557, the Mōri were masters of western Honshu and continued to battle remnants of their enemies' armies and solidify the institutional basis of their control until 1571. Beginning in 1576, Mōri Terumoto collided with Oda Nobunaga, first at Ishiyama Honganji and then in western Honshu, but after Nobunaga's assassination in 1582, Terumoto made his peace with Hideyoshi, aided in the latter's campaigns (especially in Korea), and then fought at Sekigahara.

If there is one principle that the Mōri's ascent to glory proves, it is that war is the process of destroying the enemy's ability to fight—that is, his economic base.[90] Just like for their forebears in Masakado's revolt (935–940) or the Wars between the Northern and Southern Dynasties in the 1300s, there were two basic tactics: incinerate the enemy's territory or mow down his fields. (See table 5.8.) For example, in 1525, when the Amako were the enemy, a Mōri lieutenant sent a letter boasting that "the local area had all been set ablaze *[hōka]*. . . . At Yano Village we burned everything in sight and not one enemy soldier came forth."[91] In 1540, as the Mōri engaged remnants of the Amako in Aki, the daimyo kept a diary:

> 9/5: Began to fight at Upper Yoshida Village. Burned several homes. But today there was no battle.

> 9/6: Burned the shops of Taromaru and several others. . . .

> 9/23: The Amako changed camps to Aoyama Mizuka Mountain. At this time from our first camp we burned to the ground the enemy's main camp at Mt. Kazegoe.[92]

Denying the enemy supplies and other support could also be accomplished by simply having soldiers unsheath their swords and cut down the crops in the field, perhaps then using the grain for their own provisions. Table 5.8 provides several examples of this tactic too.

To sum up, the Mōri practiced economic warfare against all comers, especially when their rivals retreated to a fortification. A Tokugawa-

TABLE 5.8
"Collateral Damage" in the Mōri Rise to Power, 1547–1582

DATE	MISDEED	PERPETRATOR	SOURCE
1547	Crops stolen	Ōuchi	*HHBE*, II, 747
1553	Crops stolen	Mōri	*HHBE*, II, 84
1555	Villages burned	Sue	*HKSKCSH*, 18
1555	Villages burned	Sue	*HHBE*, I, 350
1565	Crops destroyed	Mōri	*HHBE*, II, 863
1570	Crops destroyed	Mōri	*HHBE*, I, 268
1575	Crops destroyed	Mōri	*HHBE*, II, 428
1575	Arson/crops stolen	Mōri	*HHBE*, II, 924
1577	Harvest destroyed	Mōri	*OKKS*, I, 177; *HHBE*, III, 214
1580	Harvest destroyed	Mōri	*HHBE*, III, 214
1580	Arson/crops stolen	Mōri	*HHBE*, III, 180, 441
1580	Harvest destroyed	Mōri	*HHBE*, III, 446
1581	Arson	Mōri	*HHBE*, II, 392
1582	Arson	Hideyoshi	*HHBE*, I, 592–593
1582	Arson	Mōri	Yamamoto[a]

[a]Noted in Yamamoto Hiroaki, "Hōka inekari mugikari," p. 20.

period source describes Mōri tactics succinctly: "In the spring, they overturned seedling beds and decimated fields. In the summer, they mowed down the wheat and made people work harder by interfering with transplanting. In the autumn, they took the crops of dry fields or cut them off and blocked tax payment. In the winter, they broke into granaries, burned peasant homes, and forced them to freeze or starve to death."[93]

Yet the reader should keep in mind that these actions did not take place all the time and that workers could eventually repair the devastation. For one thing, the Mōri never did this to lands that they controlled; there the object was to nurture crops and attract farmers and artisans. Moreover, surviving cases of Mōri depredations amount to only about 1 percent of the total extant documentation.[94] Of course, since arson and pillage did not jibe with the presumed samurai sense of "honorable combat," many events undoubtedly went unrecorded. Without exaggeration, however, it seems fair to say that the wars hampered both demographic and economic growth to a considerable degree in certain times and places.

Hineno Estate

In the early years of the sixteenth century, the peasants of Hineno Estate found themselves trapped amid forces mostly beyond their control. First there was their penurious proprietor, Kujō Masamoto, who had borrowed money from his servant *(kerai)* and when he was unable to repay, killed him. Kujō also took a loan from the monks of Negoroji, with whom he could not dispense so easily. Then there were two constables for northern and southern Izumi Province, in which Hineno was located, who were constantly seeking provisions and men for their war machines. A hoodlum named Satō Sōbei ransacked Hineno too. Finally, there was nature, which, as we have already noted, caused a series of harsh famines in the late 1490s and early 1500s.

Fortunately for historians, Masamoto became so desperate to defend his ever-shrinking estate from marauders and the court was so angered by his homicidal behavior that the literate aristocrat left Kyoto and went to Hineno to live from 1501 to 1504. His diary *(Masamoto kō tabi hikitsuke)* conveys the most realistic and poignant sense of what it was like to live as a peasant in the hotly contested Kinai during the mid-Warring States era.[95]

Hineno Estate was founded in 1234 with the Kujō family as proprietor, and by the late Kamakura era it was composed of four settlements.[96] During the Wars between the Northern and Southern Dynasties, the Kujō lost control of Hineno to the local constable, and it was not until the 1400s that they even considered trying to reassert their rights. Eventually two of the hamlets, Iriyamada and Hineno, were returned to the Kujō portfolio, and when Masamoto fell into debt and the court banished him from Kyoto, he decided to live on the property and collect taxes directly.

Masamoto's diary details a constant litany of intrusions, kidnapping, and violence against the villages from several different forces. Within a month of arriving at the estate office, Masamoto issued a directive to the constable in charge of southern Izumi, Hosokawa Masahisa, that (1) his men were not to collect extra taxes; (2) if they stole more than three coins, they would be killed on sight; and (3) they were to stop raping the women of the village.[97] The next month the constable demanded tax payment, but Masamoto connived to have the Muromachi shogunate, which still held some authority in the area, stop him. Within days, however, rumors abounded that either the constable or the armed monks of Negoroji, to whom Masamoto owed money, would enter the premises.

On the tenth day of the sixth month in 1501, both constables sent soldiers into the western end of Hineno at the height of the growing season. On the seventeenth day, they captured three peasants from nearby Ōki Village, and in retaliation peasants threatened to burn a local market with whose safety the responsible constable was charged. At the beginning of the next month, two of the captured peasants escaped. The constable then offered to sell the third (who was only twelve or thirteen years old) back to the village, assuming that he could find the road on his own. Finally, on the sixth day of the seventh month, the peasant boy returned.[98]

On the fifteenth day of the eighth month, the local constable raised havoc *(rōzeki)* at a local shrine, killing several people observing a Shinto rite. Masamoto also issued an order to block the constable from selling the farmers he had kidnapped there and managed to obtain the support of the shogunate in the person of Hosokawa Masamoto *(kanrei,* prime minister).[99] No matter: on the twenty-eighth day, the same constable entered Hineno again, without authorization, and captured more cultivators.

Fed up with the kidnappings and demands for more taxes, on the fourth of the ninth month all the residents of the eastern end of Hineno Village fled to the neighboring hills, taking their most precious belongings with them. On the nineteenth, the village head of the western half put a query to Kujō: "Everyone says, 'We might flee not because of you [the proprietor, *ryōke*], but because when the constable's men stop by and kidnap our wealthier peasants [daimyo]; burn our homes; and pillage our personal belongings, various tools, and livestock, we can not stand it.' Therefore ought we to flee?"[100] Finally, on the twenty-third, Masamoto discovered that from ten at night to four in the morning on a day earlier in the ninth month, the constable had brought over one thousand men to launch arrows against the farmers of the eastern part of Hineno; the farmers returned to defend the village when they learned of the attack. Surprisingly, the farmers held their own in the battle, wounding eighty-nine of the constable's men but losing only one of their own to a slight wound.

Still, the constable demanded provisions *(hyōrō)*. After viewing the damage to fields throughout eastern and western Hineno, residents of the western half fled as well on the twenty-fourth of the ninth month. Now no one was left in Hineno, and 200–300 peasants were hiding in the nearby hills. In the tenth month a few inhabitants of the western half of Hineno came back temporarily to their homes and began to plant wheat. Somehow, they gathered in the harvest. By the end of the year, the farmers had returned and even paid some dues to Kujō, but the constable still entered Hineno as he pleased, a fact the peasants used to resist paying Masamoto all that he demanded.[101]

As 1502 dawned, cultivators protested to Kujō about having to provide the constable with porters. In the fourth month, Kujō expressed the fear that life was so bad for his farmers that they might again decide to leave. On the twenty-second of the fifth month, more discussion of constabulary incursions took place, and then on the fifth of the sixth month, when the constable tried to collect his half of the taxes *(hanzei)*, the farmers went on strike by taking refuge in their homes and lowering the blinds.[102]

While struggling with the constable and his men, on the twenty-sixth of the seventh month the residents of Hineno heard of threats to enter and burn down the settlements by the armed Negoroji monks. Although Kujō was able to stave off the angry clerics, the constable of southern Izumi (Hosokawa Masahisa) and his men threatened the same a bit later. As these dangers mounted, the most despicable character of all—Satō Sōbei, an erstwhile Masahisa vassal—burned Sano Market and part of the western end of Hineno on the sixth of the eighth month. Satō then joined forces with Negoroji and used Hineno as his base of operations; the peasants discussed matters, and Kujō fled his armed creditors on the twenty-first. From his hiding place, Masamoto told Satō and his company of about two hundred to move elsewhere or he would be willing to see his holdings put to the torch. On the twenty-third, Satō retreated and things returned to normal.[103] Eventually Kujō and his underlings tried to bribe Sōbei, even as the constable of northern Izumi demanded provisions on the twenty-ninth.

So far Kujō had collected some dues, and the residents of Iriyamada and Hineno looked upon him as a protector. On the third of the ninth month, one elder was quoted as saying that "if Kujō returned to Kyoto [as he was considering doing], it would be like taking a mother's breast away from her suckling infant."[104] This statement was an indirect reference to Satō and his threats to take provisions and porters *(ninpu)* from Hineno. On the seventh, despite the earlier bribe, Satō returned and demanded a rapid fulfillment of his needs. On the eighth, Kujō had placards placed around his settlements prohibiting anyone from making camp in Iriyamada or causing mischief. On the eighteenth of the tenth month, war broke out between the two constables and the northern one was slain, but the armies put the entire province to the torch in the process. Kujō worried that peasant living standards were dropping to a new low as the year drew to a close.[105]

In 1503, new and more terrible enemies appeared: drought and crop failure. The year 1501 had also been poor, but now things reached a new low.[106] The spring started off well enough, as a pouring rain flooded the estate on the twentieth of the fifth month; peasants were busy bargaining with the constable over taxes. From that date, however, the weather was clear and dry. By the fourteenth of the sixth month, Kujō was writing of drought, and by the seventh month over half the fields were said to be damaged. Despite the pitiful conditions, on the twenty-third of the seventh month the constables kidnapped more farmers while others simply fled. Cultivators tried trading straw for grain at market.[107]

In the ninth month, footsoldiers employed by Negoroji were reported in the vicinity, but a threat never materialized. Meanwhile, peasants were reduced to digging for bracken *(warabi)* roots and selling ash as fertilizer. Even in these straitened conditions, the constable appeared on the horizon, ready to ransack Hineno, and he kidnapped a person again on the seventeenth of the tenth month. As Kujō calculated the harvest of 1503 at 20 percent of a normal year, cultivators again prepared to flee the constable and his men on the twenty-sixth. The rest of the year passed uneventfully for Hineno, but on the twenty-sixth of the twelfth month Kujō heard that soldiers had burned 610 homes near Sakai.[108]

By 1504, order was breaking down everywhere: robbery and arson were common. For this year, Masamoto's diary mostly addresses the issue of punishment of peasant thieves guilty of stealing a sword and dried bracken roots. (See chapter 6.) In the fourth month, the monks of Kokawadera entered the estate and peasant homes, searching for provisions and trying to incinerate the place. The constable sided with Kokawadera, but then soldiers from Negoroji appeared after having put three villages to the torch. Eventually, all these forces left Hineno in a somewhat charred state.[109]

Fortunately, by the seventh month a good harvest seemed in the offing. Pleas were made to aid those who had suffered most during the famine, and Kujō stated that some of his men had even joined military forces in Kii during 1503 to get enough to eat. Then the constable reappeared, looking for lumber, but the random pillaging and arson at Hineno did not stop. As the seventh month came to an end, the constable's forces and Negoroji soldiers fought over the surplus; peasants barricaded the village. The confrontation ended when the farmers agreed to pay taxes, and Negoroji became Kujō's representative at Hineno. Even as this rapprochement was achieved, Satō Sōbei reentered the picture on the tenth of the ninth month, and arson took place widely. On the fourteenth, Negoroji conscripted four farmers as porters. A month later, Kokawadera killed rebellious locals. Peasants continued to flee Hineno through the end of the year.[110]

At the end of 1504, the diary concludes with Kujō's return to Kyoto. His stay in Hineno was largely a defeat; he had been unable to protect his holdings from various predators, especially the constables; on the second of the eleventh month Kujō wrote that "the violence of the constables knows no bounds." The following poem, written by one of Hosokawa Masamoto's followers who was forced to commit suicide, summed up Kujō's feelings toward the *bakufu*, the titular authority in the region.

> Thinking that there might be
> A good lord for me
> In hell,
> Should I don my traveling clothes
> For today's journey?

Even when he returned to Kyoto, misfortune haunted Kujō: his youngest child committed suicide in 1507, nine years before Masamoto's own death in 1516.[111]

As in the Mōri domains, pillaging, warfare, arson, and kidnapping were constantly interrupting life in Hineno, and these were hardly activities designed to encourage demographic growth or boost the local economy. While historians have no way of knowing how "representative" Hineno was, it stands as a good example of a village trapped among the self-seeking forces of the Kinai. Yet it is notable that the cultivators were not mere pawns: they went on strike, played one predator off against another, and were even victorious in battle. Even so, peasants at Hineno must have welcomed peace when it eventually came.

The Takeda

One of the most daring and famous warlord families of eastern Honshu made their home in the Kōfu basin. Descended from the Minamoto and participants in the Civil War of 1180–1185, they became the hereditary constables of Kai and remained there for the rest of their days. In the 1400s, they were nearly ousted from the province, but Takeda Nobutora managed to regain control and bring the local men of influence *(kokujin)* to heel. Nobutora eventually fell victim to his renowned son

Shingen, who carried Takeda fortunes to their apogee in 1573 with a march on Kyoto. Shingen expired along the way, however, and Oda Nobunaga destroyed his heir, Katsuyori, in 1582.

As with Kujō's diary of Hineno, historians are fortunate to have fine source material for Kai. In particular, monks at a temple—probably Jōzaiji, located in lonely and isolated Tsuru District in eastern Kai—kept a detailed journal, *The Record of Katsuyama (Katsuyama ki)*, from the onset of the Ōnin War in 1467 until 1558. This record pays particular attention to economic and political matters, although sometimes we can only infer the complicated relationships among such factors as starvation, war, and transportation blockages.[112] The following will describe the tactics used by the Takeda and show their effects on the local economy. Because *The Record of Katsuyama* covers such an extended time, it is possible to gain an overview of Tsuru for almost a century.

From the 1470s until 1520, the Takeda had yet to assert their dominance in Kai, and battles took place among warring factions within the Takeda family and between the Takeda and *kokujin*. This period seems to have witnessed the most damage to the land and people of Kai. It is not surprising, for instance, that during 1472–1473, when Takeda troops were on the move, Tsuru experienced a severe famine, with grain prices hitting the ceiling. Famine again struck there in 1492, a year in which a major *kokujin* insurrection occurred. In 1494, as a Takeda scion fought with a relative for control of the province, the journal reads, "Half the arable land [in Tsuru] was not even planted." During 1504–1505, more famine and high prices were prevalent amid war.[113]

Beginning in 1507, fourteen-year-old Takeda Nobutora began to consolidate control. In 1508, the harvest failed in Tsuru District, no doubt in part because Nobutora was campaigning there in the tenth month. The next spring naturally saw prices climb, and Takeda forces poured into Tsuru and burned Kawaguchi Village to the ground. Rebellion continued in Tsuru in 1510–1511 because armies blocked the roads and prevented grain from reaching the beleaguered cultivator class. In the tenth month of 1515, Nobutora took on both a prominent *kokujin* and the Imagawa invading from Suruga, and by the end of the year Kai peasants were digging for tubers and gathering vegetables amid a severe famine. The harsh conditions lasted into 1516, partly because the Imagawa had cut roads into Kai from the south and west.[114] The Imagawa proved more than a match for Nobutora's forces in 1517 as well, incinerating the Kōfu basin and chasing Nobutora into hiding.[115] At last, late in 1517,

Nobutora managed to unite most other samurai of Kai, and together they drove the Imagawa out of the province. Yet in Tsuru commerce remained sluggish, and residents planted no crops.

From 1519 to 1531, Nobutora at last managed to unite the Kai *kokujin* and drive the Imagawa out of the province, gaining a measure of peace for his beleaguered domain. Then the Takeda began their advance into Shinano, but a closed road network hindered commerce in Tsuru *(hitobito tsumaru koto kagiri nashi)*. In 1533, villages were burned in Kai, and in 1534 a severe famine raged in concert with a failure of transportation and commerce into Tsuru. The next year, the Go-Hōjō and Imagawa united against Nobutora, with the Takeda suffering 270 casualties out of a reported force of 2,000. Invaders burned both Upper and Lower Yoshida Villages and routed Nobutora's forces. He counterattacked in 1536, murdering countless Go-Hōjō men and capturing about one hundred women, children, elderly, and handicapped persons.[116]

From 1541, when Shingen ousted his father, *The Record of Katsuyama* yields valuable insights into Takeda war profiteering. In his later years, Nobutora had eyed Shinano, and Shingen shared his father's vision. While famine was prevalent and commerce frequently sluggish throughout the 1540s, the most notable phenomenon occurred in 1546: "Previously all the world has been starving. There is nothing left to say. [When the Takeda had won in Shinano,] we took men and women prisoner, hauled them back to Kai, and received from relatives two, three, five, or ten strings of cash for each."[117] The same fate undoubtedly befell those captured in 1536; war might mean famine within Kai, but when expeditions ventured beyond the borders, the Takeda found a way to make a profit for their war machine.

Conflict with the Ogasawara, Suwa, and Murakami of Shinano lasted for the next ten years. In 1548, *The Record of Katsuyama* states, "That the world is not rich goes without saying. . . . In that period, we killed five thousand and captured an unknown number of males and females. We tied them up and packed them onto the horses of our men from Kai."[118] These poor individuals were likely either put up for sale or used as servants or soldiers.

In 1551, as the Shinano campaigns drew to a close, a bad famine struck, and there were not enough persons to plant the fields. Many died as grain prices skyrocketed, but the war in Shinano continued. Whole villages emptied in Tsuru District, yet Kai's population received an unexpected boost: "This year too troops advanced on Shinano. . . . We attacked and breached a fort named Koiwatake and cut off five hundred heads. No one knows how many weak [*ashiyowashi*—i.e., women, children, and elderly] we captured."[119] Takeda troops probably hauled these hapless individuals back to Kai and sold them into servitude. And the next year, more of the same followed: "In one day we forced sixteen fortresses to capitulate. There will never be anything like it in the future in terms of the samurai [*kōmyō*] we killed and the weak we took prisoner."[120] As above, the "weak" referred not to footsoldiers but to noncombatants such as children, women, old people, and the handicapped.

While *The Record of Katsuyama* basically ends in 1554, later sources confirm that the Takeda operated in much the same way when they began to expand beyond Shinano. The early Tokugawa-period source *The Military Mirror of Kai (Kōyō gunkan)* reveals Takeda battle tactics and goals. For example, during the Battles of Kawanakajima between the Takeda and Uesugi, "We [the Takeda] brought the army of that vicinity in and burned all the way to Mt. Sekino. We advanced close to the fort of [Kenshin]. We pillaged the Echigo folks' [settlements]. . . . We burned right up to [Kenshin's] fortress and capriciously stole women and children and then took them back home."[121] Uesugi sources confirm such actions.

There are numerous other tales of Takeda plunder, rape, arson, and kidnapping for profit.[122] While such tales reinforce previous impressions of the devastation of war, the Takeda show just how valuable captives (and not corpses) could be for an up-and-coming Warring States daimyo. In this sense, the wars were part of the growing commercial market that had started in earnest in the late thirteenth century. By taking "the weak" captive rather than killing them, the Takeda probably lessened potential mortality during the wars.

Taken together, these examples suggest that the violence of the Warring States era frequently made life unbearable for noncombatants.[123] To the extent that this is true, civil war was a demographic and economic disaster for the archipelago. This is not to argue that there was no growth during these 150 years, but simply to note that violence, pillage, arson, kidnapping, and forced conscription are not conducive to demographic, agricultural, or commercial expansion.[124]

Ending the Mayhem

Rural folk knew that hostilities were bad for their livelihoods, and as the war wore on, they developed strategies to lessen its deleterious effects. These strategies have come to be known as the village "survival system" *(seimei iji sōchi)* or "disaster control" *(kiki kanri).*[125] For example, one reason for the spread of the Ikkō sect may have been that its adherents united to resist famine better than did most commoners; evidence suggests that peasant believers protected vulnerable Ikkō artisans such as bucket makers, iron workers, and bladesmiths by saving grain for them. Similar behavior may have played a role in the diffusion of Christianity. Such organization probably is one reason that Nobunaga and Ieyasu (who even borrowed organizational ideas from the Ikkō sect) were so keen to destroy it.[126]

Unaffiliated peasants also took precautions to survive the constant depredations of the samurai. I have already mentioned several tactics, such as flight from the land and strikes. When armies were rumored in the area, villagers sent one of their members to a mountaintop to scout for troopers; this happened in the case of Hineno.[127] Before the armies appeared, peasants hid their belongings and fled to the hills or a local temple for safety. Temples were especially good places to hide or "loan" valuables *(azukarimono)* and land documents since superstitious warriors often would not trespass. Moreover, peasants stowed their livestock, furniture, and other belongings in the mountains to prevent martial predators from laying their hands on them.[128]

When cultivators used their most effective tactic—flight or work stoppage—where did they go? Villages in danger of attack often built a small fort in the mountains *(yama no koya)*, where they stowed grain and other necessities. Jesuit priest João Rodriguez wrote of these small refuges; one stood at Suganoura in Ōmi. Archaeologists and geographers have discovered many of these mountain hideaways.[129]

Peasants were also clever enough to play warring sides off against each other or to employ bribery.[130] There was a saying that peasants were just like the grasses because they switched sides as often as their safety necessitated. Furthermore, when all else failed, reluctant peasants took up their weapons and tools, barricaded their villages, and repelled or punished predatory hosts.[131] This tactic was the peasant version of the medieval practice of "self-help" *(jiriki kyūsai).* Despite not being as well armed or trained as the samurai, cultivators and other rural folk had ways to resist warrior demands for supplies, men, and grain. I would argue that just as commerce and institutional food relief helped to ameliorate the dire effects of famine, so the peasantry learned to diminish the devastation of war. In both cases, demographic and economic growth must have occurred more readily because of the concrete actions taken by concerned individuals.

Nevertheless, for those areas targeted by warring armies—especially border lands within and between domains *(hande)*—the advent of hungry warriors must have been equivalent to a small, localized famine, especially when they were provisioning through "self-help." Fortunately for residents of the archipelago, however, the tactics of the peasant class described above helped high-ranking samurai around the archipelago to realize the negative consequences of "helping oneself" to provisions, scorched-earth tactics, and kidnap and ransom. As soon as Warring States daimyo consolidated control over an area, they issued strict laws to prohibit the very tactics they had just employed.[132]

The Go-Hōjō from eastern Honshu are a particularly well-documented case, and their records reveal a constant concern to prevent pillage *(ranbō, rōzeki)*, arson, peasant flight *(kakeochi)*, and the needless stripping of upland forests within their territory. From their origins in 1495 until their destruction in 1590, the Go-Hōjō issued approximately 127 orders against plundering, 5 documents mentioning arson, 29 on peasant flight, and 37 prohibiting lumbering.[133]

> We ought to return the peasants at once to their homes and strictly prohibit individuals in the army from plundering and pillaging.[134]

> The people of [certain villages in] Ehara District of Musashi Province should not have to pay taxes *[shoyaku, kuji]* at all beginning next year. The peasants who fled should be called back . . . and caused to stay there.[135]

Musashi was well within the Go-Hōjō domain, and the daimyo was trying to resettle a vacant territory by giving tax relief.

In the case of the Mōri, the first prohibition to stop wayward "men of the province" in Aki from ravaging their rivals' lands went out in 1557:

> *Point:* On plundering by our armies, even though we have strictly forbidden it, it does not stop. Henceforth housemen and samurai units *[shūchū]* who commit even a little pillaging will be killed right away.

> *Point:* When it is difficult to decide whether or not to plunder a certain spot, the matter may be permitted only upon general agreement.[136]

This policy was tied to the return of wayward peasants to the villages they had left. The Date and even Nobunaga tried to prevent wanton devastation as well.[137]

As leader of the massive army that eventually pacified and unified Japan, the hegemon Hideyoshi had the most to gain by banning plunder and resettling the populace. So he issued orders when he defeated the Go-Hōjō in 1590 to keep his troops from taking up lodging in peasant villages, stealing money from commoners, or pillaging fields.[138] He also joined other successful daimyo, such as the Mōri, Tokugawa, and Go-Hōjō, in eventually comprehending the devastating effects of the age-old custom of "self-help" and establishing his own provisioning territory *(kurairi chi),* from which he oversaw the doling out of grains.[139] Armies and navies no longer had to forage as they advanced or collect their provisions as landlords. This new policy, which dated from as early as the 1550s, was much more effective than the strategies of either the Kamakura or Muromachi shogunates, which permitted samurai to grab all that they could from lands where they were stationed or fought. Peasants could count on keeping a substantial portion of every harvest; the stability and predictability of the new system could only encourage demographic and economic growth in the latter decades of the sixteenth century.

Japanese society thereby solved a basic problem of the medieval period: how to provision the military in a reliable and responsible way.[140] Along with the even more fundamental problem of how to feed a growing populace, it was one of the two great issues with which inhabitants of the islands had been struggling since 1150. After 1550, samurai leaders improved upon Yoritomo's (or from a world historical perspective, Hammurabi's) solution in a way favorable to the peasantry and future demographic and economic growth. Warlords not only ended the "forage-as-you-go" policy associated in world history with Sargon of Akkad, but they even did Yoritomo (and Hammurabi) one better by intervening between the soldier and his source of food and income. And when their vassals moved to castle towns, warriors were cut off from the spoils of war for good in most of Japan.

To be sure, it is easy to adopt a "top-down" attitude to the slow but sure working out of the problem of how to provision armies without any "collateral damage." At the same time, however, innumerable peasants—by their striking, absconding, hiding, bribing, negotiating, and in the last resort fighting—were equally important partners to the solution of this age-old difficulty. From the give-and-take of both sides came the new "macroparasitic" relationship forged in 1600. And peasants were the prime beneficiaries, whether through a temporary escape from chronic malnutrition or the routinization of their daily lives.[141]

How should we assess the impact of the Warring States conflict on population? There can be little doubt that it was harmful, as the tactics and behaviors described above imply. The question is how devastating? A certain and precise answer is unavailable at the current level of research, but if most arson and plundering took place only in contested territory, then the war may have become a smaller and smaller factor as daimyo established control over their vassals and domains. Of course, during the battles for supremacy in daimyo domains between 1490 and 1520, most of Japan was likely "contested territory" at one time or another, suggesting a wide circle of devastation. Moreover, with daimyo on campaign virtually every year, fertility may have dropped and mortality risen even more. Given the relatively modest numbers of combatant deaths per battle for most of the epoch; the various systems of peasant "survival and maintenance"; and the ultimate realization forced upon high-ranking warriors that wanton pillage, arson, and kidnapping could damage as well as help their chances for hegemony, however, it seems reasonable to conceive of the war as a barrier to growth that was sometimes sizable but more usually localized and periodic, rapidly receding as greater political unity approached and peace prevailed after 1600.

This chapter has described an apparent paradox. While I have argued that Hayami's population estimate of 12.3 million for 1600 is too low and that the proper range should be about 15–17 million, I have simultaneously offered plentiful evidence that mortality from disease, famine, and war exceeded that during the "Muromachi Optimum." To be sure, there were mitigating circumstances in each case: there is no evidence that syphilis was ever epidemic; trade and charity lessened starvation so that the "spring hungers" were rarer by 1600; and the worst war devastation may have taken place only in battle zones. In a word, examining death rates leads us only part way to a viable theory. To explore the question further, we must consider a myriad of background factors, beginning with agriculture.

TABLE A.1

Comparative Deaths by Decades: Hitachi, 1426–1694

DECADE	MALE	FEMALE	CHILDREN	TOTAL
1426–1435	28	10	0	38
1436–1445	33	3	0	36
1446–1455	62	9	5	76
1456–1465	69	14	2	85
1466–1475	42	4	3	49
1476–1485	46	3	2	51
1486–1495	55	6	1	62
1496–1505	104	8	3	115
1506–1515	16	6	5	27
1516–1525	16	3	2	21
1526–1535	23	12	2	37
1536–1545	30	9	0	39
1546–1555	25	8	0	33
1556–1565	85	17	0	102
1566–1575	35	9	0	44
1576–1585	34	6	0	40
1586–1595	38	7	0	45
1596–1605	68	1	0	69
1606–1615	27	8	0	35
1616–1625	33	17	1	51
1626–1635	31	13	1	45
1636–1645	59	15	0	74
1646–1655	32	19	0	51
1656–1665	71	17	0	88
1666–1675	15	10	0	25
1676–1685	22	26	0	48
1686–1694	19	24	0	43
Total	1,118	284	27	1,429
Average	41.5	10.4	1	52.9

Source: Akahama myōhōji kakochō.

TABLE A.2
Deaths by Month: Hitachi, 1426–1600

MONTH	MALE	FEMALE	TOTAL
1	49	31	80
2	55	15	70
3	50	14	64
4	58	11	69
5	42	21	63
6	46	14	60
7	52	12	64
8	36	17	53
9	37	4	41
10	56	18	74
11	40	20	60
12	32	14	46
Total	553	191	744
Average	46	15.9	62

Source: Same as table A.1.

TABLE A.3
Deaths by Month: Hitachi, 1600–1694

MONTH	MALE	FEMALE	TOTAL
1	30	12	42
2	25	17	42
3	22	13	35
4	34	15	49
5	21	10	31
6	23	16	39
7	33	14	47
8	31	13	44
9	20	11	31
10	22	8	30
11	21	5	26
12	28	9	37
Total	310	143	453
Average	25.8	11.9	37.75

Source: Same as table A.1.

TABLE A.4

Comparative Deaths by Half-Decade: Kyoto and Environs, 1476–1530

YEARS	MALE	FEMALE	CHILDREN	TOTAL
1476–1480	10	1	0	11
1481–1485	7	1	0	8
1486–1490	40	2	0	42
1491–1495	99	7	1	107
1496–1500	152	16	5	173
1501–1505	131	20	5	156
1506–1510	127	16	3	146
1511–1515	125	11	9	145
1516–1520	99	8	1	108
1521–1525	38	1	0	39
1526–1530	30	1	0	31
Total	858	84	24	966
Average	78	7.6	2.2	87.8

Source: Tōji kakochō, as provided by Umata Ayako.

TABLE A.5

Deaths by Month: Kyoto and Environs, 1476–1530

MONTH	DEATHS
1	61
2	48
3	48
4	50
5	79
6	63
7	59
8	63
9	68
10	52
11	39
12	28
Total	658
Average	54.8

Source: Same as table A.4.

TABLE A.6
Comparative Deaths by Decade: Kai and Western Kanto, 1380–1709

DECADE	MALE	FEMALE	CHILDREN	TOTAL
1380–1389	14	7	0	21
1390–1399	7	8	0	15
1400–1409	12	7	0	19
1410–1419	21	8	0	29
1420–1429	7	7	0	14
1430–1439	108	23	0	131
1440–1449	83	39	0	122
1450–1459	47	22	0	69
1460–1469	3	7	0	10
1470–1479	61	47	0	108
1480–1489	84	90	0	174
1490–1499	100	58	0	158
1500–1509	82	57	0	139
1510–1519	40	28	0	68
1520–1529	58	38	0	96
1530–1539	63	47	0	110
1540–1549	26	27	0	53
1550–1559	5	5	0	10
1560–1569	13	6	0	19
1570–1579	4	1	0	5
1580–1589	11	11	0	22
1590–1599	11	8	0	19
1600–1609	37	38	0	75
1610–1619	72	48	0	120
1620–1629	38	42	0	80
1630–1639	55	60	0	115
1640–1649	55	37	0	92
1650–1659	70	55	0	125
1660–1669	65	24	0	89
1670–1679	19	0	0	19
1680–1689	80	23	36/3[a]	142
1690–1699	35	24	2/2[a]	63
1700–1709	13	15	4/1[a]	33
Total	1,399	917	48	2,364
Average	43.9	27.8	—	71.6

Source: Takano, *"Ichirenji kakochō."*
[a]Males/females.

TABLE A.7

Deaths by Month: Kai and Western Kanto, 1380–1590

MONTH	MALE	FEMALE	TOTAL
1	64	44	108
2	124	78	202
3	67	50	117
4	80	54	134
5	77	28	105
6	46	33	79
7	56	42	98
8	59	37	96
9	64	30	94
10	77	44	121
11	40	40	80
12	60	37	97
Total	814	517	1,331
Average	67.8	43.1	110.9

Source: Same as table A.6.

TABLE A.8

Deaths by Month: Kai and Western Kanto, 1591–1702

MONTH	MALE	FEMALE	TOTAL
1	46	39	85
2	47	35	82
3	38	34	72
4	58	27	85
5	43	13	56
6	40	28	68
7	60	31	91
8	44	31	75
9	35	30	65
10	48	28	76
11	27	23	50
12	46	37	83
Total	532	356	888
Average	44.3	29.7	74

Source: Same as table A.6.

TABLE A.9
Comparative Deaths by Decade: Shimōsa, 1395–1705

DECADE	MALE	FEMALE	CHILDREN	TOTAL
1395–1405	15	4	1	20
1406–1415	43	12	0	55
1416–1425	50	23	1	74
1426–1435	43	24	1	68
1436–1445	75	48	2	125
1446–1455	73	39	1	113
1456–1465	79	61	9	149
1466–1475	146	87	12	245
1476–1485	83	66	5	154
1486–1495	147	73	13	233
1496–1505	114	69	2	185
1506–1515	80	49	4	133
1516–1525	65	48	6	119
1526–1535	52	24	0	76
1536–1545	38	18	0	56
1546–1555	40	14	1	55
1556–1565	14	8	0	22
1566–1575	35	7	0	42
1576–1585	76	16	1	93
1586–1595	112	43	0	155
1596–1605	118	28	0	146
1606–1615	48	12	0	60
1616–1625	48	22	1	71
1626–1635	37	11	0	48
1636–1645	52	21	0	73
1646–1655	51	22	1	74
1656–1665	49	18	1	68
1666–1675	26	7	1	34
1676–1685	12	5	0	17
1686–1695	12	3	1	16
1696–1705	20	7	2	29
Total	1,853	889	66	2,808
Average	59.8	28.7	2.1	90.6

Source: Hondoji kakochō in CKS.

TABLE A.10
Deaths by Month: Shimōsa, 1395–1600

MONTH	MALE		FEMALE		TOTAL	
1	442	(149)[a]	149	(69)	591	(218)
2	395	(124)	133	(55)	528	(179)
3	432	(141)	153	(69)	585	(210)
4	469	(161)	139	(68)	608	(229)
5	407	(131)	125	(51)	532	(182)
6	496	(169)	163	(78)	659	(247)
7	410	(119)	123	(59)	533	(178)
8	409	(144)	118	(54)	527	(198)
9	286	(102)	102	(42)	388	(144)
10	289	(95)	97	(46)	386	(141)
11	366	(121)	73	(27)	439	(148)
12	320	(97)	108	(49)	428	(146)
Total	4,721	(1,553)	1,483	(667)	6,204	(2,220)
Average	393.4	(129.4)	123.6	(55.6)	517	(185)

Source: Same as table A.9.
[a]Figures in parentheses represent entries including both year and month of death.

TABLE A.11
Deaths by month: Shimōsa, 1600–1707

MONTH	MALE	FEMALE	TOTAL
1	44	12	56
2	40	15	55
3	48	15	63
4	53	21	74
5	61	18	79
6	63	24	87
7	86	39	125
8	61	22	83
9	56	17	73
10	74	25	99
11	40	15	55
12	50	10	60
Total	676	233	909
Average	56.3	19.4	75.8

Source: Same as table A.9.

TABLE A.12
Infant Mortality at Kokubunji and Hida's Ōgenji, 1785–1970

KOKUBUNJI			
YEARS	TOTAL	CHILDREN	PERCENT
1785–1799	214	93	43.5
1800–1819	234	85	36.3
1820–1839	250	94	38
1840–1859	239	105	43.9
1860–1879	253	100	39.5
1880–1899	347	161	46.4
1900–1919	521	278	53.4
1920–1940	774	370	47.8

ŌGENJI	
YEARS	PERCENT TO AGE FIVE
1781–1800	47.7
1801–1820	47.3
1821–1840	42.1
1841–1860	55.5
1861–1880	50.4
1881–1900	43.1
1901–1920	33.1
1921–1940	32.6
1941–1960	21.5
1961–1970	3.8

Source: *Kokubunji-shi shi*, pp. 358, 362.

TABLE A.13
Adult Deaths in Kokubunji, 1785–1940

YEARS	MALE	FEMALE	RATIO (F=100)
1785–1799	65	56	116
1800–1819	77	72	107
1820–1839	79	77	103
1840–1859	67	67	100
1860–1879	85	68	125
1880–1899	94	92	102
1900–1919	120	123	98
1920–1940	216	188	115

Source: *Kokubunji-shi shi*, pp. 358, 362.

6

The Brighter Side of Life

Agriculture, Commerce, and
Family Life, 1450–1600

Deaths from disease, famine, and war were common during the last century and a half of the medieval age, but scholars may read these factors in various ways, and there is a limit to what these data can tell demographers. Furthermore, there may have been compensating variables, such as a rise in the birthrate or an increase in the number of infants and young children surviving to adulthood. Without an examination of a multitude of other economic and social components, the picture is incomplete, and it is difficult to be confident about the previously proposed population range of 15–17 million for 1600.

This chapter attempts to describe and analyze the society and economy of the period 1450–1600. Scholars have long supposed that the Warring States epoch saw considerable expansion in agriculture as new and better engineering techniques combined with a further dispersion of the agronomic and social changes of the preceding epoch to lead to a more plentiful and nutritious food supply. Other economic background variables, such as trade, industry, and cities, all strongly suggest growth. Case studies show how commerce came to be a central aspect of daimyo economic policy. There were also numerous advances in industry, especially in mining, architecture, and the manufacture of cotton cloth. With the expansion of trade and industry, Japan continued to urbanize, more so during these 150 years than at any previous time. Regarding fertility, there is as usual nothing concrete on which to base any conclusions, but the corporate village and stem family both continued to spread, perhaps providing stronger support systems for children. At the same time, more people falling into the servant class probably meant at least a temporary drop in the birthrate. A visible improvement in the physical well-being of commoners, however, implies a greater chance of survival for all. In sum, the catalogue of background factors generally fits a picture of growth and supports a higher figure for Japan's population in 1600.

AGRICULTURE

With the apparently constant mayhem of the era 1467–1590, it might seem as though agricultural development would have been minimal at best, nil at worst. The Warring States era was not an easy time to make a living for cultivators—at least until daimyo domains took shape—and then various reforms were effected in the late sixteenth century. The surprising point is, however, that even a conflict as all-embracing as that described in chapter 5 could not put an end to what had started in the late Kamakura period.[1] Farmers continued to clear small parcels of land, build more and better irrigation works, and raise a variety of crops, enhancing productivity little by little. What follows is an assessment of agricultural development on a regional basis, beginning with western Japan.

Satsuma

Among the most renowned of all land records are those of giant Iriki Estate in southern Kyushu. The case of Kiyoshiki Village in the Iriki complex reveals how peasants of the late medieval period opened this region.[2] One of nine villages in Iriki, Kiyoshiki had basically four land forms. At the bottom lay about sixty square kilometers of alluvial fan, fed by several rivers; the settlement was nestled in the uplands to avoid flooding. The alluvial area contained swamps *(teishitsu den),* but most of it was well drained *(kanden)* by the seventeenth century. Moreover, near the mountains the plains rose in plateaus, allowing for easy irrigation from the nearby mountain runoff. Finally, Kiyoshiki had dry fields spread in the higher reaches, while villagers farmed the mountains in swidden style.

Two records, one dating from 1322 and the other from just after 1500, suggest how Kiyoshiki developed. First, the area under rice cultivation jumped dramatically from 61 to about 192 *chō* over these two centuries, more than trebling the arable. These new rice paddies could be found in the alluvial plains, where farmers were able to work the low-lying land because of better irrigation works and widespread use of the Champa species. They also originated in the higher reaches of the plain because land that had once depended upon the amount of rainfall to determine whether or not farmers planted now benefited from more constant access to water. A final major advance came in the conversion of dry fields to rice paddies. In some cases, peasants turned even lands once used only for slash-and-burn cropping first into semiannual dry fields, then to yearly producers, and finally into rice paddies.

Figures from the early Tokugawa period indicate that these trends continued throughout the sixteenth and seventeenth centuries. Dominated by the Shimazu family and relatively untouched by civil war, Kiyoshiki Village stands as a good example of what happened in those parts of Japan where the trends of the "Muromachi Optimum" were allowed to play themselves out unimpeded by constant disasters.[3] By 1750, the area under cultivation had multiplied several times, although farming was still not as intensive as more productive areas of the archipelago.

Western Honshu

It has become a truism that Warring States daimyo led the way in land clearance, riparian works, and intensification of agrarian techniques.[4] Presumably, warlords knew that expansion of the arable would supply them with more grain and soldiers, and therefore they pursued such policies eagerly. While research over the last twenty years has generally shown that daimyo were more interested in destruction than in construction, the Mōri of western Honshu, who practiced economic warfare so ruthlessly, occasionally invoked their authority to facilitate agrarian development.

For instance, the Mōri used the construction of roads and irrigation works in Aki to gain better control of the "men of the province."[5] An oath *(kishōmon)* signed by 32 local notables in 1532 suggests that the Mōri were able to coordinate efforts to have ditches dug and sluices built in flood-prone lands. The oath stated that the river changed its course practically every year, resulting in one *kokujin*'s fields receiving the right amount of water in one year, none the next, and too much the third. In return for a pledge to fight for the daimyo, the Mōri agreed to collect fees from each local lord and coordinate river control efforts. Apparently this policy was successful because in 1550 another oath directed to the Mōri and signed by 238 former "men of the province" pledged that the signatories would work under the Mōri in all matters pertaining to "sluices, ditches, and roads." In effect, the Mōri bought their vassals' loyalty in battle by helping them solve their agrarian problems.

Shikoku

The seventh chapter of *Seiryō ki,* a military tale set in the sixteenth century, contains what may be the most detailed portrayal of contemporary agriculture. Once widely called "Japan's first agrarian treatise," this chapter, also independently known as *A Collection of Monthly Agrarian Instructions for a New People (Shinmin kangetsu shū),* presents daunting problems of dating and authenticity, however.

According to the introduction, Doi Seiryō (1546–1629), a vassal of the Saionji warrior family in Iyo, asked one of his erstwhile followers, Matsuura Sōan, several questions about agriculture to aid the local peasants, and the *Agrarian Instructions* was the result.[6] Unfortunately, several points indicate that this text is the product of the mid- to late seventeenth century at the earliest. First, it is not mentioned in other sources until somewhere between the 1660s and 1680s. Second, it is clear that the author considered peasants a separate class from warriors, a development that did not take place until the late sixteenth century. Third, various points about the agricultural technology described in *Agrarian Instructions* seem too advanced or out of place. For example, the percentage of paddies double-cropped in wheat is too high; the treatise listed the watermelon *(suika),* which did not enter Japan until sometime between 1661 and 1680, as a garden vegetable.[7] Finally, the conclusion contains a long passage encouraging "lazy farmers" to cultivate the three Confucian virtues of knowledge, benevolence, and courage. There can be little doubt that *Agrarian Instructions* achieved its present form almost a century after the Warring States era had ended and that it reflects many Tokugawa-period practices.[8]

Before we totally reject this text as having no value for an understanding of sixteenth-century agriculture, however, it is important to recognize that some sections certainly do exemplify conditions of that era. First, there is the reason for its composition:

In 1564, when Master Seiryō was nineteen, he called together the elders and asked their opinions:

We bannermen of the Saionji House—Lord Sanemitsu and Lord Kimihiro—have no resolve and are idlers; our enemies take us lightly. Yet this is certainly an evaluation done by those who do not know conditions here. They need to think thoroughly. The Ichijō of Tosa and the Ōtomo of Bungo have established marital ties and work together. We have great rivals east and west. In Awa and Sanuki there is Miyoshi Sakyōdayū; in western Honshu there is Mōri Terumoto; are not both of these enemies that allow us no rest? Originally the Saionji were a proud family; thus great enemies on all sides never squeezed our territory, and we were never under the control of any general. We struck and pacified several strong rivals attacking our branch families, even occupying twelve provinces.

Even that House of Saionji, however, had strong enemies on all sides, and recently we have been driven to prepare fortresses. *When we take refuge there, the enemy forces plan their attacks according to when our wheat and rice fields have just ripened. Then they pillage until there is no more to take. For that reason, our peasants have no time to rest, and they are wasted even as they want the harvest that they suffered so mightily to produce. Rich and poor, high and low status alike, are driven to poverty, and many die along the roads.*

Investigating conditions, I have found this to be the truth. *Now the realm is in great disorder; it is the same in every province. Over half the dead have starved to death. The lord [ryōshu] thinks that military and economic affairs are unrelated and has no will to press for more cultivation. Because of this, the enemy plans the time when the harvest in that province will mature and knowing the proper season, attacks. It is always like this.*[9]

Later, the informant Matsuura states that he prefers early ripening rice to keep enemy troops from timing their raids so easily.[10] An important reason that the author compiled this text was to help farmers deal with the depredations of Warring States samurai.

Moreover, other facts hint at a Warring States core within *Agrarian Instructions*. The measurements utilized are those from before Hideyoshi's great Taikō surveys; the names of estate officials *(namoto)* all come from the sixteenth century and earlier. The structure of the peasant class also reflects Warring States society: there are well-to-do cultivators *(jōnō)* and dependent, "lazy" ones *(genō)*. The latter term probably refers to the dependent class of farmers in servitude, the *ge'nin*. There is no mention of a middle class of peasants dwelling in nuclear families, such as scholars would expect for the Tokugawa period. Finally, only about 10 percent of the *Agrarian Instructions* is devoted to technological issues;

rather, the contents are closer to the agricultural customs described in chapter 1, *kannō*, or "encouraging farming." This text belongs midway between the practices of the Kamakura period and Japan's tradition of agricultural treatises dating from the early modern era.[11]

If *Agrarian Instructions* represents cultivation practices in Iyo in the late sixteenth century *to a certain degree*, then what does it tell us?[12] First, it advises peasants to choose the location of their homes with reference to paddy irrigation; this point alone made the difference between a good peasant and a dependent. The treatise also encourages the application of fertilizer, twice during planting. Peasants were to use livestock to break up the soil and produce a fine mud, but dependents suffered because few had animals. Once cultivators prepared the soil, they should learn the proper season to plant; the difference between wealthier farmers and the dependent class was that the latter always acted too early or too late. From the lord's point of view, reducing the number of dependents, who farmed extensively, and increasing the productive "upper-class farmers," who cropped their lands intensively, was a constant concern.

The text relates a long list of crops and when to plant them—vegetables of all types (among them beans, radishes, turnips, and eggplant), millet, barley, wheat, and of course rice (ninety-six strains). There was upland rice; Champa rice; and early-, midseason, and late-ripening rice. There were eight varieties of Champa rice alone, and the author sings its praises for its resistance to drought, winds, and insects. *Agrarian Instructions* did not neglect dry crops; there were twelve strains of barley, for instance. It also referred to tubers, indigo, and a large variety of fruits (including melons). Agrarian historians have checked these plants with those being grown between 1550 and 1650 and found a generally high correlation between the two.[13]

One of the most convincing passages discusses the different types of soils, judged by their color, shape, and consistency. The best soil was purple, and the worst was white; there follows a description of volcanic and sandy soils and trash *(gomi)*. Unlike in the section on crops, however, there was little attempt at soil improvement; there are no suggestions to apply more fertilizer or labor. This section was close to sixteenth-century conditions because it hinted at limitations in irrigation and other technologies that might have brought greater yields had they been utilized.[14]

Concerning rice farming, results from *Agrarian Instructions* indicate a mixture of earlier and later technologies. Four different types of paddies received attention: those that could be double-cropped with wheat;

dry paddy yielding one harvest; low-lying, swampy rice fields; and mountain fields. While this variety seems authentic for sixteenth-century Iyo, the percentage of paddy double-cropping is too high at 30 percent.[15] Yet the twelve varieties of early-ripening rice loomed much larger than the mere 1 percent farmed in the Tokugawa period, and the text specifically advised peasants to plant these strains to avoid plundering by troops. The repeated references to Champa rice also fit trends of the late medieval age. The early modern customs of fertilizing dried-out paddy fields, soaking seedlings prior to planting, employing deep plowing, and then planting late-ripening rice are not evident in the *Agrarian Instructions*.[16]

One final authentic passage deals with the amount of labor expended per *chō* of paddy land and 1.25 *chō* of dry field. For paddies, farmers utilized 493 labor units, of which 200 came from women. In other words, it required about forty-nine days of one person's labor to harvest rice from one *tan*, with variations factored in for each type of paddy. This discussion fits a society concerned about peasant migration and flight.

In sum, no one can deny that *Agrarian Instructions* shows Iyo agriculture in a transitional period. Yet the description of peasant society, the emphasis upon early-ripening and Champa rice, and the variety of other grains and vegetables all reflect the late Warring States era. A text detailing everything from soils to tools to crops to labor units suggests a more sophisticated, "scientific" attitude toward agrarian activities than was evident in the ancient or early medieval eras.[17]

The Kinai

The Screen Showing Scenes within and outside of the Capital (Rakuchū rakugai byōbu) is a source similar to *Agrarian Instructions* in that it portrays Kinai society in the late sixteenth and seventeenth centuries.[18] It is difficult to distinguish earlier from later agrarian practices, but several scenes are of interest. First, both husband and wife sow the seedbeds for rice; livestock eat the stubble after peasants have harvested the field. The screen also depicts oxen plowing and smoothing the rice paddy, even as peasants use spades. Wheat fields are also noticeable, both as they ripen and as they are harvested.

None of this should be surprising, but a third group of panels suggests that there was a considerable market in selling vegetables to urban residents. In one screen, cultivators apply two buckets of manure; others show planting and harvesting. These final scenes indicate that the area around Kyoto had already come to specialize in truck gardens by the 1500s. Such regional specialization indicates that both agricultural and commercial progress was taking place.

Ōmi

Ōmi Province, located on the doorstep of the capital, contains many interesting examples of agricultural development for the 1450–1600 period. One, Tokuchin *ho,* lay within Imabori Village.[19] In fourteenth-century Tokuchin, there were four types of fields: dry fields, dry plots mixed with rice paddies, rice lands cropped fully in some years and much less in others, and stable rice fields. The primary reason for the fluctuations in the third category was an inadequate supply of water, probably because of poor irrigation or an overreliance upon rainfall.

Between 1351 and 1400, Imabori had thirteen parcels producing exclusively dry crops and only two rice paddies. Over the next fifty years, the number of parcels more than tripled to forty, adding seventeen new dry fields and five rice paddies. From 1451 to 1500, when war ravaged the Kinai, dry fields remained about the same (twenty-seven), while stable rice lands multiplied to thirteen. Even in 1556, when daimyo were struggling for control over Ōmi, the number of dry fields was higher than in the fourteenth century at seventeen, and rice paddies remained on a par with the mid-fifteenth century at six. By the 1570s, there were twenty-five *chō* of wet paddies and twenty-eight of dry fields. Development took place rapidly during the late sixteenth century, after a more difficult period between 1500 and 1556. Just as in the Iriki case, farmers first converted land to dry cropping and then to wet-rice production. Finally, documents show that cultivators sold harvests from dry fields at market.[20]

Eastern Honshu: The Takeda

When historians of the Warring States period want to emphasize the agrarian accomplishments of daimyo, they always give "Shingen's dike" *(Shingen zutsumi)* as the classic example. According to this view, the Kamanashi River, flowing south, came crashing into the Midai River, running eastward from the Japan Alps, causing constant flooding.[21] Shingen presumably had giant stones moved to stabilize the course of both rivers and eventually separated them into two different streambeds. He had a samurai overseer *(shōgi gashira)* supervise the carving of these giant stones. He then built another dike at Ryūō called Kasumi Wall. Eventually there was a whole complex, all raised at Shingen's behest. These labors purportedly took place between 1542 and 1557.

Such efforts would naturally have required great numbers of workmen and quantities of stones and other materials. Yet none of Shingen's fortifications used stones, much less the giant ones proposed for Shingen's dike. Moreover, there is not a single document discussing the project. Finally, given the fragmented nature of landholdings in the area, it is doubtful that Shingen could have summoned the power to move villages and change people's hereditary lands. In sum, it is highly unlikely that Shingen singlehandedly saved the day by having a whole complex of dikes and dams constructed.[22] Like so many other agrarian works attributed to daimyo, the story of Shingen's dike is primarily a product of Tokugawa-period lore.

Just because Shingen was not the main actor, however, does not mean that he did not have a role to play in advancing irrigation projects. In 1560, Shingen issued a one-line exemption from taxes *(munabechi sen)* for peasants in return for their bringing the waters around Ryūō under control. In 1563, he ordered villagers who wanted to build dams and dikes "to use their own legs." Like the Mōri, Shingen encouraged and managed the ongoing efforts of cultivators most concerned with flooding. The same was also true of Shingen's heir Katsuyori.[23]

Flooding was a common problem in Kai, according to the reliable *Katsuyama ki*. Even in the Ichirenji death register, which records the demise of many people from Kōfu, a common occupation was "flood engineer" *(kawayoke)*. In other words, the daimyo did not create the vaunted Shingen dike system, but it was the product of the constant efforts of farmers and others over the entire Warring States era. The land was not Shingen's direct domain; "men of the province" and peasant landlords controlled the fields. The Takedas' contribution was to coordinate and facilitate local efforts, as a way of obtaining recognition from the populace.[24]

Moreover, there are similar examples for another region in the Takeda domain—Shinano in 1569 and 1579. The energy and materials for the water control efforts came from the farmers; in the words of one author, it was as if Shingen threw a net over the entire region and linked the individual efforts into a single, state-recognized work. Shingen and the other daimyo were first concerned with winning battles, which meant destroying their enemies in economic terms; cultivators, who lived and died on the basis of their productivity, provided the primary impetus for the agricultural growth of Kai and Shinano in this epoch.[25]

Eastern Honshu: The Go-Hōjō

There are at least twenty-six cases of land development within the Go-Hōjō domain (mostly Musashino and the Tamagawa, Arakawa, and Tonegawa plains), dating from 1556 to 1590. Often cultivators returned to abandoned villages on Go-Hōjō orders to redevelop previously productive fields. One document reads as follows:

> Concerning Zuishin's house [*yashiki*] in Ōgidani [in Kamakura in Sagami], we [the Go-Hōjō] have received your request. You ought to make progress right away. We order the cultivators to open lands. This deed is for future reference.

> 4/18 [1571] [Go-Hōjō] Yasunari.[26]

Like the Takeda and other daimyo, the Go-Hōjō were primarily facilitators representative of central power; peasants, often organized by merchants or local lords, did the hard work.[27] There are thirty-one examples of the opening of new lands or the redevelopment of abandoned paddies in Musashino, with farmers applying for the right to convert the land to fields and then receiving an order from the Go-Hōjō to do so.[28]

In addition to these cases, scholars often cite the Imagawa and Date as promoting land clearance and the building of irrigation facilities; the prominence of those daimyo should come as no surprise since eastern Honshu was relatively undeveloped as late as the sixteenth century.[29] As scholarship stands now, however, the Warring States lords have lost their role as the primary agents of agricultural development to those who supplied the labor, tools, and know-how and stood to benefit the most by the activities—that is, merchants, "men of the province," and peasants.[30]

Population and Agriculture, 1450–1600

I drew the above examples from all over the archipelago, and they suggest a continuation of the expansive trend of the previous era. Moreover, because many documents did not survive the mayhem of war, this list undoubtedly does not exhaust the actual number of cases. To evaluate the argument that demographic and agricultural growth continued despite a greater toll from war and famine, a closer examination of Hayami's calculations for land under cultivation and total product in 1600 is in order. (See tables 5.1 and 5.2 above.)

First, tables 5.1 and 5.2 imply that a higher population figure for 1600 fits more smoothly with early-Tokugawa aggregate agricultural data than does Hayami's count of about 12 million. According to his reasoning, in 1600 it required 1.721 *tan* to sustain one person; that number then dropped precipitously to 1.37 *tan* for 1650 and to 1.026 *tan* for 1700. In contrast, if we accept Kitō's estimate of around 15 million inhabitants (as in table 6.1), the number of *tan* per person in 1600 comes to 1.38, a much smaller and (I would argue) more realistic average than Hayami's. At the same time, Kitō's average still leaves considerable room for improvement in the seventeenth century. Saitō's estimate of 17 million yields a figure of 1.22 *tan* per person, still indicating progress during the early Tokugawa, but not as much. Kitō's and Saitō's averages for early Tokugawa-period *koku* per person are 1.32 and 1.16 respectively. These numbers are also considerable reductions from Hayami's averages and consequently diminish the impact of the demographic expansion and agrarian improvements of the seventeenth century—some might argue by too much. Yet even they do not deny all-important advances for the 1600s.

Second, the figures in table 5.1 help us to evaluate agricultural growth over the Warring States period. Table 6.2 converts Hayami's figures on total arable and *kokudaka* for 1600 from Tokugawa to Nara measurements to make them commensurate with the numbers used above in this book. Because the Tokugawa-period *tan* was about 30 percent smaller than that of the ancient and medieval periods, I adjusted Hayami's total

TABLE 6.1

Kitō's, Saitō's, and Fujino's Population Estimates and Hayami's Farming Data for 1600

	POPULATION (N) (MILLIONS)	ARABLE (R) (THOUSANDS OF *chō*)	KOKUDAKA (Y) (THOUSANDS OF *koku*)	R/N (*Tan*)	Y/N
Kitō	15	2,065	19,371	1.38	1.32
Saitō	17	—	—	1.22	1.16
Fujino	19	—	—	1.09	1.04

Note: All figures are Tokugawa-era units.

TABLE 6.2
Pre-1600 Conversions for Hayami's Figures for 1600

ARABLE (R)[a] (THOUSANDS OF CHŌ)	KOKUDAKA (Y)[b]	Y/R	AREA TO SUPPORT ONE PERSON (TAN)
1,589	49,327,500	3.1	1.10
1,589	44,394,750 (-10%)	2.79	1.23
1,589	41,928,375 (-15%)	2.64	1.29
1,589	39,462,000 (-20%)	2.48	1.38
1,589	36,995,625 (-25%)	2.33	1.47
1,589	34,529,250 (-30%)	2.17	1.57

[a]The comparable pre-1600 arable was calculated by reducing Hayami's figure by 30 percent as per J.I. Nakamura, *Agricultural Production and Economic Development.*
[b]The conversion to Nara *koku* was done at one Tokugawa unit=2.5 Nara units. The calculations for this table assume that Hayami's total for arable is correct but that the *kokudaka* numbers include other economic activities in addition to agriculture. From row one to row two, *kokudaka* were reduced by 10 percent and then by 5 percent thereafter.

down to 1,588,462 Nara-period *chō* under cultivation in 1600.[31] By comparison, *Shūgai shō* noted that in 1150 acreage under cultivation was a mere 956,000 *chō*. While much of the advance undoubtedly took place between 1280 and 1450, it seems unrealistic to assume that there was no expansion between 1450 and 1600. For instance, if half the increase took place before 1450 and half after, then land under cultivation would have jumped by an impressive 28 percent over the last century and one-half of the medieval epoch.[32]

Third, rice productivity seems to have grown, perhaps substantially according to pre-1600 units, depending upon several factors. (See table 6.2.) The Tokugawa *koku* was 2.5 times larger than that of the Nara period, resulting in a total of 49,327,500 ancient *koku* in 1600 when we use Hayami's figure from table 5.1. Simple division computes to 3.1 *koku* per *tan* (all Nara units), or a leap of .82 *koku* over the 2.28 *koku* per *tan* computed for 1450. Of course, this computation presumes that Hayami's count for *kokudaka* in 1600 is accurate and includes only agricultural yields.

For example, the 3.1 *koku* average may drop if we retain Hayami's total figure for arable but place less faith in his *kokudaka* tally or adjust to account for nonagricultural production. Reducing Hayami's *kokudaka* number by various percentages to account for industrial or other production, as in table 6.2, provides less room for growth in per unit yields, as well as a higher figure for the area needed to support one person, during the Warring States period. Subtracting as much as 30 percent leads to a net loss in per unit yields and a consequent increase in the arable necessary to support a person over the epoch 1450–1600—an unlikely but not impossible outcome. Even when we take these variables into consideration, however, most figures would be considerably higher than the 2.28 *koku* average harvest calculated for 1450, suggesting substantial growth in wet-rice productivity and a decrease in rice acreage necessary to maintain an individual over the Warring States period. Omitting the bottom number, I found that increases in productivity ranged from 2 to 36 percent.

Viewed in this way, the gain in per-unit rice productivity between 1450 and 1600 appears to have been sizable. Even the smaller average of 2.79 *koku* per *tan*, for instance, means that over the 150 years, rice productivity grew by about .15 percent per year—much faster than the snail's pace from 700 to 1280 (.05 percent) although somewhat less than in the era from 1280 to 1450 (.24 percent). Moreover, according to the 2.79 *koku* average, in 1600 it required 1.23 *tan* in rice to sustain a person, whereas it took 2.17 *tan* in 700, 1.81 *tan* in 1280, and 1.50 *tan* in 1450. Almost whatever pre-1600 value we assume, it should be clear that *from this point of view*, despite the warfare and famine from 1450 to 1600, arable land and rice productivity continued to record gains, as described in the cases outlined above.

There is, however, a catch to this line of thinking. (See table 6.3.) When the pre-1600 productivity figures are converted to Tokugawa *koku* per *tan*, the period from 1450 to 1600 records a large diminution. Even if we attribute all of Hayami's *koku* to agrarian production, the drop is still .275 *koku* per *tan*. Why should this be so? One possibility is that the Kamakura and Muromachi figures are incorrect; either the calculations for 1280 and 1450 were too optimistic or the medieval measuring units were smaller than anticipated. We may attempt to compensate in several ways. For example, if the measuring unit used in 1450 was only 1.5 times the Nara volume—and not 1.75, as posited in chapter 4—then the yield in 1450 drops to .9 Tokugawa *koku* per *tan*, a much more reasonable estimate, at least in terms of early modern units. The new number also fits better with those from 1700 and 1720. Even then, however, the period from 1450 to 1600 may still record a slippage, depending on how we interpret Hayami's figures.

TABLE 6.3

Agricultural Productivity in Tokugawa-Period Measures, 700–1720

YEAR	YIELD[a]
700	0.48
1280	0.85
1450	1.23
1600	0.955[b]
1650	0.983
1700	1.078
1720	1.094

[a]Yield is computed in *koku/tan,* assuming that the Nara *koku* was 0.4 and the Kamakura and Muromachi units were 0.6 of the Edo-period measures. The rate of conversion for the *tan* is noted in the text.
[b]This figure and those below are all Hayami's. See table 5.1. The 0.955 number is the highest possible, assuming all *koku* were agricultural.

What is more, reducing the per-unit yield for 1450 causes another problem. The new tally for 1450, .9 Tokugawa *koku* per *tan,* is just barely above that calculated for 1280 (.85 *koku*). The new yield for 1450 is probably too low, given the sizable agrarian improvements of the era 1280–1450.[33] In essence, when Tokugawa units are utilized, we are trapped in a dilemma regarding the per-unit rice yield of 1450: either the number is too high for 1600 or too low for 1280.

Another possibility is that the numbers for 1600 are just plain wrong. After all, that year witnessed the end of a long period of turmoil, and no one can guarantee that the tax collector or land surveyor was honest or accurate. Even Hayami admits that numbers for arable and product in 1600 are mere estimates.

If the numbers in table 6.3 are correct, then at least two explanations come to mind for the unexpected drop in productivity from 1450 to 1600. First, the figures for 1600 could be showing the effects of the long civil war. In chapter 5 we discussed the everyday struggle of commoners for survival among armies bent on plunder, rape, and arson. Productivity may have declined moderately despite the evidence of land clearance and the construction of riparian works. Yet the Muromachi figure is still too high—higher than that for 1720, when statistics are good and everyone agrees that the agrarian economy had been growing for at least a century. Second, since most of the land clearance occurred in eastern Honshu, there is a strong possibility that dry fields predominated. Because yields are much smaller for crops such as wheat, barley, and millet than for wet rice, the shrinkage in productivity may have been the result of more non-rice food crops. In any case, the loss of productivity from 1450 to 1600 as measured in Tokugawa units, if real, constitutes a difficult puzzle.

As in previous chapters, the degree of error for even the early Tokugawa-period numbers is apt to be high. Two points seem certain, however. First, the late fifteenth and sixteenth centuries witnessed sizable increases in arable and rice productivity. Second, that growth was probably accompanied by a considerable demographic expansion—more than Hayami's figure of 12.3 million. The main characters in this story were Japan's commoner men and women.

COMMERCE, INDUSTRY, AND CITIES

If the record on agriculture is subject to varying interpretations, there is less doubt that trade, manufacturing, and urban centers all grew noticeably during the period 1450–1600. In a sense, conflict itself stimulated commerce and industry even as armies devastated rural borderlands; there was an ever-growing demand on the part of daimyo for provisions, cash, guns, uniforms, and other products—a true continuation of the Muromachi boom. And we have seen that the war even revived a market in human beings—for services of all kinds. Together with increases in trade and manufacturing, the archipelago witnessed probably its greatest period of urbanization so far, with nearly a million persons resident in towns and cities by 1600.

Trade

As I implied in the discussion of Takeda trafficking in humans, it is convenient to characterize commerce during the late fifteenth and sixteenth centuries as part of a war economy.[34] To be more specific, Warring States daimyo, whose main concern was the prosecution of hostilities, tried to guarantee that they were the major organizers of and chief beneficiaries from economic activity. There were both "rational" and "irrational" aspects to this control; Warring States lords were Janus-faced figures looking toward both the future and the past. Under this system, Kyoto and the Kinai remained important centers for consumer goods, but centrifugal forces pulling toward the myriad domains increased in importance.

The continuing vitality of commerce is part of the demographic story, but since others have already outlined it in English and it deserves book-length treatment on its own, I will limit this discussion to some generalizations followed by four specific cases.[35]

To begin with, many Warring States daimyo collected taxes in coin, especially in central Honshu and the Kanto. Major warlords, such as the Go-Hōjō and Takeda, assessed land values in cash and then used their revenues to purchase war materiel and other goods. They surveyed parts of their domains, and when they had finished, the monetary tax rate was frequently higher than previous levies had been. Daimyo also utilized this cash land tax *(kandaka)* as a lever to obtain more fighting men and more thorough control over village life. The lords of eastern Honshu had a greater incentive and were more successful in adopting this system, in contrast to those of western Japan, because coins were fungible and rare in their large, agrarian domains.[36] In sum, the application of this monetary land tax stimulated market development in the backwaters of eastern Honshu, expanding the Muromachi commercial boom into new territory. Kyoto and the greater Kinai were still the hub, but market forces were achieving greater penetration into new areas.[37]

In such circumstances, markets continued to spring up all over the archipelago, especially in the Kanto. In Musashino alone, evidence exists for over sixty such entities, set up at intervals of two or three miles. Records indicate that as many as three hundred merchants sold their wares there.[38] In addition to these regular markets, periodic ones opened for business six times a month; there are data for twenty-three, mostly in central and eastern Honshu.[39]

Warring States lords wrote laws governing commerce and markets.[40] Notably, they undertook the unification of weights and measures in their domains, a system later followed by Hideyoshi on a wider scale. At the same time, Warring States daimyo acted as mercantilists in trade, prohibiting the export of certain products essential to the war effort, such as grains, lumber, iron, and silver. A counterpart to this policy was the preferential treatment given to traders hawking rare goods, such as fish, salt, and seaweed in landlocked provinces like Kai. Warlords also tried to prevent merchants from buying or selling directly to consumers outside of recognized markets. Despite the enforcement of their own controls, daimyo generally banned their vassals (erstwhile "men of the province") from interrupting the free flow of goods, labor, and cash at home.

The multiplication of new commercial centers was due in no small part to a reduction in or elimination of toll barriers. As the Muromachi shogunate declined, it attempted to throw up more barriers in the Kinai to increase its revenues. The experiment merely reduced the volume of trade through its barriers along the Yodo River and in Hyōgo, and soon they were recognized as failures.[41] Cunning merchants switched to the free city of Sakai to transship their wares, and the port prospered until the late 1500s.[42] By 1550, free markets *(rakuichi)* were open for business throughout central Honshu and along the Eastern Sea Route *(Tōkai dō)*; twenty-six extended from Aizu in northeastern Japan to Hakata in northern Kyushu.[43]

Free markets placed pressures on the old arrangement of "guilds" *(za)*, wherein the shogunate, an aristocratic family, or a religious institution had recognized and protected a special group of merchants in return for a steady supply of certain goods. As they stabilized their domains, Warring States daimyo appointed their own official merchants, often from the ranks of their vassals. These *goyō shōnin*, as they were known, acted as general purchasing agents and collected and supervised domain trade.[44] Now there were not only free markets, but also greater competition among traders *(rakuza)*.

An increase in the numbers and kinds of commercial centers and merchants could not have been effected without better transportation. While the technology of land transport changed little, allusion has already been made in chapter 4 to the development of more capacious and seaworthy boats by 1400. Their number certainly grew in successive centuries. For land transport, most Warring States lords built systems of post stations *(shukueki)*, along with improving roads and bridges. In particular, the Go-Hōjō, Takeda, Imagawa, Uesugi, and Tokugawa of eastern Honshu devoted time and resources to their post stations.[45] Most were homes to wholesalers *(toi)*, who transported goods overland.[46]

Lest this expansion of the market sound too good to be true, it is worth noting that hardship also resulted. There was a vigorous commerce in humanity, as with the Takeda and Hineno examples cited in chapter 5. Moreover, just as had occurred in the Kinai in the early and mid-fifteenth century, even when people willingly entered the market, they sometimes lost control of their finances and themselves. In the Kinai, the second half of the fifteenth century witnessed a tug-of-war between creditors and debtors, with the shogunate in the middle issuing its "Orders for Virtuous Rule" or debt cancellations *(tokusei rei)*. For three months in the fall of 1454, for example, the entire province of Yamashiro revolted, demanding a moratorium. The government complied, much to the chagrin of lenders; related violence continued in Yamashiro until 1490. As the Muromachi *bakufu* crumbled and prices deflated further, revolts multiplied and helped bring on chaos. Between 1450 and 1500, there were at least fifteen such riots in the Kinai, with five *tokusei rei* issued.[47] These altercations were an apt measure of the penetration of the market into people's everyday routines.

Even in distant and isolated Kai, the market was an unpredictable factor in daily life. *The Record of Katsuyama* contains numerous notations about how easy or difficult it was to buy and sell grain. In 1518, for instance, the crop was damaged and trade halted; "there was not a single grain bought or sold that fall" in Tsuru District. By contrast, in 1528 *The Record of Katsuyama* stated that grain was cheap in the spring, indicating a good harvest the previous year and open markets. Just as surely as peasants of western Japan were caught up in a market they could not influence individually, so residents of eastern Honshu were enmeshed in their own commercial network.[48] To delineate commercial life in a little more detail, I shall refer to four case studies: the Mōri of western Honshu; daimyo relations with Ise and Kii in central Honshu; the Uesugi of Echigo; and the Takeda of Kai.

The Mōri unified cities and towns, rebuilt the transportation network, formed official merchant and artisan organizations, and then turned the entire system to the benefit of their fisc.[49] Trusted vassals *(ichi mokudai)* oversaw local towns as early as 1554; it was no accident that some vassals were pirate commanders with access to boats. One critical market met on the twentieth of each month *(hatsuka ichi)*; another was located at Itsukushima Shrine.[50] Ports such as Yamaguchi (Suō), Akamanoseki (Nagato), and Onsentsu (Iwami) also fell under similar supervision.

The Mōri established control of both the Japan and Inland Seas by setting duties on each port *(seki)*. On the one hand, they banned *kokujin* barriers, but on the other, the daimyo established their own at strategic points. Again vassals were in charge, and they were free to tax or grant remissions as warranted. These ports were Mōri direct domain, and the benefits of any dues went straightway to the daimyo.[51] In addition, the Mōri developed post stations and other forms of emergency land transport, based upon conscription. They also had bridges constructed.[52]

The Mōri placed trusted vassals over merchants and artisans. Offices overseeing traders came into being by the 1550s and had their own regulations. Merchants dealt in gold, livestock, cloth, ocean products, and tubers and melons, with a total of 328 items so registered in one document. Although they gave traders remission of the most onerous taxes, the Mōri still collected some goods and services to run the transportation network. Artisans in the Mōri domain included cannon and bomb makers, carpenters, ironworkers, and roofers.[53]

The Mōri turned the entire system to their benefit by having merchants move rice and cash, as well as borrowing each in considerable amounts and storing them in their warehouses *(kuramoto)*.[54] Mōri Terumoto was even reported to have said that these loans were more important than weapons for continuing the war. To justify the interest-bearing loans, the Mōri always stated that they were due as "collateral" for the land tax. Merchants in turn sought expansion of their lands or appointment to salaried offices.

Three phenomena serve to reveal the success of Mōri efforts to encourage commercial expansion.[55] First, from 1576 to 1582, they managed to break through Nobunaga's navy in the Inland Sea to succor the fortress at Ishiyama. These operations took considerable resources and entrepreneurial management. Second, they opened new businesses based on long-distance connections, including medicine (moxibustion) and tourism to shrines at Ise and Itsukushima. Third, special local products such as iron, lacquer, paper, salt, bronze, and vegetable oils became everyday household items in the domain. Based upon Muromachi foundations, the market in Mōri lands expanded and was a vital force in enhancing the daimyo's military and political power.

Ise and Kii, bordering on the Kinai, comprised a crucial trading sphere and staging ground for war.[56] Daimyo located in eastern Honshu openly competed for business with Ise's port at Ōminato. For instance, the Go-Hōjō commissioned large freighters operating there; it was also a shipbuilding center, sending products to Izu. The Go-Hōjō were particularly interested in Ise because they felt they could use the ships to transport provisions for their troops and hire pirates there. In 1561, they depended upon Ise ships and agents to ferry provisions to their domain, as fears of a Takeda attack mounted. That year had seen crop failure in the Kanto, and the Go-Hōjō paid Ōminato merchants dearly with silk. The Kanto daimyo also developed relations with Kumano in Kii, where they had large ships built for crews overseeing stores of lumber.

The Tokugawa and Takeda organized pirate forces and carried on shipping with Ōminato too. The Chiga, later a Tokugawa vassal, originally hailed from Shima, carrying out commercial activities throughout the Kii peninsula and demonstrating the way that war and commerce went hand in hand. The Takeda signed up the Ise Obama, and Katsuyori gave them land confirmations in 1573. The Obama had at least fifteen ships and sent men and materiel to the Takeda throughout the 1570s. To gain their trade, the Takeda gave tax relief; the Obama received three thousand strings of cash from Katsuyori in return for aid in the war and material goods shipped from Ise.

The Ise-Kii region was the focus of many powerful daimyo of eastern Honshu, who gave cash, land, status, and tax remissions in return for the aid of these pirate traders. Why were the traders of Ōminato and Kii also interested in the Kanto? Evidence suggests that Kanto ships docking in Ise carried a special prize: raw cotton. Utilized widely for uniforms, this new product was shipped westward from Kanto fields to weavers in the Kinai, while rice for military units and Kyoto fineries for daimyo went eastward. Uncontrolled by any strong warlord and highly developed economically, the Ise-Kii region became the focus of commercial and military competition for the daimyo of eastern Honshu, proving that hegemons not only concentrated narrowly on their own domains but looked to the outside world as well.

The Uesugi of Echigo developed close ties to purchasing agent Kurata Gorōzaemon and his family, who played a crucial role in developing Echigo's economy.[57] Their speciality was the indigo for which Echigo was so justly renowned; prior to the Uesugi's rise to power in 1530, Kurata had marketed the dye to the aristocratic Sanjōnishi family in Kyoto. At the time this special product of Echigo was becoming more commercialized, and demand was growing in the Kinai. In 1530, the assistant constable, Nagao Tamekage, completed his domination of Echigo and then took the surname Uesugi and the symbolic position of Kanto minister *(Kantō kanrei)*. From that time until 1560, the daimyo family granted tax remissions on a variety of goods but retained a levy on Kurata's indigo.

The Uesugi thought that the Kurata were so important that they granted them vassal status and a salary, in addition to their profits from business.[58] Within the domain, Kurata Gorōzaemon was not only in charge of affairs when Uesugi Kenshin was at war, but he also oversaw the treasury *(onkura)* and construction *(bushin)*. In his wisdom, he stockpiled gold and silver bullion, and when a succession struggle erupted after Kenshin's death in 1578, the Uesugi house remained on solid financial footing.

In 1582, Uesugi Kagekatsu, the adoptive heir of Kenshin, guaranteed the Kurata exclusive rights to market indigo, in return for a substantial sum. It was the only product so treated in Echigo, and yet the Kurata continued to supply large quantities to the Sanjōnishi as well, to maintain good relations in Kyoto and to reinforce Uesugi legitimacy in Echigo. These relations were especially important to Gorōzaemon because to get the indigo to Kyoto, he passed through Obama in Wakasa and across Lake Biwa and needed the cooperation of various authorities.

The Kurata were in effect the power behind the throne in Echigo. As noted in chapter 5, Kenshin went on campaigns nearly every year, and his domain lagged far behind others in agrarian development. The Uesugi were able to stay in the war and make the transition into the Tokugawa era in no small part because of the Kurata and domain policies on trade, markets, and merchants.

Like the Uesugi, the Takeda controlled and benefited from trade and crafts.[59] They maintained relations with several mercantile families, the most prominent in Kai being the Yatamura, who received confirmation of their rice and dry fields, their expansive home, livestock, and a large boat. They operated a wide-ranging trading network, including long-distance exchange, and like the Kurata for the Uesugi, they served as treasurers and made frequent loans to the Takeda. The Takeda treated them with more respect than most vassals, and they received tax remissions as a matter of course. Their reach extended into Sagami and Go-Hōjō territory.

Suwa Haruyoshi of Shinano was a trader who kept a complement of seventy footsoldiers and oversaw the Takeda storehouses in Shinano. In addition to aiding the Takeda in controlling Shinano, Suwa used his great wealth and extensive contacts to promote building projects there. Ina Shufu was another rich Shinano merchant who originally dealt in tea and helped operate the Takeda fisc *(kuramoto shū)*. In presiding over the Takeda treasury, he collected the land tax (in coins) and proceeded to acquire goods for the Takeda cause, including muskets, silk, and even grain from the Kinai. The Takeda granted all these merchants tax remissions and freedom from tolls, and they cracked down on barriers put in place by "men of the province" as well. Like the Mōri, Go-Hōjō, and Uesugi, the Takeda were linked to the highly advanced commercial economy.

The Takeda policy for dealing with artisans was no less lucrative or domineering. At first the daimyo brought weapons makers under their control, then construction experts, and finally those who made weights and measures. This order reflects how the Takeda came to power: first by warfare, then by engineering, and at last by administration. Kai and Shinano were home to all sorts of craftspeople: ironmongers, carpenters, miners, stonemasons, dyers, bucket makers, roofers, and leather workers, among others. Of those associated with the Takeda, twenty-seven were carpenters—the greatest number by far; then came miners (seventeen associated). The daimyo organized the carpenters, iron workers, roofers, bucket makers, dyers, and mat makers according to their skills. They gave arrow makers, plasterers, and lacquer painters exemption from some taxes, made others vassals or near-vassals, and almost always freed them from manual labor. The Takeda also formed such units when they conquered Shinano and advanced into Suruga. Another way for the Takeda to assert control was by unifying the domain's weights and measures; gauges of volume, balancing scales, and monetary units were so strongly entrenched by 1582 that the Tokugawa shogunate merely left them intact.[60]

In sum, war and trade went hand in hand. Warring States daimyo had mercantile bases, enticed traders and artisans into their service, and gained great material and monetary benefits from these arrangements. Even more than agriculture, the evidence on commerce bolsters a conclusion that the era 1450–1600 was one of growth for both the archipelago's economy and population.

Industry

Warring States daimyo developed new organizations for the control of artisans. The Takeda and Go-Hōjō together boasted metal workers, carpenters, leather makers, stonemasons, shipwrights, miners, lumbermen, dyers, lacquer painters, roofers, paper workers, silversmiths, potters, plasterers, tile makers, bronze casters, arrow and armor makers, and many others. These men and women were participating in an industrial expansion that had started in the late Kamakura era and continued more or less uninterrupted into the Tokugawa period. To be succinct, three major new sectors came to symbolize and underpin Warring States manufacturing: cotton, monumental construction, and the mining and refining of ores.

Cotton growing and cloth making were industries that took off as the wars proceeded.[61] As noted in chapter 4, cotton was first introduced to Japan prior to 1429, and like the other technologies described briefly here, it spread rapidly thereafter. As the Ōnin War erupted, Muromachi daimyo such as the Hosokawa, Yamana, and Hatakeyama soon recognized its value for military apparel. By the late 1400s, cotton imported from Korea could no longer fill demand; farmers were already growing it in the Kinai by 1480, and by the 1580s the crop was common in the Kanto. In the sixteenth century, cultivators planted it mainly in dry fields, but cotton required a great deal of fertilizer, and the risk of failure was substantial. As noted above, peasants raised raw cotton in both western and eastern Japan for shipment to the Kinai, where most of the cloth was woven.

Architecture and castle building were rapidly improving industries tied to the wars.[62] The great saws and other tools described in chapter 4 were already in use by 1450, and they spread rapidly thereafter. As it became necessary to produce lumber from pine and zelkova *(keyaki)* with the exhaustion of cedar and cypress stands, carpenters used the new saws and axes to make larger, flatter boards and to separate them more readily from the bark. As productivity rose, builders developed a uniform system of measurement *(kiwari sei)* beginning in 1489.[63] It was based on a set distance between pillars and improved a building's safety, balance, and beauty. It made carpentry into an industry that could be learned and spread more easily all over the islands, and it was critical for the building boom of the sixteenth and seventeenth centuries.

In castle building, construction moved from earth and wood to stone. This change implied progress in stone cutting and fitting and a growing population to provide the labor to move boulders and build castles. The excavation of Warring States castles has become more common throughout Japan; the Asakura's Ichijōdani is the most frequently cited example. Located in Echizen, it was a feat of engineering skill, guarded by an outer wall and trench at least seventy meters in length. Great stones shaped like measuring boxes *(masugata)* formed the western exterior wall, and rounded rocks served as the foundation for numerous buildings. The grounds also encompassed gardens, temples, and warrior dwellings.[64]

Mining and metallurgy were the newest and most crucial sector.[65] During the seventeenth century Japan may well have been the world's largest producer of silver, the technology for which had entered the islands during the sixteenth century. The first improvement was a transition to horizontal shaft mining. It may come as a surprise that workers simply gathered the gold and silver ore used in the ancient and early medieval periods from the earth's surface, as in the case of the famous discovery of gold in Mutsu in 749 that enabled Emperor Shōmu to proceed with the Great Buddha of Tōdaiji. Perhaps introduced into Japan from China, the new technique allowed Warring States daimyo to dig reinforced shafts to mine their silver, gold, copper, and iron. Moreover, they learned to pump water out of mines lying below the water table, as well as to improve ventilation.[66]

Once miners collected the ore, another advance guaranteed purer fine metals. A Japanese merchant trading out of Hakata introduced this Chinese method, in which workers added lead to ore and then melted it in a large furnace. After the mixture was liquified, the slag separated, and laborers poured water on the compound lead-silver. They then reheated the mixture and added ash where the lead became trapped; pure silver or gold was the result. These new technologies had come together by at least 1542.

Better iron-working skills accompanied these developments. In the early 1500s, the Chinese visitor Zheng Shun-gong had noted that iron cast in Japan was too inferior to use for cannons. This soon began to change, as a new, bigger furnace with a sizable chimney came into use, an even closer replica of the *tatara* (furnace) of the Tokugawa period than the bloomery of the Kamakura era. In comparison with its smaller predecessors, it produced a larger amount of better iron and used a more advanced bellows, often pedaled. The furnace, constructed from plastered mud with a large roof, could achieve higher temperatures than ever before, and repeated castings were unnecessary, raising productivity. The reason for the advance in iron smelting was the demand for swords (also exported to China) and muskets (introduced by the Portuguese in 1543 and reproduced by Japanese artisans soon thereafter). As it happens, the archipelago's richest iron deposits were located in western Honshu in Mōri territory, and it must have given the daimyo an added advantage in the wars. By the early 1600s, the Englishman Richard Cocks wrote that Japanese cast iron was as good as that of his home. The increased supply of iron had other spinoffs, such as better agricultural and carpentry tools.[67]

This brief review of three new industries hardly does them justice. Furthermore, these three basic technologies had ripple effects throughout the economy. Cotton provided jobs and raised the standard of living in general. Better architecture and castle building redounded to the benefit of peasants and daimyo trying to build secure riparian works. More and better iron meant improved tools and weapons; more gold and silver further enriched a commercial sector that needed no more stimulus. In this sense, the Warring States era was a true boon to the Japanese economy in the way that scholars have traditionally thought. If there had been no problems of provisioning or satisfying the troops' other lusts, perhaps the population would have grown even more rapidly. As it is, the growth of industry gives ample reason to believe that Japan's population in 1600 was closer to 17 than to 12 million.

Cities

The unprecedented multiplication of urban centers also supports the idea that Japan's population was larger and grew more rapidly than Hayami allowed.[68] Even in 1942, scholars tabulated 321 cities in the archipelago for 1590; 202 first appeared in documents from the era between 1450 and 1600. Breaking them down by category, we find that 67 arose as political centers, 51 developed from temples or shrines, 47 were post stations, 26 were ports, and 11 were market towns. Given sixty years of work by dedicated historians and archaeologists since then, this total would undoubtedly be higher today.[69]

Of course, there are at least two problems with these figures. First, there is no guarantee that a city or town did not exist prior to its first appearance in written materials; if it did, it would tend to lower the total number of urban centers founded in the Warring States era. Second, there is no size listed for virtually any of these entities; many may have counted fewer than five thousand residents and been little more than glorified villages. Still, they convey the general notion of exponential growth in urban population at this time.

Kitō has tried to estimate the number of Japan's city dwellers as of 1590.[70] Early in the Meiji period, the statistically minded government counted the population of its urban centers, which it defined as having 5,000 inhabitants or more; the total came to 13 percent of Japan's residents, or about 4,450,000. Given that there were 321 towns and cities in 1590 and basing his figures upon contemporary records of various kinds and analogy with the Meiji case, Kitō inferred that the total urban population probably fell between 1.1 and 2.2 million. When he limited the sample to towns above 5,000, a total urban populace of 500,000–700,000 was the result. At a population of 12.3 million for the archipelago, about 5 percent of Japan's residents then lived in what might have been called cities in 1600.

To be sure, these methods include many assumptions, but as of the present they represent the only quantitative attempt to estimate the degree of urbanization around 1600. Given the argument presented in this book that 12.3 million is too low a population figure for 1600, it seems likely that Japan's urban population was much more than 600,000. If the archipelago-wide population was 15 million, then (at 5 percent) city dwellers would have numbered 750,000; a total of 17 million would increase the total to 850,000. Since I estimated the urban populace in 1450 at about 379,000, the Warring States period would have seen about a twofold increase in townspeople. By 1600, Japan was already one of the world's highly urbanized regions and would become even more so.

The causes of this trend toward increased urbanization were both political and commercial. Daimyo founded new administrative centers like Kōriyama, Kōfu, and Nirayama as castle towns; post stations also sprang up. Market, port, and temple/shrine towns and cities came into existence primarily for commercial reasons. As in the case of trade and industry, there is a congruence of military, political, and economic factors. Another reason for urbanization must have been better access to a larger food supply, suggesting that peasant attempts to clear land and build riparian works were real enough. It is interesting to note that the decrease in famines, expansion of irrigation works, and growth of cities and towns seem to coincide, all three trends beginning about 1520.

The demographic effects of these new centers were probably diverse. On the one hand, construction jobs multiplied, creating economic opportunities that could have stimulated the birthrate. On the other hand, workers at the sites were probably single or married males separated from their spouses, reducing the number of families or breaking them apart and limiting fertility. Furthermore, evidence from both world and Japanese history suggests that cities—even relatively clean ones like Japan's— tended to be foci of infectious diseases, with higher mortality than in the countryside.[71] In sum, however, the notable increase in townspeople between 1450 and 1600 seems like one more sign that larger estimates of total population in the archipelago are more reasonable than smaller ones.

VILLAGE AND FAMILY

Like the rest of the medieval age, the Warring States and Unification eras provide no census or parish records containing data revealing the birthrate. In the absence of this crucial information, the only course is to describe and analyze factors that may have affected fertility. I have already touched on some of these variables, such as the introduction of syphilis or the impact of repeated famines and continuous expeditions and warfare. The marked advances in farming, trade, and industry affected the birth and infant mortality rates more positively. In this section, I shall deal with structures, analyzing community first and then the family, women, children, and the unfree.

Community

The creation of communities running their own affairs was one of the significant developments of the period 1280–1450, and it continued in the Warring States era, with some significant qualifications. As always, villages in western Japan and eastern Honshu were somewhat different. In the former, clustered settlement was the rule and spread from the Kinai throughout most of the region. Moats surrounded many villages. There seems to have been a disjunction in the establishment of western Japanese settlements in the sixteenth century, with many older communities disappearing while peasants were founding those of the Tokugawa period. Good examples of new villages are the excavations of Ōmi's Furu-yashiki and Myōrakuji sites, each circumscribed by earthen walls about thirty meters square. Within the walls were roads, posthole dwellings, and buildings with foundation stones (probably storehouses). Both residential centers were also served by the Uso River.

Eastern Honshu was another story. There it was not unusual for fields to be interspersed among the dwellings; small hamlets were also common. There were essentially three types of settlements: compact ones containing posthole dwellings; compact centers composed primarily of ancient pit dwellings; and villages comprised of houses made with miscanthus reeds for pillars, walls, and roofs. Examples include Honyashiki Village in Mutsu, where a Date vassal maintained roads for a populace that resided in closely fitted pit dwellings, and Minami Nakada D Site in Etchū, where pit houses again predominated. At both sites, a trend toward compactness became more evident over time.[72]

Villagers also organized themselves differently in eastern and western Japan. In the Kinai and westward, especially around Kyoto, the trend toward corporate rule advanced the fastest and furthest, in step with demographic, agricultural, and commercial gains. Hineno in Izumi, discussed above for its troubled relations with local warriors, is probably the best example.[73] Recall that there were two major villages in Masamoto's estate, Hineno and Iriyamada, with a total population of about 1,500. Each in turn was composed of several subdivisions, such as the Eastern and Western blocks in Hineno. Hineno and Iriyamada each had its own office *(mandokoro)*, and when a major problem appeared, peasants first gathered at these offices in a meeting of the entire community *(sō no yoriai)*. Masamoto named wealthier farmers to the position of head *(bantō)* for each subdivision, to collect residential taxes and pass along the proprietor's requests. In addition, heads led worship at community shrines and festivals and summarized villagers' opinions when an issue was at stake.

Age ranking was prominent: male cultivators were classified as youths *(wakamono)*, adults *(chūrō)*, or elders *(korō)*. On these men fell the heavy duties of construction, portage, and fighting, but each of these levies took the household as a unit. Hineno and Iriyamada also had class divisions, with small and dependent cultivators being most common.[74]

Two crimes indicate the importance peasants placed on continuation of the family line.[75] On the eleventh day of the first month in 1504, a resident was accused of stealing a sword from a peasant official, and the other functionaries gathered with Masamoto and decided to try an ordeal by boiling water, in which the accused thrust his hand into the pot, proving his innocence if he went unscalded. The accused turned out to be "guilty," and despite the pleading of village officials, Masamoto wrote as follows:

> I had the sword thief arrested. . . . Officials suggested that it might be best to be lenient in this case *since each peasant's life is important.* . . . However, I replied . . . we must not forget that the sword of a representative of Ōki Village had been stolen. . . . Cut off his head at once. How sad! How pathetic! . . .
>
> Afterward, the headmen came and expressed sympathy with my decision, saying it was the proper disposition.
>
> The criminal had a son eight years old. *I ordered that the household headship be held in trust for him and protected against seizure by others.* However, all his property was divided among my commissioners.[76]

The crucial point here is that just as continuity of the family line was all-important in the Tokugawa village, so it was at Hineno in 1504. The concern evident here undoubtedly helped more children and youths to survive, while at the same time maintaining equitable and stable labor, grain, and other levies.

The second crime occurred at Iriyamada in the third month of 1504. The accused family was composed of an elderly mother, older and younger adult sons, and a married daughter living nearby. The younger brother, named Shōen Uma, had been married and was raising his three children without his wife, who had divorced him. He had three homes and more than three *tan* of fields, placing him among the wealthier peasants. As noted above, 1503 was a terrible time, in which crops had failed and peasants had gathered bracken root, ground it into flour, and were preparing to eat it to survive.

Pressed by hunger, Shōen Uma stole a certain Genshichi's bale of life-saving rice. Officials discovered the bale in Uma's possession, and he admitted to stealing more rice and tools, but when he was found out, he returned the stolen merchandise. Nevertheless, by this time the peasants were seething with anger and executed Uma. Masamoto was not pleased because he felt the village had violated due process. After Masamoto had several long discussions with peasant headmen and Uma's relatives, the legal niceties were settled, but now the children were orphans:

> After Shōen Uma had been executed, his three children sat weeping the night through in their home, clinging to one another's hands. Finally, as dawn approached, the eldest, a girl of fourteen, went out with her two-year-old sister and six-year-old brother. They sought help from their neighboring aunt, since Shōen Uma had left what little rice and goods they had at home. But the children's mother had separated from Shōen Uma, and the aunt obstinately refused to help them. Therefore these pathetic children were forced to wander about in the mountains. I had the headman and his assistant check into the matter. *After ordering that the children be given some of the brown rice the aunt had stored, I assigned their uncle Ōya Ukon and their grandmother to be their guardians. It is really a pity it has come to this, but there is no alternative but to punish robbers harshly. However, since Shōen Uma's family has lived as our cultivators for generations, his descendants should not lose their title of householder. It would be best to have the title have held in trust.*[77]

On the next day, "The headman . . . reported that the villagers had made another petition about Shōen Uma's property, including his rice fields and other cultivation rights. They asked that the household title should not be confiscated, and that his cultivation rights should be held in joint trust by the children's uncle, Ōya Ukon, and the village during the children's minority."[78] As in the previous case, the village community resolved, even in the case of a food robber during a famine, to continue the line for the children's, the village's, and Masamoto's sake.

A whole constellation of new powers accrued to corporate villages in western Japan during the Warring States era.[79] First, at least in villages like Hineno and Iriyamada in the Kinai, a new, Tokugawa-like form of tax collection developed. Previously, estate lords had surveyed their lands and then charged taxes on each peasant with a field. By 1500, the estate lords, constable daimyo, and others in search of rents went to the village council, composed of officials *(bantō)*, and dealt with them. They relied upon village officials to arrive at a fair assessment for their entire village and then divide up the taxes due from each cultivator. This development had much to do with the increasing number of landlords collecting "added rent" *(kajishi)*; they were involved in the commercial economy of the Kinai region and made loans themselves. Many *bantō* must have been from this class.

Second, villages had self-defense arrangements, also led by the official class. Whether against Satō Sōbei or the *shugo daimyō*, the village managed to produce as many as 70–80 percent of its men for defense. One basis for these activities was the village common property. Since villagers did not deliver their entire surplus to lords like Masamoto, the portion that they held back could serve to pay for weapons, bribe hostile samurai, and maintain irrigation works. Expenses even went toward festivals to pray for rain or pay for rice wine. Peasants had become a force to be reckoned with politically and militarily as they played one elite off against the other.

In western Japan from 1500 onward, we could multiply these examples endlessly. At Nagaya Estate in Yamato, villagers dealt with irrigation works and crimes according to their own rules.[80] At Shinjuen, a property of Daitokuji in Yamashiro, the tax system described for Hineno and Iriyamada was in place by about 1530; fragmented parcels destroyed in the Ōnin War were gradually unified, a landlord class charged "additional rents," and the officials-cum-landlords doled out responsibilities for payment of taxes and the maintenance of irrigation facilities.[81]

In eastern Honshu, there were some similar trends, although the evidence is more sparse and difficult to read. In the Takeda domain, local adult males *(jige'nin; gō no otona shikimonodomo)* supported the daimyo, and the Takeda recorded them in surveys.[82] There were struggles between the local "men of the province" and the Takeda for control of this class. Local wealthy peasants organized themselves and strove to uphold precedents *(senrei)*, as well as to serve in the Takeda military. In terms of class, most held widespread household lands, as well as dry and paddy fields. In 1561, when a quarrel over water rights erupted among three villages, cultivators were unable to solve the problem on their own and turned to the Takeda for help. In the end, the elders of each village met under the watchful eyes of Takeda warriors to resolve the dispute according to precedent. In 1576 a conflict entailed two villages struggling over their borders. They again called upon the daimyo, and exact written records, instead of memory, noted the boundaries from then on.

We can see a process of assimilation to Takeda rule in these cases. While the villages were under control of only the elders at first, disputes over resources tended to drive these upper-class peasants into the hands of the Takeda. The daimyo immediately made warriors of the leading adult males, also placing them in charge of the village as a whole.[83] In this way, the Takeda divided warrior from peasant and instituted their own quota system for taxes for each village. To be sure, village unity was far looser. The overall trend was similar to that in western Japan, but daimyo used disputes as a wedge to open and control communities.

Village solidarity may not have been as strong in eastern Honshu, but evidence indicates a similar concern for household continuity.[84] At Kurosawa Village, located near the Takeda castle town of Kōfu, the daimyo collected residential levies. Within a long report on these cash taxes, there were several notations indicating three types of residences: a main family house *(honke),* new additions *(shinyashiki),* and vacated houses *(aki-yashiki).* Although two Takeda vassals signed the record, it is clear that villagers drew it up and then sent it to the daimyo. Next to each type of dwelling was the name of the responsible party. In cases where the household was empty, the peasants took it upon themselves to appoint someone to inherit and continue the farm, in a move reminiscent of Hineno. Sometimes the heir was from an unrelated main family, sometimes a junior member living within the "empty" building. There were also examples of main families splitting off branches—perhaps younger or older brothers—to open new lands and construct houses.

By 1584, Kurosawa gave evidence of class division within a basic unity. The wealthiest few families had many buildings and strove to maintain their status within the corporate entity. These families also possessed large numbers of servants *(ge'nin).* Many boasted surnames; served as lowly Takeda vassals; and saw to the maintenance, administration, and revival of vacant homes. Others still called themselves main families but had no surnames or great riches. Like Hineno and Iriyamada in Izumi, peasants decided the affairs of the village in broad consultation, with the well-to-do holding the keys in decision making. The wealthy also supplied expenses for community festivals and rites.

Kurosawa was akin to the corporate villages of the Kinai and western Japan but not nearly as united or strong. Both the Takeda and their archenemy, the Tokugawa, managed to penetrate these villages, taking advantage of their self-governing tendencies and at the same time siphoning off labor, personnel, and rents. The further development of village self-rule in the Warring States era laid the foundation for Tokugawa local government in the 1600s. The trends manifesting themselves in the 1500s, however, were products of demographic and economic factors that had been in place for several centuries. At the same time, the appearance of corporate villages reinforced population growth by helping to protect peasants from rampaging warriors, controlling common property such as irrigation facilities and forest rights, and nurturing offspring and ensuring the continuation of family lineages.

Family, Women, and Class

As noted in chapter 4, the structure of Japanese peasant families had begun to change as early as the 1300s. By 1450, there are several hints that commoner stem households (*ie*) were starting to develop in some places in and near the Kinai. Families in central Honshu were taking up surnames based upon their places of residence, accumulating a patrimony, and demarcating graveyards for their ancestors. The evidence presented above for both Hineno and the Takeda domain suggests that households were composed of a male head, who brought his dowry-bearing wife to live and mate with him, and that family status and lineage were important by the 1500s. In essence, the general outline of the Tokugawa-period stem household seems to have been in existence among the peasantry by 1500 in the Kinai and perhaps by the mid-1500s in central and western Japan.

There is little information about peasant family structure for this era, but the records of the Nishi family of Yamakuni Estate, an imperial property located in Tanba, provide a glimpse.[85] Documents from 1672 suggest that beginning in the early sixteenth century, the Nishi took care to note the male family head for each generation, along with the names of his sons, the year of the head's death, and the status of the wife. The Nishi also kept these facts in their ancestral tablets (*ihai*) and perhaps in village death registers.

During the Muromachi age, as imperial estates began to fall prey to warriors, the court commenced naming prominent adult peasants (*otona hyakushō)* to aristocratic rank and office. In 1550, Nishi Hyōetarō and his younger brother, Konishi Tarōjirō, both of whom lived in Yamakuni and were members of the local shrine organization *(miyaza)*, obtained such appointments. Moreover, in 1551, Hyōetarō served as guarantor when Tarōjirō bought several parcels of land. Even though Hyōetarō was older and in the Tokugawa period would have held higher status as the head of the main household, the genealogy drew no distinction between the two brothers. Formation of a clear main-branch family hierarchy was not yet common at Yamakuni, unlike in late sixteenth-century Kurosawa Village in the Takeda domain. Furthermore, the Nishi placed emphasis not simply on the male line, but also on collateral relatives and wives over five generations.

In essence, the Warring States era was an intermediary stage in the development of the stem family. The main characteristics were present among the Nishi in the early and mid-1500s, but unlike in the Tokugawa period, status distinctions were not clear-cut. The war was the major reason for greater equality among male offspring in the sixteenth century household, with each brother acting as a protector for the other. In the ensuing Pax Tokugawa, it was easier to break away and form branch units.[86]

The gradual development of the commoner *ie* likely relates to population change in complex ways. On the one hand, as households accumulated a patrimony, they tended to move to unigeniture by the 1500s, leaving the noninheriting siblings to fend for themselves. Such an arrangement suggests a growing ratio of persons to land, implying that population increase was in part responsible for the formation of the stem household.[87] Moreover, because elders placed emphasis on the continuation of the lineage, it is likely that mothers cared for children better, breast-feeding them for longer periods and lowering infant mortality. On the other hand, the days of easy access to sexual liaisons were probably over for women, perhaps reducing overall fertility.

The stem family, even as it shaped up in the 1500s, revolved around males and patrilineal succession. How did its continuing formation affect women? The conventional view is that after 1300 women lost their rights to inherit and hold property or to maintain their own domiciles. They went to live with their husbands, to whom they provided a dowry. In effect, they were not much better than household slaves, desired for their ability to produce male heirs and not much else. Men could divorce their wives by whim, especially if they failed to produce a son. A wife's adultery was punished by the death of both adulterors; men could take on concubines as they pleased.[88]

Over the last twenty years, however, women in general, and peasant women in particular, have been receiving less stereotypical treatment from scholars. For example, it has been established that several females donned armor and fought in battles for the Mōri, Shimazu, and even Hideyoshi.[89] Among the farming populace, women performed many functions. In the case of Hineno it has already been shown that women divorced their husbands, abandoned their children, and worked and managed fields. *Agrarian Instructions,* the Iyo treatise of somewhat doubtful provenance, gave women a major role in planting and harvesting, with 200 of the 493 labor units needed to cultivate a one-*chō* rice paddy coming from females.

Because their labor was essential for the village, wives still had political power in the late 1400s and 1500s. Many held seats in the shrine institutions of their corporate villages, although they were not as powerful as their spouses. Comical sketches *(kyōgen)* hint that many women did not begin to lose their higher status until the very end of the sixteenth and seventeenth centuries.[90]

In the 1500s, the Jesuit priest Luis Frois had his own perspective on what he called "women's problems."[91] He listed ten of them, but basically they were the birth and care of children; poverty arising from frequent famines; and disease, partially stemming from the commodification of sex and the importation of syphilis. To be sure, the last two problems would probably have had the effect of lowering the birthrate and raising mortality. Still, men shared these dangers; the only sign in Frois' writing of hardship specifically for women living in an *ie* was the pressure to produce a male heir.

In fact, a woman's lot may not have been so harsh right up to 1600. Peasant women could rid themselves of an undesirable mate simply by leaving, as happened to Shōen Uma at Hineno. They could make land transactions, albeit through various subterfuges, such as selling to a temple as an act of piety. They could even manage their own farms, provided they could find a male guarantor. This more optimistic view concerning late medieval women comes in light of the realization that Tokugawa-period peasant women may not have had it so bad as the laws dictated.[92]

Still, it is prudent to remember the various dangers facing women in the Age of the Country at War. The constant battling was harmful to many women, as they were among the most common captives during and after conflicts, sold into slavery or raped by soldiers.[93] Even when peace prevailed, peasant women faced special challenges, including child care and labor in the fields. In sum, mortality for women probably remained high, even as fertility fell somewhat and they took better care of their infants and children.

Bearing children was one of a woman's primary functions, but the evidence on children's lives is sparse and subject to varying interpretations.[94] As in previous centuries, an offspring was not considered an adult until age fifteen; as noted above, until the age of seven a child "belonged to the gods," implying that his or her survival was doubtful. As had been true since 1150 or so, the newborn were the chief victims of infectious diseases such as smallpox, measles, and influenza. Infant mortality must have been frightening even in the late 1500s.[95]

Add to these dangers, apparent throughout the medieval period, the suffering of long-term war and the possible increase of abortion and infanticide. Since children were weak, armies kidnapped them regularly, as in the examples cited for Hineno and the Takeda. These unfortunates were then either sold or used for their labor. As for rudimentary family planning, at least according to the Jesuit Luis Frois—a biased source to be sure—women who lived in poverty or were ill often did not possess the strength to bear or raise their young, turning to medicinal or other means to terminate their pregnancies. As earlier in the medieval age, busy parents called upon young women or elders to watch their children, and no one can be certain how long mothers suckled or cared for their babies.[96] When one of the many famines of this era struck, parents in starving families often sold their offspring. One such sale of a young female is recorded for Satsuma in 1511, for example.[97] The practice of selling children into service to avoid starvation must have had decidedly mixed results for both the child and his/her family.

If a child survived to age ten, then he or she was expected to work. Farmers' children labored right alongside their parents in the fields; the same was true of the trades. During the refurbishing of Amano Shrine on Mt. Kōya in 1411, children composed about one-fifth of the roofers and one-third of the carpenters and bronze workers.[98] The demands and dangers of these jobs could have increased youth mortality.

Yet most improvements in industry and in other aspects of material culture, to be discussed below, gradually enhanced the chances of survival for infants and youth over the 1500s. The dispersion of corporate communities to eastern Honshu and the development of stem units may have promoted the survival of children. What is more, by the 1500s some village children could acquire the rudiments of an education. Learning to read and write and do simple arithmetic had to improve the lives of those lucky few, usually aged seven to thirteen, who were chosen for schooling. Education took place most commonly in local temples.[99] Most advances were apparent by the last decades of the sixteenth century.

It seems important not to place too much importance on these positive aspects, though, because the twin abominations of famine and war intervened to create more broken and homeless families during the Warring States era than at any time since the great Kamakura famines. This rise in broken and homeless families not only may have harmed children, but it may also have led to a sizable increase in the servile class *(ge'nin)*. Kidnapping was common practice during the battles of the Warring States era, from the Shimazu and Sagara of Kyushu to the Date of northeastern Honshu.[100] Daimyo all over Japan wrote laws skirting the issue or openly permitting the sale of humans, suggesting that such behavior was rampant.[101]

Recall that this class of unfree began to appear in the late Heian period and expanded considerably during the three great famines of the Yōwa, Kangi, and Shōga eras. Further note that *ge'nin* were heritable, that they could be sold away from their families, and that many dwelled in lean-tos within their master's household lands. While the era from 1280 to 1450 shows little evidence of further growth of this class, it is unlikely that it disappeared, but rather that families merely passed servants along from one generation to the next. Then came the social unrest and warfare beginning in 1467. Common sense would suggest that by the late 1500s the number of those in bondage was at an all-time high. For a village near Kyoto in 1433 the unfree totaled about 20 percent of the inhabitants.[102]

It is unclear how this growth in the unfree class affected society. The lynchpin of Hayami's argument for massive population expansion during the late sixteenth and seventeenth centuries is that Hideyoshi's surveys freed those people and gave them their own land, boosting fertility just as the death rate was falling.[103] One critical ingredient in Hayami's hypothesis is the assumption that *ge'nin* of the era 1450–1580 were miserable and unable to reproduce. Yet during 1473–1591, the Itomura family from Ōmi farmed twenty-one parcels (composing about three *chō*) and held numerous unfree cultivators, but the servants all functioned within the larger Itomura enterprise and had small plots to cultivate for themselves.[104] Moreover, in exchange for cropping their own land as well as helping with the master's fields, the *ge'nin* received remission of their rent. To be sure, they dwelt in small huts and lean-tos *(soeya, kadoya),* where living conditions could not have been good. And they could be bought and sold. Yet the lot of many *ge'nin* seems to have been better than previously thought.[105]

Literature on servants presents them as "unattached" *(muen),* outsiders living beyond the bounds of the rest of society.[106] Yet while the existence of a substantial market in human beings could have depressed the birthrate and the lot of these unfree servants may have been worse than that of most independent peasants, it is hard to judge the overall impact demographically from the small number of extant examples. It is probably best to view the slippage of more people into bondage during the Warring States era as a small drag on fertility, depending on their lot and the effects of hostilities.

Community, family, and class placed countervailing pressures on Japan's population between 1450 and 1600. Villages continued a trend toward corporateness until they were general in western Japan; settlements in eastern Honshu remained more fluid. These new communities, along with the formation of more stem families, may have helped save lives, especially among infants fortunate enough to receive better care. At the same time, many women and children may have fared worse, as war and famine reduced fertility and raised mortality. What is more, the constant food crises and wars created a substantial class of unfree cultivators, who may not have produced all the children they wished or could. In a word, frequent harvest failures and war slowed demographic increase prior to the early 1500s, postponing premodern Japan's largest population boom until after 1600.

MATERIAL CULTURE

Trends commencing during the "Muromachi Optimum" continued to play themselves out ever so slowly, hampered by the wars but eventually leading to an uneven and incremental rise in people's physical well-being. Diet changed little between 1450 and 1600, with the same basic foods being grown, gathered, fished, or hunted. Crops noted in *Agrarian Instructions* and confirmed for the late 1500s were not much different from those cultivated in 1450. Indeed, as noted above, depending upon what figures we utilize, we can even posit a drop in per-unit rice productivity, although this seems to be a statistical aberration. Yet because double-cropping, irrigation works, the planting of Champa rice, and other techniques advanced noticeably and better nets and technology improved fishing catches, there was undoubtedly more food to go around by 1600. The booming commercial economy and food relief institutions helped spread food to those who needed it most. Finally, the slow change in the late sixteenth century away from the "spring hungers" toward an early-modern death pattern also suggests a general rise in caloric intake.[107]

Peasant garb made slow progress. As cotton raising and cloth production became industries native to Japan, some peasants were probably able to discard their rough hemp clothing for warm, soft cotton. As cotton clothes became available in markets, it is hard to imagine that some wealthier peasants would not have bought them or made their own from the cotton that they raised.[108]

The physical setting in which families of the late fifteenth and sixteenth centuries lived has already been generally described. In both western and eastern Japan, archaeologists have found that peasants used a wide variety of pots, bowls, and utensils, mostly made of wood and lacquer, with iron goods becoming increasingly common after 1300, especially in the Kanto. Domiciles with flooring spread throughout the islands, even though a considerable mass of those living in eastern Honshu still resided in pit dwellings first known to their Jōmon ancestors. There was a transition in rural and urban home building toward greater size and better construction between the 1520s and 1580s.[109] Specific improvements included the building of taller residences, with tiled roofs and plastered walls, and much more storage space. There was, however, another major difference between homes east and west: residents of western Japan almost universally preferred the boiler *(kamado)* with which to heat and cook, while those living in eastern Honshu utilized a fireplace *(irori),* centered in the floor.[110]

Sanitation and bathing were better as well. Whereas once Kyoto was the filthiest place in the islands, pictorial and archaeological evidence from the later sixteenth century shows public toilets that were scooped regularly *(kumitori shiki)* when they filled up.[111] Similar examples have been uncovered in northern Kyushu, Bingo, Sakai, Ōmi, and Ichijō-dani.[112] Given that these toilets generally have been excavated in what was also the most agriculturally developed region of the archipelago, it is easy to envision the increasing use of night soil for fertilizer as one reason for the cleaning up of those western Japanese regions. As a Spanish visitor to Japan remarked in 1609, "It is a certainty that one cannot see streets and homes this clean anywhere else in the world."[113] He might have also commented on personal hygiene since the trend toward the opening of public baths was ongoing from the fourteenth century.[114]

All these improvements added to the physical comfort of residents, but it is important to indicate that progress was not limited to material life. The sixteenth century witnessed a substantial rise in literacy and numeracy.[115] Until 1300, village temples and shrines served primarily as places of worship, although they already acted to inform locals of the newest fads in big cities too. Village notables were especially anxious to learn of city customs, and in the period after 1300 a few temples essentially became the equivalent of local schools for those who had the time and ability to study. As the corporate village spread first into western and then eastern Japan, peasants had to be trained to read and write their own rules about crime, taxes, defense, and cultivation. By the Warring States period, communities were storing these rules in special containers, as at Imabori in Ōmi and Esaka in Settsu.

The offspring of local notables and wealthy peasants were the most frequent students. At Hineno, local officials seemed to know how to read and write simple Japanese. Even Luis Frois wrote, "All the children in Japan study at temples."[116] Undoubtedly Frois was exaggerating, yet his fellow Jesuit Luis Almeida wrote that among his converts every child over age ten knew how to read and write and that schools were to be found everywhere in Kyushu.[117] Without the foundation laid in education in the 1500s, it is hard to imagine the development of new industries or even the operation of the Tokugawa shogunate, which required so much paper shuffling.

At the same time that schooling was spreading, Japanese mathematics *(wasan)* was developing. The abacus entered Japan from China, possibly as early as 1550. It is hard to describe just what a major advance the abacus was over the previous method of notched sticks; its importation removed the esoteric field of mathematics exclusively from the hands of Buddhist monks and gave the same abilities to warriors, merchants, and rich peasants. New industries such as architecture, castle building, and riparian works are unthinkable without this basic improvement in quantitative methods.

Along with these two undeniable changes in education and mathematics came transformations in the perception of time and space. Jesuits brought the first mechanical clock to Japan in 1552. From 1588, references to time appear in the rules of corporate communities; they were essential for castle life, where everything depended on the precise timing of the changing of the guard. The view of space changed as well, units of measurement became more uniform, and the *kiwari* system diffused throughout the islands. The physical well-being of commoners improved by education and inventions, as well as by advances in diet, housing, clothing, and sanitation.

Chapter 5 presented an apparent paradox: an increase in Japan's population of 5–7 million between 1450 and 1600 at the same time that extraordinary mortality from disease, famine, and war may have risen. In a word, numerous improvements in background variables such as agriculture, trade, industry, community, family, and physical well-being seem to have more than offset whatever may have been the harsh effects of the new mortality regime. Measured in Nara units, both arable and per-unit rice productivity registered sizable increases between 1450 and 1600. Commerce and industry presented a most positive aspect, as the Muromachi boom broadened and deepened to include eastern Honshu and even more commoners. By 1600, perhaps 5 percent of the population—between 750,000 and 850,000 persons—lived in towns of at least five thousand.

Corporate communities and stem families evolved from their pre-1450 roots and may have helped more people survive amid the misery of famine and war. Because of these twin disasters, however, the number of those in bondage undoubtedly expanded, although no one knows how difficult their lives were. Incremental improvements in diet, housing, clothing, and sanitation also helped to offset the negative impact, particularly after 1520. Greater access to education and new inventions such as the abacus also added to the well-being of some.

Table 6.4 uses Kitō's and Saitō's estimates to show how population trends may have acted over the uneven course of the Warring States epoch. For comparison's sake, I calculated the annual rate of demographic growth from 1280 to 1450, an era at the start of this growth cycle, at .297 percent. For a tabulation of 15 million for 1600, the argument advanced in this book would suggest that population may have increased by only 2 million during the harsh conditions of 1450–1550, equaling a yearly rate of merely .18 percent. Even with an expansion of 3 million between 1550 and 1600, the annual rate of increase would have risen to only .447 percent—not much different from later in the Tokugawa period. Only the rate from 1600 to 1721 (15–31.3 million) jumps noticeably (.61 percent)

Even if we allow for Saitō's higher figure of 17 million for 1600, if the population expanded by 3 million between 1450 and 1550 and by 4 million from 1550 to 1600, then the annual rates of growth equal .26 and .537 percent respectively. Both rates are higher than Kitō's but still

TABLE 6.4
Demographic Growth Rates According to Kitō and Saitō for
1450–1550, 1550–1600, and 1600–1721

1280–1450	If population increased from 6.1 to 10.1 million, then r = 0.297
1450–1550	(Kitō) If population increased from 10 to 12 million, then r = 0.18
	(Saitō) If population increased from 10 to 13 million, then r = 0.26
1550–1600	(Kitō) If population increased from 12 to 15 million, then r = 0.447
	(Saitō) If population increased from 13 to 17 million, then r = 0.537
1550–1721	(Kitō) If population increased from 12 to 31.3 million, then r = 0.56
	(Saitō) If population increased from 13 to 31.3 million, then r = 0.51
1600–1721	If we accept a figure of 15 million, then from 1600 to 1721, r = 0.61
	If we accept a figure of 17 million, then from 1600 to 1721, r = 0.505

Note: Here r = rate of demographic growth. It is calculated, from figures presented above, according to Shryock and Siegel, *Methods and Materials of Demography,* 2, pp. 377–380.

correspond closely to the argument made in this book. Furthermore, the posited rate for 1550–1721 is .51 percent—much more realistic than the 1 percent proposed by Hayami, given what scholars already know about population expansion even in optimal times in the Tokugawa period.

If these figures are plausible, there seem to be at least two ways to evaluate social and economic trends between 1450 and 1600. On the one hand, we can see the Warring States and Unification eras as a missed opportunity, arguing that a truly massive breakthrough would have come if only crop failures had not been so frequent and the samurai had found a peaceful way to resolve their disagreements. On the other hand, we can emphasize the advances made, especially in agriculture, commerce, industry, and community and family formation. In all these areas, the last 150 years of the medieval age helped lay the foundation for early Tokugawa society.

Epilogue

I have argued in the preceding pages that a fundamental transformation swept the Japanese archipelago during the medieval age, symbolized by a trebling of the population from a mere 5.5–6.3 million in 1150 to 15–17 million by 1600. While I have focused upon deriving defensible numbers for demographic fluctuations over half a millennium, I have also touched upon many aspects of society and economy affecting birth and death rates, including factors of extraordinary mortality, such as disease, famine, and war, and indirect or background variables, such as agriculture, commerce, industry, the village and family, and the physical well-being of commoners. It has been a daunting undertaking, in part because there are few quantifiable materials, and in part because there are so many elements that affect population. I hope that this monograph will be viewed not as the final word on this subject but rather as a hypothesis to be tested and criticized by scholars to come.[1] The main findings of this monograph appear in tables E.1, E.2, and E.3.

TABLE E.1
Population Estimates for Japan, 1150–1721[a]

YEAR	ESTIMATE (MILLIONS)
1150	5.5–6.3
1280	5.7–6.2
1450	9.6–10.5
1600	15–17
1721	31.3

[a]Refers to the archipelago without Hokkaido or the Ryukyu chain.

TABLE E.2
Estimates for Japan's Total Arable, 1150–1721
(Pre-1600 *chō*)

YEAR	ARABLE
1150	956,000
1280	977,000[a]
1450	1,241,379[a]
1600	1,588,462
1721	2,251,539

[a]Figures estimated from approximate total rural population and per-person *tan* requirements. See chapter 2, note 49, and chapter 4, note 59.

TABLE E.3
Estimates for Rice Yields per *tan,* 730–1720

YEAR	NARA *KOKU*	TOKUGAWA *KOKU*
730	1.57	0.48
1280	1.88	0.85
1450	2.28	1.23
1600	2.33–3.10[a]	0.955
1720	3.55[a]	1.094

[a]The figures in Nara units were arrived at by multiplying Hayami's figures for total *koku* by 2.5 and assuming that a Nara *tan* was 1.3 times larger than a Tokugawa *tan.*

What generalizations can we draw from this narrative of medieval Japanese demographic and economic development? As is true for all history, there is no single answer to this question; instead, there are multiple answers depending on the perspective. In considering this question, I would like to emphasize three points. First, I cannot help noticing the depth and sophistication of the population and economic evidence (as opposed to numbers) for "medieval" Japan. Even though data-poor in comparison to later epochs, the period between 1150 and 1600 is far from a so-called "Dark Age." To be sure, many will doubt the reliability of the figures calculated in this monograph, but at least this discussion is possible for Japan, as it is not for so many other parts of the globe for these centuries. If we accept the estimates derived and supported in this monograph as even a starting point, then the overall population record for medieval Japan is surprisingly good—equal to or better than any other place in the world.

Second, my analysis suggests that the medieval period as defined in this book encompassed a critical turning point. For the first 450 years of Japan's documented history, between 700 and 1150, the population was essentially static, hovering around 5–6.5 million. This stability was primarily the result of killer infections attacking a populace with no immunities, although famine and political instability played some role. At the same time, even if we accept Kitō's or Saitō's new figures for 1600, the age from 1600 to 1721 stands out as an epoch of strong demographic, agricultural, and economic growth in Japan's premodern past. Only the dramatic expansion of the Yayoi period can surpass the early Tokugawa epoch in percentage terms, and it took place over a much longer period of time.

The medieval epoch falls between these two very different periods. In other words, the inhabitants of the archipelago witnessed a crucial reversal of fortunes over the course of these four and one-half centuries. In Kitō's theory, the medieval era represented the end of a second cycle of population growth and the beginning of the third and final premodern cycle. According to information currently available, the turning point from stasis to expansion seems to have occurred in the late thirteenth century.[2] And the demographic growth commencing around that time reverberated throughout the economy, stimulating agrarian, commercial, and industrial improvements, as well as improvements in the society, where the corporate village and stem family were two of its eventual products.

Third, scholars may draw upon world history in numerous ways to place medieval Japan in context. For instance, an economic schema borrowed from European history would see the late medieval era as an earlier extension of Japan's Tokugawa heritage, helping to lay the foundations for what was to come.[3] To borrow a phrase from David Landes, we can view the epoch from 1280 to 1600 as Japan's era of "multicentennial maturation."[4] Historians of Western Europe now agree that the roots of the demographic and economic growth propelling much of the continent into the early modern era lay in the time from about 1000 to 1500. During this half millennium, peasants opened up new frontiers; farming became more intensive and geared for the market; commerce reawakened from its long slumber; and towns and cities sprang up throughout the region. To be sure, the agricultural regime reached its limits by 1250 or so and then was dealt a harsh blow by plagues lasting from about 1350 to 1500. Still, everyone agrees that without the development of the 1000–1500 era Western Europe's history would have been very different.

In a similar way, we can envision Japan after 1280 as commencing its own "multicentennial maturation." In the area of mortality, immunities continued to rise for almost all infections, and while we cannot know the death tolls arising from disease, it seems likely that they took a lesser toll on the overall population than before 1150. In agriculture, double-cropping, the *shimahata,* the planting of Champa rice, and the building of more and better irrigation works (including the waterwheel) led to greater output and more expansive arable, eventual banishing "spring hungers" and creating a more benign mortality pattern. The corporate village came into existence and spread, as did the stem family. A commercial boom began in the 1300s and continued more or less uninterrupted through the Tokugawa age. Industry became technologically more sophisticated and productive. Cities multiplied. And the physical well-being of commoners and aristocrats alike ascended to new heights. In all these ways the period beginning around 1280 links ahead to what James McClain has called "the fertile seedbed" of Tokugawa Japan.[5]

There may be limits, however, to how far we can press this parallel. For example, some will seize upon the comparison with Western Europe to assert that Japan was the quintessential "late developer," with all the advantages and handicaps that that presumably entailed.[6] To be sure, the initiation of a new growth cycle around 1280 is later than the beginning of Western Europe's "maturation" in 1000, and if scholars choose to emphasize Japan's late development, then that is one point of view. We should note at the same time, however, that (1) all parts of Western Europe did not begin the process at the same time or maintain it at the same pace, and (2) China, along with possibly the Middle East and India, began to grow and was more inventive than either Western Europe or Japan even earlier, but then for various reasons—most of which are the subject of controversy—it moved along another path.

Korea provides another intriguing comparison.[7] The peninsula underwent its own "multicentennial maturation" beginning in the fourteenth century; peasants overcame fallowing, and land clearance, especially for rice paddies, boomed as never before. Village communities sprang up, and a new balance between the rulers and the ruled was struck with the growth of a Neo-Confucian elite. A population boom enhanced by advances in medicine borrowed from Sung China provided the drive for this transformation.

A survey of world history suggests that there were several different routes to modernity; Japan followed one, parts of Western Europe another, China a third, and Korea yet another. The mirror image shape of demographic curves in preindustrial Japan and Western Europe would seem sufficient to show that there is no single, universal path to modernity.[8] Deeming or implying that one way, particularly the European, is paradigmatic would seem to constitute an important potential drawback to this approach.

Yet another drawback is its teleological emphasis on growth as an unalloyed good. The deaths from famine and war in medieval Japan should make this clear. To take another example, by 1600 Japan had already sustained considerable ecological damage, especially to its forests and soil. Cypress and cedar, the preferred building materials, were becoming more and more difficult to harvest, and much of the archipelago had been stripped bare. Limited water resources were the source of friction between villages. Mines were soon exhausted too. "Progress" should never be a given of history nor provoke unreflective cheers from humanity.

A second, anthropological theory outlined in the introduction may be a more useful way to put "medieval" Japan into world historical perspective. This notion holds that the Middle Ages were a time when Japanese society slowly and painfully overcame a "macroparasitic imbalance."[9] To elaborate, just as invisible viruses and bacteria have preyed upon humans for millennia, meriting the sobriquet of "microparasites," much more visible agents have also been the bane of humans for about as long. Before the advent of agriculture, these "macroparasites" were carnivores, such as lions or bears, but soon hunters learned to band together to kill those predators.

When humans invented agriculture and a class of primary producers came into existence, however, a new macroparasitic threat appeared: other humans. They stole part or all of a cultivator's meager harvest, giving nothing in return and leaving the hard-working peasant to face hunger and death. Fortunately, just as humans eventually reached equilibria with various pathogens, reducing them to childhood diseases, so such modulated relationships were also possible with humans who seized food and land. Eventually, elites learned to collect rents and taxes in a more or less regular fashion, a far more palatable form of "macroparasitism" than plunder. The working out of this balance, with its implication of reciprocity between elites and primary producers, necessarily took centuries.

In Japan during the years from 1150 to 1600, evidence suggests that such macroparasitism was moving from a highly unstable to a more predictable and bearable form. The frequent wars, with their arson, plundering, and kidnapping, represented the imbalance in its most extreme form, but the great famines of the Kamakura or Warring States periods were no less an expression of disequilibrium. After all, while the elite may have lost some of their income during a famine, none suffered the starvation that was the lot of many peasants. For the first half of this period, the macroparasitic basis of civilization remained stark and clear; hard-pressed tax producers received little or nothing in return for their support of civil aristocrats, highly placed priests, or warriors. Moreover, unlike the first two groups of elites, most warriors contributed to the mayhem by constantly abusing primary producers and fighting wars. At least the civil aristocrats left us great poetry and art and the priests elaborate rituals and spiritual comfort; most warriors were not part of the solution but part of the problem for many centuries.

Slowly over the medieval epoch, however, greater reciprocity came to characterize the relations between the elites and primary producers. Food relief institutions were created to care for orphans and the hungry hordes. Commercial markets came into existence and allowed peasants to exchange their hard-earned surplus for material benefits, such as clothes, tools, and fertilizer. Eventually, an early modern death pattern replaced the chronic malnutrition of "spring hungers." And from 1590, one obvious sign of disequilibrium—war—was banished from the islands to Korea and then transmogrified into the Pax Tokugawa after 1639. A greater sense of reciprocity was made even more secure and explicit by the victorious Tokugawa shogunate and its adoption of a new ideology.[10] Notably, famine receded for only a time but reappeared later in the form of the famous Kyōhō, Tenmei, and Tenpō disasters.

No matter what perspective we train upon Japan's medieval economy and society, one thing is clear: they are important and interesting topics. This work is intended to add to the excellent monographs already available on these subjects. Unlike those other studies, however, this book has focused on that most imponderable of all imponderables: population. For most of the era, elites rode waves of stasis and expansion as best they could, but their contribution was negligible. Common folk provided a large degree of the impetus for social and economic developments, and it is to them that this story really belongs.

Endnotes

ABBREVIATIONS USED FOR PRIMARY SOURCES IN NOTES AND TABLES

ASS	*Aou-shi shi*
CKS	*Chiba-ken shiryō*
DNS, with series number in Roman numerals and volume in Arabic numbers	
	Dai Nihon shiryō
GKS	*Gifu-ken shi*
HHBE	*Hagi-hanbatsu etsuroku*
HI	*Heian ibun*
HKS	*Hyōgo-ken shi*
HKSKCSH	*Hiroshima-ken shi: Kodai chūsei shiryō hen*
	(kengai monjo hen)
HSS	*Hennen sabetsu shi shiryō shūsei*
JK	*Jishū kakochō*
KI	*Kamakura ibun*
KSS	*Kōfu-shi shi: Genshi kodai chūsei hen*
MKM	*Mōrike monjo*
MKTH	*Masamoto kō tabi hikitsuke*
MSS	*Maizuru-shi shi: shiryō hen*
NBCICS	*Nanboku chō ibun: Chūgoku Shikoku hen*
NBCIK	*Nanboku chō ibun: Kyushu hen*
OKKS	*Okayama-ken komonjo shū*
SIGH	*Sengoku ibun: Go-Hōjō hen*
ZGR	*Zoku gunsho ruijū*

INTRODUCTION

1. The application and dating of the term "medieval" for Japan is hotly contested. I adopted the traditional periodization merely because population totals can be adduced for 1150 and 1600. For another perspective, see Mass, *Origins of Japan's Medieval World*, introduction.

2. Hayami, "Jinkō shi," p. 122. The Japanese term for dark ages is *ankoku jidai.*

3. Yokoyama, "Honchō." On his other estimates, see work in note 14 below.

4. Yoshida Tōgo, *Ishin shi,* pp. 25-26. For a handy table of prewar estimates, see Takahashi Bonsen, *Jinkō shi,* pp. 35-81.

5. Taeuber, *Population of Japan,* pp. 14 and 20.

6. McNeill, *Plagues,* p. 126.

7. Hayami: "The Population at the Beginning of the Tokugawa Period"; *Kinsei nōson,* pp. 18-24; *Nihon ni okeru keizai shakai,* pp. 82-85; *Nihon keizai shi,* pp. 71-113.

8. Hayami, Nishikawa, and Shinpo, *Sūryō keizai shi,* pp. 42-49.

9. Hanley and Yamamura, *Economic and Demographic Change,* pp. 44-45.

10. Sawada, *Nara chō jidai,* pp. 143-309; *Kanoko C iseki,* pp. 105-110.

11. Kitō first elaborated this theory in *Nihon nisen nen* and refined it in *Jinkō kara yomu.* It should be noted that at the time of the writing of this book, archaeologists were engaged in a debate about the origin of the Yayoi period, with a growing number supporting carbon-dating of rice grains at 900 BCE. For the sake of convenience, I have retained the traditional date.

12. Hanley and Yamamura, *Economic and Demographic Change,* pp. 44-45.

13. McNeill, *Plagues,* pp. 5-13. It is interesting to note that as recently as 2001 Fujiki, *Kiga to sensō,* pp. 3-16, characterized Japan's medieval period as an era of "famine and war."

14. This section briefly summarizes my *Population of Ancient Japan.*

15. Hanihara, "Estimation of the Number of Early Migrants"; Seki Akira, *Kikajin.*

16. McNeill, *Plagues,* pp. 124-125.

CHAPTER 1: NEW PROBLEMS, SAME RESULT

1. *Gaki sōshi; jigoku sōshi; yamai sōshi.*

2. For the computation and corroboration of the figures in these sources, see Farris, *Population of Ancient Japan.*

3. On *Shūgai shō,* note Iyanaga, *Kodai shakai keizai shi,* pp. 363-367.

4. Japanese research on these records is voluminous. The most well-known analyses are Ishii Susumu, *Nihon chūsei kokka,* pp. 118-173; Amino, *Nihon chūsei tochi seido,* pp. 31-38, 141-180, 425-523, 584-586; and Nakano Hideo, "Ōtabumi kenkyū." In addition to these general studies, there is voluminous research on individual *ōtabumi:* Gomi Satsuo: "Hyūga no kuni," "Ōsumi no kuni," and "Satsuma no kuni"; Mino, "Noto no kuni"; Ebisawa: "Kamakura jidai ni okeru Bungo no kuni" and "Hyūga no kuni"; *MSS,* pp. 533-564; Kamoshida, "Hitachi no kuni"; Shimazu, "Chūsei Hitachi"; Morimoto, "Hizen no kuni"; Nishikōri: "Betsumyō sei" and "Ōtabumi"; Kuwahara, "'Ōtabumi' denseki"; Itoga, "Hitachi no kuni"; Watanabe Sumio, "Nihon no shōen"; Nakano Hideo: "Awaji no kuni ōtabumi" and "Kagen yo'nen Hitachi no kuni tabumi"; Saitō Masao, "'Awaji no kuni ōtabumi'"; Inoue Hiroshi,

"Jōō ninen Iwami no kuni"; *Hidaka chōshi: Shiryō hen,* pp. 929–948; Homuda, "Ōtabumi to kokugaryō"; and Nakano Hatayoshi, "Kenkyū no Buzen Bungo." Also note various articles in Amino et al., *Kōza Nihon shoen shi,* vols. 5–7 and 9, and Ebisawa's *Shōen kōryō sei,* pp. 41–201.

    5. For the twofold analyses of both *Wamyō shō* and *Shūgai shō,* see Farris, *Population of Ancient Japan.* Essentially, these methods are variations of a system first devised by Kitō Hiroshi in 1983. See Kitō, *Nihon nisen nen,* pp. 46–47. In the first, it is assumed that the rice acreage listed in the record is a unit of account representing all economic activity within the province and embracing almost all of its populace. Once I computed a satisfactory cipher for the mean area of paddy rice necessary to sustain an individual, I merely divided by it and then added totals for infants and urbanites to achieve an overall estimate. In the second, I read the figures as reflecting merely all wet-rice paddies. I then subtracted a percentage for abandoned fields, used the same number as in the first method for the average rice acreage necessary to support one person, divided that figure into the total rice land under cultivation, and then added totals for those subsisting by means other than rice farming, children, urbanites, and others. These methods are far from perfect, and many objections may be fairly lodged against them, but to make use of the quantitative sources currently available, these methods seem to take into consideration the most variables.

    6. Furthermore, I utilized the fragmentary Buzen register because a reliable Tokugawa-period copy contains the total rice fields within the province. I analyzed the 1306 rather than the 1279 Hitachi record because the 1306 register is complete, but the 1279 document provides invaluable corroboration for the early-fourteenth-century list. Finally, the Tango register includes unmistakable notations from the Muromachi era, even though the province-wide total lists the date 1288. The Buzen record may be found in Nakano Hatayoshi, "Kenkyū no Buzen Bungo," p. 39. On the 1279 Hitachi *ōtabumi,* see Nakano Hideo, "Kagen yo'nen Hitachi no kuni tabumi." The best text for the Tango record appears in *MSS,* pp. 533–552.

    7. Amino, *Nihon chūsei tochi seido,* pp. 35–36; Tanuma Tatsumi: "Muromachi bakufu to shugo ryōkoku," pp. 92–93, and "Chūseiteki kōden taisei"; Homuda, "Ōtabumi to kokugaryō," pp. 530–544; Irumada, "Kōden to ryōshu sei." Of these authorities, Tanuma and Irumada seem to believe that the freezing of numbers became commonplace after 1300, Amino seems to accept the general accuracy of the *ōtabumi* for the period to 1250 or so, and Homuda casts doubt upon their reliability even from the time of compilation. Current opinion as represented by Ishii Susumu and the series *Kōza Nihon shoen shi* (Amino et al.) would seem to support the general veracity of the Kamakura Great Land Registers.

    8. The leading authority on estate surveys was Hōgetsu, "Chūsei kenchi." Also note Hosokawa Kameichi, "Chūsei shōen no kenchi"; Tomizawa, *Chūsei shōen to kenchū;* and Hōgetsu, "Kenchi" and "Kenchū chō." More recently, see Suzuki Tetsuo, *Kaihatsu to hyakusei,* pp. 97–124

9. Figures on the estate survey came from Amino, *Chūsei shōen no yōsō*, pp. 56–59; the original records may be found in *KI*, 11, pp. 57–62.

10. The *ōtabumi* figures for Iriki appear in *KI*, 2, p. 241; the survey numbers were included in *Iriki monjo*, p. 39.

11. The 1282 Hitachi Great Land Register is contained in *KI*, 18, pp. 280–287.

12. Inoue Hiroshi, *Chūgoku chihō no shōen*, p. 398. Also note Asaka Toshiki, *Hokuriku chihō no shōen Kinki chihō no shōen*, pp. 39–50; and Tsutsui Teiko, *Tōhoku Kantō Tōkai chihō no shōen*, pp. 107–125. These authors—whose works are volumes 9, 6, and 5 respectively in the multi-volume compendium in *Kōza Nihon shōen shi*, edited by Amino et al.—confirm the accuracy of the land registers.

13. Yamamoto Takashi, *Shōen sei no tenkai*, pp. 104–118.

14. J.I. Nakamura, *Agricultural Production and Economic Development*, pp. 75–77. Note that Nakamura assumed that the Kamakura *koku* and early modern *koku* held the same volume. Nakamura's study was thoroughly criticized by Rosovsky, "Rumbles in the Rice Fields."

15. Yamamura, "The Decline of the *Ritsuryō* System," p. 12.

16. *Dai Nihon sozei shi*, p. 242.

17. Hōgetsu, *Chūsei ryōsei shi*, pp. 28–170.

18. It should be noted that the editors of *Dai Nihon sozei shi* assume that all measures in the records it cites were made according to the *senshi to* (p. 248).

19. Hōgetsu, "Hōken jidai zenki no sangyō keizai," p. 21.

20. Furushima, *Nōgyō gijutsu shi*, pp. 197–198. Hōgetsu, "Hōken jidai zenki no sangyō keizai," p. 21, asserts that the maximum yield was 1.6 *koku*. It should be noted that Hōgetsu states that it is not absolutely certain that the proprietor received all the harvest. For another, even lower estimation of Kamakura yields, see Minegishi, "Nengu, kuji, to utokusen," pp. 69–71.

21. In terms of the Nara measurement, one *tan* of high-grade paddy produced 2.5 *koku*; medium-grade paddy produced 2 *koku*, low-grade, 1.5, and very low-grade, .75. Since the authorized legal mix of grades yielded 1.57 *koku*, it computes that high-grade paddy made up 23 percent of the paddy fields; medium-grade, 36 percent; low-grade, 27 percent; and very low-grade, 13 percent. For simplicity's sake, in calculating the Kamakura percentages of the mix, I have combined the last two categories (40 percent). Overall, therefore, the Kamakura mix cited above reduces inferior paddy land by 5 percent and increases medium-grade by 4 percent and high-grade by 2 percent, thus supporting the conclusion that Kamakura agriculture saw *some*, but not major, improvement.

22. Yamamura, "The Growth of Commerce," p. 392, states that the effort to standardize the *senshi to* "had little effect," but Hōgetsu, *Chūsei ryōsei shi*, p. 172, seems to contradict Yamamura, stating that the measure was widely used until the end of the Kamakura era. For one example, see *KI*, 40, p. 52.

23. Yamamura, "The Growth of Commerce," p. 392.

24. On the figure of 2.17 *tan* of rice paddy to sustain an individual grantee, see Farris, *Population of Ancient Japan.*

25. On this issue, see ibid. and Kitō, *Nihon nisen nen,* p. 47. As noted, there is the possibility, enunciated by Amino and others, that the numbers in the *ōtabumi* record not just rice production but all economic activity converted into rice equivalencies. More so than in the case of Heian records, this conclusion seems particularly apt for the Kamakura Great Land Registers. Amino, *Nihon chūsei tochi seido,* pp. 36–65. Amino believes that the *ōtabumi* were compiled to raise labor gangs and therefore would have included most of the populace.

26. Farris, *Population of Ancient Japan;* Hayami, "The Population at the Beginning of the Tokugawa Period," p. 22. Note that Amino, *Chūsei minshū no seigyō to gijutsu,* pp. 44–45, argues that fishing communities were omitted from the Great Land Registers if they did not contain fields.

27. Ishii Susumu, "Bunken kara saguru jinkō," pp. 59–61; Kōno, "Hakkutsu kara shisen shita jinkō," pp. 61–63. On Kamakura also note Ono Masatoshi *Chūsei iseki,* pp. 10, 16–17, and Kōno, *Kamakura.*

28. Tanaka Migaku, *Heijō-kyō,* pp. 125–165; Farris, *Sacred Texts,* p. 164.

29. One might argue that Japan was more urbanized in the Kamakura period, but even as late as 1875 only about 13 percent of Japan's population lived in centers with more than five thousand inhabitants. It is probable that the percentage was much lower in the late thirteenth century; the estimate of about two hundred thousand for Japan's urban residents in 1280 works out to 3.3 percent in urban centers if we assume that the total population was 6 million. See Kitō, *Edo jidai no jinkō,* pp. 77–78.

30. Personal communication from Saitō Osamu, August 15, 2000.

31. McNeill, *Plagues,* pp. 124–126; *Hyakuren shō,* Gennin 1/4/13, p. 161; Kangen 1/5/19, p. 199.

32. Hattori, *Kamakura jidai,* pp. 80–86. Hattori notes the declining trend especially among the elite classes. Also note Ōsumi, *Shinjin no sekai,* pp. 49–68, 194–212.

33. Burnet and White, *Natural History of Infectious Disease,* pp. 118–119.

34. Jannetta, *Epidemics and Mortality,* p. 68. Jannetta argues that measles never became endemic to the islands, a view that has much to recommend it but that I do not share. Anecdotal evidence can be found in Farris, "Diseases of the Premodern Period in Japan," pp. 381–382.

35. Jannetta, *Epidemics and Mortality,* p. 134. On malaria in this period, see Ueno Katsuyuki, "Nihon kodai chūsei ni okeru shippei ninshiki."

36. Burnet and White, *Natural History of Infectious Disease,* pp. 118–119. These authors also list a fourth factor: "the number of organisms shed by the patient or carrier and the period over which such liberation persists, the physical form in which the organisms are shed into the environment and how long the material will remain infectious under existing environmental circumstances." Some of these variables may be subsumed under the quality of the microorganism, along with such characteristics as the means by which the

pathogen is spread and the dose needed to initiate symptomatic infection. Unfortunately, however, sources for the medieval epoch are usually too general to permit specific comments about most of these points.

37. Farris, "Diseases of the Premodern Period in Japan," pp. 381–382. On tuberculosis, note Johnston, *Modern Epidemic*, pp. 40–42.

38. See Evans and Brachman, *Bacterial Infections of Humans*, pp. 377–378.

39. Hattori, *Kamakura jidai*, p. 85.

40. Farris, *Population of Ancient Japan*. See also Gomi Fumihiko, *Insei ki shakai*, pp. 285–311.

41. Fujikawa, *Shippei shi*, pp. 250–253.

42. McNeill, *Plagues*, p. 198.

43. *Gaki sōshi*, pp. 1–38. *Jigoku sōshi* contains similar figures, pp. 39–76.

44. The first English-speaking work to treat the Civil War of 1180–1185 in detail was Shinoda, *Founding of the Kamakura Shogunate*. Mass then wrote *Warrior Government*. Also see Farris, *Heavenly Warriors*, pp. 252–310. Recently, Mass has issued *Yoritomo*, a revised version of *Warrior Government*. Also note Friday, *Samurai, Warfare and the State*.

45. My narration of the Yōwa famine follows two sources: Nishimura Makoto and Yoshikawa, *Nihon kyōkō*, pp. 102–109, and Sasaki Junnosuke, *Kikin to sensō*, pp. 19–21. All quotations originate from these two sources unless otherwise noted. Also note Souyri, *World Turned Upside Down*, pp. 33–35.

46. *Hōjō ki*, pp. 29–32; Keene, *Anthology of Japanese Literature*, pp. 201–203.

47. Farris, *Heavenly Warriors*, pp. 305–307.

48. See Kitō, *Nihon nisen nen*, pp. 54–55. Kitō, *Jinkō kara yomu*, pp. 65–67, claims that until 1200 the weather was hotter and drier than in earlier times.

49. Yamamoto Takeo: "Rekishi no nagare"; *Kikō*, pp. 11–21.

50. Most Japanese historians agree that the late eleventh and twelfth centuries were an unusually warm time, leading to frequent droughts and the opening of more land in eastern and northern Japan. See Ishii Susumu, *Chūsei no katachi*, pp. 14–17; Minegishi, *Chūsei saigai senran*, pp. 31–40; Gomi Fumihiko, "Chūseiteki tochi shoyū," pp. 77–80, and Nishiyachi Seibi and Iinuma Kenji, "Chūseiteki tochi shoyū," pp. 81–85—both in Gomi Fumihiko and Watanabe, *Tochi shoyū shi*.

51. For Europe, see Gottfried, *Black Death*, pp. 22–23. For China and the Western Hemisphere, see Farris, "Famine, Climate, and Farming." Also note Isogai Fujio, *Nōgyō to kikō*, pp. 250–257. In eustatic terms, this age conforms to the Rottnest Terrace, with a submergence under the ocean of lands from western Australia to Maine. See Fairbridge, "Eustatic Changes," pp. 171–172.

52. HI, 11, pp. 342–344. Unless otherwise noted, translations are mine.

53. Ibid., p. 342.

54. Ibid., 8, p. 3104.

55. Ibid., p. 3058.

56. Ibid., p. 3059.

57. As examples of records on dry fields and crops, see ibid., pp. 3001, 3030, 3050, 3063. For nonpayment of taxes, see ibid., pp. 2993, 3000–3001, and 3013–3014. On labor dues, see ibid., pp. 3019–3020, 3029, and 3034–3035.

58. Higashijima, "Toshi ōken to chūsei kokka," pp. 169–177. All quotations here originate from this source unless otherwise noted. In an entry for the first month of 1184, Kanezane wrote that he had heard that "because the Kanto suffered from famine, just a few military forces were headed for the capital." This quotation raises the possibility that the drought and famine reached into eastern Honshu. Because Yoritomo controlled the Kanto and communications with the court had been severed, Kanezane added that "it was hard to tell if it were true or not." Given the historical record as it has survived, with most documentation of the famine surviving for Kyoto and Taira-controlled western Japan, it seems likely that that region, and not eastern and northern Honshu, suffered the brunt of the crisis and the highest mortality rates. Arakawa, *Kikin,* pp. 40–41, was one of the first to propose that the bumper harvest of eastern Honshu played a crucial role in the outcome of the civil war. It should be noted, however, that aristocratic diaries and chronicles contradict Arakawa's view by using the vague phrase "all under heaven" *(tenka)* repeatedly to denote that everyone was suffering.

59. *Gyokuyō,* Juei 2/Int. 10/18, p. 644.

60. Ibid., Juei 2/9/3, p. 626.

61. Sources for the following narration of the Kangi famine include Nishimura Makoto and Yoshikawa, *Nihon kyokō,* pp. 112–123; Sasaki Junnosuke, *Kikin to sensō,* pp. 33–51; and DNS, V, 5 and 6. Unless otherwise specified, all quotations come from these sources.

62. *Hyakuren shō,* Kangi 3/6/17, p. 168; Kangi 2/10/29, p. 167. Later it was compared to the Yōwa years.

63. This quotation is inaccurately ascribed to Fujiwara Teika in *Meigetsu ki* in Sasaki Junnosuke, *Kikin to sensō,* p. 34. The proper attribution can be found in DNS, V, 6, pp. 720–721. The term *guro* (mounded hill) is explained in Kinda, "Shōen sonraku no keikan," pp. 146–147.

64. Yamamoto Takeo, *Kikō,* pp. 177–200, claims that the late twelfth century witnessed dry, hot weather. In his earlier "Rekishi no nagare," pp. 119–141, he constructed a graph implying that temperatures were falling in the 1200s, but he makes no direct statement. Also advocating a warm early medieval period are Nishiyachi, "Chūsei zenki no ondanka," and Tamura, "Zaichi shakai to tenkō." Saitō Osamu, "The Frequency of Famines," combines the tenth through fourteenth centuries and thus his data mask climatic changes.

65. *Kishiwada shishi,* p. 405.

66. Isogai Fujio: "Nihon chūsei shi kenkyū to kikō hendō ron"; *Nōgyō to kikō,* pp. 193–275; Minegishi, *Chūsei saigai senran,* pp. 38–39; Gomi Fumihiko, Nishiyachi, and Kawai, "Chūsei zenki no tochi shoyū"; Fujiki, *Kiga to sensō,* p. 13.

67. For more on the topic of climate in the ancient epoch, see Farris, "Famine, Climate, and Farming." The weighting of terms used to express heat is ex-

plained in table 5 in the article and table 1.4 in this work. Most are either prayers for rain or Japanese words such as *kan* (drought) or *kansho* (drought and heat).

68. Atwell, "Volcanism and Short-Term Climatic Change." See also Gomi Fumihiko, Nishiyachi, and Kawai, "Chūsei zenki no tochi shoyū," pp. 155–157; Minegishi, *Chūsei saigai senran,* pp. 38–39; Fujiki, *Kiga to sensō,* pp. 13–14.

69. Historians and archaeologists of medieval Europe have been measuring changes in glaciers and tree pollen in peat bogs for over twenty-five years, and these indicators show evidence of a "Little Ice Age," marked by advancing glaciers, increased ice floes, and retreating forest cover high in the mountains as the glaciers grew. It is now basic knowledge among these scholars that the years from 1150/ 1200 to 1300/1350 were colder and wetter than earlier centuries, provoking several major famines in Western Europe on the eve of the Black Death. See Gottfried, *Black Death,* pp. 23–24. In eustatic terms, this begins the age of the Paria Emergence, so named for a peninsula in Venezuela. See Fairbridge, "Eustatic Changes," pp. 172–173. Descriptions of climate in thirteenth-century Japanese materials seem to confirm that historians are dealing with a worldwide ecological event.

70. *Meigetsu ki,* 3, Kangi 3/7/15, p. 304.

71. On the area of Koazaka, see Amino et al., *Kōza Nihon shōen shi,* 6: *Hokuriku dō no shōen Kinki chihō no shōen* I, p. 338.

72. *KI,* 1, pp. 212–321.

73. Uchida, "Chūsei shoki Kinai sonraku to nōgyō keiei," p. 5.

74. *KI,* 8, pp. 82–98, 121–142.

75. This explanation differs considerably from Yamamura, "Tara in Transition," pp. 356–358, who emphasizes the power of the proprietor and a high man-land ratio as explanations for equivalent units. While the proprietor, Kasuga, may have been responsible for the reorganization at Esaka, the man-land ratio declined even as farming units became equalized. I find an argument based upon the cost of labor more convincing than Yamamura's view.

76. *KI,* 6, p. 297 (Buzen); p. 301 (Settsu).

77. Isogai Fujio, "Kangi no kikin to kōbu no jinshin baibai seisaku." On countermeasures, also see Gomi Fumihiko, Nishiyachi, and Kawai, "Chūsei zenki no tochi shoyū," pp. 158–160.

78. *KI,* 6, pp. 315–329.

79. *Azuma kagami,* Kangi 3/4/21, p. 106.

80. *Tsuika hō,* 1, pp. 97–100.

81. *KI,* 6, pp. 299–300. For another complaint in Shinano, see *Azuma kagami,* Katei 2/7/17, p. 177

82. *KI,* 7, pp. 68–70. Tōdaiji went away empty-handed from an estate in Suō in 1233. See ibid., p. 39.

83. Ibid., pp. 386–387.

84. Ibid., 8, p. 102. Also see ibid., 6, pp. 225–226.

85. *KI,* 6, pp. 313–314.

86. Ibid., pp. 345–346, 365. Jeffrey Mass translated the documents from some of these disputes. See *Kamakura Bakufu,* pp. 57, 133–134, 163–164.

87. *KI*, 7, pp. 51–55; Isogai Fujio, "Kangi no kikin to Jōei shikimoku," pp. 11–13.

88. *KI*, 8, pp. 170–172.

89. *Azuma kagami*, Kangi 3/5/13, p. 107; *Tsuika hō*, p. 67.

90. *Azuma kagami*, Jōei 1/4/7, p. 115; *KI*, 6, pp. 357–358.

91. *Azuma kagami*, Jōei 1/4/21, p. 116.

92. Ibid., Jōei 1/7/10, pp. 116–117.

93. Hazard, "The Wako," pp. 260–270.

94. *KI*, 6, pp. 257–258. Lands in Harima had the same problem in that year. See ibid., p. 299.

95. Ibid., 7, pp. 48–49. Also note Kaya Village in Aki Province in western Honshu, where a record from the fall of 1230 showed thirteen of eighteen *chō* uncultivated, gone to waste, or damaged. See ibid., 6, pp. 229–230.

96. See Farris, "Famine, Climate, and Farming."

97. Irumada, *Hyakusei mōshijō to kishōmon*, pp. 279–303. Yasutoki first experimented with this policy during the crop failure of 1201.

98. *DNS*, V, 6, pp. 365–366.

99. Fujiki, *Kiga to sensō*, pp. 27–34. In this light, it is important to note that the *Mirror* is actually a paean to the virtues of the Hōjō leaders and should be read with great care. See Ishige, "*Azuma kagami* no seiji shisō," and Katō Michiko, "*Azuma kagami* ni okeru 'dōri.'"

100. Texts of the Jōei Formulary are legion. See *KI*, 6, pp. 374–388; *Goseibai shikimoku*, pp. 7–41; J.C. Hall, "Japanese Feudal Laws."

101. Isogai Fujio, "Kangi no kikin to Jōei shikimoku no seiritsu."

102. Ibid., pp. 18–19. Ōyama, *Kamakura bakufu*, pp. 345–346, has explicitly tied the Jōei Formulary to the famine. Takeuchi, "Jōei shikimoku no hizuke," has argued that the formulary was compiled between Jōei 1/7/10 and 1/8/10 and implemented by Jōei 2/5/14. For Mass' opinion, see *Development of Kamakura Rule*, pp. 102–112.

103. *Tsuika hō*, 1, pp. 87–89. The translation is mine.

104. For the 676 prohibition, see Nishimura Makoto and Yoshikawa, *Nihon kyokō*, p. 3; for the one for 1226, see Sasaki Junnosuke, *Kikin to sensō*, p. 25. On this slave market, also note Sasamoto, *Ikyō o musubu shōnin to shokunin*, pp. 205–214.

105. *KI*, 8, pp. 195 and 327. Isogai Fujio, "Kangi no kikin to kōbu no jinshin baibai seisaku," p. 17.

106. *Tsuika hō*, 1, p. 31; J.C. Hall, "Japanese Feudal Laws," pp. 38–39. This translation is my own.

107. Isogai Fujio: "Kangi no kikin to Jōei shikimoku," pp. 23–24; "Nihon chūsei shakai to dorei sei," pp. 26–33; "Hyakusei mibun no tokushitsu to dorei e no tenraku," pp. 74–75; and "Nihon chūsei dorei hō."

108. Fujiki, *Kiga to sensō*, pp. 21–26.

109. Minegishi, "Chūsei shakai no kaikyū kōsei," p. 41.

110. *Goseibai shikimoku*, p. 31; J.C. Hall, "Japanese Feudal Laws," p. 39.

Note that my translation differs from Hall's. The phrase that I apply to the flee-ing peasant and translate as "If even after having been invited back" Hall inter-prets as referring to the Kamakura courts, a view that commentator Kasamatsu Hiroshi finds doubtful. The final statement, concerning the freedom of going or staying, is a hotly debated issue among Japanese historians. For a good recent summary of the various postures, see Kuroda Hiroko, *Josei kara mita,* pp. 129–220; Suzuki Tetsuo, *Kaihatsu to hyakusei,* pp. 135–198.

111. Jannetta, "Famine Mortality in Nineteenth-Century Japan."

112. For this brief summary, I am relying upon Sasaki Junnosuke, *Kikin to senso,* pp. 46–56; and Nishimura Makoto and Yoshikawa, *Nihon kyoko,* pp. 122–124.

113. *Azuma kagami,* Kencho 3/4/26, p. 474. Of course, there are many im-ponderables, such as the amount of ash and gas belched forth and the direction of the winds.

114. *KI,* 11, p. 262.

115. Atwell, "Volcanism and Short-Term Climatic Change," pp. 46–50; Gomi Fumihiko, Nishiyachi, and Kawai, "Chusei zenki no tochi shoyu," pp. 153–158; Isogai Fujio, *Nogyo to kiko,* pp. 193–277.

116. *KI,* 12, p. 99.

117. For the Kamakura order, see *KI,* 12, pp. 55–65; for Emperor Kame-yama's, see ibid., pp. 277–285. In general on the Shoga famine, see Isogai Fujio, "Bun'ei gannen tamugi kazei kinshi rei," pp. 110–115; Gomi Fumihiko, Nishi-yachi, and Kawai, "Chusei zenki no tochi shoyu," pp. 157–160.

118. On tax arrears in the fifth month of 1257 in northern Kyushu, see *KI,* 11, pp. 226–227; for Ategawa, see *KI,* 12, pp. 17–18; for Tara, see *KI,* 12, pp. 182–183; a document from the third month of 1263 states Kaga owed fifty *koku* of rice to the court for a state Buddhist ceremony from 1257. See *KI,* 12, pp. 263–265. The last record lists several provinces in western Japan where taxes had not been paid.

119. Note *KI,* 11, pp. 363–364, and *KI,* 12, p. 38. The order from the tenth month of 1259 was repeated by Kamakura in 1261; *KI,* 12, p. 65. In the third month of 1258, when the Kyoto aristocrat named titular head of the Kamakura administration *(shogun)* was intending to make a progress to Kyoto, vassals *(goke'nin)* were warned to be on the lookout for local people fleeing required labor duties. See *KI,* 11, pp. 265–266.

120. See *KI,* 12, p. 14 and 160–171, and numerous disputes, such as *KI,* 11, pp. 302–303. Also cf. *KI,* 11, p. 351, for the order concerning excessive pa-perwork, dated in the sixth month of 1259. In the twelfth month of 1257, an as-sistant land steward *(jito dai)* was ordered to appear in Kyoto on charges of violent activities. Note *KI,* 11, pp. 254–255.

121. *KI,* 11, p. 336; *Tsuika ho,* p. 92. Also note Fujiki, *Kiga to senso,* pp. 34–38.

122. *KI,* 11, p. 363.

123. Hazard, "The Wako," pp. 272–277.

124. *Azuma kagami,* Bun'o 1/6/1, p. 741.

125. *KI*, 11, p. 295; also note ibid., 12, pp. 76-77, 194-195, 263. Also note Harrington, "Social Control and the Significance of *Akutō*."

126. Amino, "Kamakura makki no shomujun," pp. 29-31. Amino is famous for his thesis that the Mongol Invasions of 1274 and 1281 represented a turning point in Japanese history. See his *Mōko shūrai*. Also note Mass, "Of Hierarchy and Authority at the End of Kamakura," in *Origins of Japan's Medieval World*, pp. 17-38.

127. Cited in Sasaki Junnosuke, *Kikin to sensō*, p. 63.

128. *Azuma kagami*, 1, Kennin 1/8/23, p. 590, for the severe famine of 1201. For 1272, See *KI*, 14, p. 393, for an instance of peasants abandoning agriculture and p. 399 for difficulties encountered in repairing Chūsonji at Hiraizumi.

129. There is an abundance of work in English on these various conflicts. See Farris, *Heavenly Warriors*, pp. 263-273, 289-307, 313-335; Varley, *Warriors of Japan*, pp. 46-158; and Friday: *Samurai, Warfare and the State* and "Valorous Butchers." Both the Hōgen and Heiji Insurrections lasted for a matter of days and were fought mainly in the capital; the Northern Expedition lasted for two months, much of which was taken up in preparations and marching; the Jōkyū War took only one month, while the first Mongol Invasion of 1274 lasted for only two weeks, one day in Kyushu. Fighting during the second invasion lasted for about one month.

130. *Ōmi no kuni Banbanoshuku Rengeji kakochō*, pp. 243-253. Conlan, *State of War*, pp. 10-11, notes this document and lends implicit support to my analysis by describing how the Hōjō managed to keep their army intact despite devastating defeats at the hands of Go-Daigo's supporters. According to Conlan, the staying power of the Hōjō army was "remarkable."

131. Farris, *Heavenly Warriors*, pp. 320-324, 436.

132. The conventional view among Japanese historians over the last forty years has been that single, mounted battle was the rule, with forces small, skirmishes infrequent, and relatively few deaths among warriors. See Ishii Susumu: *Kamakura bakufu*, pp. 113-150, and *Chūsei bushidan*, pp. 16-226; Ishii Shirō: "Kassen to tsuibu," and *Nihon jin no kokka seikatsu*, pp. 38-72. Following these authors, Farris, *Heavenly Warriors*, pp. 263-343, argued that the predominant mode of fighting was single and mounted, and although each equestrian samurai had two or three attendants *(shojū)*, the role of these servants in warfare was secondary and they were often not reliable soldiers.

Beginning in the early 1990s, however, a new generation of historians examined weapons, defenses, and tactics during the late twelfth and thirteenth centuries and voiced criticisms of this paradigm. See Kawai: "Jishō Juei no nairan"; "Tsuwamono no michi to hyakusei no narai," pp. 34-43; *Genpei kassen*; and "Jishō Juei no sensō to Kamakura bakufu." See also Kondō: "Buki kara mita chūsei bushi ron"; *Yumiya to tōken*; and "Bugu no chūsei ka to bushi no seiritsu," pp. 140-184. Moreover, in 2004 Karl Friday wrote *Samurai, Warfare and the State*, an important survey of warrior life in the early medieval age synthesizing a broad range of material—including the work of Kawai and Kondō—while strongly criticizing the accepted wisdom.

In particular, these scholars argue that the nature of warfare was transformed between 1100 and the Civil War of 1180–1185. While the single, mounted mode of combat, undoubtedly invented in the Kanto, had prevailed as late as 1100, over the next century a tactical evolution took place. See Kawai, "Jishō Juei no sensō to Kamakura bakufu," pp. 63–64. Also note *Enkyō bon Heike monogatari*, p. 517, and Kondō, *Yumiya to tōken*, pp. 136–221.

New tactics were intimately bound up with the assertion that the Civil War of 1180–1185 witnessed violence on an unprecedented scale. The war involved many more soldiers than ever before; as a result, the fighting reached down in rural society to those unskilled in the old-fashioned single, mounted combat. What is more, barricades, trenches, and palisades played a more prominent function in the Civil War and Northern Expedition of 1189, suggesting greater efforts to enlist commoner muscle. See Kawai, "Jishō Juei no sensō to Kamakura bakufu," pp. 65–69. Friday appears to agree with Kawai, arguing that the armies of the late twelfth century could be counted in the thousands or even tens of thousands, whereas battles before 1100 involved several dozen or perhaps a hundred mounted archers (*Samurai, Warfare and the State*, pp. 119–132). Larger armies were apt to mean greater casualties; thus war was an even more important component in mortality than I had originally thought.

These arguments are open to question, however. For instance, the construction of palisades and ditches, about which Kawai and Friday supply plentiful testimony for northeastern Honshu, was not a new tactic. It had long been practiced in that region, having been employed against the "barbarians" in the seventh and eighth centuries, by the Abe and Kiyowara in the eleventh, and both by and against the Northern Fujiwara in the twelfth. To complicate matters, Kawai, Kondō, and Friday all admit that mounted archers were "the finely honed troops forming the main element of attack" during the Civil War. Cf. Kawai, "Jishō Juei no sensō to Kamakura bakufu," p. 68; Kondō, *Yumiya to tōken*, pp. 219–220; Friday, *Samurai, Warfare and the State*, pp. 128–131. The differences between the older and newer paradigms probably have minimal meaning for overall death rates.

133. Karl Friday has emphasized this point in *Samurai, Warfare and the State*, pp. 115–118; 155–162.

134. Gomi Fumihiko, *Kamakura to kyō*, pp. 143–145.

135. *Azuma kagami*, Genryaku 1/2/25, p. 104.

136. Kawai: "Tsuwamono no michi to hyakusei no narai," pp. 39–42, and "Kamakura shoki no sensō to zaichi shakai."

137. Adolphson, *Gates of Power*, pp. 125–239. Other specific examples of the destruction of peasant dwellings can be found on pp. 164, 168–170, 218, 225, 229–230, and 233–234.

138. Most of this paragraph comes from Miura Hiroyuki, *Zoku hōsei shi*, pp. 703–750. Also see Ishimoda, "Kamakura bakufu ikkoku jitō shiki," pp. 1–13; Mass, *Yoritomo*, pp. 129–180, 216.

139. Farris, *Heavenly Warriors*, pp. 286–289.

140. Conlan, *In Little Need of Divine Intervention*, p. 240.

141. For a definition of this term, especially as it applies to warriors, see Katsumata, *Ikki*, pp. 76–77. Kobayashi Keichirō, "Gun'yaku to hyōrō," p. 26, stresses warrior provisioning from their own properties or at the battle site during the Kamakura period. On self-help, also note Friday, *Samurai, Warfare and the State*, p. 30.

142. As general Buddhist terms, *jiriki* and *tariki* were associated with more than one sect. In Pure Land Buddhism, Hōnen referred to them, eventually emphasizing "the aid of another." Both terms are also commonly found in Zen, especially *jiriki*.

143. Ishii Ryōsuke, "Chūsei no 'karita rōzeki'"; Haga, "Karita rōzeki"; Kuramochi, "Karita rōzeki no hongen," pp. 132–150.

144. Oda, "Roji rōzeki."

145. McNeill, *A History of the Human Community*, 1, pp. 41, 43–44.

146. Mass: *Yoritomo*, pp. 102–130, and *Warrior Government*, pp. 93–167, provide the most detailed and nuanced discussion in English.

147. See Ishimoda, "Kamakura bakufu ikkoku jito shiki." Also see Mass: *Yoritomo* and *Warrior Government*.

148. Mass: *Yoritomo*, pp. 102–130; *Warrior Government*, pp. 93–167.

149. McNeill, *A History of the Human Community*, 1, pp. 43–44.

150. Jeffrey Mass has listed several cases of harmful behavior during peacetime: *Yoritomo*, pp. 225–252; *Warrior Government*, pp. 171–202. Also see selected documents translated in his *Kamakura Bakufu* and *Development of Kamakura Rule*. Fujiki, *Kiga to sensō*, pp. 4–5, quotes from a nineteenth-century maxim that "Even though one might meet up with Famine seven times, one ought not encounter War even once."

151. *KI*, 16, pp. 137–138. In English on this protest, note Frohlich, "Rulers, Peasants and the Use of the Written Word in Medieval Japan," pp. 118–203.

152. Amino, *Mōko shūrai*, pp. 177–182. Also note Kuroda Hiroko, *Mimi o kiri hana o sogi*.

153. Nakamura Ken, "Jūtaku hakyaku."

CHAPTER 2: CHANGE WITHIN BASIC CONTINUITY

1. Toda, "Jū-jūsan seiki no nōgyō rōdō," pp. 309–332; Yamamoto Takashi: "Chūsei nōmin no seikatsu no sekai," pp. 131–166, and "Shōen seika no kōchi nōhō." On the Kamakura estate, also see Keirstead, *Geography of Power*. Also on Kamakura agriculture, see Souyri, *World Turned Upside Down*, pp. 84–91.

2. Kuroda Hideo, *Chūsei kaihatsu*, pp. 406–446.

3. Toda, "Jū-jūsan seiki no nōgyō rōdō," pp. 314–316; 327–328, and Kuroda Hideo, *Chūsei kaihatsu*, pp. 412–414, 418, 421–423, 430–435, cite numerous poems sung as part of the agricultural cycle, many of them tied to *arata uchi*. It is plausible to question how rhythmic this work might be. It probably ruined many tools and backs!

4. Toda, "Jū-jūsan seiki no nōgyō rōdō," pp. 319–326. This time frame may seem long, but the cultivators undoubtedly did not concentrate on it every day.

5. There are many articles on this practice. See, for example, Yamamoto Takashi: *Shōen sei no tenkai,* pp. 73–154, and "Kamakura jidai no kannō to shōen shihai"; Ōta, "Kamakura ki no shōen to kannō"; Kuroda Toshio, "Kamakura jidai no shōen no kannō."

6. *Myōden* could consist of either wet-rice or dry fields. Many estates had both.

7. Kuroda Toshio, "Kamakura jidai no shōen to kannō," pp. 3–10.

8. Kelly, *Water Control in Tokugawa Japan.*

9. Farris, *Population, Disease, and Land,* pp. 102–104.

10. Kuroda Hideo, *Chūsei kaihatsu,* pp. 252–253. Also note Sasamoto, *Ikyō o musubu shōnin to shokunin,* pp. 38–43, for the impact of more iron on the production of hoes and spades.

11. Farris, *Population of Ancient Japan.*

12. Kuroda Hideo, *Chūsei kaihatsu,* pp. 254–255, uses the outdated Hasegawa Kumahiko, *Waga kodai seitetsu,* pp. 133–137, to make sweeping statements about advances in this industry at this time. My narrative is based on the much more recent archaeological survey, Ono Masatoshi, *Chūsei iseki,* pp. 102–104.

13. Amino: *Nihon chūsei no hinōgyōmin,* pp. 432–465; *Chūsei minshū no seigyō to gijutsu,* pp. 238–257; Sasamoto, *Ikyō o musubu shōnin to shokunin,* pp. 38–54; Sakurai, "Tennō to imoji," pp. 209–231, is critical of Amino's views.

14. Furushima, *Nōgyō gijutsu shi,* pp. 201–205. The subject of livestock in Japanese farming is tricky. Depending upon nutrient sources, it may or may not be an improvement. Given the scarcity of documentation, I have chosen to call this a technological "change" and consider it a minor one at best.

15. Farris, *Population of Ancient Japan.*

16. *KI,* 8, p. 40.

17. Ibid., 23, pp. 158–159.

18. Furushima, *Nōgyō gijutsu shi,* p. 204; *Shaseki shū; Sand and Pebbles.*

19. Furushima, *Nōgyō gijutsu shi,* pp. 205–216.

20. *Shaseki shū,* p. 214; *Sand and Pebbles,* p. 158.

21. Furushima, *Nōgyō gijutsu shi,* pp. 209–242. There were limits to how much common lands could produce or contribute to growth. A particularly interesting record written by a shrine official and dating from the early fourteenth century states that cultivators in Ōsumi Province "recently have damaged pine trees, cut down grasses, and harvested even the undergrowth *[shimokusa].* While they were committing these outrageous acts, the growth of small trees has been insufficient, the mountain has been wasted, and there is not a living thing on it." Only by enforcing restrictions did Iwashimizu Shrine return the mountain forest to its previous lush condition; *KI,* 32, p. 156. One may infer the position of the author of the document, as well as the location of the mountain, through *KI,* 29, pp. 336–337.

22. Troost, "Peasants, Elites, and Villages," pp. 93–94.

23. The conversion of dry fields into paddy, as noted by Kimura Shigemitsu in *Hatake to Nihonjin,* pp. 122–130, would also qualify as a more intensive method. See Troost, "Peasants, Elites, and Villages," p. 93. Note that the *shima-hata* was different from the mounded rows upon which wheat was planted.

24. *KI,* 25, pp. 239–240.

25. Kimura Shigemitsu, *Hatake to Nihonjin,* pp. 137–149. Kimura has related the same interpretation in *Nihon kodai chūsei hatasaku shi,* pp. 188–232, and "Chūsei zenki no nōgyō seisanryoku to hatasaku."

26. *Tsuika hō,* p. 105.

27. Furushima, *Nōgyō gijutsu shi,* p. 235.

28. Isogai Fujio, "Bun'ei gannen tamugi kazci kinshi rei," pp. 107–125. Isogai has reiterated his view in *Nōgyō to kikō,* pp. 161–191.

29. Fujiki, *Kiga to sensō,* pp. 38–42.

30. Furushima, *Nōgyō gijutsu shi,* p. 232.

31. *KI,* 16, pp. 254–255.

32. Isogai Fujio: "Jūsan-yon seiki Kii no kuni Kinokawa engan chiiki no tamugi shiryō"; "Kodai chūsei ni okeru zakkoku no kyūhōteki sakutsuke"; "Kamakura makki nanboku chō ki suiden nimōsaku tenkai jōkyō ka no nōgyō seisanryoku." These essays also appear in *Nōgyō to kikō,* pp. 57–160.

33. Minegishi, "Jūgo seiki kōhan no tochi seido," pp. 397–401; Kuroda Hideo, *Chūsei kaihatsu,* p. 69.

34. See, for example, Kagose, *Tei shitchi;* Ogawa Naoyuki, "Kantō chihō ni okeru tsumida no denshō."

35. Furushima, *Nōgyō gijutsu shi,* pp. 243–244.

36. Ibid. Takagi Tokurō, "Chūsei ni okeru sanrin shigen to chiiki kankyō," notes the battle between two communities over mountain wasteland in the Kamakura era.

37. *KI,* 24, p. 179.

38. Furushima, *Nōgyō gijutsu shi,* pp. 217–234, 257–274. Recently, Hirakawa Minami, an authority on ancient archaeology and history, has pointed out that a tabulation of rice strains found on wooden tablets and in poetry collections from the eighth and ninth centuries reveals nearly as many as were grown in the Edo period. They were dispersed from northern Kyushu to northeastern Honshu, and their use was likely adapted to climate and local insect conditions. It also should be noted, however, that the names of the strains are often regional, with different varieties sporting variant names in different places. Different varieties may also have the same name in different places. With this important caveat, we might argue that Kamakura peasants saw little in the way of amelioration; indeed Hirakawa's discovery may eventually lead to revised thinking about the ingenuity and productivity of Nara agriculturalists. Hirakawa, "Shin hakken no 'shushi fuda' to kodai no inasaku."

39. Itō Toshikazu, "Kodai chūsei no 'nohata'"; "Heian Kamakura jidai no yamahata (yakibata)."

40. *Azuma kagami,* Bunji 5/2/30, pp. 319–320.

41. Ibid., Shōji 1/4/27, p. 557.
42. Ibid., Shōgen 1/2/20, p. 635.
43. Ibid., Kangi 2/1/26, p. 91; En'ō 1/2/14, p. 237.
44. Ibid., Ninji 2/10/22, pp. 287–288. On all the above orders for land clearance, note Gomi Fumihiko, Nishiyachi, and Kawai, "Chūsei zenki no tochi shoyū," pp. 145–153.
45. Fukuda, *Chiba Tsunetane,* pp. 75–83.
46. Miura Keiichi, *Chūsei minshū seikatsu,* pp. 57–64.
47. Kuroda Hideo, *Chūsei kaihatsu,* pp. 55–61, 156–157.
48. *KI:* 7, p. 70 (Satsuma 1233); 8, p. 317 (Harima 1241); 11, p. 303 (Harima 1258); 14, p. 222 (Settsu 1271). Also note Imai, "Chūsei ni okeru kaikon"; Harada Nobuo, "Tōgoku no chūsei sonraku ni okeru kaihatsu to saigai"; and Suzuki Tetsuo, *Kaihatsu to hyakusei,* pp. 75–124. Conlan, *State of War,* pp. 205 and 219, speaks of increase in acreage under cultivation, especially paddy fields, but presents no examples. On p. 209, he also notes the existence of fraudulent claims to field development.
49. Speculation based upon the inferred population and rice yield figures for 1280 may suggest about how much land was available for planting rice. If we posit a population of about 6.25 million (an average of my estimate and Saitō Osamu's), then allowing for the 40 percent of the population that did not crop rice, we arrive at a total rice-farming population of 4,464,286. Subtracting 16 percent to allow for those below age six, as per above, leaves a total of 3,848,522. If the yield of rice land sufficient to sustain one person averaged 1.81 *koku* per *tan* and only 75 percent of paddies were cultivated, then total area could have been as low as 928,777 *chō,* 3 percent less than the figure in *Shūgai shō.* This number could imply that a smaller amount of land was being more intensively farmed, but if we do not make allowance for infants, then the tally calculates at 1,077,381 *chō,* a 13 percent increase over the arable of 1150. It seems likely that the acreage of paddy land was about the same in 1280 as in 1150.
50. Kinda, *Jōri to sonraku,* pp. 339–486. Harada Nobuo, *Chūsei sonraku,* pp. 82–258, has completed a thorough typology of medieval villages.
51. Troost, "Peasants, Elites, and Villages," p. 99. Also note Troost's excellent dissertation, "Common Property and Community Formation."
52. Iwamoto Yoshiaki, "Ijū to kaihatsu no rekishi," pp. 359–462; Keirstead, *Geography of Power,* pp. 25–45. Also on Kamakura *rōnin,* note Makino, *Buke jidai shakai,* pp. 30–40; Yamamoto Takashi, "Rōnin to chūsei sonraku"; Mizukami, *Chūsei no shōen to shakai,* pp. 91–154; and Suzuki Tetsuo, *Kaihatsu to hyakusei,* pp. 43–74.
53. Based upon research he did almost fifty years ago on Hideyoshi's surveys of the late sixteenth century, Araki Moriaki has held that peasants of the late Heian and Kamakura eras were members of a "patriarchal slave society," tied to the land and their masters; he reads Article 42 as a vain effort by the Kamakura *bakufu* to stop lords, primarily land stewards, from turning all their agriculturalists into slaves. Araki's original view can be found in "Taikō kenchi

no rekishiteki zentei—1." Araki has been especially vehement in his criticism of Amino, the leading advocate of peasant freedom of movement. See "Shikimoku yonjū ni jō kaishaku to idō no jiyū"; "Amino Yoshihiko shi no kingyō ni tsuite hihanteki kentō"; "Amino Yoshihiko shi kingyō ni tsuite no hihanteki kento." For Amino's views, see "Chūsei no futan taikei," pp. 86–90; *Nihon chūsei no minshū*, pp. 92–101. Fujiki Hisashi, Ōyama Kyōhei, Minegishi Sumio, and others emphasize the freedom of cultivators to move. See Kuroda Hiroko, *Josei kara mita*, pp. 131–134; Suzuki Tetsuo, *Kaihatsu to hyakusei*, pp. 135–197.

54. Kuroda Hiroko, *Josei kara mita*, pp. 129–153. For a prewar view, see Suzuki Ryōichi, "Chūsei ni okeru nōmin no chōsan." Also note Kuroda Hiroko, "Chōsan tōbō soshite kyoryū no jiyū," where the author concedes that migration was common no matter what the legal reality was; Yanagihara, "Hyakusei no chōsan to shikimoku yonjū ni jō"; Nakano Hideo, "Chūsei hyakusei to jitō shihai"; and Tamura, "Tsuibu oboegaki—Heian makki Kamakura ki no hyakusei ie chōsan," later included in Tamura, *Zaichi ron no shatei*, pp. 249–270.

55. Kuroda Hiroko, "Chūsei no chōsan to josei." When a peasant cultivator changed his residence in accordance with Article 42, he might bring his family with him or not.

56. Domar, *Capitalism, Socialism, and Serfdom*, pp. 225–238.

57. For general discussions of unfree persons, see Minegishi, "Chūsei shakai no kaikyū kōsei"; Takigawa, "Chūsei no jūsha ge'nin to no seido," in *Nihon rodo hosei shi*, pp. 85–124; Takahashi Masaaki, "Nihon hōken shakai." For a helpful legalistic perspective, see Maki, *Jinshin baibai*, pp. 89–186; some terminological difficulties are cleared up in Yasuno, "Jinshin baibai ninjō 'tenkō' bungen," and Hidemura, "Chūsei jinshin baibai monjo." Two excellent older studies are Ishii Ryōsuke, "Chūsei jinshin hōsei zakkō," and Egashira, "Chūsei ni okeru ge'nin no baibai"; see also Egashira, *Kōyasan ryō shōen*, pp. 377–427. More recently, see Kimura Shigemitsu and Sonobe, "Chūsei no shodankai shomibun," pp. 235–247; Minegishi, "Chūsei mibun sei kenkyū to ge'nin mibun tokushitsu," pp. 238–253; and Yasuno, *Ge'nin ron*, for a more imaginative, literary approach. Finally, my interpretation of the terms *hyakusei* (tax-paying commoner) and *ge'nin* (the unfree) varies considerably from that advanced by Conlan, *State of War*, pp. 111–123. I believe that my usage conforms much more closely to normal definitions employed by Japanese historians. See, for example, Nagahara, *Iwanami Nihon shi jiten*, p. 380 *(ge'nin)* and p. 974 *(hyakusei)*.

58. Mizukami, *Chūsei no shōen to shakai*, pp. 91–154.

59. Isogai Fujio: "Aki no kuni zaichō kanjin Tadokoro shi," pp. 50–84; "Chūsei hyakusei no saimu tenraku," pp. 379–426.

60. Ishii Susumu, *Chūsei no katachi*, pp. 208–217; Suzuki Tetsuo, *Kaihatsu to hyakusei*, pp. 364–382.

61. Hotate, "Fukuro mochi kasa mochi tsubo tori."

62. Isogai Fujio: "Nihon chūsei shakai to dorei sei"; "Hyakusei mibun no tokushitsu to dorei e no tenraku."

63. Kawane, *Chūsei hōken sei seiritsu shi,* pp. 392–396, has discovered another example related to the Shōga crisis.

64. Mizukami, *Chūsei no shōen to shakai,* pp. 91–154.

65. Kimura Shigemitsu and Sonobe, "Chūsei no shodankai shomibun," pp. 239–246. See also Ishii Susumu, *Chūsei no katachi,* pp. 216–217.

66. Isogai Fujio, "Nihon chūsei dorei hō." The terminology for unfree persons is complex. Generally speaking, it is assumed that the word *zōnin,* used in Article 41 along with *nuhi,* included other unfree people, such as *ge'nin* and *shojū.*

67. Most pessimists are of the old school: see Takigawa, *Nihon rōdō hōsei shi,* pp. 85–124. Among current scholars, Isogai Fujio appears to be the most pessimistic; see "Chūsei hyakusei no saimu tenraku," pp. 379–426. Optimists include Takahashi Masaaki, "Nihon hōken shakai," pp. 73–96; Minegishi, "Chūsei shakai no kaikyū kōsei," pp. 36–49; and Ishii Susumu, *Chūsei no katachi,* pp. 216–217.

68. Hosokawa Ryōichi, *Chūsei no risshū jiin to minshū,* pp. 177–179. Dōgyo was a member of the Regulations *(risshū)* Sect.

69. I am relying upon Nagamura, *Chūsei Tōdaiji no soshiki to keiei,* pp. 341–348; Ōyama, *Kamakura bakufu,* pp. 144–156; and Ishii Susumu, *Kamakura bakufu,* pp. 239–255. The quotation in this paragraph can be found in Ishii's work.

70. Farris, *Population of Ancient Japan.*

71. On iron, see note 12 above. On salt, see Amino, "Chūsei no seien to shio no ryūtsū," pp. 52–68; on pottery, see Ishii Susumu, "Chūsei yōgyō no shosō," pp. 123–152. On silk, see *Meiji zen Nihon sangyō gijutsu shi,* pp. 7–8; Ito Toshio, *Kinu,* pp. 163–183. Note imports were especially popular under Kiyomori and that Yoritomo made frequent gifts of silk to Buddhist orders. Yet most warrior clothing was not made of silk. On travel, see Wakita Haruko, "Chūsei no kōtsū un'yu," pp. 102–105. For a brief English summary, see Souryi, *World Turned Upside Down,* pp. 91–100. Finally, Amino has gathered and revised his previous essays in *Chūsei minshū no seigyō to gijutsu.* He stresses the importance and growth of these industries, especially in the latter half of the medieval age.

72. Sasaki Gin'ya, "Sangyō no bunka to chūsei shōgyō," pp. 143–188. Also see Sakurai Eiji: "Chūsei no kahei shin'yō," "Chūsei kinsei no shōnin," and "Chūsei no shōhin ichiba,"—all in Sakurai and Nakanishi, *Ryūtsū keizai shi,* pp. 42–77, 112–148, and 199–234; and Maehira Fusaaki, "Chūsei kinsei no bōeki," in Sakurai and Nakanishi, *Ryūtsū keizai shi,* pp. 331–339, for the most recent summary of this topic.

73. Cited in Nagahara Keiji, "Shōen ryōshu keizai no kōzō," p. 84. It should be noted that the number dropped to fifty-seven in 1351–1400.

74. Yamamura, "The Growth of Commerce," pp. 372–373.

75. Amino and Yokoi, *Toshi to shokunōmin no katsudō,* pp. 137–175. Note that Ishii Susumu, *Chūsei no katachi,* pp. 50–83, provides up-to-date in-

formation on Tosa. In addition to this list, Ashiya and Kamisaki in northern Kyushu may also qualify as urban areas.

76. Ogawa Makotō, *Chūsei toshi "fuchū."*

77. Ono Masatoshi, *Chūsei iseki,* pp. 16 and 26. On the rise of Toba and Yodo, note Ōmura, "Chūsei zenki no Toba to Yodo." For further information on medieval cities, also note Niki, *Toshi,* and Satō Makoto and Yoshida, *Toshi shakai shi.*

78. Kitō, *Edo jidai no jinkō,* p. 78.

79. The topics of kinship and marriage reveal a broad range of opinion, from scholars asserting the ubiquity of patrilineal arrangements to Takamure Itsue's matriarchy, with newer views taking a third position for bilateral relations. Historians emphasizing the trend for men to become increasingly dominant among farming families—whether as symbolized by a man's operation of the ox-drawn plow, the increasing number of virolocal marriages, or a patriarch's control of numerous servants—include Nishimura Hiroko, "Yometori kon e no ugoki," pp. 87–89; Suzuki Kunihiro, "Chūsei zenki shinzoku ron josetsu"; and Isogai Fujio cited in Minegishi, "Chūsei no kazoku to kyōdōtai," (1992), p. 460. Iinuma, "Josei mei kara mita chūsei no josei no shakaiteki ichi," made a painstaking study of women's names appearing in transfer documents throughout the late Heian and Kamakura periods, and the rise of childlike names during the thirteenth century suggested infantilization and declining status and inheritance powers for women.

Early in the postwar period, Takamure, *Nihon kon'in shi,* pp. 175–204, was the most articulate supporter of matrilineal kinship and matrilocal sexual relations. In her view, "artificial" matrilocal marriage prevailed during the thirteenth century, but most of her examples came from the elite. When it came to peasants, she seemed to argue for a high incidence of nightly visitation *(tsumadoi kon)* and matrilocal marriage *(mukotori kon).*

Recently, Gomi Fumihiko has expressed his doubt that the term "patriarchal" ever applied correctly to the medieval family. See "Chūsei no ie to kafuchō sei," p. 45. Also note the dissent of Kuroda Hiroko, *Josei kara mita,* pp. 129–293.

In English, see Wakita Haruko, "The Medieval Household and Gender Roles within the Imperial Family, Nobility, Merchants, and Commoners"; Hitomi Tonomura, "Sexual Violence against Women: Legal and Extralegal Treatment in Premodern Warrior Societies"; and Wakita Haruko et al., "Appendix: Past Developments and Future Issues in the Study of Women's History in Japan"—all in Tonomura, Walthall, and Wakita, *Women and Class in Japanese History,* pp. 81–97, 135–152, and 275–298.

80. Sakata, *Uji ie mura,* esp. pp. 77–109. Also note Sakata's recent "Chūsei hyakusei no jinmei to mura shakai."

81. On the life of the elderly, see Nishimura Hiroko, *Kodai chūsei no kazoku to josei,* pp. 389–404.

82. Tabata, *Nihon chūsei no josei,* pp. 2–82. To be fair, in "Chūsei no josei," p. 77, Tabata calls the medieval village "patriarchal." Also note Tabata

and Hosokawa, *Nyonin rōjin kodomo,* pp. 36–39, 87–96, 166–175. Tabata also maintains, however, that divorce was reserved for men; the only way for a wife to end her marriage was to take her belongings and leave. See *Nihon chūsei no josei,* pp. 176–190. Once a woman became a mother, she gained a new level of respect and responsibility to feed and care for her children.

83. Akashi, "Kodai chūsei no kazoku to shinzoku." For Iinuma's view, see note 79 above.

84. Conversation with Fukutō Sanae, June 2002.

85. On joint property ownership, see Tabata, *Nihon chūsei no josei,* pp. 58–65. On stem families, see Gomi Fumihiko, "Chūsei no ie to kafuchō sei," pp. 34–35. Amino, quoted in *Kodomo no shakai shi,* pp. 57–58, agrees with Gomi. Also see Iinuma, "Chūsei ie kenkyū." Kuramochi, *Chūsei sonraku shakai shi,* pp. 192–299, argues that wealthier cultivators *(myōshu)* comprised strong patrilineal self-help units.

86. Kuroda Toshio, *Chūsei kyōdōtai,* pp. 297–318, esp. 304–308.

87. Amino, *Muen kugai raku,* pp. 200–211. On travel, see Amino, *Igyō no ōken,* pp. 68–75. Kuroda Hideo, *Sugata to shigusa,* pp. 73–87, has questioned Amino's view. Moreover, others detect the existence of greater bonds of love between husband and wife, as symbolized by the term of endearment *en'yū,* or "related friend," used by each for the other in virilocal marrriages and signaling a willingness to care for the tablets of the spouse's ancestors. Nishimura Hiroko, "Yometori kon e no ugoki," p. 93. It should be noted that other interpretations of the term *en'yū* also exist. Cf. Tabata, *Nihon chūsei no josei,* p. 5, and Kuroda Hiroko, *Josei kara mita,* pp. 221–248. Kuroda argues for an equal place for women in village rituals of the thirteenth century.

88. Iinuma, "Chūsei zenki no josei." Also see Iinuma, "Nihon chūsei no kafuchō sei." For a recent summary of work on medieval women, see Nishio, "Josei shi to iu shiza."

89. Wakita Haruko, *Chūsei josei shi,* pp. 130–156. Tabata, *Nihon chūsei no josei,* pp. 46–50, points out that women could even receive fields in return for wet-nursing infants.

90. Tabata, *Nihon chūsei no josei,* pp. 53–54, 63. Also see Tabata, "Kamakura ki ni okeru boshi kankei to bosei kan," p. 150.

91. Iinuma, "Chūsei zenki no josei," pp. 35–36, makes this assertion based upon the *Picture Scroll of the Kasuga Deity (Kasuga gongen genki e)* and *Picture Scroll of the Tale of Saigyō (Saigyō monogatari emaki),* both of which date to the second half of the Kamakura age. His reasoning, however, may be questioned: he assumes that because infants are tied by a sash to their mother's (?) clothes, they are therefore being breast-fed. There is also no indication that the infants have reached the age of three. On a related note, Iinuma agrees with Tabata that infant and maternal mortality were high at this time.

92. Nishio, "Nihon chūsei ni okeru kazoku to kazoku ideorogii," pp. 22–25.

93. Hotate: "Chūsei no kodomo no yōiku to shujin ken"; "Zadan kai"; Tajima, "Minshū no kosodate no shūzoku to sono shisō," pp. 20–22.

94. On prostitution, see Narahara, "Chūsei no 'yūjo'"; Amino, "Yūjotachi no kyozō to jitsuzō," pp. 70–71.

95. Miura Keiichi, *Nihon chūsei no chiiki to shakai*, p. 339.

96. On orphanages, see Kume Yoshio, "Hiden'in no enkaku to shūen"; Amino, "Kodai chūsei no hiden'in."

97. Hosokawa Ryōichi, *Onna no chūsei*, pp. 34–58. Also see Iinuma works listed in note 88. Nishio Kazumi believes that the generalization about broken families is closer to the truth. See "Chūsei kazoku to kojin."

98. On nunneries, see Ushiyama, "Chūsei no amadera to ama"; Hosokawa Ryōichi, "Kazoku o kōsei shinai josei"; and Katsuura, "Josei no hosshin shukke to kazoku."

99. Tabata, *Nihon chūsei no josei*, p. 6. The proposition that *ge'nin* families produced few children comes from Hayami, "Taikō kenchi."

100. Isogai Fujio, "Ge'nin no kazoku to josei," pp. 111–151.

101. Conversations with Kuroda Hideo (March 1999) and Amino Yoshihiko (September 1999).

102. On toilets, see *Toire no kōkogaku*, pp. 41–55. Among the finds, there were two that washed away the droppings. Yet neither of them was likely used by the common population, as one was found in Hōjō Yasutoki's villa in Kamakura and the other on Mt. Kōya. On a different note, cotton did not enter Japan until the Muromachi age.

103. Oka Yōichirō made the report at the Historiographical Institute of Tokyo University. See Oka, "Toshi no nioi." See also Kōno, *Kamakura*, p. 40. On these various cities and towns, see Gomi Fumihiko and Saiki, *Chūsei toshi Kamakura to shi no sekai*. For the influx of rural migrants to towns, see Takahashi Shin'ichirō, "Chūsei no toshi mondai." Takahashi connects the in-migration to the market in children in most urban centers.

104. Harada Nobuo, *Chūsei sonraku*, pp. 447–472. Takagi Harufumi, "Shomin no kodomo," pp. 179–180.

105. Takagi Harufumi, "Shomin no kodomo," pp. 180–181. Harada Nobuo, *Chūsei sonraku*, pp. 473–484, on housing. On the *irori*, see Kōno, *Kamakura*, pp. 175–178, and Ono Masatoshi, *Chūsei iseki*, p. 130. For its advantages, see Hanley, *Everyday Things*, pp. 35–36, 60, 63–64.

106. Itō Teiji, "Chūsei nōson no sumai." Also note Hirai Kiyoshi, *Zusetsu Nihon jūtaku*, pp. 81–83, for diagrams. For a more general discussion, see Hirai, *Nihon jūtaku*.

CHAPTER 3: THE DAWN OF A NEW ERA

1. On *Tokushi yoron*, see Brownlee, *Political Thought*, pp. 122–128. Other scholars holding such views include Amino Yoshihiko and Naitō Konan. See Amino, Nagahara, and Ōzaki, "Naitō Konan no 'Ōnin no ran ni tsuite' o megutte." For a recent American view, see Mass, *Origins of Japan's Medieval World*.

2. I am indebted to Professor Hongō Kazuto of the Historiographical Institute at Tokyo University for suggesting the following materials and estimates for the number of soldiers in 1450.

3. The term *nobushi* literally means "one who lies [in wait] in the moors." This suggests a kind of guerrilla fighter. Conlan, "Largesse and the Limits of Loyalty in the Fourteenth Century," p. 42, writes that even though they fought and died, the *nobushi* did not belong to a warrior lineage. In "Nanboku chō ki kassen," pp. 419–420, Conlan cites a passage from a military loyalty report in which the characters for *nobushi* are placed in opposition to those for "horse rider," and he states that the term could mean footsoldier. I believe that that is the definition most applicable here. For an extended discussion of this term, see Conlan, *State of War*, pp. 70–71. There Conlan insists *nobushi* were not infantry but "skirmishers." It is clear that they were not disciplined, organized troops, but neither did they fight on horseback. "Disorganized footsoldiers" seems closest to Conlan's meaning.

4. *Mansai jūgo nikki*, 3, p. 705.

5. *DNS*, VIII, 9, p. 743.

6. J.W. Hall, "The Muromachi Bakufu," p. 219. The estimate of 28,250 for the *bakufu* army is calculated on the assumption that the number of mounted warriors was 3,250 and that shogunate footsoldiers totaled 25,000.

7. Farris, *Heavenly Warriors*, p. 50. For the total population in 730, see Farris, *Population of Ancient Japan*.

8. For comparison's sake, consider two other examples from different periods of Japanese history. If we assume, based upon Farris, *Heavenly Warriors*, p. 341, that Kamakura fighters could have numbered as many as 30,000 and that the total population in 1280 was about 5.7 million, as calculated above, then the minimum estimate of Japan's population in 1450 would have been 25.1 million and the maximum 37.6—both unreasonable figures. If we apply the same thinking to the Tokugawa period around 1700, when warriors numbered about 2 million (Totman, *History of Japan*, p. 226) and the total population amounted to 31.3 million, then we arrive at 1450 estimates ranging from 2.1 to 3.1 million for the archipelago—clearly inaccurate. In the Kamakura case, I would argue that Japanese society was not close to its capacity for exploiting the total population to raise armies, whereas in the Tokugawa era, most believe that the line between samurai and peasant had been drawn too far down the social scale, leading to bloated military forces and the attendant problems noted by numerous scholars.

9. Fujiki, *Zōhyōtachi*, pp. 106–109. Also on this question, see sources cited in note 3. Recently, Fujiki, *Kiga to sensō*, pp. 73–86, has asserted that commoners and villagers began to call themselves *ashigaru* and *zōhyō* (footsoldiers) by the 1460s and 1470s. Also note that Itō Toshikazu argues that the status of *ji-zamurai* (local samurai) came into existence only in the latter half of the fifteenth century ("Chūsei kōki no tochi shoyū," in Gomi Fumihiko and Watanabe, *Tochi shoyū shi*, pp. 209–215). See also Kojima, "Ashigaru to Ōnin Bunmei no ran," pp. 191–216, on the status of these lowly warriors in the village.

10. Letter from Saitō Osamu, August 15, 2000.

11. Saitō Osamu, "Kikin to jinkō zōka sokudo"; in English, "The Frequency of Famines." For the figures for 1000, 1250, and 1450, see note 10.

12. Farris, "Diseases of the Premodern Period in Japan," p. 383.

13. Jannetta, *Epidemics and Mortality,* pp. 116–141.

14. Farris, "Diseases of the Premodern Period in Japan," p. 383.

15. The narration of this epidemic follows Iwasaki, "Gojō tenjin kō," pp. 127–129.

16. *Chūsei minshū to majinai,* esp. pp. 17, 30–31, and 50–52. More recently, note Ueno Katsuyuki, "Nihon kodai chūsei ni okeru shippei ninshiki," pp. 109–112, on "cures" for malaria.

17. Kusakawa, "Hōsō no kami okuri"; Kikuchi Yōko, "Ekibyō okuri minka ryōhō nenchū gyōji shiryō"; Misaki, "Shōgatsu gyōji ni okeru ekishin chinsō ni tsuite," pp. 39–44; Takahashi Masaaki, "Hōsō no kami—yaaai"; Nagaoka, "Minka iryō"; Ōshima, *Ekishin to sono shūhen.*

18. Note Kitagawa and Matsumoto, "Climatic Implications," whose findings for the giant Japanese cedar in Yakushima generally support the conclusions of this paragraph for the fourteenth and fifteenth centuries.

19. Yamamoto Takeo: "Rekishi no nagare"; *Kikō,* pp. 131–176; 201–230.

20. Isogai Fujio, "Nihon chūsei shi kenkyū to kikō hendō ron." Note that this essay has been included and expanded upon in Isogai Fujio, *Nōgyō to kikō,* pp. 193–277.

21. Almost all the scholars noted in this section on climate base their reasoning at least in part on Fairbridge, "Eustatic Changes," pp. 171–172. The shifts in ocean levels that Fairbridge noted, including the Rottnest Terrace and the Paria Emergence, can be calculated only in relative terms. This is a major reason for the differences of opinion among scholars.

22. Atwell, "Volcanism and Short-Term Climatic Change," pp. 50–55. Maun et al., "Global-Scale Temperature Patterns," seem to draw the same conclusion for the world in the mid-fifteenth century.

23. Isogai Fujio, "Nihon chūsei shi kenkyū to kikō hendō ron," pp. 41–43.

24. Yamamoto Takeo, *Kikō,* pp. 227–228. Of course, the statistics presented in table 3.1 do not support Yamamoto's contention clearly.

25. Minegishi, *Chūsei saigai senran,* pp. 31–42.

26. Sasaki Junnosuke, *Kikin to sensō,* pp. 72–137.

27. The following descriptions are drawn from Sasaki Junnosuke, *Kikin to sensō;* Nishimura Makoto and Yoshikawa, *Nihon kyōkō,* pp. 134–158; and *HSS,* 3–4, passim. For the late Kamakura period, see related documents in *KI.* For 1287, for example, see *KI,* 21, p. 272, where crop damage was reported at Yugenoshima Estate in Shikoku, and p. 342, where a land steward is accused of stealing the wheat crop in Awaji. For 1294, note *KI,* 24, p. 172, where the Fushimi Emperor accuses cultivators of using poor weather as an excuse not to go to work. For 1298, see *KI,* 26, pp. 152–153, where Harima's Ōbe Estate reported crop damage, delinquent tax payments, and peasant suffering owing to two

years of drought, and pp. 200 and 219, where crop damage is announced for Mino's Akanabe Estate and peasants seem to have fled. For 1314, note *KI*, 33, pp. 47–48, 72, and 84, where crop damage is mentioned for Tara Estate and Wakasa in general, and pp. 68–69, where violence is noted at Tara; in *KI*, 33, p. 84, unusual crop damage was announced for "the entire realm" in this year.

28. Signs of a substantial starving and floating populace in Kamakura appear as early as the second month of 1317 (*KI*, 34, p. 148). In 1320, the well-documented problem of "floating people" *(rōnin)* erupted at Katsuragawa in Ōmi (*KI*, 35, pp. 326–327). Fields were also damaged in Etchū (*KI*, 35, p. 331), and peasants fled at Kurami Estate in Wakasa (*KI*, 35, p. 339).

29. *Taihei ki*, 1, p. 38; *The Taihei ki*, pp. 6–7. I follow Higashijima, "Toshi ōken to chūsei kokka," in my interpretation of this passage in *Taihei ki*.

30. Higashijima, "Toshi ōken to chūsei kokka," pp. 190–191.

31. During the famine of 1330, Go-Daigo restricted the production of rice wine to save on grain and forced merchants to sell their provisions to starving Kyotoites. See *KI*, 40, pp. 51–52, 58, 60, and 104. For related documents, see ibid., p. 77, where a land steward resisted taxes; p. 99, where a land steward damaged fields at Kuroda Estate; and pp. 161–162, where the sale of a person is noted. Also see Higashijima, "Toshi ōken to chūsei kokka," pp. 191–194, where records state that Go-Daigo ordered the elimination of barrier fees around Kyoto, especially at Hyōgo.

32. Murai, *Bunretsu suru ōken to shakai*, p. 130, also describes a link between the wars and famine, noting a family selling a member into servitude in return for food. So does Fujiki, *Kiga to sensō*, p. 163. *HSS*, vol. 3, p. 644, includes a shogunate law written in 1333 regulating the kidnapping and sale of hapless commoners.

33. *HSS*, 3, pp. 661–662, reports the pawning of a male during famine conditions in 1338. The monk Nichizō wrote of famine in the same year, p. 663.

34. Ibid., pp. 666–667. Nichizō recorded 1340 as a year of hunger.

35. Ibid., 4, p. 132, records a human sale in Hitachi in the tenth month of this year. Less reliable sources also name 1356–1357 as a time of suffering.

36. Tōji noted much land out of cultivation in the eleventh month. *Ibid.*, pp. 152–157.

37. Ibid., p. 217; *The Laws of the Muromachi Bakufu*, p. 66.

38. *HSS*, 4, pp. 277–278, wherein is noted the transfer of *ge'nin* in 1401–1402; in 1402, persons also dwelt in cemeteries, and a ban was placed on excessive labor dues. In 1403, *ge'nin* were transferred in Musashi (p. 280).

39. Ibid., pp. 290–291. Later in 1408 a man and woman were sold in Hyūga for 4.5 *koku* of rice. In 1409 peasants at Kamikuze Estate in Yamashiro failed to pay taxes and fled (p. 298). Finally, in 1412 peasants absconded from an estate in Kii, and the land became vacant (p. 302).

40. Fujiki, *Kiga to sensō*, pp. 48–50.

41. Ibid., pp. 49–50; Fujiki notes the characteristics of this new form of famine but is decidedly more pessimistic about their meaning.

42. Ibid., p. 50.

43. In 1422, relief and disposal of the dead continued along *Gojō kawara* with a brawl erupting between monks and outcasts. *HSS,* 4, p. 344. Doles of grain were given to *ge'nin* and others in both 1422 (p. 343) and 1423 (p. 345). It should also be noted that the Nara and early Heian courts frequently provided grain relief *(shingō)* to the residents of their respective cities. However, even though starving persons may well have migrated to the capitals under those circumstances, the sources of the times do not indicate large-scale movements of people into the capital in search of food.

44. Fujiki, *Kiga to sensō,* pp. 60–62. Also note Kanda Chisato: *Sengoku ransei o ikiru chikara,* pp. 16–91, and "Do ikki no saikentō," which examine the link between hunger and the riots. On these riots in English, see Davis: "*Ikki* in Late Medieval Japan," and "The Kaga *Ikkō-Ikki,*" pp. 1–36.

45. Katsumata, *Ikki,* pp. 154–155, 164–165. Itō Toshikazu ("Chūsei kōki no tochi shoyū," in Gomi Fumihiko and Watanabe, *Tochi shoyū shi,* pp. 204–209), describes how the market led to foreclosures and an increasing concentration of holdings in the hands of a few wealthy peasants and merchants. Also see chapter 4.

46. The year 1441 witnessed starvation and an outbreak of measles in the capital region, ill-timed because the position of shogun was once again vacant, this time because of assassination. Fujiki, *Kiga to sensō,* pp. 62–64. As in 1428, cultivators poured into the capital, begging for food and burning and looting. At sixteen locations around Kyoto mobs gathered, and they demanded grain and debt relief as they tore up contracts. Rioters were so numerous that food merchants had difficulty reaching the capital; even samurai of the Kyōgoku family could not break through the angry crowds.

47. Ibid., pp. 50–51, 64. *HSS,* 4, p. 386, notes peasant flight in Suō for 1439.

48. On *kakochō* for the medieval period, see Nakayama, "Chūsei no kakochō ni tsuite"; Tamura: *Nihon chūsei sonraku,* pp. 374–411, and "Chūsei jin no 'shi' to 'sei.'"

49. The Hondoji register can be found in *CKS.*

50. *Akahama Myōhōji kakochō* appears in *ZGR,* pp. 445–468; Shida, *Chūsei Hitachi,* is a helpful analysis of this document. The *Tōji kakochō* has not been published, but Professor Umata Ayako of Umehara Women's College in Hyōgo has transcribed it and kindly provided me with a copy. The *Ichirenji kakochō* is found in part in *KSS,* 1, pp. 933–954, but is completely intact in Takano, "*Ichirenji kakochō.*" It contains listings for persons from Shinano, Musashi, and Sagami. The *Yūgyōji kakochō* is available in *JK.*

51. See Hotate, "Chūsei minshū no raifu saikuru," pp. 226–227.

52. For a simple visual reference, see the maps in Hongō, "Nanboku chō dōran zu," pp. 16–17. I also consulted Satō Shin'ichi, *Nanboku chō no dōran,* and Satō Kazuhiko, *Nanboku chō nairan.*

53. Tamura Noriyoshi was the first person to verify this demographic fact, which many historians had long suspected. Collecting his data from the immense

Hondoji death register, Tamura tabulated long-term deaths from 1394 to 1592 and coordinated those statistics with descriptive accounts of starvation in the Kanto and the rest of Japan. More important, he made use of the recorded month of a person's demise to demonstrate that people were most susceptible to death in the spring and early summer—precisely the result obtained from the Yūgyōji register (which Tamura has yet to analyze). According to Tamura, when deaths from medieval registers were plotted on a graph, they all showed a characteristic N-shape—i.e., rising numbers of deaths in the spring and summer, falling after the harvest until the end of winter and the exhaustion of food supplies. The reader should note that although the Yūgyōji register does not really conform to this shape, it does seem to support the idea of "spring hungers." Based on his work on the Hondoji document, Tamura argued that the general populace during the medieval age suffered from "chronic famine conditions." *Nihon chūsei sonraku,* pp. 374–411, esp. p. 404.

54. It should be noted that the Ichirenji register contains such wild swings in death statistics that its value as a tool in any discussion may appear dubious.

55. *KI,* 21, pp. 276–277.

56. Ibid., p. 359.

57. Ibid., pp. 340–343.

58. In 1294, land stewards of Suō became violent in a similar way; see ibid., 24, p. 173; for 1298, see ibid., 26, p. 101.

59. Ibid., 33, p. 127.

60. Ibid., p. 213.

61. Ibid., 36, p. 13.

62. Ibid., p. 39.

63. Ibid., p. 317, and pp. 329–330 for Satsuma.

64. Ibid., 21, pp. 305–307.

65. Ibid., p. 310.

66. In 1314, the land steward's representative of Ōnari Estate in Owari perpetrated unnamed brutal outrages on the populace. See ibid., 33, p. 25, and pp. 54–56 for Iyo.

67. Ibid., 36, p. 86.

68. On "evil bands," see *Akutō no chūsei;* Watanabe Akifumi, "Kamakura chūki made no 'akutō'"; Kuroda Toshio, *Nihon chūsei hōken,* pp. 304–329; Arai, *Chūsei akutō;* and Kaizu, *Chūsei no henkaku to tokusei,* pp. 215–236. In English, note Harrington, "Social Control and the Significance of *Akuto*"; and Conlan, *State of War,* pp. 200–202; 209–218.

69. The "evil band" to which incidents I refer can be found in *KI:* 20, pp. 120–121; 21, p. 233; 24, pp. 146–147; 26, pp. 104, 121–122, 134–135, 137, 153–154, 180; 31, pp. 245–246, 290, 295, 321; 33, pp. 23–24, 32, 46, 108, 137, 194, 233–234, 246, 247–248, 249–256; 34, pp. 27, 32, 68–69, 72, 160–162, 255; 35, pp. 323, 336; 36, pp. 39, 174, 266, 267, 278, 288–289; 37, pp. 27, 119–120, 132–134, 156–157, 187–188; 40, pp. 65–66, 110, 138, 154–155, and 185.

70. Ibid., 24, pp. 125–126.

71. Ibid., 31, pp. 268–269.

72. Ibid., 34, pp. 186–187. Other documents concerning this dispute can be found in ibid., 35. On this conflict, see Murayama, "Katsuragawa myōōin to sono jūmin no rekishi."

73. Mass, *Origins of Japan's Medieval World*, pp. 17–38. The quotation appears on p. 4 of Mass' introduction. Also note Conlan, *State of War*, pp. 194–221, for a legalistic and institutional explanation for the rising tide of violence.

74. See Hongō, "Nanboku chō dōran zu," pp. 16–17. Conlan's description (in *State of War*) and Hongō's map correspond closely. On the wars, also note Murai, *Bunretsu suru ōken to shakai*, pp. 13–120.

75. Conlan, "Nanboku chō ki kassen," pp. 421–426. Also see Conlan: "The Nature of Warfare in Fourteenth-Century Japan"; "State of War," pp. 14–86; and *State of War*, pp. 48–82, esp. figure on p. 56. For another recent account of the wars in English, see Souyri, *World Turned Upside Down*, pp. 101–120.

76. Conlan, *State of War*, describes the military loyalty reports and battle wound lists as an "unparalleled body of evidence" (p. 49) but later writes of them as limited (p. 53). Yet Kondō, *Chūseiteki bugu*, pp. 240–244, criticizes Conlan for his dependency on these often vague reports and lists.

77. Conlan, "Nanboku chō ki kassen," pp. 422–423.

78. Shakadō, "Nanboku chō ki kassen ni okeru senshō."

79. Such conclusions about combatant death rates obscure general disagreement about the way military forces moved and fought during the wars. In Thomas Conlan's view, battles were usually small-scale, much more similar to combat during the Civil War of 1180–1185 than that of the Warring States period (1467–1568). Mass formations were not important; Conlan counted the soldiers named in the military loyalty reports and arrived at a total of only 8,634. Moreover, mounted fighters composed the major and most effective units, with organized infantry nearly nonexistent. While archery was the deadliest form of attack, the sword was more frequently utilized, although soldiers resorted to that weapon less and less as the fourteenth century wore on. The pike *(yari)* was too short to have been employed on a wide scale. If Conlan's interpretation is correct, death among combatants in the Wars between the Northern and Southern Dynasties would have had little impact demographically. See Conlan: "Nanboku chō ki kassen," pp. 426–430; "State of War," pp. 73–74; *State of War*, pp. 12–82, 223. For Conlan, the Wars between the Northern and Southern Dynasties witnessed organizational but no tactical changes. Karl Friday, *Samurai, Warfare and the State*, pp. 87, 126–133, 164–168, appears to agree. For other scholars whose work supports Conlan, see Friday, ibid., p. 132.

Several Japanese scholars disagree with Conlan's formulation, however. In 1965, Satō Shin'ichi (*Nanboku chō no dōran*, pp. 193–200) advanced the most venerable interpretation, maintaining that the wars marked the beginning of a fundamental transition in the Japanese military arts. (Also note Satō Kazuhiko, *Nanboku chō nairan*, pp. 23–24.) This transition began with the "evil bands," who fought in guerrilla units. Based on the militarization of these bands and others, Satō Shin'ichi argued for a sizable increase in the warrior class, with most of the new recruits being footsoldiers, including the new *nobushi*. Mass tactics first came into prominence in the wars of the fourteenth century; the pike was a central weapon in infantry battles. Satō pointed to traditions such as those associated with the Kikuchi of northern Kyushu, who became famous for their prowess with the weapon. (See Shakadō, "Nanboku chō ki kassen ni okeru senshō," p. 38, who thinks the Kikuchi learned the tactic from the Mongols.) Satō also argued that armor for infantry improved, further suggesting the widespread activities of massed forces. Seki Yukihiko also invoked the Satō paradigm; "Busō," pp. 13–18.

One weakness with Satō Shin'ichi's thesis is its reliance on the oft-fanciful *Record of the Great Peace (Taihei ki)*. See *Taihei ki,* 1, pp. 105 and 320–335; *The Taihei ki,* pp. 75 and 274–289. Also note Satō Kazuhiko, *Nanboku chō nairan,* pp. 67–71. It is not unusual to find figures such as 207,600 warriors departing Kamakura for the Battle of Kasagi against Go-Daigo in 1331, 50,000 riders (a force of 500,000 or more?) at Yoshino Castle in 1333, and even three Hōjō armies with a combined strength of 240,000 defending their city later that same year. On the other hand, casualties in *Taihei ki* are always listed in much more realistic numbers, such as 273 or 432. See *Taihei ki,* 1, pp. 52–53, 413; *The Taihei ki,* pp. 23, 269. Such exaggerations and inconsistencies have undoubtedly been one reason that historians once concluded that this classic was worthless as a historical source. See Kume Kunitaka, "*Taihei ki* wa shigaku ni eki nashi." There is a rebuttal by Inoue Yoshinobu, "*Taihei ki* to ryōshu sō."

Kondō Yoshikazu, one of a cohort of Japanese scholars reassessing premodern warfare and weapons in light of more recent material and documentary evidence, has come down between Satō and Conlan to typify a third group. He has criticized Conlan and others for overreliance on the often vague military loyalty reports and battle wound lists, as well as for an inadequate consideration of weapon relics surviving from the 1300s. Basing his analysis on documents, weapons, and the descriptions of battle found in *Taihei ki,* Kondō has asserted that (1) armies consisted of unorganized but specialized groups of both cavalry and infantry; (2) horse riders preferred swords or wrestling their opponents to the ground over the bow and arrow; and (3) footsoldiers numbering in the hundreds used a new, more powerful bow to engage in long-range archery contests. Most important for any consideration of demography, Kondō argued that the specialization of bow-and-arrow-shooting infantry and sword-wielding horse riders implied an increase in the size of armies. Kondō, "Buki kara mita nairan ki no sentō," pp. 66–67. Kondō does an expert job of analyzing combat in the fourteenth century in *Chūseiteki bugu,* pp. 237–276.

The difference among these views ultimately comes down to matters of documentation and how far historians wish to generalize from the available data. Ultimately, each contains an element—either larger armies or lower combatant deaths—consistent with the idea that a growth cycle continued through the fourteenth century. With either model, the wars represent a spike in mortality between 1331 and about 1363 and then a swift decline. The hypothesis about the "Muromachi Optimum" may work with Satō, Conlan, or Kondō.

80. Friday states that "there was no fourteenth-century military revolution comparable to the upheavals sweeping through the political, social and economic structures" (*Samurai, Warfare and the State*, p. 133). Conlan also seems to hold this view, as he speaks of "rising prosperity" and the immense importance of commerce for supplying armies (*State of War*, pp. 83–106). Conlan describes the Wars between the Northern and Southern Dynasties as having a transformative effect on all aspects of society, an interpretation that seems at odds with his views of tactics and the organization and small size of fourteenth-century armies (*State of War*, pp. 1–11). On p. 223, he states that "the impact of war was greater than the[se] aggregate numbers would imply." It should also be stated that Conlan seems to believe that a fundamental transformation in the size and organization of armies took place precisely during the "Muromachi Optimum," as the wars wound down (*State of War*, pp. 72–82). Moreover, *DNS*, VI, 4, pp. 306–307 and 779, contains reliable documentary accounts mentioning "several hundred" or even "several thousand" horse riders.

81. *Taihei ki*, 1, p. 116; *The Taihei ki*, p. 87.

82. *Taihei ki*, 1, p. 191; pp. 255, 303; *The Taihei ki*, pp. 158, 216, and 262.

83. *Taihei ki*, 1, pp. 214–226, 352–354; *The Taihei ki*, pp. 179–189, 305.

84. Farris, *Heavenly Warriors*, p. 136; Friday, "Pushing beyond the Pale," pp. 17–20, makes the same point for the campaigns of the 700s. Also note the ordinances of the Kenmu era *(Kenmu shikimoku)*, as well as *Muromachi bakufu hō*, p. 4 *(Kenmu shikimoku)* and pp. 11, 13, 17, 151, 153, 167, and 185 *(Tsuika hō)*. Also note *The Laws of the Muromachi Bakufu*, p. 17. Conlan (*State of War*, pp. 26, 29, 30, 72, 85, 92–100, 103–106, and 224) also notes references to arson, pillage, and blockade. Generals encouraged followers to extort supplies, "harvesting the provisions of neighboring *shōen*,... conscripting the residents as laborers...," and "seiz[ing] the autumn harvest."

85. *NBCIK*, 2, p. 80.

86. *GKS*, p. 889. See also Satō Shin'ichi, *Nanboku chō no dōran*, pp. 167–168; Conlan, "State of War," p. 103. For even more examples of the harmful effects of war on commoners, see Murai, *Bunretsu suru ōken to shakai*, pp. 128–135.

87. *NBCIK*: 3, p. 323, for Ōsumi in 1353; 4, p. 142, for Ōsumi in 1359; and 5, p. 73, for Aki.

88. *NBCICS*, 2, p. 320. *Kenmu shikimoku* and *Tsuika hō*, pp. 155–156; 158–161; *Muromachi bakufu hō*, pp. 11–13, 14, 17, 22–23, 24, 26–27, 39–40; *The Laws of the Muromachi Bakufu*, pp. 25–29, 31, 34, 40–41, 43, 46–47, 60–61.

89. *NBCICS*, 3, p. 118.

90. *NBCIK*, 2, p. 392.

91. *NBCICS*, 4, p. 101.

92. Conlan: "State of War," p. 109; *State of War*, pp. 85 and 106. Articles in Japanese are legion, but note especially Shimada, *Nihon chūsei no ryōshu sei to sonraku*, vol. 1, pp. 303–335; Ikeda, "Hanzei ka."

93. Ikeda, "Hanzei ka." Also note *Muromachi bakufu hō*, pp. 70–71; *The Laws of the Muromachi Bakufu*, pp. 93–94. Conlan, *State of War*, pp. 224–225, seems to leave open the possibility for warrior abuse of the "half-tax."

CHAPTER 4: THE BEST OF TIMES

1. Postan, *Medieval Economy and Society*, p. 42. Also on peasants during this era, see Souyri, *World Turned Upside Down*, pp. 128–134.

2. Kuroda Hideo, *Chūsei kaihatsu*, pp. 47–49. Furushima, *Nōgyō gijutsu shi*, pp. 199–217; on livestock, see pp. 274–275.

3. Furushima, *Nōgyō gijutsu shi*, pp. 238–241. The example from Upper and Lower Kuze Estate was figured from a 1568 document. There is no direct evidence for the 1300s, but other arguments presented below make this seem likely.

4. Amino, *Chūsei shōen no yōsō*, pp. 217–230.

5. *ASS*, 8(1), pp. 3–728. For autumnal wheat, see p. 3; for summer wheat, pp. 103, 203, 399, 413, 428, 523, and 728. My interpretation is that the seasons refer to the time when the wheat was harvested, but the term need not be read that way. Japanese scholars debate this issue even recently; note Kuroda Satoshi, "'Akimugi' to wa nani ka."

6. Isogai Fujio, "Jūsan-yon seiki Kii no kuni Kinogawa engan chiiki no tamugi shiryō." These essays are included in Isogai Fujio, *Nōgyō to kikō*, pp. 57–160.

7. Miura Keiichi, "Jūyon go seiki ni okeru nimōsaku hatten."

8. Furushima, *Nōgyō gijutsu shi*, pp. 257–258.

9. Ibid., pp. 238–241.

10. Sŏng Hi-kyŏng, *Rōshōdō Nihon kōroku*, p. 144. Note that Sŏng wrote of a third crop planted in late autumn and reaped in the winter. I know of no other source mentioning triple-cropping.

11. Koide, *Tonegawa to Yodogawa*, p. 77; Ogawa Naoyuki, "Kanto chihō ni okeru tsumida no denshō"; Kimura Motoi, *Tokyo teichi no chūsei*; Kagose, *Tei shitchi*. Also see Harada Nobuo, *Chūsei sonraku*, pp. 75–78, 259–286, and Yamamoto Takashi, "Shōen sei ka no kōchi nōhō."

12. Takahashi Takashi, "Chūsei ni okeru natsu mugi."

13. The first to discuss Champa rice was Hōgetsu, "Honpō Champa mai," pp. 167–177. I follow Arashi, *Akagome*. Note that the presumed period for the introduction of Champa rice (1100–1300) precedes considerably the first attested mention of the new grain (1397). The earlier introduction seems probable given that it was known in Sung China by 1100 and that there were numerous contacts between Japanese and Sung Chinese traders and Buddhist monks.

14. Kuroda Hideo, *Chūsei kaihatsu*, pp. 431–433.

15. Yagi, *Suiden nōgyō*, pp. 89–90.

16. For Higashi Nagao Estate in Sanuki, see Hōgetsu, "Honpō Champa mai," p. 171. On Yano Estate, see *ASS*, 8(1), pp. 327, 341.

17. Saitō Osamu, "Inasaku to hatten no hikaku shi," pp. 212–240. Also

note Arashi, *Akagome,* pp. 23–26. Harada Nobuo, "Tōgoku no chūsei sonraku ni okeru kaihatsu to saigai," stresses the frequency of natural disasters on Kanto flood plains.

18. There were many reasons for the first cultivators to prefer mountain paddies. They were located well above the water table, where dwellings were less prone to flood or other natural disasters. Residents could supplement a diet of brown rice with game animals and wild berries, roots, and nuts from nearby hills; they might also do slash-and-burn cropping. Most important, mountain paddies were easy to irrigate, often relying exclusively on natural watering. They might require some leveling, ditching, and perhaps even simple pond building, but the water was generally warmer, which was better for Japanese strains.

19. This hypothesis on developmental lag would help to explain the distribution of Champa-related place names *(daitō ta; tōboshi ta):* eight from the Kanto and northern Honshu and three from the western tip of Honshu or Kyushu. See Yanagita, *Teihon Yanagita Kunio shū,* pp. 217–218. Although the cultivation of *akagome* began in the Kinai and western Japan, eventually it declined as Kinai farmers became adept at raising more delicious and profitable native strains in river bottoms. Sources show that Champa rice was no longer being widely grown in the Kinai as early as the 1700s. Changes in farmers' preferences occurring during the Edo and early Meiji periods led to the obliteration of these terms in most of western Japan by the early 1900s, and they remained only in peripheral regions that adopted the practice later and continued thereafter.

20. Kinda, *Bichikei to chūsei sonraku,* pp. 161–223. Also see Kinda, *Jōri to sonraku,* pp. 309–315. See also Ono Masatoshi, *Chūsei iseki,* p. 234, for an example in Kawachi.

21. Saitō Osamu, "Inasaku to hatten no hikaku shi," pp. 225–227.

22. Kimura Osamu, "Izumi no kuni Hineno no shō ni okeru kaihatsu to shokaisō no dōkō." Also in Izumi note the construction of an irrigation pond and land clearance by the Wada at Ōshima Estate around 1300. Iikura, "Kinai zaichi ryōshu." See also Koyama Harunori, "Izumi no kuni Hineno no shō," in Ishii Susumu, *Chūsei no mura,* pp. 118–123, and Miura Keiichi, "Kamakura jidai ni okeru kaihatsu to kanjin." For more recent examinations of Hineno's beginnings, see Hattori Hideo, "Hineno mura ezu to kōya no kaihatsu," and Iinuma Kenji, "Ezu ni miru jinja to shōen kaihatsu"—both in Gomi Fumihiko and Watanabe, *Tochi shoyū shi,* pp. 172–188.

23. Tsubunouchi, "Chūsei ni okeru shōen no kaihatsu to kōkogaku."

24. Koide, *Tonegawa to Yodogawa,* pp. 73–74.

25. Kobayashi Motonobu, "Muromachi ki ni okeru Nishidai no saikaihatsu to keiei"; Mizuno Shōji, "Tanba no kuni Ōyama no shō," in Ishii Susumu, *Chūsei no mura,* pp. 65–82. The classic study is Ōyama, *Nihon chūsei nōson shi,* pp. 288–319.

26. Kobayashi Motonobu, "Suiri to shōen."

27. Kuroda Hiroko, "Kamakura kōki ni okeru ike chikuzō to sōson no seiritsu"; Hōgetsu, "Chūsei ni okeru yōsui ike no chikuzō."

28. Suzuki Kunihiro et al., "Kii no kuni Arakawa no shō chōsa hōkoku sho."

29. Murata, "Yōsui shihai to sho ryōshu rengō."

30. Takahashi Manabu, "Kodai matsu ikō ni okeru chikei kankyō no henbō to tochi kaihatsu."

31. Ebisawa Tadashi, "Bungo no kuni Tajiri no shō," and Iinuma Kenji, "Bungo no kuni Tokō no shō"—both in Ishii Susumu, *Chūsei no mura,* pp. 153-186.

32. Imatani, "Waga kuni chūsei shiyō yōsui mizukuruma." Imatani has investigated those few machines still operating in rural prefectures today and finds the water-driven type to be common.

33. *Yijo sillok,* 1: *Sejong changhŏn taewang sillok,* Sŏndŏk 4/12, p. 260.

34. Hōgetsu, *Chūsei kangai shi;* Nakamura Kichiji, *Chūsei shakai,* pp. 90-228.

35. Watanabe Hisao, "Yamato heiya ni okeru kangō shūraku no keisei." For other studies of Yamato villages, see Kinda, *Jōri to sonraku,* pp. 397-442, and Mizuno, "Nihon chūsei sonraku." A good general reference on settlement patterns is Ono Masatoshi, *Chūsei iseki,* pp. 40-57. Nagahara, "Shōen sei shihai to chūsei sonraku," argues that records from several other estates indicate that compact settlements were a product of population growth beginning in the late Kamakura era. Also see Nagahara, *Nihon chūsei shakai kōzō.*

36. Haraguchi, "Kodai chūsei no shūraku."

37. Shimada, *Nihon chūsei sonraku shi,* pp. 276-287. Also see Hirose's general endorsement, "Chūsei sonraku no keisei to tenkai," and Takagi Tokurō, "Chūsei ni okeru sonraku keikan no hen'yō to chiiki shakai." For an even more recent statement, see Gomi Fumihiko and Itō Toshikazu, "Tenkanki no tochi shoyū," in Gomi Fumihiko and Watanabe, *Tochi shoyū shi,* pp. 165-171.

38. Yoshida Toshihiro, "Chūsei sonraku no kōzō to sono hen'yō katei."

39. Harada Nobuo, "Chūsei ni okeru sonraku no keikan—hōkō."

40. Sakuma: "Hakkutsu sareta chūsei no mura to machi"; "Kinai no chūsei sonraku to yashiki chi." Also note Kinda, *Jōri to sonraku,* pp. 499-503.

41. Ishio, "Chūsei teichi shūraku no keisei to tenkai."

42. Farris, *Sacred Texts,* pp. 36-42.

43. Tonomura, *Community and Commerce,* pp. 37-95. Note that Kuroda Hiroko, *Josei kara mita,* pp. 221-248, places the start of this pattern somewhat earlier in the thirteenth century, on rather dubious evidence.

44. A good general study is Miura Keiichi, *Chūsei minshū seikatsu,* pp. 201-273. Also note Katō Mieko, "Women's Associations and Religious Expression in the Medieval Japanese Village," in Tonomura et. al, *Women and Class in Japanese History,* pp. 119-134.

45. Sakata, *Uji ie mura,* pp. 182-303. For separate treatments of the same area in Ōmi, see Sakata, "Chūsei sonraku kyōdōtai no kōzō," and Ebara, "Chūsei zenki sonraku."

46. Tabata, *Chūsei sonraku no kōzō,* pp. 19-65; also note Tabata's analysis of two Ōmi corporate communities, pp. 286-306.

47. Shimada, *Nihon chūsei sonraku shi,* pp. 222-333.

48. Itō Masatoshi, *Chūsei kōki no sonraku,* pp. 100-152.

49. Kuroda Hiroko, *Chūsei sōson shi.* For another example from Kii Province, see Kaneko, "Mura no tanjō to zaichi kantō," pp. 324-351.

50. Troost: "Common Property and Community Formation," pp. 434-444; "Peasants, Elites, and Villages." Troost cites other examples (not included in this work) and support for her thesis in literature on peasants living in various other parts of the globe. For a similar idea in Japanese, note Amino, *Chūsei shōen no yōsō,* p. 287.

51. Kuroda Hideo, "Sengoku Shokuhōki," pp. 303-304. See also Frohlich, "Rulers, Peasants and the Use of the Written Word in Medieval Japan."

52. Amino: *Muen kugai raku,* pp. 254-263; *Mōko shūrai,* pp. 441-445. Amino was not the first or only scholar to point this out. See, for example, Inoue Toshio, *Ikkō ikki,* pp. 56-94, 649-656; Saitō Osamu, "Inasaku to hatten no hikaku shi," pp. 228-230. In English, note Keirstead, *Geography of Power,* pp. 34-38, and Farris, *Population, Disease, and Land,* pp. 118-131.

53. Yagi, *Suiden nōgyō,* p. 88.

54. Uejima, *Kyōkō shōen sonraku,* pp. 206-210.

55. I derived the relative mix of different grades of paddies as follows. First, since more land had to have been cleared between 1280 and 1450 to support a dramatically larger population, the percentage of inferior grade land was raised from 35 to 45 percent. At the same time, because of all the innovations mentioned above, the percentage of medium-grade paddy was also increased, from 40 to 45 percent. The figure of 10 percent seemed about right for paddy producing "added rent" since this was primarily a phenomenon of the Kinai and vicinity. Of course, different weights are plausible or even likely, but given the large growth in measuring units as adumbrated in the text, both medium- and high-grade paddies in 1450 were greatly outproducing their Nara and Kamakura counterparts.

56. Hōgetsu, *Chūsei ryōsei shi,* pp. 171-179; Yamamura, "The Growth of Commerce," pp. 392-393.

57. See, for example, Uejima: *Kyōkō shōen sonraku,* pp. 71-333, and "Harima no kuni Yano no shō ni okeru hyakushō myō no seiritsu to myōshu hyakushō"; Shimada, "Shōenseiteki 'shiki' taisei no kaitai," pp. 316-338; and Masaki, "Niimi no shō ni okeru shinden to nōmin." For more recent work critical of this thesis, see Kurushima, "Kuze no shō." Also note Nishitani: "Chūsei Nihon no tochi baibai to tochi shoyū"; "Chūsei kōki ni okeru Kyōkō shōen no shūshu to zaichi dōkō."

58. Amino, *Chūsei shōen no yōsō,* p. 282.

59. Not only is it possible to quantify a rise in rice yields, but the amount of paddy land may also have increased sizably. If we use an average for Japan's population in 1450 (10 million) and assume that the islands' urban dwellers amounted to about 4 percent of the total, then the population of rural Japan equaled 9.6 million. Previous calculations about the farming populace not engaged in rice farming and the area of fields left out of cultivation stated that the

former amounted to about 40 percent and the latter about 25 percent. As the population grew and agriculture improved, however, both figures would have tended to shrink. For convenience's sake, assume that the two numbers roughly offset each other at 20 percent by 1450. Moreover, although more children were probably surviving infancy by the mid-Muromachi era, let us employ Kitō's figure of 16 percent for the population below age six.

We arrive at a sum of 8,275,862 persons aged six and above supported on an average of perhaps 1.50 *tan* each. By that logic, simple multiplication shows that in 1450 there would have been at least 1,241,379 *chō* under wet-rice cultivation. In contrast, *Wamyō shō* tabulated only 860,000 such units around 925, and the *Shūgai shō*'s total for 1150 was merely 956,000 *chō*. An inferred total for 1280 was about 1,003,079 *chō*. The amount of arable had grown by 30 percent in three hundred years, with the lion's share (24 percent) occurring after 1280, along with the diffusion of the tools, technologies, and organizations outlined above. Also see chapter 1, note 5.

60. It may also be too large. While Yamamura, "The Growth of Commerce," p. 392, argues that almost all the growth in units of measurement had taken place by 1450, it should be noted that using a multiplier of 1.75 leads to problems when the volumes are converted to Tokugawa units. If we arbitrarily raise the mean rice yield too high, there is less and less room for productivity advances between 1450 and 1700, as we near well-documented numbers for rice harvests associated with the mid-Tokugawa period. (See chapter 6.)

61. North and Thomas, *Rise of the Western World,* p. 26.

62. Amino, *Mōko shūrai,* pp. 441–445. More recently, see Amino and Yokoi, *Toshi to shokunōmin no katsudō,* pp. 174–194. As noted in chapter 3, many scholars besides Amino have discerned a turning point in the fourteenth century.

63. Yamamura, "The Growth of Commerce," pp. 376–393. Yamamura also describes the standardization of units of measurement, which I leave to him. In addition, the research of numerous Japanese and American scholars writing both before and after Yamamura confirms and enriches this story, which on its own deserves book-length treatment for an English-speaking audience. Also note Wakita Haruko, "Towards a Wider Perspective on Medieval Commerce," and Souyri, *World Turned Upside Down,* pp. 148–151, 153–160. For more recent analyses of the commercial economy, see Sakurai, "'Mimono' no keizai," who looks at the role of gift giving; for a recent general treatment, see Sakurai and Nakanishi, *Ryūtsū keizai shi,* esp. pp. 42–80, 112–148, and 199–234.

64. Farris, "Trade, Money, and Merchants in Nara Japan."

65. Sasaki Gin'ya, *Chūsei ryūtsū shi,* pp. 1–70.

66. Conlan, *State of War,* pp. 89–95; Toyoda, *Chūsei shōgyō,* pp. 115–120. In English, note Toyoda's *History of Pre-Meiji Commerce.* Toyoda first published his research almost fifty years ago, before many new documents had been discovered or archaeological evidence had come to light.

67. Sasaki Gin'ya, *Chūsei ryūtsū shi,* pp. 71–97, provides the material for

Kii and the next three paragraphs; see also pp. 379–430, Tonomura, *Community and Commerce*, pp. 126–130. Also see Toyoda, *Chūsei shōgyō*, pp. 130–134. Toyoda even quotes a peasant song about going to market.

68. On the *toimaru*, see Toyoda, *Chūsei shōgyō*, pp. 196–267, and Usami, *Chūsei ryūtsū to shōgyō*, pp. 105–196.

69. For an account of the Ōyamazaki *za*, see Yamamura, "The Development of *Za* in Medieval Japan." Yamamura also lists many other products available at markets in Kyoto and the provinces.

70. On traveling merchants, see Sasamoto, *Ikyō o musubu shōnin to shokunin*, pp. 87–125.

71. Gay, "The Muromachi Bakufu in Medieval Kyoto," pp. 84 and 102. For the most expert and detailed study in English, see Gay's *Moneylenders*, pp. 35–148. These moneylenders often operated in local society too and sold goods on consignment. See Nakajima, "Chihō kara mita dosō." Often the merchants of Kyoto were women. See Sasamoto, *Ikyō o musubu shōnin to shokunin*, pp. 126–172.

72. On Kyoto's population, see Yamamura, "The Growth of Commerce," p. 377; Sasaki Gin'ya, *Muromachi Bakufu*, p. 267.

73. Yamamura quotes Toyoda on the variety of merchants and artisans in 1460 in "The Growth of Commerce," p. 378. The figure for interest rates comes from Gay: "The Muromachi Bakufu in Medieval Kyoto," p. 125, and *Moneylenders*, p. 48.

74. Among the numerous studies, see Toyoda, *Za*; Ono Kōji, *Nihon chūsei shōgyō shi*; Gay: "The Muromachi Bakufu in Medieval Kyoto," pp. 81–90, and *Moneylenders*, pp. 56–61; and Yamamura, "The Development of *Za*," pp. 438–465.

75. Farris, "Shipbuilding." To be sure, the ancient, hollowed-out log boat was still more popular and plied Japanese coastal waters until as late as the 1960s. And both Koreans and Chinese carried their shares of cargo and passengers, usually in sophisticated junks.

76. Shinjō, *Chūsei suiun shi*, p. 424.

77. Ibid., pp. 575–706, for a discussion of barriers. Also note Usami, *Chūsei ryūtsū to shōgyō*, p. 29, who indicates that the rate at Udono Barrier near modern Osaka was 5 percent in the 1300s. For a recent detailed analysis of the Hyōgo barrier in 1445, including both freight and destinations, see Fujita, "Hyōgo shūhen no fune ni yoru jūgo seiki chūyō no kaijō yusō," pp. 267–279.

78. Sasaki Gin'ya, *Muromachi bakufu*, p. 167.

79. Goble, *Kenmu*, pp. 199–210.

80. Sasaki Gin'ya, *Chūsei ryūtsū shi*, pp. 81–85. It should be noted that the number of documents decreases after 1351 (twenty-two examples). The explanation offered by Sasaki, pp. 346–347, is that when the Wars between the Northern and Southern Dynasties erupted in 1331, powerful warrior leaders *(shugo daimyō)* demanded payments in rice provisions rather than money.

81. *Yijo sillok*, 1: *Sejong changhŏn taewang sillok*, Sŏndŏk 4/12, p. 260.

Yamamura, "The Growth of Commerce," pp. 383-384, misinterprets this writing.

82. Sasaki Gin'ya, *Chūsei ryūtsū shi,* pp. 124-126.

83. Watanabe Hirochika, "Harima no kuni Yano no shō no 'akamai' to washi." On Champa rice at Yano, also see *ASS,* 8(1), p. 327.

84. Uejima, *Kyōkō shōen sonraku,* pp. 206-270; Shimada, "Shōenseiteki 'shiki' taisei no kaitai," pp. 334-335. Kurushima, "Kuze no shō," pp. 4-24, critiques Uejima's interpretation. Also note Kamiki, *Shōhin ryūtsū shi,* pp. 130-139.

85. Sasaki Gin'ya, *Chūsei ryūtsū shi,* pp. 126-130.

86. On deflation, see Yamamura and Kamiki, "Silver Mines and Sung Coins." One remedy for bankrupt peasants was to issue an "order of virtuous government" *(tokusei-rei).* For a recent article on an early example, see Suzuki Tetsuo, "Kenmu tokusei-rei to chiiki shakai," pp. 166-190.

87. Yamamura, "The Growth of Commerce," pp. 388-389. See also Gay: "The Muromachi Bakufu in Medieval Kyoto," pp. 98-132, and *Moneylenders,* pp. 127-148; and Souyri, *World Turned Upside Down,* pp. 161-166. For a recent Japanese treatment, see Itō Toshikazu, "Chūsei kōki no tochi shoyū," in Gomi Fumihiko and Watanabe, *Tochi shoyū shi,* pp. 204-209.

88. Sakai, *Nihon chūsei no zaichi shakai,* p. 98. Amino, *Chūsei shōen no yōsō,* pp. 267-292 and 333-346, also deals with a riot at Tara.

89. For the comparison with European bread riots, see Bohstedt: "The Pragmatic Economy" and "The Moral Economy." Also note Miskimin, *Economy of Early Renaissance Europe,* p. 107.

90. See Ono Masatoshi, *Chūsei iseki,* pp. 84-127, for an overview of the archaeological record. This work has especially detailed coverage of the many villages specializing in ceramics. Also note Amino, *Chūsei minshū no seigyō to gijutsu,* for updated versions of many of his earlier articles.

91. Toyoda Takeshi, "Ringyō," and Nakamura Yūzō, "Kenchiku gyō"—both in Toyoda, *Sangyō shi,* pp. 372-375, and 419-436 respectively. Tamura, "Chūsei 'zaimoku,'" stresses the widespread market for lumber throughout the archipelago in the fourteenth and fifteenth centuries.

92. Watanabe Norifumi, "Seien gyō," in Toyoda, *Sangyō shi,* pp. 396-402; Amino, "Chūsei no seien to shio no ryūtsū," pp. 43-92 (reprinted in Amino, *Chūsei minshū no seigyō to gijutsu,* pp. 81-130); Kanō and Kinoshita, "Shio tetsu no seisan to kōnō," pp. 185-206.

93. On the ancient process, see Farris, *Population of Ancient Japan.*

94. Amino Yoshihiko, "Gyogyō," in Toyoda, *Sangyō shi,* pp. 380-396; also see Amino: "Kodai chūsei kinsei shoki no gyorō to kaisan butsu no ryūtsū," pp. 219-272, and *Chūsei minshū no seigyō to gijutsu,* pp. 3-80. Amino also treats fishing in his classic *Nihon chūsei no hinōgyōmin,* pp. 239-430.

95. Ishii Susumu, "Chūsei yōgyō no shosō," pp. 119-152.

96. Harada Tomohiko, *Chūsei ni okeru toshi,* pp. 3-64, 239-249. Also note Harada's *Nihon hōken seika no toshi to shakai,* pp. 1-40. Harada never

explicitly states his definition of a town, and many centers he cited probably had fewer than five thousand residents. This accounts for the discrepancy between Harada's tally of towns and the total urban population figured below. For the most recent archaeological evidence, see Ono Masatoshi, *Chūsei iseki,* pp. 8–33; *Toshi no kyūshinryoku,* esp. the articles by Itō, Yamamura, and Mizusawa. Also note Ogawa Makoto, *Chūsei toshi "fuchū,"* esp. pp. 3–54; and Satō Makoto and Yoshida, *Toshi shakai shi,* pp. 47–86, 199–256.

97. Sasaki Gin'ya, *Muromachi bakufu,* p. 267.

98. On Kamakura, see Kōno, *Kamakura,* pp. 251–260.

99. Cf. map, in Totman, *History of Japan,* p. 156; Gay: "The Muromachi Bakufu in Medieval Kyoto," pp. 77–135, 210–214, and *Moneylenders,* pp. 9–33; Berry, *Culture of Civil War,* esp. pp. 1–105. Also note Wakita Haruko, *Nihon chūsei toshi ron,* pp. 119–180.

100. Tsuji, "Iseki kara mita Muromachi ki Kyoto no kōsei"; Yamada, "Chūsei toshi Kyoto no hen'yō." More recently, note Yamamoto Yoshikazu, "Chūsei Kyoto no gairō to gaiku," and Ōmura Takuo, "Chūsei Kyoto ni okeru kyojū keitai to jūmin ketsugō"—both in Niki, *Toshi,* pp. 51–72, 181–202.

101. Yasuda, *Chūsei no Nara,* pp. 23–137; Morita Tatsuo, "Chūsei Nara no gō gōmin jisō," in Niki, *Toshi,* pp. 203–228.

102. Orio, "Chūsei no Hakata"; Ōba, "Tairiku ni hirakareta toshi Hakata"; Saeki, "Chūsei toshi Hakata no hatten to Okinohama."

103. Mesaki Shigekazu, "Anotsu no minato kenshō"; Isobe Masaru, "Tsu shi—kaigan wa kako ni chinmotsu shita"; and Nitta Yasuji, "Nemureru chūsei toshi Anotsu no minato"—all in "Tokushū"; Yata: "Meiō shichi nen Kishū ni okeru jishin tsunami to Wada ura," and *Nihon chūsei sengoku ki no chiiki to minshū,* pp. 171–216.

104. Shimozuma, "Kusado Sengen ni miru shōgyō katsudō"; Ishii Susumu, "Mokkan kara mita chūsei toshi 'Kusado Sengen'"; Iwamoto Shōji, "Kusado Sengen no hakkutsu seika kara"; Murakami Masana, *Kusado Sengen chō;* Amino, *Nihon chūsei toshi,* pp. 265–275; and Matsushita Masashi, *Kusado Sengen machi iseki.*

105. For a recent article on economic activity at Kusado Sengen, see Shimozuma, "Kusado mokkan ni miru ryūtsū kin'yū katsudō."

106. The history of Southeast Asia also strongly suggests a tie among the dearth of labor, bilateral kinship, and the consequent high status of women. See K. Hall, "Economic History of Early Southeast Asia," pp. 190–191. I elaborate on these connections in *Population of Ancient Japan.* Naturally, when population increased and labor became more plentiful, both kinship and the status of women underwent change.

107. Although many of these same generalizations held true for elite lineages of civil aristocrats and warriors, most experts agree that by 1200, if not somewhat earlier, those two classes were forming stem families. See Fukutō, "'Ie' no seiritsu to josei"; Takahashi Hideki, *Chūsei no ie to shinzoku;* Ishii Susumu, "Chūsei shakai ron," pp. 348–350; Satō Shin'ichi, *Nihon no chūsei kokka.*

Samurai households appeared to be strongly patriarchal. I entertain considerable doubt about much of this research, but it constitutes the main line of Japanese inquiry. Also see Sakata, "Chūsei hyakusei no jinmei to mura shakai."

108. Sakata: *Uji ie mura*, pp. 60–76, 110–133; "Chūsei no ie to josei"; and "Chūsei sonraku ni okeru ie to josei." Note that Tabata and Hosokawa, *Nyonin rōjin kodomo*, pp. 36–39, place the establishment of commoner *ie* a bit earlier than Sakata.

109. Sakata has recently buttressed this argument in "Chūsei hyakusei no jinmei to mura shakai."

110. On the definition of *ie,* see Nakane, *Japanese Society,* pp. 4–8; R. Smith, *Ancestor Worship,* pp. 32–34, 69–70; Hanley, "Family and Fertility in Four Tokugawa Villages," pp. 196–198. Note that Nakane, *Kazoku no kōzō,* believes that all Japanese always had stem families and that it was a basic characteristic of Japanese civilization. Also see Murakami Yasusuke, "*Ie* Society as a Pattern of Civilization"; Wakita Haruko, "The Medieval Household and Gender Roles within the Imperial Family, Nobility, Merchants, and Commoners," in Tonomura et al., *Women and Class in Japanese History,* pp. 81–98.

111. Despite the gradual ascendancy of the adult male and his line in the medieval and early modern eras, Japanese kinship even today retains bilateral characteristics, and these are more than just relics of a bygone era. The terms used for relatives and the widespread practice of male adoption—in other words, continuing the lineage through a female—are just two examples. The modern Japanese state mandated a facade of patriarchy, but in reality kinship in the islands has always been fluid and completely unlike the quintessential patrilineal unit, the Chinese clan. To borrow from Robert Bellah, in Japan the traditional family was "political," whereas in premodern China the government was "familistic." Bellah, *Tokugawa Religion,* pp. 13–19, 46–48, 183, 188–189. See also Yoshida Takashi, "Ritsuryō sei to sonraku," pp. 144–162, and Yoshida's notes to *Ritsuryō,* pp. 225–240, 548–569; R. Smith, "Japanese Kinship Terminology." On Chinese kinship, see the classic: Feng, *The Chinese Kinship System.*

112. Sakata, "Chūsei no ie to josei," p. 200. Also note Miura Keiichi, *Nihon chūsei no chiiki to shakai,* pp. 358–359. The gradual establishment of the *ie* in a few places by 1450 should not be taken as an indication that more distant relatives did not matter. Sakata, *Uji ie mura,* pp. 306–343; Sakata is criticizing Suzuki Kunihiro: "Chūsei zenki shinzoku ron josetsu"; "Chūsei no shinzoku to 'ie,'"; "Chūsei no 'uji' to myōjizoku"; "Chūsei zenki no kazoku=shinzoku keitai to sono igi." A host of relatives and in-laws, centered on the elders *(korō),* aided each other in agriculture, crime prevention, the collection of timber and grasses, and numerous other tasks. Sakata, *Uji ie mura,* pp. 121–126.

113. Katsuda, "Sonraku no bosei to kazoku," pp. 196–205. On village cemeteries, also note Sakamoto, "Sōbo kara miru chūsei sonraku."

114. Takamure, *Nihon kon'in shi,* pp. 205–242. Another early advocate of the position that virolocal institutions became common in the fourteenth century is Nagahara, "Josei shi ni okeru nanboku chō Muromachi ki." Also note Sakata,

"Chūsei no ie to josei," p. 202, and Iinuma, "Josei mei kara mita chūsei no josei no shakaiteki ichi." More recently, see Tabata and Hosokawa, *Nyonin rōjin kodomo,* pp. 141–143, 154–174. It should be noted that there is dissent from this view. For example, Kuroda Hiroko argues that peasant *ie* came into existence in the eleventh and twelfth centuries but that this structure did not adversely affect women's status or freedoms in the medieval period. For Kuroda, the decline in women's position in society did not come until the sixteenth century or later. See *Josei kara mita,* pp. 221–293; "Chūsei kōki no mura no onnatachi." Also see Fujiki, *Zōhyōtachi.*

115. Tonomura, "Women and Inheritance in Japan's Early Warrior Society." Also see Tonomura's "Sexual Violence against Women: Legal and Extralegal Treatment in Premodern Warrior Societies," in Tonomura et al., *Women and Class in Japanese Society,* pp. 135–152.

116. Sakata, "Chūsei no ie to josei," pp. 192–194. On the formation of the corporate community at Eastern Village, see Kuroda Hiroko, "Kamakura kōki ni okeru ike chikuzō to sōson no seiritsu."

117. See, for example, Kuroda Hiroko, "Minshū josei no hataraki kurashi"; in *Josei kara mita,* pp. 251–193, Kuroda describes the prominence of women's roles in village shrine associations. See also Wakita, *Chūsei josei shi,* pp. 152–230; Tabata Yasuko, "Women's Work and Status in the Changing Medieval Economy," in Tonomura et al., *Women and Class in Japanese History,* pp. 99–118.

118. Wakita Haruko, "Bosei sonchō shisō to zaigo kan." Also note Nishio, "Nihon chūsei ni okeru kazoku ideorogii." Wakita Haruko, "*Ie* no seiritsu to chūsei shinwa" (English translation: "The Formation of the *Ie* and Medieval Myth"), discusses how the Empress Jingū myth in *The Chronicles of Japan* became amalgamated with the idea of safe birth and spread throughout the archipelago.

119. On the separate language, see Ōno Susumu, *Nihongo no nenrin,* pp. 65–77. More recently, Nishimura Hiroko, *Kodai chūsei no kazoku to josei,* pp. 321–388, has utilized medieval stories *(kana zōshi)* to describe the emotional life of women during this period. While she depicts the society as patriarchal and polygamous, the heroines display independence and strength.

120. Ushiyama, "Chūsei no amadera to ama," and Tsuchiya, "Negainushi to ama"; Hosokawa Ryōichi: *Chūsei no risshū jiin to minshū,* pp. 100–168, and "Kazoku o kōsei shinai josei" ("women who did not form families"), pp. 220–226. Also see Katsuura, "Josei no hosshin shukke to kazoku," pp. 260–261; Hosokawa Ryōichi, "Medieval Nuns and Nunneries: The Case of Hokkeji," in Tonomura et al., *Women and Class in Japanese History,* pp. 67–80. More recently, see Tabata and Hosokawa, *Nyonin rōjin kodomo,* pp. 245–276; for households headed by single women, see pp. 207–211.

121. *Kodomo no shakai shi,* pp. 7–82; Tajima, "Minshū no kosodate no shūzoku to sono shisō"; Hotate, "Chūsei minshū no raifu saikuru," pp. 222–233; Kagoya, "Ransei no kodomo no hibi," pp. 251–255. For more recent and detailed articles, see *Nihon bungaku: Tokushū: Chūsei ni okeru kodomo,* esp.

articles by Ono, Tanaka, and Kuroda; Hotate, "Zadan kai" and Tabata and Hosokawa, *Nyonin rōjin kodomo,* pp. 103–108.

122. Hattori, *Heian jidai igaku,* pp. 233–250; Tanba, *Ishin pō.*

123. Hattori, *Kamakura jidai,* pp. 93–170.

124. Kagoya, "Ransei no kodomo no hibi," pp. 251–255.

125. Amino, "Kodai chūsei no hiden'in"; Kume Yoshio, "Hiden'in no enkaku to shūen."

126. Gay: "The Muromachi Bakufu in Medieval Kyoto," pp. 27–77, and *Moneylenders,* pp. 9–35; Berry, *Culture of Civil War,* pp. 212–220; Hayashiya, "Kyoto in the Muromachi Age."

127. On the Kumano *bikuni,* note Katō Emiko, "Chūsei no josei to shinkō," p. 280; Kagoya, "Ransei no kodomo no hibi," pp. 244–248; Shinmura, *Nihon iryō shakai shi,* pp. 384–386.

128. On the silence in Muromachi law, see Minegishi, "Chūsei shakai no kaikyū kōsei." For a few documents, see Isogai Fujio, "Hyakusei mibun no tokushitsu to dorei e no tenraku," pp. 70–71; Tanahashi Mitsuo, "Jinshin baibai monjo niten"; Takahashi Masaaki, "Nihon hōken shakai"; Maki, *Jinshin baibai,* pp. 138–147; more recently, see Suzuki Tetsuo, *Kaihatsu to hyakusei,* pp. 355–363. Suzuki's records include hereditary and short-term servants, as well as children and adults.

129. For example, see Takahashi Masaaki, "Nihon hōken shakai," p. 93.

130. The point about labor supply is made by Maki, *Jinshin baibai,* p. 148. Kuroda Hiroko, *Josei kara mita,* pp. 150–161, gives examples of the application of *Goseibai shikimoku* article no. 42 to peasant flight in the Muromachi period.

131. Maki, *Jinshin baibai,* pp. 149–162.

132. *Yijo sillok,* 1: *Sejong changhŏn taewang sillok,* Sŏndŏk 4/12, p. 261.

133. On the infantile status, see Amino's comment in *Kodomo no shakai shi,* p. 57; on family formation, see Takahashi Masaaki, "Nihon hōken shakai," pp. 87–88.

134. Minegishi, "Chūsei shakai no kaikyū kōsei," pp. 41–42.

135. Nagahara, "Chūsei kinsei ikōki no gijutsu seisanryoku no hatten," pp. 235–237; Kuroda Hideo, "Sengoku Shokuhōki," pp. 286–287.

136. Furushima, *Nōgyō gijutsu shi,* pp. 217–234; Kuroda Hideo, "Sengoku Shokuhōki," pp. 282–283.

137. *Toire no kōkogaku,* pp. 65–72.

138. Kuroda Hideo, *Sugata to shigusa,* pp. 130–133.

139. Furushima, *Nōgyō gijutsu shi,* p. 207; Kuroda Hideo: *Sugata to shigusa,* pp. 133–136, and "Sengoku Shokuhōki," p. 283.

140. Takahashi Masaaki, "Yogore no Kyoto." For Kamakura, see Gomi Fumihiko and Saiki, *Chūsei toshi Kamakura to shi no sekai.* Also note chapter 2.

141. *Yijo sillok,* 1: *Sejong changhŏn taewang sillok,* Sŏndŏk 4/12, pp. 260–261. The ambassador concludes by noting that even bathers used cash.

142. Nakakiri, *Furo,* pp. 136–150.

143. Itō Teiji: *Chūsei jūkyo shi*, pp. 111–205; "Chūsei nōson no sumai," p. 66. There is a strong possibility that the house described in the second work belonged to a warrior and not a cultivator.

144. Tashiro, "Shimo furudate iseki." See also Ono Masatoshi, *Chūsei iseki*, pp. 50–57. More recently, see Ishii Susumu, *Chūsei no katachi*, pp. 254–267, who argues that Shimo Furudate may have been a market.

145. On China, see McNeill, *A History of the Human Community*, 1, pp. 321–337, for a simple and succinct summary; for Western Europe, see North and Thomas, *Rise of the Western World*; for Korea, see Yi Tae-jin, "Social Changes" and "The Influence of Neo-Confucianism."

CHAPTER 5: RETURN OF THE DEMONS OF YORE

1. Kitō, *Jinkō kara yomu*, pp. 16–17.

2. Hanley and Yamamura, *Economic and Demographic Change*, pp. 43–44. Much of the following discussion is based upon this source.

3. For Hayami's views, see "The Population at the Beginning of the Tokugawa Period"; *Kinsei nōson*, pp. 18–24; *Nihon ni okeru keizai shakai*, pp. 82–85; *Nihon keizai shi*, pp. 71–113. Hayami, Nishikawa, and Shinpo, *Sūryō keizai shi*, pp. 42–49, contains the 1975 estimate. Recently, Hayami has published his work in English. See *Historical Demography*, esp. pp. 39–65.

4. Hanley and Yamamura, *Economic and Demographic Change*, pp. 44–45. Also note Hanley's doubts about the growth rate, pp. 348–349. For the record, Hayami, *Historical Demography*, pp. 43–44, has given himself "wiggle room" of plus or minus 2 million.

5. Totman, *Early Modern Japan*, p. 140, is a recent example.

6. Hanley and Yamamura, *Economic and Demographic Change*, pp. 44–45. Note the inexact citation of Sawada's estimate.

7. Ibid., p. 45.

8. Hayami: "Nihon keizai shi ni okeru chūsei kara kinsei e no tenkan"; "Taikō kenchi."

9. Saitō Osamu, "Dai kaikon jinkō shōnō keizai," pp. 187–199.

10. Fujino, "Nōgyō kensetsu toshi katsudō to keizai seichō," pp. 41–57.

11. Conversation with Kitō Hiroshi, June 2000. Fujino took his data from Umemura, "Tokugawa jidai no jinkō sūsei to sono kisei yōin."

12. Kitō, *Jinkō kara yomu*, pp. 83–84.

13. Saitō Osamu, "Kikin to jinkō zōka sokudo"; in English see "The Frequency of Famines."

14. Correspondence with Saitō Osamu, August 15, 2000.

15. Also note Tomobe, "Tokugawa zenki no jinkō zōka to 'ie' no seiritsu."

16. Farris, "Diseases of the Premodern Period in Japan," pp. 383–384. I supplemented these data with Sasaki Junnosuke, *Kikin to sensō*, pp. 117–208. Local epidemics included an outbreak in 1486 in Nagato, 1475 in Kyoto, 1491 in Kii and Nara, 1499 in Kyoto, 1502 in Kyoto (measles), 1509 in Aizu, 1528 in

Kai (smallpox), 1543 in the Kanto, 1562 in Noto and Musashi, 1577 in Noto, and 1584 in Hyūga.

17. *Katsuyama ki*, p. 60. This source was formerly called the *Myōhōji ki*. Another even better example occurs on pp. 94-95, where there is a battle in Shinano, the roads into Tsuru District are blocked, and a smallpox outbreak takes place.

18. Fujiki, *Kiga to senso*, pp. 159-161, lists a few more cases from the writings of Luis Frois.

19. *Katsuyama ki*, p. 124.

20. Ibid., pp. 141-144.

21. Crosby, *Columbian Exchange*, pp. 125-126.

22. McNeill, *Plagues*, pp. 193-194. McNeill believes the demographic impact of this malady to have been small.

23. Crosby, *Columbian Exchange*, pp. 151-152.

24. Ibid., p. 149.

25. Evans and Brachman, *Bacterial Infections of Humans*, p. 720. Much of my discussion is borrowed from this helpful source.

26. These statistics come from Takao Suzuki, *Study of Osseous Syphilis in Skulls of the Edo Period*, pp. 38-40.

27. For the sources used, see Sasaki Junnosuke, *Kikin to senso*, pp. 117-208. Assigning a value of one to a general famine and one-half to a local outbreak, we find that there was famine somewhere almost once every three years. Saitō Osamu, "The Frequency of Famines," pp. 26-27. The weighted average for the epoch from 1451 to 1600 is also higher than for either previous era. The weighted totals for 1150-1280, 1281-1450, and 1451-1600 are 24, 43, and 48.5 respectively. Of course, we must remember that not only are the time periods of different length, but also many more sources have survived for the later eras.

28. These statistics on famine are derived from Sasaki Junnosuke, *Kikin to senso*, pp. 117-208; Ogashima, *Nihon saii*, pp. 28-33; Nishimura Makoto and Yoshikawa, *Nihon kyokō*, pp. 158-212; *HSS*, 4 and 5. According to Saitō Osamu's weighting system, the ninety years from 1451 through 1540 witnessed 38.5 years of crop failure, a figure equaled only by the well-documented eighth and ninth centuries.

29. See note 28. Saitō's weighting system yields a figure of 12.5 hungry years.

30. Yamamoto Takeo: *Kikō*, pp. 226-229; "Rekishi no nagare." Nagahara, *Nairan to minshū no seiki*, pp. 384-388, has lent his support to this general outline.

31. Isogai Fujio, "Nihon chūsei shi kenkyū to kikō hendō ron." See also Isogai's *Nōgyō to kikō*, pp. 193-277.

32. Atwell, "Volcanism and Short-Term Climatic Change," argues for three periods of unusually frigid weather: 1444-1465, 1584-1610, and 1636-1644. The historical evidence for Japan for 1584-1610 is thin, however, putting Atwell with those who see a warm era from 1470 to 1600. His data for the Kan'ei famine of 1636-1644 are more convincing and undermine the idea that

the seventeenth century was a time of unrestrained growth. Implicitly, Atwell's data support considerable demographic growth in the 1500s and a higher population in 1600.

33. Fairbridge, "Eustatic Changes."

34. Kitagawa and Matsumoto, "Climatic Implications," p. 2157. Michael Maun et al., "Global-Scale Temperature Patterns," argue that the late fifteenth and sixteenth centuries were slightly cooler than later times.

35. Minegishi, *Chūsei saigai senran*, pp. 31–42. Mizuno, "Hito to shizen no kankei shi sobyō," criticizes Minegishi and argues that climate warmed around 1500 and then became progressively cooler until 1600. Mizuno correlates his conclusions with changes in the level of Lake Biwa.

36. Akamatsu, "Muromachi bakufu," p. 405.

37. The sources for the following discussion are listed in note 28.

38. Fujiki, *Kiga to sensō*, pp. 66–69. Fujiki lists a riot and debt relief for 1454 but does not mention famine. Still, the riots of 1454 and a food shortage in 1455 may have been related. The 1457 crisis was caused at least partially by an epidemic, the first and only time disease has been linked to one of these riots. Also note Kanda, *Sengoku ransei o ikuru chikara*, pp. 21–32, who argues that quarrels over leadership among elite warrior houses also figured in riots.

39. For other descriptions of the Kanshō famine, see Fujiki, *Kiga to sensō*, pp. 51–59, 69–71; Tabata and Hosokawa, *Nyonin rōjin kodomo*, pp. 175–180. Fujiki is far more pessimistic about the extent and mortality from the Kanshō famine than I am.

40. Tsang, "Corpses Clog the River."

41. Ibid., p. 12. Fujiki, *Kiga to sensō*, p. 53.

42. Akamatsu, "Muromachi bakufu," pp. 405–407. On the riot, see Fujiki, *Kiga to sensō*, pp. 69–71.

43. Atsuta, "Kanshō no kikin to Yamato," pp. 148–169.

44. *Daijōin jisha zōjiki*, Kanshō 2/7/20, p. 11.

45. The figure of one *tan* producing 100 coins' worth of grain or other goods is taken from Akamatsu, *Kodai chūsei shakai keizai shi*, pp. 507–510. Nishio, "Kieki no shisha o kazoeru," pp. 102–106, suggests that even figures for mortality in Kyoto were more likely concocted for their religious and ideological significance than for their demographic meaning.

46. Akamatsu, *Kodai chūsei shakai keizai shi*, pp. 503–521.

47. The best work has been done by Nishio: "Kanshō ninen no kikin"; "Muromachi chūki Kyoto ni okeru kikin to minshū"; Minegishi, "Rennyo no jidai," pp. 68–72. Ramirez-Christensen, *Heart's Flower*, pp. 23, 25, and 88, notes the famine in passing. Also see Morita, *Ashikaga Yoshimasa*, pp. 74–81.

48. Fujiki, *Kiga to sensō*, pp. 55–58. Just how good starving workers would have been at their jobs is open to question.

49. Ibid., pp. 71–72. Fujiki lists Suruga as starving in 1468, but he does so on rather thin evidence.

50. According to Fujiki's data, the famine in Kyoto extended back into

1471. Ibid., p. 240. Fujiki also adds "western and northern provinces" and Musashi for 1482 (pp. 88–90).

51. In 1494, starvation combined with war between the Shiba and Go-Hōjō–Imagawa rocked Tōtōmi. On other local crises in the 1490s, see ibid., pp. 89–90. Fujiki describes a famine of 1495 as afflicting Aizu and Noto, not Kai (p. 240).

52. Ibid., p. 90, and Minegishi, *Chūsei saigai senran,* pp. 17–24. Note that a giant earthquake struck in the ocean floor off the coast of Ise in 1498, inundating the port of Anotsu and reverberating from Kai to Kii, with floods and high winds trailing in its wake.

53. Fujiki, *Kiga to sensō,* pp. 90–91.

54. Ibid., p. 241, notes that sources for both Aizu in 1505 and Kyoto in 1506 claimed that famine was widespread, but evidence does not exist for any other area during these two years.

55. Tamura, "Zaichi shakai to tenkō."

56. It is uncertain what the price of one *shō* of rice was during a good harvest. Regional variation was undoubtedly pronounced. The *Katsuyama ki,* however, notes that during a famine in Kai in 1473, a *shō* of rice cost 130 coins, while barley cost 70 coins and wheat 60. Based upon this standard, most of the prices of rice quoted in the text appear to be higher than usual, indicating a grain shortage.

57. Kobayashi Kiyoharu, "Sengoku sōran no tenkai," pp. 2–18. On the Hosokawa, see Berry, *Culture of Civil War,* pp. 44–52.

58. Fujiki, *Kiga to sensō,* pp. 91–92, gives a few examples of soldierly misbehavior that may have contributed to famine.

59. Ibid., p. 242, also mentions Kai for this year.

60. Ibid., p. 92. In 1547, famine and war combined to deal a double blow to those living in Suruga. Fujiki also notes famine in Hida in 1547.

61. Ibid., pp. 106–107; *Katsuyama ki,* p. 122.

62. Kobayashi Kiyoharu, "Sengoku sōran no tenkai," pp. 18 and 22–26.

63. Fujiki, *Kiga to sensō,* p. 243, adds Yamato for 1568. He also notes the Imagawa policy to counter peasants fleeing their unproductive lands in 1567 (p. 109).

64. For the period 1550–1590, Fujiki, ibid., pp. 107–113, describes in detail the intertwined relationship of war, natural disaster, and famine in Suruga. Many of his points are listed in the text. In addition, in 1571 and 1573, Suruga peasants fled their damaged fields for castle towns in Musashi, Sagami, and Izu; in 1576, Suruga and Mutsu farmers received tax relief due to crop damage; the Go-Hōjō followed the same tax relief policy after a bad year in 1580, while the Takeda captured and sold fleeing cultivators. In 1585, when peasants absconded in Izu, the Go-Hōjō forced those remaining behind to cultivate their lands. To counter this policy, fleeing peasants played one daimyo off against another along the domain borders. In 1590, the Tokugawa reported many abandoned fields within their domain in Tōtōmi. Also note Fujiki's linking of the Kyushu food crises to Hideyoshi's battles there (*Kiga to sensō,* pp. 161–163).

See also Kuroda Motoki, "Daimyō hikan dogōsō no rekishiteki seikaku," pp. 18–21.

65. Shida, *Chūsei Hitachi,* pp. 17–37, 61–68.

66. Tamura, "Chūsei jin no 'shi' to 'sei,'" pp. 112–114.

67. Ibid., pp. 110–111. The exact shape of the N may vary by register, usually being high in the first month, then dipping in the second or third, and rising again for the fourth, fifth, and/or sixth months.

68. Tamura, *Nihon chūsei sonraku,* pp. 374–411.

69. Ibid., pp. 393–403.

70. Hanley and Yamamura, *Economic and Demographic Change,* p. 208.

71. Fujiki: *Zōhyōtachi,* pp. 13–197; *Kiga to sensō,* pp. 60–215. Also note Souyri, *World Turned Upside Down,* pp. 202–217.

72. Birt, "Warring States," pp. 160–215.

73. Ueno Haruo, *Kai Takeda,* p. 134.

74. J.W. Hall, *Government and Local Power,* p. 270.

75. Jansen, "Tosa in the Sixteenth Century," p. 92.

76. For an all-too-brief account in English, see Friday, *Samurai, Warfare and the State,* pp. 167–168.

77. *MKM,* vol. 1, pp. 250–462. On the Battle at Kōriyama, see Wakita Haruko, *Sengoku daimyō,* pp. 398–407.

78. Yamamoto Takeshi, *Chōsokabe,* p. 35.

79. Isogai Masayoshi, *Takeda Shingen,* p. 117, 138.

80. Yamamoto Takeshi, *Chōsokabe,* p. 35. These figures include samurai and commoners.

81. Isogai Masayoshi, *Takeda Shingen,* p. 117.

82. Ibid., pp. 131–138.

83. Okuno Takahiro, *Takeda Shingen,* pp. 100–101.

84. Hanagasaki, *Uesugi Kenshin,* pp. 71–92.

85. Fujiki, *Zōhyōtachi,* pp. 19–25.

86. Fujiki, *Kiga to sensō,* pp. 79–81, links soldiering to *dekasegi* as early as the Ōnin War. He also argues that women often took part in warfare; see pp. 181–190.

87. Fujiki, *Zōhyōtachi,* p. 96.

88. The *Harvard Magazine* article (Lambert, "The Deadliest War," pp. 15–19) that gave mortality statistics was subsequently revised by the editor of that same magazine in response to a letter from Leyden, "Civil War Slaughter." To put the 18.2 figure in perspective, the death rate in the contemporary United States *from all causes* is fewer than ten per thousand per year.

89. The following brief narrative is drawn from Wakita Haruko, *Sengoku daimyō,* pp. 398–408, and Asao, *Tenka ittō.*

90. The following originates with Yamamoto Hiroaki, "Hōka inekari mugikari."

91. *HKSKCSH,* p. 421.

92. *MKM,* 1, p. 262.

93. Fujiki, *Zōhyōtachi,* p. 36.

94. Ibid., p. 38.

95. The best text of Kujō's diary is *MKTH.* It has been treated in English by Ryavec, "Political Jurisdiction in the Sengoku Daimyo Domain." Also note Tanuma Mutsumi, "*Masamoto kō tabi hikitsuke* ni miru kikin shiryō," pp. 16–19, and Kanda, *Sengoku ransei o ikiru chikara,* pp. 71–91. As study of the Warring States era has progressed, village life has received increased attention. See Fujiki, *Kiga to sensō,* pp. 99–105, 125–144, 164–178.

96. Koyama Harunori, "Izumi no kuni Hine-shō," in Ishii Susumu, *Chūsei no mura,* pp. 109–111. This source provides a good geographical analysis of Hineno's layout.

97. *MKTH,* p. 12.

98. Ibid., pp. 41–55.

99. Ibid., pp. 62–63.

100. Ibid, pp. 71–77.

101. Ibid., pp. 82–83, on the battle and provisions. Also note p. 99 for another entry. Ryavec, "Political Jurisdiction in the Sengoku Domain," pp. 47–52, shows how peasants tried to play Kujō and the constable off against each other.

102. *MKTH,* pp. 111, 117, 119, and 122 respectively.

103. Ibid., pp. 131–132 *(shugo),* 135, 138, and 141.

104. Ibid., p. 143; quotation appears on pp. 149–150.

105. Ibid., pp. 151–152, 166–167, 174.

106. Ibid., p. 196, for flood. Tamura, "Zaichi shakai to tenkō."

107. *MKTH,* pp. 192–196, 199, 201.

108. Ibid., pp. 217–221, 223, 225, 232.

109. Ibid., pp. 238–239, 256–259.

110. Ibid., pp. 280–282, 294–295, 298–299, 316–319, 339.

111. Ibid., p. 332; poem on p. 337; information on Masamoto, pp. 350–351.

112. Also note Sasamoto, *Takeda Shingen.*

113. *Katsuyama ki,* pp. 59–63, 64 (quotation), 66–68.

114. Ibid., pp. 71–72, 74, 75, 77–79.

115. Sasamoto, *Takeda Shingen,* p. 5.

116. *Katsuyama ki,* pp. 81, 85–87, 95, 98–99, 101–103. The last incident is also noted by Fujiki, *Zōhyōtachi,* p. 22.

117. *Katsuyama ki,* pp. 118–119.

118. Ibid., pp. 120–121.

119. Ibid., pp. 127–128.

120. Ibid., pp. 130–131.

121. Ibid., p. 134.

122. Fujiki, *Zōhyōtachi,* pp. 27–28. Sasamoto, *Takeda Shingen,* contains more examples.

123. These three cases are not the only ones, although they may be the best documented. Even as early as the Ōnin War, "Looting by warriors seems to have been chronic and perhaps necessary for daily sustenance." Gay, *Moneylenders,*

pp. 148-160; quotation on p. 157. Half the city was destroyed, and fires in 1494 and 1500 thwarted initial attempts to rebuild. Fujiki Hisashi and Kanda Chisato have shown the effects of pillaging by hungry hordes calling themselves foot-soldiers *(ashigaru to gōshite)* during the Ōnin War. See Fujiki, *Kiga to sensō,* pp. 73-86; Kanda, *Sengoku ransei o ikiru chikara,* pp. 40-53. Comparing a map of Kyoto in 1450 with one from 1500 reveals how war diminished the capital. See Totman, *History of Japan,* p. 156.

At Tarumi Estate in Settsu, frequent battles led to breaches in the dams that helped to irrigate paddy fields. By 1479, the dams had broken down completely and flooded the land, and the peasants fled. See Shimada, *Nihon chūsei sonraku shi,* p. 452. For another area ravaged by the Ōnin War, see Sakai, "Yamashiro no kuni Nishioka no 'Ōnin no ran.'" Only repairs initiated by the *shugo* later in the century resulted in a revival for Tarumi. For recent work on another source of violence in the latter half of the fifteenth century—provincial uprisings—see Kanda, *Sengoku ransei o ikiru chikara,* pp. 54-69.

Later in the conflict, the Shimazu and Sagara of southern and northern Kyushu respectively, the Tokugawa of Mikawa, and the Date of northeast Honshu were also guilty of similar misdeeds. Oda Nobunaga committed arson frequently and in this sense qualifies as a typical Warring States daimyo. For all these examples, see Fujiki, *Zōhyōtachi,* pp. 15-38. Recently, Fujiki, *Kiga to sensō,* pp. 88-95 and 105-121, has catalogued similar abuses by the Imagawa of Suruga and the Go-Hōjō of Izu. Hideyoshi's armies in Kyushu also utilized the full range of Warring States tactics to subdue the island. On Hideyoshi's pillaging of Kyushu, see Fujiki: *Zōhyōtachi,* pp. 44-49; *Kiga to sensō,* pp. 154-164, 173-180.

124. On forced conscription, see Fujiki, *Mura to ryōshu,* pp. 159-181. For more on pillage and village defenses, see Sakata, Ebara, and Inaba, *Mura no sensō to heiwa,* pp. 259-274.

125. For the former term, see Fujiki, "Kikin to sensō kara mita Ikkō ikki," p. 93; for the latter, see Fujiki, *Mura to ryōshu,* p. 161.

126. Fujiki, "Kikin to sensō kara mita Ikkō ikki," pp. 95-100.

127. Fujiki, *Zōhyōtachi,* p. 150.

128. Fujiki, "Mura no kakushimono azukarimono," pp. 66-94; Sasamoto, *Ikyō o musubu shōnin to shokunin,* pp. 199-205; Minegishi, *Chūsei saigai senran,* pp. 230-251.

129. The Rodriguez reference comes from Minegishi, *Chūsei saigai senran,* pp. 101-102. Fujiki also gives several other examples in *Zōhyōtachi,* pp. 152-162, 167-177, and *Kiga to sensō,* pp. 95-99, 170-172. Ihara, "Yamashiro to yama koya no kaikyūteki seikaku," first suggested the existence of hideaways. Sasamoto, "Sengoku jidai no yama no koya," argued even more vehemently for the refuge theory. Koana, "Yama no koya wa tobi ya ka" and "Sengoku jidai no yama no koya," and Yamashita, "Sengoku ki ni okeru jōkaku no rekishiteki ritchi," believe that these structures were in fact just warrior fortresses because they were too small—for example, fourteen by forty-seven meters—to have

housed many peasants and their belongings. For a good summary of the debate, see Ichimura, "Sengoku ki jōkaku to yakuwari," pp. 289-297. For recent work, see Sasamoto, "Yama no koya no shōchō"; Ihara, "Chūsei no jōkaku to minshū seikatsu." For archaeological evidence in Kai, see Nakai, " 'Minshū' to 'jōkaku' kenkyū shiron"; *Ryūgasaki.*

130. Fujiki, *Zōhyōtachi,* p. 178.

131. On armed villages and fighting peasants, see Fujiki, *Kiga to sensō,* pp. 99-105, 130-137, 164-172. Tanaka Katsuyuki, "Mura no 'hanzei' to senran tokusei ikki," shows how peasants "negotiated" the Muromachi half-tax, which supposedly went to warriors, into a tax reduction for themselves. Also note Kuroda Motoki, "Daimyo hikan dogōsō no rekishiteki seikaku," who emphasizes the role of wealthy peasants in village rejuvenation.

132. Yamamoto Hiroaki, "Hōka inekari mugikari," pp. 31-33. On villages located in the *hande,* see Inaba, "Chūsei shakai ni okeru shūshu to futan"; and Minegishi, *Chūsei saigai senran,* pp. 181-211.

133. These data come from *SIGH,* 1-6. Also note Michael Birt: "Warring States" and "Samurai in Passage." My emphasis differs from Birt's.

134. *SIGH,* 4, pp. 43-44.

135. Ibid., 1, p. 183.

136. *Mōrike monjo,* 1, p. 195.

137. Fujiki, "Kikin to sensō kara mita Ikkō ikki," pp. 109-112.

138. Fujiki, *Zōhyōtachi,* pp. 184-192.

139. Takagi Shōsaku, "Ransei." Also note Kuroda Hideo, "Sengoku Shokuhōki, p. 287; and Fujiki, *Toyotomi heiwa to sengoku shakai,* pp. 36-91. On Mōri provisioning, note Kikuchi Akiyoshi, "Sengoku daimyō Mōri shi to hyōrō," who argues for Mōri direct delivery of provisions to their troops by the 1560s. On the Tokugawa, note Totman, *Politics in the Tokugawa Bakufu,* pp. 19-20.

140. On Hideyoshi's various policies to establish a peaceful order, see Fujiki: *Toyotomi heiwa to sengoku shakai* and *Zōhyōtachi,* pp. 201-261. Also note Inaba, "Chūkinsei ikōki no sonraku fueede to heiwa." In English, see Berry, *Hideyoshi.*

141. On the "peace dividend," see Sakata, Ebara, and Inaba, *Mura no sensō to heiwa,* pp. 274-318.

CHAPTER 6: THE BRIGHTER SIDE OF LIFE

1. On this topic in English, see Yamamura, "Returns on Unification," pp. 329-339. It should be noted that while the upshot of Yamamura's essay is the same as mine, he is far more optimistic and less critical of the sources. Also note Wakita Osamu, "The *Kokudaka* System," and Yamamura, "From Coins to Rice," pp. 357-366. For a recent examination of landholding during the era 1450-1600, see Itō Toshikazu, "Chūsei kōki no tochi shoyū," and Inaba Tsuguharu, "Sengokki no tochi shoyū"—both in Gomi Fumihiko and Watanabe,

Tochi shoyū shi, pp. 204–224 and 225–244 respectively. Itō is particularly well versed in the role of *do ikki* and *jizamurai,* while Inaba stresses the formation of autonomous villages and the importance of daimyo land surveys.

2. Yoshida Toshihiro, "Chūsei sonraku no kōzō to sono hen'yō katei."

3. Nagahara, *Sengoku no dōran,* pp. 261–264.

4. Nakamura Kichiji, *Kinsei shoki nōsei shi,* pp. 400–405. Yamamura, "Returns on Unification," is at least as outdated.

5. Yata Toshifumi, *Nihon chūsei sengoku ki kenryoku kōzō,* pp. 61–70.

6. *Seiryō ki.* Note especially the excellent essay by Tokunaga, "*Shinmin kangetsu shū* no nōgyō gijutsu."

7. Nagai, "*Seiryō ki* kan shichi," argues for an early eighteenth-century date for compilation based upon the appearance of a tuber imported from Okinawa.

8. Tokunaga, "*Shinmin kangetsu shū*"; *Seiryō ki,* pp. 139–144.

9. *Seiryō ki,* pp. 5–6. Emphasis added.

10. Ibid., p. 49.

11. Ibid., pp. 13, 98, 147, 211.

12. Tokunaga, "*Shinmin kangetsu shū,*" pp. 226–233.

13. Ibid., pp. 236–239.

14. Ibid., pp. 245–247. When we turn to fertilizer types, the text is distinctively early modern. There is some mention of grasses or ash, and both were widely utilized in the 1500s, according to Furushima, *Nōgyō gijutsu shi,* pp. 213–216. Yet manure and night soil were also prominent, as they were in the Tokugawa period, and there are also bird droppings, oils, and fishcakes. All together, the section on fertilizer is either a Tokugawa tract or agriculture in the sixteenth century was far more advanced than heretofore thought.

15. Tokunaga, "*Shinmin kangetsu shū,*" p. 255. Furushima, *Nōgyō gijutsu shi,* p. 227, notes several examples from this period, but the percentages are not as high as in the Tokugawa epoch.

16. Tokunaga, "*Shinmin kangetsu shū,*" p. 267.

17. Kuroda Hideo, "Sengoku Shokuhōki," p. 282.

18. Koizumi, "*Rakuchū rakugai byōbu* no nōsakugyō fukei." Also note Nishitani, "Chūsei kōki ni okeru Kyōkō shōen no shūshu to zaichi dōkō," who argues for a greater stability in Kinai farming in the 1500s.

19. Maruyama, "Ōmi no kuni Tokuchin ho nōkata shogō ni okeru nōgyō seisan no arikata," pp. 683–696.

20. For other examples from Ōmi, see Ōwada, "Sengoku daimyō Asai shi," who describes the Asai warlords coordinating efforts at irrigation among *kokujin;* Murata, "Yōsui shihai to shoryōshu rengō," who discusses a village commune *(sōson)* developing its own irrigation works tapping the Yasu River in the 1500s; see also Makihara, "Sengoku Shokuhō ki no tochi seido to 'shoryōshu.'" Mizuno, "Hito to shizen no kankei shi sobyō," analyzes agrarian development in the lands around Lake Biwa.

21. For this older view, note Ueno Haruo, *Kai Takeda,* pp. 370–401.

22. Sasamoto, *Takeda Shingen,* pp. 154–156. Also note Sasamoto's more

scholarly *Sengoku daimyō Takeda shi,* pp. 213-245, and Harada Nobuo, *Chūsei sonraku,* pp. 82-252, for his work on the Kanto.

23. Sasamoto, *Takeda Shingen,* pp. 157-158.

24. Ibid., pp. 158-160.

25. Ibid., pp. 160-163.

26. *SIGH,* 2, p. 181.

27. Noritake, "Sengoku ki ni okeru 'kaihatsu.'"

28. Ikegami, "Sengoku jidai no Musashino ni okeru kaihatsu." Ikegami also stresses the role of what were called the *yado* or *shinjuku.* Usually translated as "inns" or "postal stations," these places served as bases from which peasants could then clear wider territories. See Ikegami, "Tenma yaku to shinjuku." On this topic, also see Ebara, *Nihon chūsei chiiki shakai,* pp. 306-345. Ikegami sees the daimyo as active, asserting that their role was not merely encouraging and legalistic, but also included leadership in the construction and repair of dams and sluices. Most other scholars, however, see the Go-Hōjō as merely molding peasant energies in a productive direction. See Asakura, "Sengoku ki no kōchi kaihatsu"; Shibatsuji, "Sengoku ki no suiri kangai to kaihatsu."

29. Ōwada, "Sengoku daimyō Asai shi," pp. 21-22. Also see Yamamura, "Returns on Unification," pp. 331-333. Many daimyo had laws in their domain codes referring to agriculture and land clearance. See, for example, Jansen, "Tosa in the Sixteenth Century," pp. 103-110, and Ryavec, "Political Jurisdiction in the Sengoku Daimyo Domain," pp. 213, 217, 236-237.

30. Furushima: *Nōgyō gijutsu shi,* pp. 242-243, and *Tochi ni kizamareta rekishi,* pp. 128-147; Koide, *Tonegawa to Yodogawa,* pp. 81-87.

31. J.I. Nakamura, *Agricultural Production and the Economic Development,* p. 76. Kitō, *Jinkō kara yomu,* p. 66, makes the difference 20 percent.

32. In chapter 4, note 59, I estimated the amount of arable in 1450 at 1,241,379 *chō.* Although this figure is only one possibility, if we accept its general validity, then the 150 years between 1450 and 1600 could have seen as much as a 28 percent increase in arable, a figure in line with substantial demographic growth, certainly more than Hayami's 2 million. This growth of cultivated lands is approximately equivalent to the 30 percent growth shown between 1150 and 1450. The slowing in growth may have been a result of the increased toll of famine and war. These figures are not meant to be definitive, merely suggestive.

33. Another problem with using a multiplier of 1.5 *(senshi to)* for 1450 is that measure was no longer being used then.

34. I borrowed the concept of war economy from Kubo, "Sengoku shakai no sensō keizai to shūshu," but my usage is closer to that of Sakurai, "Chūsei no shōhin ichiba," pp. 227-331.

35. See Yamamura: "Returns on Unification," pp. 358-370, and "From Coins to Rice"; Nagahara with Yamamura, "The Sengoku Daimyo and the Kandaka System"; and Sasaki Gin'ya with Hauser, "Sengoku Daimyo Rule and Commerce." In Japanese, see Nagahara, *Sengoku ki no seiji keizai,* pp. 302-336.

More recently, note Sakurai Eiji: "Chūsei no kahei shin'yō"; "Chūsei kinsei no shōnin"; and "Chūsei no shōhin ichiba"—all in Sakurai and Nakanishi, *Ryūtsū keizai shi,* pp. 42–80, 112–148, and 199–234 respectively. The first essay examines changes in the money supply and forms of bills of exchanges, while the second deals with the Honai and other merchants in central Japan. The third essay treats the market and is cited throughout this section.

36. Yamamura, "From Coins to Rice," pp. 353–357. Among the many reasons for this difference between eastern Honshu and western Japan, Yamamura noted (1) the relative scarcity of cash contrasted to the high grain productivity in eastern Honshu; (2) the secular deflation of the period 1450–1600, when the price of rice dropped by about 80 percent, making cash more valuable than dues paid in kind; and (3) the daimyo's desire to reduce the power of local "men of the province." On rice prices, see Kamiki, *Shōhin ryūtsū shi,* pp. 220–231. For an older but still helpful discussion of coins, see Brown, *Money Economy.*

37. For much of the Warring States era Kyoto and its vicinity were an attenuated hub. Rice-wine brewers and pawnbrokers in particular declined. See Hayashima: "Sengoku jidai no dosō sakaya yaku to Muromachi bakufu"; "Kyōkō chiiki no saimu to kōrisen."

38. For more on Warring States merchants, see Ishii Susumu, *Chūsei no katachi,* pp. 218–306; Sasamoto, *Ikyō o musubu shōnin to shokunin,* pp. 253–261.

39. Toyoda, *Chūsei shōgyō,* pp. 314–329.

40. Ibid., pp. 329–337; Sakurai, "Chūsei no shōhin ichiba," p. 228; and Nakabe, *Chūsei toshi,* pp. 91–122.

41. Shinjō, *Chūsei suiun shi,* pp. 707–752.

42. On Sakai, see Morris, "Sakai: The History of a City in Medieval Japan." Also note Morris: "Sakai: From Shōen to Port City"; "The City of Sakai and Urban Autonomy." In Japanese, note Sasamoto, *Ikyō o musubu shōnin to shokunin,* pp. 173–198.

43. Toyoda, *Chūsei shōgyō,* pp. 415–428.

44. Yamamura, "The Development of the *Za* in Medieval Japan," pp. 454–459. Sakurai, "Chūsei no shōhin ichiba," p. 230, argues that Warring States daimyo used "guild" merchants as they did others and did not adopt policies to eliminate the organizations.

45. Toyoda, *Chūsei shōgyō,* pp. 341–353. Also see Abe Kōichi, "Chūsei kōki ni okeru Kanto nairiku no suijō kōtsū to tenma," and Noritake, "Sengoku ki no ryōkoku kan tsūkō to daimyō kenryoku."

46. Usami, *Chūsei no ryūtsū to shōgyō,* pp. 106–111.

47. On these riots, a good short introduction is Katsumata, *Ikki,* pp. 152–178. Also see Gay, *Moneylenders,* pp. 127–148. Recently in Japanese, see Hasegawa Yasuko, "Sengokki ni okeru funsō saitei to sōkoku ikki."

48. *Katsuyama ki,* pp. 81 and 91.

49. On the Mōri and commerce, see Akiyama, *Mōri shi,* pp. 188–217; Kishida, "Chihō keizai to toshi."

50. Kishida, "Chihō keizai to toshi," pp. 93–94, 97–103. The date 1554 is

an inference drawn from Akiyama, *Mōri shi,* p. 194. Kishida argues that the *ichi mokudai* were more important for transportation than trade.

51. Akiyama, *Mōri shi,* pp. 194–201.

52. Kishida, "Chihō keizai to toshi," pp. 93–98, 107.

53. Ibid., pp. 103–108; Akiyama, *Mōri shi,* pp. 201–205.

54. Akiyama, *Mōri shi,* pp. 206–212.

55. Kishida, "Chihō keizai to toshi," pp. 89–93, 108–119.

56. This entire description follows Nagahara, *Sengoku ki no seiji keizai,* pp. 167–203. Even as early as 1481, Ōminato port received thirty boats laden with rice, bamboo, lumber, firewood, wheat, and soybeans. Seven originated from Owari, nine from other parts of Ise, and fourteen from Shima.

57. This discussion follows Nagahara, *Sengoku ki seiji keizai,* pp. 287–306. Members of the Kurata family were originally officials at Ise Shrine, and they collected rice for the institution and had contacts throughout the region. They gained the capital and connections to become big-time merchants and kept a residence in Kyoto, where they developed ties with civil and military aristocratic houses. Their trade routes included areas north and south of the capital, wherever attendants or officials of Ise Shrine were located.

58. The tie between the two families was so intimate that Gorōzaemon even prepared the way for Uesugi Kenshin to enter Kyoto in 1553 and again in 1559, such was the merchant's reputation in and along the way to the capital. Later he served in a similar role in a trip to Kii. When Kenshin went to battle in 1562, Kurata kept watch at home and sent prayers to Ise Shrine for his lord.

59. This description of the Takeda and trade follows Sasamoto, *Sengoku daimyō Takeda shi,* pp. 269–366.

60. By so controlling these craftspeople, the Takeda were making a statement to powerful *kokujin:* "We are the sole rulers of Kai and Shinano, and our power is domain-wide." There are many more examples of commerce during this epoch. See work on the Asakura and Go-Hōjō in Usami, *Chūsei no ryūtsū to shōgyō,* pp. 255–296; Nagahara, *Sengoku no dōran,* pp. 225–228, 236–238. On the Honai merchants, see Tonomura, *Community and Commerce,* pp. 122–156; Suzuki Tsuruko, *Nihon chūsei shakai no ryūtsū,* pp. 201–249.

61. Nagahara: "Chūsei kinsei ikōki no gijutsu seisanryoku no hatten," pp. 235–237, and "Mensaku no tenkai"; Kuroda Hideo, "Sengoku Shokuhōki," pp. 286–287. The widespread cultivation of cotton helped to intensify farming after 1600 because farmers often planted cotton in unused rice fields by then. This practice may have been partially responsible for the disappearance of the medieval servant class *(ge'nin)* and the establishment of the "self-sufficient" early modern peasant.

62. Nagahara, "Chūsei kinsei ikōki no gijutsu seisanryoku no hatten," pp. 240–242.

63. Nakamura Yūzō, "Kenchiku gyō," in Toyoda, *Sangyō shi,* p. 435.

64. Kawahara, "Ichijōdani iseki"; Ono Masatoshi, *Chūsei iseki,* pp. 20–23. Recently on fortifications, see Senda and Kojima, *Tenka tōitsu to shiro.*

65. Nagahara, "Chūsei kinsei ikōki no gijutsu seisanryoku no hatten," pp. 237–239. Also note Kuroda Hideo, "Sengoku Shokuhōki," pp. 278–279, 293–295; Yamamura and Kamiki, "Silver Mines and Sung Coins," pp. 346–348.

66. Sasamoto, *Sengoku daimyō Takeda shi*, pp. 303–335. The Takeda were renowned for their miners *(kinzan-shū)*, possessing at least eight mines in Kai, Shinano, and Suruga. Nobutora opened them, Shingen developed them, and they began to peter out by the 1570s, suggesting one reason for Katsuyori's downfall. The miners were experts at tunneling, a technology useful in undermining enemy fortifications. Like Takeda and Go-Hōjō farmers, miners acted independently and then requested and received Takeda permission for their activities.

67. The comments by Zheng and Cocks come from Toyoda Takeshi, "Kōgyō," in Toyoda, *Sangyō shi*, p. 379.

68. There are several works on cities. In English, see Wakita Haruko with Hanley, "Dimensions of Development." In Japanese, see Ono Masatoshi, *Chūsei iseki*, pp. 8–39; for a general survey, see Wakita Haruko, *Nihon chūsei toshi ron;* for recent work, see selected articles in *Toshi no kyūshinryoku;* Satō Makoto and Yoshida, *Toshi shakai shi.* None of these sources approach cities from a demographic perspective.

69. Harada Tomohiko: *Nihon hōken seika no toshi*, pp. 1–40; *Chūsei ni okeru toshi*, pp. 3–64.

70. Kitō, *Edo jidai no jinkō*, pp. 77–79.

71. On Japan, see Sasaki Yoichiro, "Urban Migration and Fertility in Tokugawa Japan." For world history, see McNeill, *Plagues*, pp. 55–56.

72. Ono Masatoshi, *Chūsei iseki*, pp. 42–57, 62–65.

73. On Hineno, see Sugiyama, *Sengoku daimyō*, pp. 290–291. More recently, note Kanda, *Sengoku ransei o ikiru chikara*, pp. 69–91. For a more general discussion of daimyo and village life, see Inaba Tsuguharu, "Sengokki no tochi shoyū," in Gomi Fumihiko and Watanabe, *Tochi shoyū shi*, pp. 225–238.

74. For more on class and age divisions within the village, see Sakata, Ebara, and Inaba, *Mura no sensō to heiwa*, pp. 93–98, 101–118.

75. Sugiyama, *Sengoku daimyō*, pp. 293–301; Ryavec, "Political Jurisdiction in the Sengoku Daimyo Domain," pp. 59–94; *MKTH*, pp. 237–264. Also note Sakata, Ebara, and Inaba, *Mura no sensō to heiwa*, pp. 139–151.

76. The translation is taken from Ryavec, "Political Jurisdiction in the Sengoku Daimyo Domain," p. 70 emphasis added; *MKTH*, p. 237.

77. Translation from Ryavec, "Political Jurisdiction in the Sengoku Daimyo Domain," p. 89; emphasis added; *MKTH*, pp. 248–249.

78. Translation from Ryavec, "Political Jurisdiction in the Sengoku Daimyo Domain," p. 90; *MKTH*, p. 249. The emphasis placed on continuation of the family line may also be evident in the creation of separate village graveyards. See Sakamoto, "Sōbo kara miru chūsei sonraku."

79. Katsumata, "Sengoku jidai no sonraku." On village solidarity, also note Fujiki, *Kiga to sensō*, pp. 95–104, 125–136, 164–172. For a more detailed examination of villages in this period, see Sakata, Ebara, and Inaba, *Mura no sensō to*

heiwa, pp. 82–120, 135–154, 211–318. These villages policed themselves and worked cooperatively in times of famine and flood. See Sugiyama, *Sengoku daimyō,* pp. 295–296, 299–301; *MKTH,* pp. 136–148.

80. Abe Takeshi, "Chūsei kōki no Yamato no sonraku."

81. Inaba Tsuguharu, "Sengoku jidai no murauke sei to mura." For Imabori in Ōmi, see Tonomura, *Community and Commerce,* pp. 152–187. Also note Sakata, "Sanson to gyoson."

82. Hirayama, "Sengoku daimyō ryōkoku ka ni okeru gōson."

83. Fujiki, *Kiga to sensō,* pp. 102–104, argues that even villages in eastern Honshu were more successful at resisting daimyo demands for troops and porters than is usually thought. He also asserts that the line between peasant and warrior was clear even in the early sixteenth century.

84. Hirayama, "Sengoku ki tōgoku no gōson ni okeru ie."

85. Sakata, *Uji ie mura,* pp. 136–183. See also Sonobe, "Chūkinsei ikōki sonraku ni okeru miyaza to ie." Sakata has reaffirmed his conclusions in Sakata, Ebara, and Inaba, *Mura no sensō to heiwa,* pp. 9–81.

86. Sakata, *Uji ie mura,* pp. 71–76. Sakata may be trying to provide evidence to support the long-held idea of the rise of the small, independent cultivator beginning around 1600. On main and branch family relations in the Tokugawa period, see Thomas Smith's classic, *Agrarian Origins,* pp. 1–64.

87. Sakata, Ebara, and Inaba, *Mura no sensō to heiwa,* pp. 52–54. For a while younger brothers were able to clear land for their own branch households, but this trend ended in many places by the early eighteenth century.

88. Takamure, *Nihon kon'in shi,* pp. 205–242.

89. Tabata, *Nihon chūsei no shakai to josei,* pp. 226–227. Also on women warriors, see Fujiki, *Kiga to sensō,* pp. 184–190, 201–203; and Tabata, "Sengokki no 'ie' to josei." For recent work on women in English, see Tonomura et al., *Women and Class in Japanese History.* Note especially essays by Wakita, Tabata, and Tonomura and the appendix.

90. Kuroda Hiroko, "Chūsei kōki no mura no onnatachi." Also see chapter 4.

91. Quoted in Kuramochi, *Chūsei sonraku shakai shi,* pp. 266–301. The following derives from this book.

92. Cornell: "Retirement, Inheritance, and Intergenerational Conflict"; "Why Are There No Spinsters in Japan?"; "Was 'Three-and-a-Half Lines' So Bad?"

93. Fujiki, *Kiga to sensō,* pp. 190–215.

94. The narrative on children was composed from information in Yūki, *Ransei no kodomo,* pp. 173–206; Kuramochi, *Chūsei sonraku shakai shi,* pp. 270–271; and Kuroda Hideo, *"Emaki" kodomo.* Kuroda presented many of his ideas in "Jūroku seiki no tenkan." More recently, note Moriyama and Nakae, *Nihon kodomo shi,* pp. 88–151. This work uses picture scrolls and the reports of Jesuit missionaries.

95. Kuramochi, *Chūsei sonraku shakai shi,* p. 269; Yūki, *Ransei no kodomo,* pp. 245–246.

96. Kuroda Hideo, *"Emaki" kodomo,* pp. 52–64.

97. Yūki, *Ransei no kodomo,* p. 197; on this general topic, see pp. 193–199.

98. Ibid., p. 187.

99. Ibid., pp. 207–218; Kuroda Hideo, *"Emaki" kodomo,* pp. 64–79.

100. Fujiki, *Zōhyōtachi,* pp. 15–22.

101. Maki, *Jinshin baibai,* pp. 170–186. For analysis of the Yūki Code, see Suzuki Tetsuo, *Kaihatsu to hyakusei,* pp. 343–354, where Suzuki argues that the lives of these *ge'nin* were relatively good.

102. Takahashi Masaaki, "Nihon hōken shakai," p. 78.

103. Hayami: "Nihon keizai shi ni okeru chūsei kara kinsei e no tenkan"; "Taikō kenchi." On the other hand, Tonomura cites the work of Miyagawa Mitsuru on Imabori, where he finds that the Taikō survey changed little. See Tonomura, *Community and Commerce,* pp. 163–165. Tomobe has also expressed reservations about Hayami's thesis. See "Jinkō to kazoku."

104. Minegishi, "Chūsei shakai no kaikyū kōsei," p. 47.

105. Minegishi updates his work in "Chūsei no kazoku to kyōdōtai," p. 47. Also note Takahashi Masaaki, "Nihon hōken shakai."

106. Yasuno, *Ge'nin ron,* pp. 13–45, 181–224.

107. Ono Masatoshi, *Chūsei iseki,* pp. 162–163.

108. Nagahara, "Mensaku no tenkai," pp. 75–78.

109. Itō Teiji, *Chūsei jūkyo shi,* pp. 206–261.

110. Ono Masatoshi, *Chūsei iseki,* p. 53 for an eastern *irori;* p. 49 for a western *kamado.* For the utensils of everyday life, see pp. 130–164. Why the *kamado/irori* difference should have persisted is unclear, but perhaps it was related to the harsher winters in eastern Honshu.

111. Takahashi Masaaki, "Yogore no Kyoto," p. 7.

112. *Toire no kōkogaku,* pp. 57–76. Also note Ono Masatoshi, *Chūsei iseki,* pp. 246–247.

113. Cited in Takahashi Masaaki, "Yogore no Kyoto," p. 7.

114. Takeda, *Furo to yu no hanashi,* pp. 85–101. Masamoto took baths irregularly while he lived at Hineno.

115. Kuroda Hideo, "Sengoku Shokuhōki," pp. 301–311. More recently, note Ōto Yasuhiro, "Chūsei shakai ni okeru kyōiku no tamensei," in Tsujimoto and Okita, *Kyōiku shakai shi,* pp. 65–119.

116. Cited in Kuroda Hideo, "Sengoku Shokuhōki," p. 304.

117. Ibid.

EPILOGUE

1. See Totman, *Pre-Industrial Korea and Japan in Environmental Perspective,* esp. pp. 65–142, for an approach that shares certain characteristics with this work and at the same time may serve as a useful critique.

2. Naitō Konan argued in 1921 that this foundation went back only to the Ōnin War (1467–1477), basing his statement primarily upon the appearance of

"the people" in history for those years. The interpretation put forward in this book would push that divide back another two centuries. The late thirteenth century ushered in not only a new demographic cycle that continued throughout the Tokugawa period, but also many changes—growing immunities to various diseases, the beginning of more intensive agriculture through double-cropping and the introduction of Champa rice, the rise of a booming commercial economy, the formation of the stem family and corporate village, the development of better industry, the increase in urbanization, the upsurge in commoners' physical well-being—so that the search for the origins of Tokugawa Japan should move deeper into the medieval era. See Naitō, *Naitō Konan zenshū*, pp. 130–148. Also note Amino, Nagahara, and Ōzaki, "Naitō Konan no 'Ōnin no ran ni tsuite' o megutte"; and Amino and Yokoi, *Toshi to shokunōmin no katsudō*, pp. 174ff.

3. McClain, *Japan*, p. 242. To be fair to the author, he does not place great emphasis on this point.

4. Landes, *The Wealth and Poverty of Nations*, pp. 40–44. Also note North and Thomas, *Rise of the Western World*, pp. 33–89, for a more theoretical approach. The approach and perspective of this book differ from both works in important respects.

5. McClain, *Japan*, p. 242.

6. Ibid., p. 243.

7. Yi: "Social Changes"; "The Influence of Neo-Confucianism."

8. McNeill, *Plagues*, pp. 69–176.

9. Ibid., pp. 5–8.

10. Scheiner, "Benevolent Lords and Honorable Peasants."

Character List

ai 藍

akagome 赤米

akane 茜

akimugi 秋麦

akiyashiki 空屋敷

akutō 悪党

ankoku jidai 暗黒時代

arata uchi 荒田打ち

ashigaru (to gōshite) 足軽（と号して）

ashiyowashi 足弱

azukari dokoro 預所

azukarimono 預物

azukeoku 預置

Azuma kagami 吾妻鏡

bakudai hyōrō 莫大兵粮

bakufu 幕府

banmin hyakusei 万民百姓（萬民百姓）

bantō 番頭

bikuni 比丘尼

bokujū 僕従

bosei sonchō 母性尊重

bu 歩

bushin 普請

chikuden 逐電

chō 町

chōhō kei hakogata ro 長方形箱型炉

chōki 逃毀

chōsan 逃散

chūden 中田

chūgoku 中国

chūrō 中老

(dai) akusaku 大悪作

Daijōin jisha zōjiki 大乗院寺社雑事記

daikan 大官

daimyō 大名

daitō ta 大唐田

daitōmai 大唐米

dekasegi 出稼ぎ

do (tsuchi) ikki 土一揆

domin 土民

dōran 動乱

dosō 土倉

egoma 荏胡麻

ekishin 疫神

emakimono 絵巻物

emishi 蝦夷

Engi shiki 延喜式

enju 槐

en'yū 緑友

fuigo 鞴
fukuro mochi 袋持ち
(fu)rōnin 浮浪人
fusaku 不作

gaibyō 咳病
Gaki sōshi 餓鬼草子
geden 下田
gegeden 下々田
gegyō to 下行斗
gekoku jō 下剋上
ge'nin 下人
ge'nō 下農
Genpei jōsui ki 源平盛衰記
gō 郷
gō no otona shikimonodomo 郷
    之乙名敷者共
gojō kawara 五条川原
goke'nin 御家人
gomi ごみ（ミ）
gongo dodan 言語道断
Goseibai shikimoku 御成敗式目
goyō shōnin 御用商人
Gozan 五山
gun 郡
gunchū-jō 軍忠状
guro 畾
Gyokuyō 玉葉

haguchi 羽口
haimatsu 這い松
hakahara 墓原
hakogata 箱型
han chika shiki tategata ro 半地
    下式縦型炉
hande 半手
hanzei 半済

hatsuka ichi 廿日市
hiden'in 悲田院
hiki 疋
himono ya ひものや
hi'nin 非人
hitobito tsumaru koto kagiri
    nashi 人々ツマル事無限
ho 保
Hōjō ki 方丈記
hōka 放火
Hokuriku dō 北陸道
hōmen 放免
hon to 本斗
Hōnen shōnin eden 法然上人絵
    伝
honke 本家
hottate bashira 掘立柱
Hyakuren shō 百錬抄
hyakusei 百姓
Hyōgo kitaseki nyūsen nōchō 兵
    庫北関入船納帳
hyōjō shū 評定衆
hyōrō 兵粮
hyōrō mai 兵粮米
hyōrō sho 兵粮所

ibyō 夷病
ichi mokudai 市目代
ie 家
ihai 位牌
ikki 一揆
imoji 鋳物師
inu ji'nin 犬神人
iran 違乱
irihama 入浜
irori 囲炉裏
Ishin pō 医心方

jige'nin 地下人

Jigoku sōshi 地獄草紙

ji'nin 神人

jiriki (kyūsai) 自力救済

jiriki sata 自力沙汰

Jishū 時宗

jitō 地頭

jitō (dai) 地頭代

jizamurai 地侍

jōden 上田

Jōei 貞永

jōnō 上農

jōri sei 条里制

jufu 呪符

kadoya 門屋

Kaisen shikimoku 廻船式目

kaizoku 海賊

kajishi 加地子

kakeochi （闕）欠落

kakochō 過去帳

kamado 竈

kan 旱

kana 仮名（カナ）

kana zōshi 仮名草子

kandaka 貫高

kanden 乾田

kannō (chō) 勧農（帳）

kannō no tori 勧農の鳥

kanrei 管領

kansho 旱暑

Kanshō 寛正

Kantō kanrei 関東管領

karita rōzeki 刈田狼藉

kassen teoi chūmon 合戦手負い
　注文

Kasuga gongen genki e 春日権現
　験記絵

katakana 片仮名（カタカナ）

katsuo ami 鰹網

Katsuyama ki 勝山記

kawanari 河成

kawayoke 川除

kebiishi (chō) 検非違使（庁）

kegare 穢

kemi 検見

kenchū chō 検注帳

kendan sata 検断沙汰

Kenmu shikimoku 建武式目

kerai 家礼

keyaki 欅

kichijitsu 吉日

kiki kanri 危機管理

Kikki 吉記

kinzan-shū 金山衆

kishin-jō 寄進状

kishōmon 起請文

kiwari sei 木割制

ko 子

kō otsunin 甲乙人

koe oke 肥桶

koku 石

koku to 国斗

kokudaka 石高

kokudo 国土

kokujin 国人

kōmyō 高名

korō 古老

kōryō 公領

kōya 荒野

Kōyō gunkan 甲陽軍鑑

kuchiberashi 口減し

kugo'nin 供御人

Kugyō bunin 公卿補任

kuji 公事

kumitori shiki 汲取式

kumonjo 公文所

kurairi chi 蔵入地

kuramoto (shū) 倉本衆

kyōgen 狂言

machi 町
machi no furo 町の風呂
machiya 町屋
magarikane 曲尺
maguwa 馬鍬
mandokoro 政所
Mansai jūgo nikki 満済准后日記
mansaku jōtai 萬作状態
Masamoto kō tabi hikitsuke 政
　基公旅引付
masu(gata) 枡（型）
Matsuzaki tenjin engi 松崎天神
　縁起
me 女
Meigetsu ki 明月記
migyōsho 御教書
mikuriya 御厨
Minkei ki 民経記
miyaza 宮座
mo も
mokkan 木簡
monme 匁
muen 無縁
mukotori kon 婿取婚
munabechi sen 楝別銭
murasaki 紫
myō (den) 名（田）
Myōhōji ki 妙法寺記
myōji 苗字
myōshu shiki 名主職

namoto 名木
*nanatsu made wa kami no
　uchi* 七つまで神のうち
natsumugi 夏麦
nawashiro 苗代
nenbutsu 念仏

nengu (shotō) 年貢所當
Nijō kawara rakugaki 二条河原
　落書
ninpu 人夫
nisun 二寸
nobushi 野付
nōka 農家
nōmin 農民
nōsho 農書
nuhi 奴婢

ōame 大雨
oidasu 追いだし
ōimizo 大井溝
onkura 御倉・御蔵
ōnokogiri 大鋸
onnengu mai 御年貢米
ōtabumi 太田文
otona hyakushō 乙名百姓

Rakuchū rakugai byōbu 洛中洛
　外屏風
rakuichi 楽市
rakuza 楽座
ranbō 濫妨
reiboku 霊木
ri (i, li) 里
Risshō ankoku ron 立証安国論
risshū 律宗
ritsuryō 律令
ro 炉
roji rōzeki 路次狼藉
rokusai ichi 六斎市
rōzeki 狼藉
ryōke 領家
ryōshu (to) 領主斗

Saigyō monogatari emaki 西行物
　語絵巻

sakamogi 逆茂木

sakaya 酒屋

sakumō o karitoriowannu 苅取作毛畢

samurai dokoro 侍所

sanden 散田

sanjō rokushaku 三丈六尺

sanshaku 三尺

sanzoku 山賊

segaki-e 施餓鬼会

seimei iji sōchi 生命維持装置

Seiryō ki 精良記

sejō 世上

Sejong changhŏn taewong sillok 世宗荘憲大王実録

seki 関

sekisho 関所

senrei 先例

senshi to 宣旨斗

Shaseki shū 沙石集

shichigō 七郷

shidara no kami 志多羅神

shijō 四条

shiki 職

shimahata 島畑

shimokusa 下草

Shingen zutsumi 信玄堤

shingō 賑給

shinjuku 新宿

Shinmin kangetsu shū 親民監月集

shinpo jitō 新補地頭

shinsei 新制

shinyashiki 新屋敷

Shirakawa no mitachi 白川御館

shō 升

shōen 庄・荘園

shōen-kokugaryō 庄・荘園国衙領

shōgatsu sechie 正月節会

shōgi gashira 将棋頭

shōgun 将軍

shohō 諸方

shojū 所従

shoki shōen 初期庄・荘園

shōkō ki 小康期

shomu sata 所矛沙汰

shō to 庄斗

shotō 所當

shotō mai 所當米

shoyaku 諸役

shūchū 衆中

shuden-ryō to 主殿寮斗

Shūgai shō 拾芥抄

shugo daimyō 守護大名

shugo-dai 守護（代）

shujin 主人

shukueki 宿駅

shūson 集村

sō 惣

sō no yoriai 惣の寄合

soeya 添屋

sonden 損田

sōron 相論

sōson 惣村

suika 西瓜

suiko 出挙

ta asobi 田遊び

ta no kami matsuri 田の神祭

Taihei ki 太平記

taihō 台飽

Taikō 太閤

tan 反・段

tansen 段銭

tariki 他力

tatara たたら・鑢

tatari 祟り・タタリ

teishitsu den 低湿田
tenka 天下
to 斗
tōboshi (ta) とうぼし・唐法師
　　（田）・唐穂青（田）
tōgasa 唐瘡
tōgoku 東国
toi 問
toimaru 問丸
Tōji kakochō 東寺過去帳
Tōkai dō 東海道
toki no washi 時の和市
tokusei (ikki) 徳政（一揆）
tokusei (rei) 徳政（令）
Tokushi yoron 読史余論
torioi 鳥追い
tsubo 坪
Tsuika hō 追加法
tsukahara 塚原
tsumadoi kon 妻問婚
tsumida 摘田

uji 氏
ujikami 氏神
ujina 氏名
urame 裏目
urikai ウリカイ
utsugi 卯木

wakamono 若者
wakō 倭寇
Wamyō shō 和名抄
warabi 蕨
wasan 和算
washi 和市
watakushi naki no seidō 政道無
　　私

yado 宿
yama no koya 山の小屋
Yamai no sōshi 病の草紙
yamaimo 山芋
yari 鑓
yashiki 屋敷
Yata Rokubeinojō 矢田六兵衛尉
yokaki 代掻き
yometori kon 嫁取婚
youchi 夜討
Yōwa ninen ki 養和二年記
yuzuri-jō 譲状

za 座
zaike (yaku) 在家（役）
zasshō 雑掌
zōhyō 雑兵
zōnin 雑人
zuryō 受領

Works Cited

Unless otherwise noted, the place of publication for Japanese works is Tokyo.

PRIMARY SOURCES

Akahama myōhōji kakochō. In *Zoku gunsho ruijū,* vol. 33 (2). Revised edition. Zoku gunsho ruijū kansei kai, 1983.

Aou-shi shi, vols. 7 and 8 (1). Aou-shi kyōiku iinkai, 1990–1992.

Azuma kagami. In *Shintei zōho kokushi taikei,* vols. 32–33. Yoshikawa kōbunkan, 1964.

Chiba-ken shiryō: Chūsei hen: Hondoji kakochō. Chiba-ken, 1982.

Dai Nihon shiryō. Series 5, 6, 8. Tokyo daigaku shiryō hensan jo, 1925–2001. Cited in text as *DNS.*

Dai Nihon sozei shi, vol. 2. Revised edition. Chōyō kai, 1927.

Daijōin jisha zōjiki. In *Zoku shiryō taisei,* vols. 26–37. Revised edition. Edited by Takeuchi Rizō. Rinsen shoten, 1978.

Enkyō bon Heike monogatari. 2 vols. Edited by Kitahara Yasuo and Ogawa Eiichi. Bensei sha, 1990.

Gaki sōshi; jigoku sōshi; yamai sōshi; kusoshi emaki. In *Nihon no emaki,* vol. 7. Edited by Komatsu Shigemi. Chūō kōron sha, 1987.

Gifu-ken shi: Shiryō hen: Kodai chūsei, vol. 3. Gifu-ken, 1971.

Goseibai shikimoku. In *Nihon shisō taikei: Chūsei seiji shakai shisō,* vol. 21(1). Edited by Kasamatsu Hiroshi. Iwanami shoten, 1972.

Gyokuyō. 3 vols. Geirin sha, 1975.

Hagi-hanbatsu etsuroku. 5 vols. Yamaguchi-ken monjo kan, 1967–1971.

Heian ibun. 11 vols., 2 supplements, and a 2-vol. index. Edited by Takeuchi Rizō. Tokyo dō, 1974–1980. Cited in text as *HI.*

Hennen sabetsu shi shiryō shūsei. Edited by Harada Tomohiko. San'ichi shobō, 1984–1987.

Hidaka chōshi: Shiryō hen. Hidaka-chō, 1980.

Hiroshima-ken shi: Kodai chūsei shiryō hen (kengai monjo hen), vol. 5. Hiroshima-ken, 1980.

Hōjō ki. In *Nihon koten bungaku taikei,* vol. 30. Edited by Nishio Makoto. Iwanami shoten, 1957.

Hyakuren shō. In *Shintei zōho kokushi taikei,* vol. 11. Yoshikawa kōbunkan, 1929.

Hyōgo-ken shi: Shiryō hen: Chūsei, vol. 8. Hyōgo-ken, 1994.

Ichirenji kakochō. In *Kōfu-shi shi: Genshi kodai chūsei hen,* vol. 1. Kōfu-shi yakusho, 1989.

Iriki monjo. Edited by Asakawa Kan'ichi. Revised edition. Nihon gakujutsu shinkō kai, 1955.

Iwashimizu monjo. In *Dai Nihon komonjo: Iewake.* Series 4. 6 vols. Shiryō hensanjo, 1909.

Kamakura ibun. 42 vols., 4 supplements, and 5-vol. index. Edited by Takeuchi Rizō. Tokyo dō, 1971–1998. Cited in text as *KI.*

Kanoko C iseki urushigami monjo: Honbun hen. Mito: Ibaraki-ken kyōiku zaidan, 1983.

Katsuyama-son shi: Katsuyama ki. Katsuyama mura, 1992.

Kenmu shikimoku and *Tsuika hō.* In *Nihon shisō taikei,* vol. 21(1). *Chūsei seiji shakai shisō.* Edited by Kasamatsu Hiroshi. Iwanami shoten, 1972.

Kishiwada shishi: Kodai chūsei hen, vol. 2. Kishiwada-shi, 1996.

Kokubunji-shi shi, vol. 2. Kokubunji-shi, 1991.

Maizuru-shi shi: Shiryō hen. Maizuru-shi shi hensan iinkai, 1973.

Mansai jūgo nikki. 3 vols. Kyoto teikoku daigaku bungaku bu, 1920.

Masamoto kō tabi hikitsuke. In *Nihon shi shiryō sōkan,* vol. 1. Izumi shoin, 1996.

Meigetsu ki. 3 vols. Tosho kankō kai, 1912.

Mōrike monjo. In *Dai Nihon komonjo: Iewake.* Series 8. 4 vols. Shiryō hensan gakari, 1920–1924.

Muromachi bakufu hō. In *Chūsei hōsei shiryō shū,* vol. 2. Edited by Satō Shin'ichi and Ikeuchi Yoshisuke. Iwanami shoten, 1957.

Nanboku chō ibun: Chūgoku Shikoku hen. 6 vols. Edited by Matsuoka Hisato. Tokyo dō, 1987–1995. Cited in text as *NBCICS.*

Nanboku chō ibun: Kyushu hen. 7 vols. Edited by Seno Seiichirō. Tokyo dō. 1980–1992. Cited in text as *NBCIK.*

Okayama-ken komonjo shū, vol. 1. Edited by Mizuno Kōichirō et al. Shibunkaku shuppan, 1953.

Ōmi no kuni Banbanoshuku Rengeji kakochō. In *Gunsho ruijū,* vol. 29. Revised edition. Zoku gunsho ruijū kansei kai, 1986.

Ritsuryō. In *Nihon shisō taikei,* vol. 3. Edited by Inoue Mitsusada et al. Iwanami shoten, 1976.

Ryūgasaki no chūsei jōkaku, vol. 2. Ryūgasaki kyōiku iinkai, 1987.

Seiryō ki. In *Nihon nōsho zenshū,* vol. 10. Nōsangyōson bunka kyōkai, 1980.

Sengoku ibun: Go-Hōjō hen. 6 vols. Tokyo dō, 1991–1995.

Shaseki shū. In *Nihon koten bungaku taikei,* vol. 85. Edited by Watanabe Kōya. Iwanami shoten, 1966.

Shūgai shō. In *Kojitsu sōsho,* vol. 22. Revised edition. Meiji tosho, 1993.

Sŏng Hi-kyŏng. *Rōdōshō Nihon kōroku.* Edited by Murai Shōsuke. Iwanami bunko, 1987.

Taihei ki. In *Nihon koten bungaku taikei,* vols. 34–36. Edited by Gotō Tanji et al. Iwanami shoten, 1960.

Tanba Yasuyori. *Ishin pō.* In *Nihon igaku sōsho katsuji bon.* Oriento shuppan sha, 1991.

Tōji kakochō. Unpublished manuscript provided by Umata Ayako.

Tsuika hō. In *Nihon shisō taikei 21 Chūsei seiji shakai shisō,* vol. 1. Edited by Kasamatsu Hiroshi. Iwanami shoten, 1972.

Yijo sillok. In *Chūgoku Chōsen no shiseki ni okeru Nihon shiryō shūsei,* vol. 1. Kokusho kankō kai, 1976.

Yūgyōji kakochō. In *Jishū kakochō.* Kyūgaku kenkyūjo, 1964.

SECONDARY SOURCES

Abe Kōichi. "Chūsei kōki ni okeru Kanto nairiku no suijō kōtsū to tenma." In *Chūsei tōgoku no butsuryū to toshi.* Edited by Minegishi Sumio and Murai Shōsuke, pp. 85–111. Yamakawa shuppan sha, 1995.

Abe Takeshi. "Chūsei kōki no Yamato no sonraku." In *Nihon chūsei seiji shakai no kenkyū,* pp. 799–826. Zoku gunsho ruijū kansei kai, 1991.

Adolphson, Mikael. *The Gates of Power.* Honolulu: University of Hawai'i Press, 2000.

Akamatsu Toshihide. *Kodai chūsei shakai keizai shi kenkyū.* Heirakuji shoin, 1972.

———. "Muromachi bakufu." In *Taikei Nihon shi sōsho 1 Seiji shi 1.* Edited by Fujiki Kunihiko and Inoue Mitsusada, pp. 312–407. Yamakawa shuppan, 1965.

Akashi Ikki. "Kodai chūsei no kazoku to shinzoku." *Rekishi hyōron* 416 (December 1984): 5–26.

Akiyama Nobutaka. *Sengoku daimyō Mōri shi no kenkyū.* Yoshikawa kōbunkan, 1998.

Akutō no chūsei. Iwata shoin, 1998.

Amino Yoshihiko. *Chūsei minshū no seigyō to gijutsu.* Tokyo daigaku shuppan kai, 2001.

———. "Chūsei no futan taikei—nengu ni tsuite." In *Chūsei kinsei no kokka to shihai.* Edited by Nagahara Keiji et al., pp. 72–103. Tokyo daigaku shuppan kai, 1986.

———. "Chūsei no seien to shio no ryūtsū." In *Kōza Nihon gijutsu no shakai shi 2 Engyō to gyogyō,* pp. 43–91. Nihon hyōronsha, 1985.

———. *Chūsei shōen no yōsō.* Hanawa sensho, 1966.

———. *Igyō no ōken.* Heibon sha, 1986.

———. "Kamakura makki no shomujun." In *Kōza Nihon shi 3 Hōken shakai no tenkai,* pp. 21–56. Tokyo daigaku shuppan kai, 1970.

————. "Kodai chūsei kinsei shoki no gyorō to kaisan butsu no ryūtsū." In *Kōza Nihon gijutsu no shakai shi* 2 *Engyō gyogyō*, pp. 219–272. Nihon hyōron sha, 1985.

————. "Kodai chūsei no hiden'in o megutte." In *Chūsei shakai to ikkō ikki*, pp. 275–290. Yoshikawa kōbunkan, 1985.

————. *Muen kugai raku*. Revised edition. Heibon sha, 1987.

————. *Nihon chūsei no hinōgyōmin to tennō*. Iwanami shoten, 1984.

————. *Nihon chūsei no minshū zō*. Iwanami shoten, 1980.

————. *Nihon chūsei tochi seido shi no kenkyū*. Hanawa shobō, 1991.

————. *Nihon chūsei toshi no sekai*. Chikuma shobō, 1996.

————. *Nihon no rekishi* 10 *Mōko shurai*. Shōgakkan, 1974.

————. "Yūjotachi no kyozō to jitsuzō." In *Shūkan Asahi hyakka Nihon no rekishi* 3 *chūsei* 1 *Yūjo kugushi shirabyōshi*, pp. 70–71. Asahi shinbun sha, 1986.

Amino Yoshihiko and Yokoi Kiyoshi. *Nihon no chūsei* 6 *Toshi to shokunōmin no katsudō*. Chūō kōron shinsha, 2003.

Amino Yoshihiko, Nagahara Keiji, and Ōzaki Masahide. "Naitō Konan no 'Ōnin no ran ni tsuite' o megutte." *Rekishi kōron* 11 (1981): 10–37.

Amino Yoshihiko et al., eds. *Kōza Nihon shōen shi*. 7 vols. Yoshikawa kōbunkan, 1989–1999.

Arai Takashige. *Chūsei akutō no kenkyū*. Yoshikawa kōbunkan, 1990.

Arakawa Hidetoshi. *Kikin*. Kyōiku sha, 1979.

Araki Moriaki. "Amino Yoshihiko shi kingyō ni tsuite no hihanteki kentō." *Nenpō chūsei shi kenkyū* 11 (1986): 97–119.

————. "Amino Yoshihiko shi no kingyō ni tsuite hihanteki kentō." *Rekishigaku kenkyū* 538 (February 1985): 35–47.

————. "Shikimoku yonjū ni jō kaishaku to idō no jiyū." *Ōsaka furitsu daigaku daigakuin sōgō kengaku kenkyū ka* 2 (1986): 1–24.

————. "Taikō kenchi no rekishiteki zentei—1." *Rekishigaku kenkyū* 163 (May 1953): 1–17; 164 (July 1953): 1–22.

Arashi Kaichi. *Nihon akagome kō*. Yūzan kaku, 1974.

Asakura Naomi. "Sengoku ki no kōchi kaihatsu ni kansuru ichi shiron." *Komazawa daigaku shigaku ronshū* 18 (February 1988): 58–69.

Asao Naohiro. *Taikei Nihon no rekishi* 8 *Tenka ittō*. Shōgakkan, 1993.

Atsuta Kō. "Kanshō no kikin to Yamato." In *Chiiki shi to rekishi kyōiku*, pp. 147–174. Kimura Hirokazu sensei taikan kinen kai, 1985.

Atwell, William. "Volcanism and Short-Term Climatic Change in East Asian and World History, c. 1200–1699." *Journal of World History* 12 (2001): 29–98.

Bellah, Robert. *Tokugawa Religion*. New York: Free Press, 1957.

Berry, Mary Elizabeth. *The Culture of Civil War in Kyoto*. Berkeley: University of California Press, 1994.

————. *Hideyoshi*. Cambridge, MA: Harvard University Press, 1982.

Birt, Michael. "Samurai in Passage: Transformation of the Sixteenth-Century Kanto." *Journal of Japanese Studies* 11 (Summer 1985): 369–400.

————. "Warring States: A Study of the Go-Hōjō Daimyo and Domain, 1491–1590." Ph.D. dissertation, Princeton University, 1983.

Bohstedt, John. "The Moral Economy and the Discipline of Historical Context." *Journal of Social History* 26 (Winter 1992): 265–284.

————. "The Pragmatic Economy, the Politics of Provisions, and the Invention of the Food Riot Tradition in 1740." In *Moral Economy and Popular Protest*. Edited by Adrian Randall and Andrew Charlesworth, pp. 55–92. New York: Macmillan, 2000.

Brown, Delmer. *Money Economy in Medieval Japan*. New Haven, CT: Yale University Press, 1951.

Brownlee, John. *Political Thought in Japanese Historical Writing*. Waterloo, Ontario: Wilfred Laurier University Press, 1991.

Burnet, MacFarlane, and David White. *The Natural History of Infectious Disease*. Cambridge: Cambridge University Press, 1972.

Chūsei minshū to majinai. Hiroshima kenritsu rekishi hakubutsukan tomo no kai, 1990.

Conlan, Thomas. *In Little Need of Divine Intervention*. Ithaca, NY: Cornell University Press, 2001.

————. "Largesse and the Limits of Loyalty in the Fourteenth Century." In Mass, *The Origins of Japan's Medieval World*, pp. 39–64.

————. "Nanboku chō ki kassen no ichi kōsatsu." In *Nihon shakai no shiteki kōzō: Kodai chūsei*. Edited by Ōyama Kyōhei, pp. 417–440. Shibunkaku shuppan, 1997.

————. "The Nature of Warfare in Fourteenth-Century Japan: The Record of Nomoto Tomoyuki." *Journal of Japanese Studies* 25 (Summer 1999): 299–330.

————. *State of War: The Violent Order of Fourteenth-Century Japan*. Ann Arbor: University of Michigan Press, 2003.

————. "State of War: The Violent Order of Fourteenth-Century Japan." Ph.D. dissertation, Stanford University, 1998.

Cornell, Laurel. "Retirement, Inheritance, and Intergenerational Conflict in Preindustrial Japan." *Journal of Family History* 8 (Spring 1983): 55–69.

————. "Was 'Three-and-a-Half Lines' So Bad? Peasant Women and Divorce in Early Modern Japan." *Signs* 15 (1990): 710–732.

————. "Why Are There No Spinsters in Japan?" *Journal of Family History* 9 (Winter 1984): 326–339.

Crosby, Alfred, Jr. *The Columbian Exchange: Biological and Cultural Consequences of 1492*. Westport, CT: Greenwood Press, 1972.

Davis, David L. "*Ikki* in Late Medieval Japan." In *Medieval Japan: Essays in Institutional History*. Edited by John Hall and Jeffrey Mass. Stanford, CA: Stanford University Press, 1974.

————. "The Kaga *Ikkō-Ikki*, 1473–1580." Ph.D. dissertation, University of Chicago, 1978.

Domar, Evsey. *Capitalism, Socialism, and Serfdom*. Cambridge: Cambridge University Press, 1989.

Ebara Masaharu. "Chūsei zenki sonraku no ichi tokushitsu ni tsuite." *Rekishi-gaku kenkyū* 527 (April 1984): 1–14.

———. *Nihon chūsei chiiki shakai no kōzō.* Azekura shobō, 2000.

Ebisawa Makoto. "Hyūga no kuni zuden chō no seikaku." *Kamakura ibun geppō* 14 (February 1988): 4–5.

———. "Kamakura jidai ni okeru Bungo no kuni no kokugaryō ni tsuite." In *Seinan chiiki shi kenkyū,* vol. 3. Edited by Hidemura Hidemi, pp. 101–119. Bunken shuppan kan, 1977.

———. *Shōen kōryō sei to chūsei sonraku.* Azekura shobō, 2000.

Egashira Tsuneharu. "Chūsei ni okeru ge'nin no baibai." *Keizai shi kenkyū* 19 (March 1938): 63–68.

———. *Kōyasan ryō shōen kenkyū.* Kyoto: Rinsen shoten, 1972.

Evans, Alfred, and Philip Brachman, eds. *Bacterial Infections of Humans: Epidemiology and Control,* 3rd ed. New York: Plenum Medical Book, 1998.

Fairbridge, Rhodes W. "Eustatic Changes in Sea Level." In *Physics and Chemistry of the Earth,* vol. 4. Edited by L.H. Ahrens et al., pp. 99–185. New York: Pergamon Press, 1961.

Farris, William Wayne. "Diseases of the Premodern Period in Japan." In *The Cambridge World History of Human Disease.* Edited by Kenneth F. Kiple, pp. 376–385. Cambridge: Cambridge University Press, 1993.

———. "Famine, Climate, and Farming in Early Japan." In *Centers and Peripheries in Heian Japan.* Honolulu: University of Hawai'i, forthcoming.

———. *Heavenly Warriors: The Evolution of Japan's Military, 500–1300.* Cambridge, MA: Harvard University Press, 1992.

———. *Population, Disease, and Land in Early Japan, 645–900.* Cambridge, MA: Harvard University Press, 1985.

———. *The Population of Ancient Japan: Revised Estimates and Interpretive Issues.* Ann Arbor: University of Michigan, forthcoming.

———. *Sacred Texts and Buried Treasures: Issues in the Historical Archaeology of Ancient Japan.* Honolulu: University of Hawai'i Press, 1998.

———. "Shipbuilding and Nautical Technology in Japan, Origins to 1640." Paper presented at "Tools of Culture" conference, University of Oregon, Eugene, September 1997.

———. "Trade, Money, and Merchants in Nara Japan." *Monumenta Nipponica* 53 (Autumn 1998): 303–334.

Feng, Han-Yi. *The Chinese Kinship System.* Cambridge, MA: Harvard University Press, 1967.

Friday, Karl. "Pushing beyond the Pale: The Yamato Conquest of the *Emishi* and Northern Japan." *Journal of Japanese Studies* 23 (Winter 1997): 1–24.

———. *Samurai, Warfare and the State in Early Medieval Japan.* London and New York: Routledge, 2004.

———. "Valorous Butchers: The Art of War during the Golden Age of the Samurai." *Japan Forum* 5 (April 1993): 1–19.

Frohlich, Judith. "Rulers, Peasants and the Use of the Written Word in Medieval Japan." Ph.D. dissertation, University of Zurich, 2004.

Fujikawa Yū. *Nihon shippei shi.* New edition by Matsuda Michio. Heibon sha, 1969.

Fujiki Hisashi. *Kiga to sensō no sengoku o iku.* Asahi shinbun sha, 2001.

———. "Kikin to sensō kara mita Ikkō ikki." In *Kōza Rennyo,* vol. 1, pp. 93–118. Heibon sha, 1996.

———. "Mura no kakushimono azukarimono." In *Kotoba no bunka shi: Chūsei,* vol. 1, pp. 65–156. Heibon sha, 1988.

———. *Mura to ryōshu no sengoku sekai.* Tokyo daigaku shuppan kai, 1997.

———. *Toyotomi heiwa to sengoku shakai.* Revised edition. Tokyo daigaku shuppan kai, 1992.

———. *Zōhyōtachi no senjō.* Asahi shinbun sha, 1995.

Fujino Shōsaburō. "Nōgyō kensetsu toshi katsudō to keizai seichō: Keiki junkan: 1600 nen—1868 nen." *Risshō daigaku keizaigaku kihō* 49 (October 1999): 35–102.

Fujita Hirotsugu. "Hyōgo shūhen no fune ni yoru jūgo seiki chūyō no kaijō yusō." *Chizu to rekishi kūkan.* Daimei dō, 2000.

Fukuda Toyohiko. *Chiba Tsunetane.* Yoshikawa kōbunkan, 1973.

———, ed. *Chūsei o kangaeru: Ikusa.* Yoshikawa kōbunkan, 1993.

Fukutō Sanae. " 'Ie' no seiritsu to josei." In *Chūsei no seikatsu kūkan.* Edited by Toda Yoshimi, pp. 1–35. Yuhikaku, 1993.

Furushima Toshio. *Furushima Toshio chosaku shū 6 Nihon nōgyō gijutsu shi.* Tokyo daigaku shuppan kai, 1975.

———. *Tochi ni kizamareta rekishi.* Iwanami shinsho, 1967.

Gay, Suzanne. *The Moneylenders of Late Medieval Kyoto.* Honolulu: University of Hawai'i Press, 2001.

———. "The Muromachi Bakufu in Medieval Kyoto." Ph.D. dissertation, Yale University, 1982.

Goble, Andrew. *Kenmu.* Cambridge, MA: Harvard University Press, 1996.

Gomi Fumihiko. "Chūsei no ie to kafuchō sei." In *Ie to kafuchō sei,* pp. 31–48. Waseda daigaku shuppan bu, 1992.

———. *Insei ki shakai no kenkyū.* Yamakawa shuppan sha, 1988.

———. *Taikei Nihon no rekishi 5 Kamakura to kyō.* Shōgakkan, 1988.

Gomi Fumihiko and Saiki Hideo, eds. *Chūsei toshi Kamakura to shi no sekai.* Takashi shoin, 2002.

Gomi Fumihiko and Watanabe Hisashi, eds. *Shin taikei Nihon shi 3 Tochi shoyū shi.* Yamakawa shuppan, 2002.

Gomi Fumihiko, Nishiyachi Seibi, and Kawai Yasushi. "Chūsei zenki no tochi shoyū." In Gomi Fumihiko and Watanabe, *Tochi shoyū shi,* pp. 153–160.

Gomi Satsuo. "Hyūga no kuni kenkyū zuden chō sho kō." *Nihon rekishi* 148 (October 1960): 27–41.

———. "Ōsumi no kuni kenkyū zuden chō sho kō." *Nihon rekishi* 142 (April 1960): 33–54.

———. "Satsuma no kuni kenkyū zuden chō zakkō." *Nihon rekishi* 137 (November 1959): 27–48.

Gottfried, Robert. *The Black Death.* New York: Free Press, 1983.

Haga Norihiko. "Karita rōzeki kō." *Hōsei shi kenkyū* 29 (1979): 69–96.

Hall, John C. "Japanese Feudal Laws *(Go seibai shikimoku)."* *Transactions of the Asiatic Society of Japan.* First Series 34 (1906): 1–44.

Hall, John W. *Government and Local Power in Japan, 500–1700.* Princeton, NJ: Princeton University Press, 1966.

———. "The Muromachi Bakufu." In Yamamura, *The Cambridge History of Japan,* pp. 175–230.

Hall, John W., and Toyoda Takeshi, eds. *Japan in the Muromachi Age.* Berkeley: University of California Press, 1977.

Hall, John W., Nagahara Keiji, and Kozo Yamamura, eds. *Japan before Tokugawa: Political Consolidation and Economic Growth, 1500 to 1650.* Princeton, NJ: Princeton University Press, 1981.

Hall, Kenneth. "Economic History of Early Southeast Asia." In *The Cambridge History of Southeast Asia,* vol. 1. Edited by Nicholas Tarling, pp. 183–275. Cambridge: Cambridge University Press, 1992.

Hanagasaki Moriaki. *Uesugi Kenshin.* Shin jinbutsu ōrai sha, 1991.

Hanihara, Kazuro. "Estimation of the Number of Early Migrants to Japan: A Simultative Study." *Journal of the Anthropological Society of Nippon* 95 (July 1987): 391–403.

Hanley, Susan. *Everyday Things in Premodern Japan.* Berkeley: University of California Press, 1997.

———. "Family and Fertility in Four Tokugawa Villages." In Hanley and Wolf, *Family and Population in East Asian History,* pp. 196–228.

Hanley, Susan, and Kozo Yamamura. *Economic and Demographic Change in Preindustrial Japan, 1600–1868.* Princeton, NJ: Princeton University Press, 1977.

Hanley, Susan, and Arthur P. Wolf, eds. *Family and Population in East Asian History.* Stanford, CA: Stanford University Press, 1985.

Harada Nobuo. "Chūsei ni okeru sonraku no keikan—hōkō." *Sapporo daigaku joshi tanki daigaku bu kiyō* 17 (February 1991): 47–56.

———. *Chūsei sonraku no keikan to seikatsu.* Kyoto: Shibunkaku shuppan, 1999.

———. "Tōgoku no chūsei sonraku ni okeru kaihatsu to saigai." *Kokuritsu rekishi minzoku hakubutsukan kenkyū hōkoku* 96 (March 2002): 393–413.

Harada Tomohiko. *Chūsei ni okeru toshi no kenkyū.* Dai Nihon yūben kai kōdan sha, 1942.

———. *Nihon hōken seika no toshi to shakai.* San'ichi shobō, 1960.

Haraguchi Shōzō. "Kodai chūsei no shūraku." *Kōkogaku kenkyū* 92 (March 1977): 16–32.

Harrington, Lorraine. "Social Control and the Significance of *Akutō.*" In *Court and Bakufu in Japan.* Edited by Jeffrey Mass, pp. 221–250. Stanford, CA: Stanford University Press, 1982.

Hasegawa Kumahiko. *Waga kodai seitetsu to Nihon tō.* Gijutsu shoin, 1977.

Hasegawa Yasuko. "Sengokki ni okeru funsō saitei to sōkoku ikki." *Nihon shi kenkyū* 482 (October 2002): 43–70.

Hattori Toshirō. *Heian jidai igaku no kenkyū.* Kuwana bunsei dō, 1955.

———. *Kamakura jidai igaku no kenkyū.* Yoshikawa kōbunkan, 1964.

Hayami Akira. *The Historical Demography of Pre-modern Japan.* University of Tokyo, 1997.

———. "Jinkō shi." In *Iwanami kōza Nihon tsūshi 1 Nihon rettō to jinrui shakai,* pp. 117–147. Iwanami shoten, 1993.

———. *Kinsei nōson no rekishi jinkōgakuteki kenkyū.* Tōyō keizai shinpō sha, 1973.

———. *Nihon keizai shi e no shikaku.* Tōyō keizai shinpō sha, 1968.

———. "Nihon keizai shi ni okeru chūsei kara kinsei e no tenkan." *Shakai keizai shigaku* 37 (1971): 95–105.

———. *Nihon ni okeru keizai shakai no tenkai.* Keiō tsūshin, 1973.

———. "The Population at the Beginning of the Tokugawa Period: An Introduction to the Historical Demography of Pre-Industrial Japan." *Keio Economic Studies* 4 (1966): 1–28.

———. "Taikō kenchi o megutte." *Shakai keizai shigaku* 31 (1966): 24–30.

Hayami Akira and Miyamoto Matao. "Gaisetsu: Jūnana jūhasseiki." In *Nihon keizai shi 1 Keizai shakai no seiritsu jūnana jūhasseiki,* pp. 4–84. Iwanami shoten, 1988.

Hayami Akira, Nishikawa Shunsaku, and Shinpo Hiroshi. *Sūryō keizai shi nyūmon.* Nihon hyōron sha, 1975.

Hayashima Daisuke. "Kyōkō chiiki no saimu to kōrisen." *Atarashii rekishigaku no tame ni* 247 (June 2002): 20–33.

———. "Sengoku jidai no dosō sakaya yaku to Muromachi bakufu." *Nenpō chūsei shi kenkyū* 26 (2001): 35–56.

Hayashiya Tatsusaburō. "Kyoto in the Muromachi Age." In J.W. Hall and Toyoda, *Japan in the Muromachi Age,* pp. 15–34.

Hazard, Benjamin. "The Formative Years of the Wako, 1223–63." *Monumenta Nipponica* 22 (1967): 260–277.

Hidemura Senzō. "Chūsei jinshin baibai monjo no ichi kōsatsu." *Kyushu daigaku keizai gakkai keizai gaku kenkyū* 34 (March 1959): 63–93.

Higashijima Makoto. "Toshi ōken to chūsei kokka." In *Sōsho: Rekishigaku to genzai: Ō to kō—tennō no Nihon shi.* Edited by Suzuki Masayoshi, pp. 167–211. Kashiwa shobō, 1998.

Hirai Kiyoshi. *Nihon jūtaku no rekishi.* NHK bukkusu, 1974.

———. *Zusetsu Nihon jūtaku no rekishi.* Gakugei shuppan sha, 1980.

Hirakawa Minami. "Shin hakken no 'shushi fuda' to kodai no inasaku." *Kokushi gaku* 169:1–55.

Hirayama Yū. "Sengoku daimyō ryōkoku ka ni okeru gōson no kōzō ni tsuite." *Nenpō chūsei shi kenkyū* 19 (1994): 94–123.

———. "Sengoku ki tōgoku no gōson ni okeru ie ni tsuite." *Takeda shi kenkyū* 18 (October 1997): 1–23.

Hirose Kazuo. "Chūsei sonraku no keisei to tenkai." *Busshitsu bunka* 50 (May 1988): 7–27.

Hōgetsu Keigo. *Chūsei kangai shi no kenkyū.* Unebi shobō, 1943.

———. "Chūsei kenchi ni okeru ichi ni no mondai." *Shinano* 10 (May 1958): 26–32.

———. "Chūsei ni okeru yōsui ike no chikuzō ni tsuite." *Hakusan shigaku* 17 (July 1973): 1–10.

———. *Chūsei ryōsei shi no kenkyū.* Yoshikawa kōbunkan, 1961.

———. "Hōken jidai zenki no sangyō keizai." In *Shin Nihon shi kōza: Hōken jidai zenki,* pp. 1–50. Chūō kōron sha, 1952.

———. "Honpō Champa mai kō." In *Nihon nōgyō keizai shi kenkyū,* vol. 2, pp. 167–178. Nihon hyōron sha, 1949.

———. "Kenchi" and "Kenchū chō." In *Heibonsha hyakka jiten,* vol. 5, pp. 178–180. Heibonsha, 1984.

Homuda Yoshinobu. "Ōtabumi to kokugaryō no shoryō kōsei." In *Nihon kodai shi kenkyū,* pp. 527–563. Yoshikawa kōbunkan, 1980.

Hongō Kazuto. "Nanboku chō dōran zu." In *Nihon no rekishi* 12 *Chūsei* II *Go-Daigo to Takauji: Kenmu no shinsei.* Edited by Amino Yoshihiko and Kasamatsu Hiroshi, pp. 16–17. Asahi shinbun sha, 1986.

Hosokawa Kameichi. "Chūsei shōen no kenchi." *Shakai keizai shigaku* 7 (October 1934): 1–20.

Hosokawa Ryōichi. *Chūsei no risshū jiin to minshū.* Yoshikawa kōbunkan, 1987.

———. "Kazoku o kōsei shinai josei." In Minegishi, *Chūsei o kangaeru,* pp. 210–240.

———. *Onna no chūsei.* Nihon edeitaa sukuuru shuppan bu, 1989.

Hotate Michihisa. "Chūsei minshū no raifu saikuru." In *Iwanami kōza Nihon tsūshi* 7 *chūsei* 1, pp. 221–252. Iwanami shoten, 1993.

———. "Chūsei no kodomo no yōiku to shujin ken." *Kamakura ibun geppō* 24 (April 1984): 1–3.

———. "Fukuro mochi kasa mochi tsubo tori." *Rekishi chiri kyōiku* 362 (January 1984): 82–85.

Hotate Michihisa et al. "Zadan kai: Kodomo o meguru bunka shi." *Nihon no bigaku: Tokushū kodomo* 34 (2002): 1–36.

Ichimura Takao. "Sengoku ki jōkaku to yakuwari o megutte." In *Sōten Nihon no rekishi* 4 *chūsei hen,* pp. 282–300. Shinjinbutsu ōrai sha, 1991.

Ihara Kesao. "Chūsei no jōkaku to minshū seikatsu." *Gekkan bunka zai* 301 (October 1988): 34–45.

———. "Yamashiro to yama koya no kaikyūteki seikaku." *Nagano* 110 (April 1983): 14–20.

Iikura Harutake. "Kinai zaichi ryōshu no ichi kōsatsu." *Shoryō bu kiyō* 15 (October 1963): 16–39.

Iinuma Kenji. "Chūsei ie kenkyū zenshin no tame no shiron." *Minshū shi kenkyū* 23 (November 1982): 27–50; 24 (May 1983): 1–22.

————. "Chūsei zenki no josei no shōgai." In *Nihon josei seikatsu shi 2 chūsei,* pp. 31–74. Tokyo daigaku shuppan kai, 1990.

————. "Josei mei kara mita chūsei no josei no shakaiteki ichi." *Rekishi hyōron* 443 (March 1987): 44–62.

————. "Nihon chūsei no kafuchō sei ni tsuite." *Hikaku kazoku shi kenkyū* 2 (1987): 27–33.

Ikeda Yoshiharu. "Hanzei ka no shomin seikatsu." *Shirin* 42 (June 1959): 86–112.

Ikegami Yūko. "Sengoku jidai no Musashino ni okeru kaihatsu." In *Kaihatsu to chiiki minshū,* pp. 115–133. Yūzan kaku, 1991.

————. "Tenma yaku to shinjuku." *Sengoku shi kenkyū* 8 (August 1984): 1–11.

Imai Rintarō. "Chūsei ni okeru kaikon." *Shakai keizai shigaku* 8 (December 1938): 47–71.

Imatani Akira. "Waga kuni chūsei shiyō yōsui mizukuruma no fukugen." *Kokuritsu rekishi minzoku hakubutsukan kenkyū hōkoku* 4 (March 1984): 17–56.

Inaba Tsuguharu. "Chūkinsei ikōki no sonraku fueede to heiwa." *Funsō to soshō no bunka shi,* pp. 101–134. Aoki shoten, 2000.

————. "Chūsei shakai ni okeru shūshu to futan." *Rekishigaku kenkyū* 742 (October 2000): 46–55.

————. "Sengoku jidai no murauke sei to mura." *Rekishigaku kenkyū* 680 (January 1996): 1–20.

Inoue Hiroshi. "Jōō ninen Iwami no kuni sōden sū chūmon no kisoteki kentō." *San'in shidan* 18 (June 1981): 1–38.

Inoue Toshio. *Ikkō ikki no kenkyū.* Yoshikawa kōbunkan, 1968.

Inoue Yoshinobu. "*Taihei ki* to ryōshu sō." *Shirin* 40 (January 1957): 1–20.

Irumada Nobuo. *Hyakusei mōshijō to kishōmon no sekai.* Tokyo daigaku shuppan kai, 1986.

————. "Kōden to ryōshu sei." *Rekishi* 38 (March 1969): 1–23.

Ishige Tadashi. "*Azuma kagami* no seiji shisō." *Kikan Nihon shisō shi* 58 (2001): 18–32.

Ishii Ryōsuke. "Chūsei jinshin hōsei zakkō." *Hōgaku kyōkai zasshi* 65 (August 1938): 98–124; 65 (September 1938): 55–75; 65 (October 1938): 109–128.

————. "Chūsei no 'karita rōzeki.'" *Sōka hōgaku* 18 (August 1988): 3–14.

Ishii Shirō. "Kassen to tsuibu." *Kokka gakkai zasshi* 91 (August 1978): 1–27; 91 (December 1978): 1–41.

————. *Nihon jin no kokka seikatsu.* Tokyo daigaku shuppan kai, 1986.

Ishii Susumu. "Bunken kara saguru jinkō." In *Yomigaeru chūsei 3 Bushi no miyako Kamakura,* pp. 59–61. Heibonsha, 1989.

————, ed. *Chūsei no mura.* Tokyo daigaku shuppan kai, 1995.

————. "Chūsei shakai ron." In *Iwanami kōza Nihon rekishi 8 chūsei 1,* pp. 315–367. Iwanami shoten, 1976.

————. "Chūsei yōgyō no shosō." In *Kōza Nihon gijutsu no shakai shi 4 Yōgyō,* pp. 119–152. Nihon hyōron sha, 1984.

———. "Mokkan kara mita chūsei toshi 'Kusado Sengen.'" *Kokushi gaku* 130 (November 1986): 1–29.

———. *Nihon chūsei kokka shi no kenkyū.* Iwanami shoten, 1970.

———. *Nihon no chūsei* 1 *chūsei no katachi.* Chūō kōron shinsha, 2002.

———. *Nihon no rekishi* 12 *chūsei bushidan.* Shōgakkan, 1974.

———. *Nihon no rekishi* 7 *Kamakura bakufu.* Chūō kōron sha, 1965.

Ishimoda Sho. "Kamakura bakufu ikkoku jitō shiki no seiritsu." In *Chūsei no hō to kokka.* Edited by Ishimoda and Satō Shin'ichi, pp. 1–134. Tokyo daigaku shuppan kai, 1960.

Ishio Kazuhito. "Chūsei teichi shūraku no keisei to tenkai." *Hisutoria* 138 (March 1993): 73–93.

Isogai Fujio. "Aki no kuni zaichō kanjin Tadokoro shi ni tsuite no oboegaki." In Tsuda, *Kinsei kokka no seiritsu katei,* pp. 50–84.

———. "Bun'ei gannen tamugi kazei kinshi rei no haikei." *Tokyo gakugei daigaku fuzoku kōtōgakkō kenkyū kiyō* 31 (March 1994): 107–125.

———. "Chūsei hyakusei no saimu tenraku o meguru zaichi chitsujo." In *Kinsei kokka to Meiji ishin.* Edited by Tsuda Hideo, pp. 379–428. Sansei do, 1989.

———. *Chūsei no nōgyō to kikō.* Yoshikawa kōbunkan, 2002.

———. "Ge'nin no kazoku to josei." In Minegishi, *Chūsei o kangaeru,* pp. 111–151.

———. "Hyakusei mibun no tokushitsu to dorei e no tenraku o megutte." *Rekishigaku kenkyū: Minzoku to kokka* 450 (November 1977): 66–76, 93–96.

———. "Jūsan-yon seiki Kii no kuni Kinokawa engan chiiki no tamugi shiryō ni tsuite." *Tokyo gakugei daigaku fuzoku kōtōgakkō kenkyū kiyō* 23 (January 1986): 1–18; 24 (February 1987): 7–20.

———. "Kamakura makki nanboku chō ki suiden nimōsaku tenkai jōkyō ka no nōgyō seisanryoku ni tsuite." *Tokyo gakugei daigaku fuzoku kōtōgakkō kenkyū kiyō* 28 (March 1988): 129–153.

———. "Kangi no kikin to Jōei shikimoku no seiritsu." *Rekishi to chiri* 276 (September 1978): 1–25.

———. "Kangi no kikin to kōbu no jinshin baibai seisaku." *Tokyo gakugei daigaku fuzoku kōtōgakkō kenkyū kiyō* 17 (February 1980): 13–27; 18 (February 1981): 9–25; 19 (February 1982): 7–22.

———. "Kodai chūsei ni okeru zakkoku no kyūhōteki sakutsuke ni tsuite." *Tokyo gakugei daigaku fuzoku kōtōgakkō kenkyū kiyō* 26 (March 1989): 107–130.

———. "Nihon chūsei dorei hō no kisoteki kōsatsu." *Rekishigaku kenkyū* 424 (September 1975): 30–47.

———. "Nihon chūsei shakai to dorei sei." *Rekishigaku kenkyū* 664 (October 1994): 20–36, 84–87, 133.

———. "Nihon chūsei shi kenkyū to kikō hendō ron." *Nihonshi kenkyū* 388 (December 1994): 25–48.

Isogai Masayoshi. *Takeda Shingen.* Shin jinbutsu ōrai sha, 1970.

Itō Masatoshi. *Chūsei kōki no sonraku.* Yoshikawa kōbunkan, 1991.

Itō Teiji. *Chūsei jūkyo shi.* Tokyo daigaku shuppan kai, 1958.

———. "Chūsei nōson no sumai." In *Shūkan Asahi hyakka Nihon no rekishi* 2 *chūsei* 1–2 *Chūsei no mura o aruku,* pp. 66–67. Asahi shinbun sha, 1986.

Itō Toshikazu. "Heian Kamakura jidai no yamahata (yakibata) ni kansuru rekishi chirigakuteki kenkyū." *Nihon joshi daigaku bungaku bu kiyō* 45 (1995): 79–96.

———. "Kodai chūsei no 'nohata' ni kansuru rekishi chirigakuteki kenkyū." *Nihon joshi daigaku bungaku kenkyū ka* 1 (1994): 1–21.

Itō Toshio. In *Mono to ningen no bunka shi* 68-I *Kinu.* Hōsei daigaku shuppan kyoku, 1992.

Itoga Shigeo. "Hitachi no kuni tabumi no shiryōteki seikaku." *Ibaraki kenshi kenkyū* 53 (December 1984): 17–33.

Iwamoto Shōji. "Kusado Sengen no hakkutsu seika kara." In *Chūsei toshi kenkyū* 3 *Tsu tomari yado,* pp. 38–55. Shinjinbutsu ōrai sha, 1996.

Iwamoto Yoshiaki. "Ijū to kaihatsu no rekishi." In *Nihon minzoku bunka taikei* 6 *Hyōhaku to teichaku.* Edited by Amino Yoshihiko et al., pp. 359–462. Shōgakkan, 1984.

Iwasaki Takeo. "Gojō tenjin kō." *Shiron: Chū kinsei bungaku* 4 (November 1985): 110–131.

Iyanaga Teizo. *Nihon kodai shakai keizai shi kenkyū.* Iwanami shoten, 1980.

Jannetta, Ann. *Epidemics and Mortality in Early Modern Japan.* Princeton, NJ: Princeton University Press, 1987.

———. "Famine Mortality in Nineteenth-Century Japan: The Evidence from a Temple Death Register." *Population Studies* 46 (1992): 427–443.

Jansen, Marius. "Tosa in the Sixteenth Century: The 100 Article Code of Chōsokabe Motochika." In *Studies in the Institutional History of Early Modern Japan.* Edited by Marius Jansen and John Hall, pp. 89–115. Princeton, NJ: Princeton University Press, 1968.

Johnston, William. *The Modern Epidemic.* Cambridge, MA: Harvard University Press, 1995.

Kagose Yoshiaki. *Tei shitchi.* Kokin shoin, 1972.

Kagoya Tomoko. "Ransei no kodomo no hibi." In Yūki, *Nihon kodomo no rekishi* 2 *Ransei no kodomo,* pp. 219–279.

Kaizu Ichirō. *Chūsei no henkaku to tokusei.* Yoshikawa kōbunkan, 1994.

Kamata Motokazu. "Nihon kodai no jinkō ni tsuite." *Mokkan kenkyū* 6 (1984): 131–151.

Kamiki Tetsuo. *Nihon chūsei shōhin ryūtsū shi ron.* Yuhikaku, 1980.

Kamoshida Masao. "Hitachi no kuni Kōan ninen 'sakuden sō kanmon' no ichi kōsatsu." *Ibaraki kenshi kenkyū* 19 (March 1971): 10–25.

Kanda Chisato. "Do ikki no saikentō." *Shigaku zasshi* 110 (March 2001): 62–87.

———. *Nihon no chūsei* 11 *Sengoku ransei o ikiru chikara.* Chūō kōron shinsha, 2002.

Kaneko Tetsushi. "Mura no tanjō to zaichi kantō." In *Chūsei jin to seikatsu se-kai.* Edited by Katsumata Shizuo, pp. 324–351. Yamakawa shuppan, 1996.

Kanō Hisashi and Kinoshita Masashi. "Shio tetsu no seisan to kōnō." In *Kodai no chihō shi 2 San'in san'yō nankai hen.* Edited by Yagi Atsuru, pp. 172–206. Asakura shoten, 1977.

Katō Emiko. "Chūsei no josei to shinkō." In *Nihon josei seikatsu shi 2 chūsei,* pp. 259–287. Tokyo daigaku shuppan kai, 1990.

Katō Michiko. "*Azuma kagami* ni okeru 'dōri' o megutte." *Kikan Nihon shisō shi* 58 (2001): 87–104.

Katsuda Itaru. "Sonraku no bosei to kazoku." In Minegishi, *Chūsei o kangaeru,* pp. 180–209.

Katsumata Shizuo. *Ikki.* Iwanami shinsho, 1982.

———. "Sengoku jidai no sonraku." *Shakai bunka shi kenkyū* 6 (August 1985): 1–36.

Katsuura Noriko. "Josei no hosshin shukke to kazoku." In Minegishi, *Chūsei o kangaeru,* pp. 241–271.

Kawahara Sumiyuki. "Ichijōdani iseki." *Nihon no bijutsu* 214 (March 1984).

Kawai Yasushi. *Genpei kassen kyozō o hagu.* Kōdansha, 1996.

———. "Jishō Juei no nairan to chiiki shakai." *Rekishigaku kenkyū* 730 (November 1999): 2–13.

———. "Jishō Juei no sensō to Kamakura bakufu." *Nihonshi kenkyū* 344 (March 1991): 60–94.

———. "Kamakura shoki no sensō to zaichi shakai." *Chūsei nairan shi kenkyū* 12 (1992): 2–15.

———. "Tsuwamono no michi to hyakusei no narai." *Asahi hyakka Nihon no rekishi bessatsu Rekishi o yominaosu 15 Shiro to kassen,* pp. 34–43. Asahi shinbun sha, 1993.

Kawane Yoshihira. *Chūsei hōken sei seiritsu shi ron.* Tokyo daigaku shuppan kai, 1971.

Keene, Donald, ed. *Anthology of Japanese Literature from the Earliest Era to the Mid-nineteenth Century.* New York: Grove Press, 1955.

Keirstead, Thomas. *The Geography of Power in Medieval Japan.* Princeton, NJ: Princeton University Press, 1992.

Kelly, William. *Water Control in Tokugawa Japan: Irrigation Organization in a Japanese River Basin, 1600–1870.* Ithaca, NY: Cornell University Press, 1982. East Asia Papers 31.

Kikuchi Akiyoshi. "Sengoku daimyō Mōri shi to hyōrō." *Hitotsubashi ronsō* 123 (June 2000): 96–113.

Kikuchi Yōko. "Ekibyō okuri minka ryōhō nenchū gyōji shiryō." In *Tōhoku minzoku shiryō shū.* Edited by Iwasaki Toshio, pp. 127–160. Man'yō dō shoten, 1976.

Kimura Motoi, ed. *Tokyo teichi no chūsei o kangaeru.* Meicho shuppan, 1995.

Kimura Osamu. "Izumi no kuni Hineno no shō ni okeru kaihatsu to shokaisō no dōkō." *Nihon rekishi* 412 (September 1982): 31–47.

Kimura Shigemitsu. "Chūsei zenki no nōgyō seisanryoku to hatasaku." *Nihon-shi kenkyū* 280 (June 1991): 1–40.

———. *Hatake to Nihonjin.* Chūō kōron sha, 1996.

———. *Nihon kodai chūsei hatasaku shi no kenkyū.* Azekura shobō, 1992.

Kimura Shigemitsu and Sonobe Toyomoto. "Chūsei no shodankai shomibun no tōsō." In *Ikki 3 Ikki no kōzō,* pp. 235–286. Tokyo daigaku shuppan kai, 1981.

Kinda Akihiro. *Bichikei to chūsei sonraku.* Yoshikawa kōbunkan, 1993.

———. *Jōri to sonraku no rekishi chirigaku kenkyū.* Daimei dō, 1985.

———. "Shōen sonraku no keikan." In *Nihon shi 2 Chūsei.* Edited by Toda Yoshimi, pp. 127–158. Yuhikaku, 1978.

Kishida Hiroyuki. "Chūsei kōki no chihō keizai to toshi." In *Kōza Nihon reki-shi* 4 *chūsei* 2, pp. 83–123. Tokyo daigaku shuppan kai, 1985.

Kitagawa Hitoshi and Matsumoto Eiji. "Climatic Implications of Delta 13C Variations in a Japanese Cedar (Cryptomeria japonica) during the Last Two Millennia." *Geophysical Research Letters* 22 (August 15, 1995): 2155–2158.

Kitō Hiroshi. *Edo jidai no jinkō to shakai.* Jōchi daigaku, 1990.

———. *Jinkō kara yomu Nihon no rekishi.* Kōdan sha, 2000.

———. *Nihon nisen nen no jinkō shi.* PHP Paperbacks, 1983.

Koana Yoshimi. "Sengoku jidai no yama no koya kō." *Shinano* 42 (March 1985): 47–53.

———. "Yama no koya wa tobi ya ka." *Shinano* 36 (October 1984): 41–48.

Kobayashi Keiichirō. "Gun'yaku to hyōrō." *Nihon rekishi* 221 (October 1966): 25–36.

Kobayashi Kiyoharu. "Sengoku sōran no tenkai." In *Iwanami kōza Nihon reki-shi* 8 *chūsei* 4, pp. 1–44. Iwanami shoten, 1976.

Kobayashi Motonobu. "Muromachi ki ni okeru Nishidai no saikaihatsu to keiei." In *Chūsei shōen no sekai: Tōji-ryō Tanba no kuni Ōyama no shō.* Edited by Ōyama Kyōhei, pp. 225–244. Shibunkaku shuppan, 1995.

———. "Suiri to shōen." In *Egakareta shōen no sekai,* pp. 80–99. Shin jinbutsu ōrai sha, 1995.

Kodomo no shakai shi kodomo no kokka shi. Shinhyōron, 1984.

Koide Hiroshi. *Tonegawa to Yodogawa.* Chūkō shinkō, 1975.

Koizumi Yoshihiro. "*Rakuchū rakugai byōbu* no nōsakugyō fukei." *Nihonshi kenkyū* 337 (September 1990): 80–91.

Kojima Akira. "Ashigaru to Ōnin Bunmei no ran." In *Sōkoku no chūsei,* pp. 191–216. Tokyo dō, 2000.

Kondō Yoshikazu. "Bugu no chūsei ka to bushi no seiritsu." In *Insei no tenkai to nairan.* Edited by Motoki Yasuo. Yoshikawa kōbunkan, 2002.

———. "Buki kara mita chūsei bushi ron." *Nihonshi kenkyū* 416 (April 1997): 26–47.

———. "Buki kara mita nairan ki no sentō." *Nihonshi kenkyū* 373 (September 1993): 60–74.

————. *Chūseiteki bugu no seiritsu to bushi.* Yoshikawa kōbunkan, 2000.

————. *Yumiya to tōken.* Yoshikawa kōbunkan, 1997.

Kōno Shinjirō. *Chūsei toshi Kamakura.* Kōdan sha, 1995.

————. "Hakkutsu kara shisen shita jinkō." In *Yomigaeru chūsei 3 Bushi no miyako Kamakura,* pp. 61–63. Heibon sha, 1989.

Kubo Ken'ichirō. "Sengoku shakai no keizai to shūshu." *Rekishigaku kenkyū* 754 (October 2001): 58–69.

Kume Kunitaka. "*Taihei ki* wa shigaku ni eki nashi." *Shigaku zasshi* 17 (April 1891): 28–38; 18 (May 1891): 7–20; 20 (July 1891): 21–25; 21 (August 1891): 7–21; and 22 (September 1891): 6–22.

Kume Yoshio. "Hiden'in no enkaku to shūen." *Nihon ishigaku zasshi* 25 (January 1979): 32–52.

Kuramochi Shigehiro. "Karita rōzeki no hongen." In *Chūsei no hakken.* Edited by Nagahara Keiji, pp. 132–150. Yoshikawa kōbunkan, 1993.

————. *Nihon chūsei sonraku shakai shi no kenkyū.* Azekura shobō, 1996.

Kuroda Hideo. *"Emaki" kodomo no tōjō.* Kawade shobō, 1989.

————. "Jūroku seiki no tenkan ni tsuite." Paper presented at the Historiographical Institute of Tokyo University, July 6, 2001.

————. *Nihon chūsei kaihatsu shi no kenkyū.* Azekura shobō, 1984.

————. "Sengoku Shokuhōki no gijutsu to keizai hatten." In *Kōza Nihon rekishi* 4 *chūsei* 2, pp. 275–316. Tokyo daigaku shuppan kai, 1985.

————. *Sugata to shigusa no chūsei shi.* Heibon sha, 1986.

Kuroda Hiroko. "Chōsan tōbō soshite kyoryū no jiyū." *Minshū shi kenkyū* 33 (May 1987): 11–40.

————. "Chūsei kōki no mura no onnatachi." In *Nihon josei seikatsu shi* 2 *chūsei,* pp. 187–222. Tokyo daigaku shuppan kai, 1990.

————. "Chūsei no chōsan to josei." *Rekishi hyōron* 467 (March 1989): 15–30.

————. *Chūsei sōson shi no kōzō.* Yoshikawa kōbunkan, 1985.

————. *Josei kara mita Nihon chūsei shakai to hō.* Azekura shobō, 2002.

————. "Kamakura kōki ni okeru ike chikuzō to sōson no seiritsu." In Tsuda, *Kinsei kokka no seiritsu katei,* pp. 85–123.

————. *Mimi o kiri hana o sogi.* Yoshikawa kōbunkan, 1995.

————. "Minshū josei no hataraki kurashi." In *Nihon josei no rekishi: Onna no hataraki,* pp. 81–92. Kadokawa sensho, 1993.

Kuroda Motoki. "Daimyō hikan dogōsō no rekishiteki seikaku." *Sengoku shi kenkyū: Bessatsu* (2001): 18–29.

Kuroda Satoshi. "'Akimugi' to wa nani ka." *Minshū shi kenkyū* 54 (November 1997): 67–80.

Kuroda Toshio. *Chūsei kyōdōtai ron mibun sei ron.* In *Kuroda Toshio chosaku shū,* vol. 6, pp. 297–318. Hōzō kan, 1995.

————. "Kamakura jidai no shōen no kannō to minshū sō no kōsei." *Rekishigaku kenkyū* 261 (January 1962): 1–19; 262 (February 1962): 29–38.

————. *Nihon chūsei hōken sei ron.* Tokyo daigaku shuppan kai, 1974.

Kurushima Noriko. "Tōji-ryō Yamashiro no kuni Kuze no shō no myōshu shiki ni tsuite." *Shigaku zasshi* 93 (August 1984): 1–46.

Kusakawa Takashi. "Hōsō no kami okuri." *Nihon minzokugaku* 5 (1957): 1–8.

Kuwahara Kiminori. "'Ōtabumi' denseki no rekishi chiri gakuteki kenkyū." *Hanazono daigaku kenkyū kiyō* 12 (1981): 139–170.

Lambert, Craig. "The Deadliest War." *Harvard Magazine* 102 (May–June 2001): 15–19.

Landes, David. *The Wealth and Poverty of Nations.* New York: W.W. Norton, 1998.

The Laws of the Muromachi Bakufu. Translated by Kenneth Grossberg. Sophia University Press, 1981.

Leyden, R.W. "Civil War Slaughter." *Harvard Magazine* 103 (July–August 2001): 4.

Maki Hidemasa. *Nihon hōshi ni okeru jinshin baibai no kenkyū.* Yuhikaku, 1961.

Makihara Shigeyuki. "Sengoku Shokuhōki no tochi seido to 'shoryōshu.' " *Nihonshi kenkyū* 472 (December 2002): 1–25.

Makino Shinnosuke. *Buke jidai shakai no kenkyū.* Toe shoin, 1928.

Maruyama Yoshihiko. "Ōmi no kuni Tokuchin ho nōkata shogō ni okeru nōgyō seisan no arikata." In *Kokushi ronshū.* Akamatsu Toshihide kyōju taikan kinen jigyō kai, 1972.

Masaki Kisaburō. "Niimi no shō ni okeru shinden to nōmin." *Kyushu shigaku* 9 (July 1958): 21–33.

Mass, Jeffrey. *The Development of Kamakura Rule, 1180-1250.* Stanford, CA: Stanford University Press, 1979.

———. *The Kamakura Bakufu: A Study in Documents.* Stanford, CA: Stanford University Press, 1976.

———, ed. *The Origins of Japan's Medieval World.* Stanford, CA: Stanford University Press, 1997.

———. *Warrior Government in Early Medieval Japan.* New Haven, CT: Yale University Press, 1974.

———. *Yoritomo and the Founding of the Kamakura Bakufu.* Stanford, CA: Stanford University Press, 1999.

Matsushita Masashi. *Nihon no bijutsu: Kusado Sengen machi iseki* 215 (April 1984).

Maun, Michael, et al. "Global-Scale Temperature Patterns and Climate Forming over the Past Six Centuries." *Nature* 392 (April 23, 1998): 779–787.

McClain, James. *Japan: A Modern History.* New York: W.W. Norton, 2002.

McNeill, William. *A History of the Human Community,* 2nd ed. 2 vols. Englewood Cliffs, NJ: Prentice-Hall, 1987.

———. *Plagues and Peoples.* New York: Doubleday, 1976.

Meiji zen Nihon sangyō gijutsu shi. Nihon gakujutsu shinkōkai, 1960.

Minegishi Sumio. "Chūsei mibun sei kenkyū to ge'nin mibun tokushitsu." *Chūsei shi kōza* 4 *Chūsei no hō to kenryoku,* pp. 238–253. Gakusei sha, 1985.

———. "Chūsei no kazoku to kyōdōtai." In *Rekishi ni okeru kazoku to kyōdōtai*. Edited by Hara Hidesaburō and Sasaki Junnosuke, pp. 455–463. Aoki shoten, 1992.

———. "Chūsei no kazoku to kyōdōtai." *Rekishi hyōron* 441 (January 1987): 43–49.

———, ed. *Chūsei o kangaeru: Kazoku to josei.* Yoshikawa kōbunkan, 1992.

———. *Chūsei saigai senran no shakai shi.* Yoshikawa kōbunkan, 2001.

———. "Chūsei shakai no kaikyū kōsei." *Rekishigaku kenkyū* 312 (May 1966): 36–49.

———. "Jūgo seiki kōhan no tochi seido." In Takeuchi, *Taikei Nihon shi sōsho 6 Tochi seido* 1, pp. 395–446.

———. "Nengu, kuji, to utokusen." In *Nihon no shakai shi 4 Futan to sōyo*, pp. 55–92. Iwanami shoten, 1986.

———. "Rennyo no jidai." *Kōza Rennyo*, vol. 1, pp. 67–93. Heibon sha, 1996.

Mino Akizumi. "Noto no kuni densū mokuroku ni tsuite." *Chihō shi kenkyū* 32 (April 1958): 22–33.

Misaki Kazuo. "Shōgatsu gyōji ni okeru ekishin chinsō ni tsuite." *Tōhoku minzoku* 5 (May 1970): 39–44.

Miskimin, Harry. *The Economy of Early Renaissance Europe, 1300–1460.* Cambridge: Cambridge University Press, 1975.

Miura Hiroyuki. *Zoku hōsei shi kenkyū.* Iwanami shoten, 1926.

Miura Keiichi. *Chūsei minshū seikatsu shi kenkyū.* Shibunkaku shuppan, 1984.

———. "Jūyon go seiki ni okeru nimōsaku hatten no mondai ten." In *Kokushi ronshū*, pp. 670–681. Akamatsu Toshihide kyōju taikan kinen jigyō kai, 1972.

———. "Kamakura jidai ni okeru kaihatsu to kanjin." *Nihonshi kenkyū* 195 (November 1978): 1–30.

———. *Nihon chūsei no chiiki to shakai.* Shibunkaku shuppan, 1993.

Mizukami Kazuhisa. *Chūsei no shōen to shakai.* Yoshikawa kōbunkan, 1969.

Mizuno Shōji. "Hito to shizen no kankei shi sobyō—chūsei kōki no kan Biwako chiiki o chūshin ni." *Minshū shi kenkyū* 61 (May 2001): 33–60.

———. "Nihon chūsei sonraku ni kansuru ni san no mondai." *Atarashii rekishigaku no tame ni* 166 (March 1982): 17–26.

Morimoto Masanori. "Hizen no kuni Saga goryō to betsumyō." *Shien* 110 (December 1972): 111–136.

Morita Kyōji. *Ashikaga Yoshimasa.* Izumi shoin, 1993.

Moriyama Shigeki and Nakae Kazue. *Nihon kodomo shi.* Heibon sha, 2002.

Morris, V. Dixon. "The City of Sakai and Urban Autonomy." In *Warlords, Artists, and Commoners.* Edited by George Elison and Bardwell Smith, pp. 23–54. Honolulu: University of Hawai'i Press, 1981.

———. "Sakai: From Shoen to Port City." In J. W. Hall and Toyoda, *Japan in the Muromachi Age*, pp. 145–158.

———. "Sakai: The History of a City in Medieval Japan." Ph.D. dissertation, University of Washington, 1970.

Murai Shōsuke. *Nihon no chūsei* 10 *Bunretsu suru ōken to shakai.* Chūō kōron shinsha, 2003.

Murakami Masana. *Maboroshi no chūsei shūraku Kusado Sengen chō.* Kokusho kankō kai, 1980.

Murakami Yasusuke. "*Ie* Society as a Pattern of Civilization." *Journal of Japanese Studies* 10 (Summer 1984): 279–364.

Murata Shūzō. "Yōsui shihai to sho ryōshu rengō." *Nara joshi daigaku bungaku bu kenkyū nenpō* 16 (1972): 27–48.

Murayama Shūichi. "Katsuragawa myōōin to sono jūmin no rekishi." *Shisō* 16 (January 1960): 22–41.

Nagahara Keiji. "Chūsei kinsei ikōki no gijutsu seisanryoku no hatten." In *Kokushi gaku ronshū.* Imai Rintarō sensei kijū kinen ronbun shū kankō kai, 1988.

———, ed. *Iwanami Nihon shi jiten.* Iwanami shoten, 1999.

———. "Josei shi ni okeru nanboku chō Muromachi ki." In *Nihon josei shi* 2 *chūsei,* pp. 137–171. Tokyo daigaku shuppan kai, 1982.

———. "Mensaku no tenkai." In *Kōza Nihon gijutsu no shakai shi* 3 *bōseki,* pp. 69–102. Nihon hyōron sha, 1983.

———. *Nihon chūsei shakai kōzō no kenkyū.* Iwanami shoten, 1973.

———, ed. *Nihon keizai shi kenkyū* 2 *chūsei.* Tokyo daigaku shuppan kai, 1965.

———. *Nihon no rekishi* 14 *Sengoku no dōran.* Shōgakkan, 1975.

———. *Sengoku ki no seiji keizai kōzō.* Iwanami shoten, 1997.

———. "Shōen ryōshu keizai no kōzō." In Nagahara, *Nihon keizai shi taikei* 2 *Chūsei,* pp. 57–102.

———. "Shōen sei shihai to chūsei sonraku." *Hitotsubashi ronsō* 48 (March 1962): 51–72.

———. *Taikei Nihon no rekishi* 6 *Nairan to minshū no seiki.* Shōgakkan, 1996.

Nagahara Keiji with Kozo Yamamura. "The Sengoku Daimyo and the Kandaka System." In J.W. Hall, Nagahara, and Yamamura, *Japan before Tokugawa,* pp. 27–63.

Nagai Yoshiaki. "*Seiryō ki* kan shichi no kisoteki kenkyū." *Nōson kenkyū* 57 (September 1983): 76–88; 58 (March 1984): 89–98; 59 (September 1984): 39–52; 60 (March 1985): 72–84.

Nagamura Makoto. *Chūsei Tōdaiji no soshiki to keiei.* Hanawa shobō, 1989.

Nagaoka Hiroo. "Minka iryō." *Nihon minzokugaku taikei: seikatsu to minshū,* vol. 2, pp. 311–326. Heibon sha, 1959.

Naitō Konan. *Naitō Konan zenshū,* vol. 9. Chikuma shobō, 1969.

Nakabe Yoshiko. *Chūsei toshi no shakai to keizai.* Nihon hyōron sha, 1992.

Nakai Hitoshi. "'Minshū' to 'jōkaku' kenkyū shiron." *Teikoku daigaku Yamanashi bunka zai kenkyū jo kenkyū hōkoku* 5 (1994): 1–38.

Nakajima Keiichi. "Chihō kara mita dosō." *Mita chūsei shi kenkyū* 7 (October 2000): 94–110.

Nakakiri Kakutarō. *Furo.* Yūzan kaku, 1927.

Nakamura, James I. *Agricultural Production and the Economic Development of Japan, 1873-1922.* Princeton, NJ: Princeton University Press, 1966.

Nakamura Ken. "Jūtaku hakyaku ni tsuite." *Dōshisha daigaku jinbun kagaku kenkyū jo kiyō* 8 (June 1964): 59-82.

Nakamura Kichiji. *Chūsei shakai no kenkyū.* Kawade shobō, 1939.

————. *Kinsei shoki nōsei shi kenkyū.* Iwanami shoten, 1938.

Nakane Chie. *Japanese Society.* London: Weidenfeld and Nicolson, 1970.

————. *Kazoku no kōzō.* Tokyo daigaku tōyō bunka kenkyū jo, 1970.

Nakano Hatayoshi. "Kenkyū no Buzen Bungo zuden chō." *Nihon rekishi* 118 (April 1959): 38-42.

Nakano Hideo. "Awaji no kuni ōtabumi o megutte." *Hōsei daigaku bungaku bu kiyō* 32 (1986): 45-82.

————. "Chūsei hyakusei to jitō shihai." *Nihon rekishi* 434 (July 1984): 38-54.

————. "Kagen yo'nen Hitachi no kuni tabumi no tekisuto ni tsuite." *Okayama daigaku kyōiku gakubu kenkyū shūroku* 52 (October 1979): 49-55.

————. "Ōtabumi kenkyū no genjō to kadai." *Shinano* 33 (July 1981): 52-83.

Nakayama Fumihito. "Chūsei no kakochō ni tsuite." *Matsudo shiritsu hakubutsukan kiyō* 3 (March 1996): 3-36.

Narahara Junko. "Chūsei no 'yūjo.'" In *Nihon josei no rekishi: Sei ai kazoku,* pp. 78-85. Kadokawa sensho, 1992.

Nihon bungaku: Tokushū: Chūsei ni okeru kodomo 51 (July 2002): 1-59.

Niki Hiroshi, ed. *Mono kara miru Nihon shi: Toshi.* Aoki shoten, 2002.

Nishikōri Tsutomu. "Betsumyō sei ni kansuru ichi kōsatsu." *Shigaku kenkyū* 142 (October 1978): 1-28.

————. "Ōtabumi no chōsō gata kisai to heiretsu gata kisai ni tsuite." *Hiroshima daigaku bungaku bu kiyō* 38 (December 1978): 24-51.

Nishimura Hiroko. *Kodai chūsei no kazoku to josei.* Yoshikawa kōbunkan, 2002.

————. "Yometori kon e no ugoki to fūfu no jōai." In *Nihon josei no rekishi: Sei, ai, kazoku,* pp. 87-95. Kadokawa sensho, 1992.

Nishimura Makoto and Yoshikawa Ichirō, eds. *Nihon kyokō shi kō.* Maruzen, 1936.

Nishio Kazumi. "Chūsei kazoku to kojin." *Rekishi hyōron* 503 (March 1992): 2-14.

————. "Josei shi to iu shiza." *Rekishi hyōron* 479 (March 1990): 16-39.

————. "Kanshō ninen no kikin ni tsuite." *Rekishi to chiri* 373 (September 1986): 1-14.

————. "Kieki no shisha o kazoeru to iu koto." *Nihonshi kenkyū* 387 (December 1994): 98-106.

————. "Muromachi chūki Kyoto ni okeru kikin to minshū." *Nihonshi kenkyū* 275 (July 1985): 52-80.

————. "Nihon chūsei ni okeru kazoku to kazoku ideorogii." *Hisutoria* 133 (December 1991): 20-38.

Nishitani Masahiro. "Chūsei kōki ni okeru Kyōkō shōen no shūshu to zaichi dōkō." *Fukuoka daigaku jinbun ronsō* 32 (December 2000): 1-52.

————. "Chūsei Nihon no tochi baibai to tochi shoyū." *Shigaku zasshi* 109 (October 2000): 35–64.

Nishiyachi Seibi. "Chūsei zenki no ondanka to manseiteki nōgyō kiki." *Minshū shi kenkyū* 55 (May 1998): 5–22.

Noritake Yūichi. "Sengoku ki ni okeru 'kaihatsu' ni tsuite." *Shikai* 37 (1990): 17–29.

————. "Sengoku ki no ryōkoku kan tsūkō to daimyō kenryoku." In *Sōkoku no chūsei*, pp. 246–269. Daimei dō, 2000.

North, Douglass, and Robert Thomas. *The Rise of the Western World: A New Economic History*. Cambridge: Cambridge University Press, 1973.

Ōba Yasutoki. "Tairiku ni hirakareta toshi Hakata." In *Chūsei fūkei o yomu 7 Higashi Shina kai o kakomu chūsei sekai*. Edited by Ishii Susumu and Amino Yoshihiko, pp. 20–53. Shinjinbutsu ōrai sha, 1995.

Oda Yūzō. "Roji rōzeki ni tsuite." *Nenpō chūsei shi kenkyū* 6 (1981): 1–37.

Ogashima Minoru, ed. *Nihon saii shi*. Nihon kōgyō kai, 1894.

Ogawa Makoto. *Chūsei toshi "fuchū" no tenkai*. Kyoto: Shibunkaku dō, 2001.

Ogawa Naoyuki. "Kantō chihō ni okeru tsumida no denshō." *Shizen to bunka* 3 (1980): 93–134; 4 (1981): 45–126.

Oka Yōichirō. "Toshi no nioi hama no nioi." In Gomi Fumihiko and Saiki, *Chūsei toshi Kamakura to shi no sekai*, pp. 237–245. Takashi shoin, 2002.

Okuno Takahiro. *Takeda Shingen*. Yoshikawa kōbunkan, 1959.

Ōmura Takuo. "Chūsei zenki no Toba to Yodo." *Nihonshi kenkyū* 459 (November 2000): 1–29.

Ono Kōji. *Nihon chūsei shōgyō shi no kenkyū*. Hōsei daigaku shuppan kyoku, 1989.

Ono Masatoshi, ed. *Zukai Nihon no chūsei iseki*. Tokyo daigaku shuppan kai, 2001.

Ōno Susumu. *Nihongo no nenrin*. Shinchō sha, 1966.

Orio Manabu. "Chūsei no Hakata." *Nihon rekishi* 434 (July 1984): 83–89.

Ōshima Takehiko. *Ekishin to sono shūhen*. Iwasaki bijutsu sha, 1985.

Ōsumi Kazuo. *Nihon no chūsei 2 Shinjin no sekai tonseisha no kokoro*. Chūō kōron shinsha, 2002.

Ōsumi Kazuo and Nishiguchi Junko, eds. *Shiirizu josei to bukkyō 1 Ama to amadera*. Heibon sha, 1989.

Ōta Junzō. "Kamakura ki no shōen to kannō." *Rekishigaku kenkyū* 9 (September 1971): 23–33; 10 (October 1971): 20–29.

Ōwada Tetsuo. "Sengoku daimyō Asai shi no kangai shihai." In *Seisan no rekishi chiri*, pp. 19–38. Rekishi chiri gakkai, 1969.

Ōyama Kyōhei. *Nihon chūsei nōson shi no kenkyū*. Iwanami shoten, 1978.

————. *Nihon no rekishi 9 Kamakura bakufu*. Shōgakkan, 1974.

Postan, Michael. *The Medieval Economy and Society*. New York: Pelican, 1972.

Ramirez-Christensen, Esperanza. *Heart's Flower*. Stanford, CA: Stanford University Press, 1994.

Rosovsky, Henry. "Rumbles in the Rice Fields: Professor Nakamura vs. the Official Statistics." *Journal of Asian Studies* 27 (February 1968): 347–360.

Ryavec, Carol. "Political Jurisdiction in the Sengoku Daimyo Domain: Japan, 1477–1573." Ph.D. dissertation, Columbia University, 1978.

Saeki Hirotsugu. "Chūsei toshi Hakata no hatten to Okinohama." In *Nihon chūsei shi ronkō*, pp. 419–450. Bunken shuppan, 1987.

Saitō Masao. "'Awaji no kuni ōtabumi' no genpon ni tsuite." *Onko sōshi* 31 (November 1977): 8–19.

Saitō Osamu. "Dai kaikon jinkō shōnō keizai." In *Iwanami Nihon keizai shi shiriizu* 1 *Keizai shakai no seiritsu,* pp. 171–215. Iwanami shoten, 1988.

———. "The Frequency of Famines as Demographic Correctives in the Japanese Past." *Institute of Economic Research, Hitotsubashi University Discussion Papers Series A* 386 (January 2000): 1–32.

———. "Inasaku to hatten no hikaku shi." In *Tōnan Ajia kara no chiteki bōken,* pp. 195–240. Libro, 1986.

———. "Kikin to jinkō zōka sokudo." *Keizai kenkyū* 51 (January 2000): 28–39.

Sakai Kimi. *Nihon chūsei no zaichi shakai.* Yoshikawa kōbunkan, 1999.

———. "Yamashiro no kuni Nishioka no 'Ōnin no ran.'" In *Sōkoku no chūsei,* pp. 217–245. Daimei dō, 2000.

Sakamoto Ryōta. "Sōbo kara miru chūsei sonraku." *Hisutoria* 182 (November 2002): 53–84.

Sakata Satoshi. "Chūsei hyakusei no jinmei to mura shakai." *Chūō daigaku bungaku bu kiyō: Shigakka* 45 (February 2000): 31–54.

———. "Chūsei no ie to josei." In *Nihon tsūshi* 8 *chūsei* 2, pp. 171–214. Iwanami shoten, 1993.

———. "Chūsei sonraku kyōdōtai no kōzō to sono henka ni tsuite." *Rekishi hyōron* 428 (April 1985): 40–56.

———. "Chūsei sonraku ni okeru ie to josei." In *Ie to josei,* pp. 161–195. Sansei dō, 1989.

———. *Nihon chūsei no uji ie mura.* Azekura shobō, 1997.

———. "Sanson to gyoson." In *Nihon sonraku shi kōza* 2 *keikan* 1 *genshi kodai chūsei,* pp. 295–314. Yūzan kaku, 1990.

Sakata Satoshi, Ebara Masaharu, and Inaba Tsuguharu. *Nihon no chūsei* 12 *Mura no sensō to heiwa.* Chūō kōron shinsha, 2002.

Sakuma Takashi. "Hakkutsu sareta chūsei no mura to machi." *Nihon tsūshi* 9 *chūsei* 3, pp. 175–206. Iwanami shoten, 1994.

———. "Kinai no chūsei sonraku to yashiki chi." *Hisutoria* 109 (December 1985): 1–19.

Sakurai Eiji. "Chūsei no shōhin ichiba." In Sakurai and Nakanishi, *Ryūtsū keizai shi,* pp. 199–234.

———. "'Mimono' no keizai." *Kokuritsu rekishi minzoku hakubutsukan kenkyū hōkoku* 92 (February 2002): 113–130.

———. "Tennō to imoji." In *Iwanami koza Tennō to ōken o kangaeru* 3 *Seisan to ryūtsū.* Iwanami shoten, 2002.

Works Cited   353

Sakurai Eiji and Nakanishi Satoru, eds. *Shin taikei Nihon shi* 12 *Ryūtsū keizai shi.* Yamakawa shuppan sha, 2002.

Sand and Pebbles. Translated by Robert Morrell. Albany: State University of New York Press, 1985.

Sasaki Gin'ya. *Chūsei shōhin ryūtsū shi no kenkyū.* Hōsei daigaku shuppan kyoku, 1972.

———. *Nihon no rekishi* 13 *Muromachi bakufu.* Shōgakkan, 1975.

———. "Sangyō no bunka to chūsei shōgyō." In Nagahara, *Nihon keizai shi taikei* 2 *Chūsei,* pp. 143–188.

Sasaki Gin'ya with William Hauser. "Sengoku Daimyo Rule and Commerce." In J.W. Hall, Nagahara, and Yamamura, *Japan before Tokugawa,* pp. 125–148.

Sasaki Junnosuke, ed. *Nihon chūsei kōki kinsei shoki ni okeru kikin to sensō no kenkyū.* Waseda daigaku kyōiku gakubu, 2000.

Sasaki Yoichiro. "Urban Migration and Fertility in Tokugawa Japan: The City of Takayama, 1773–1871." In Hanley and Wolf, *Family and Population in East Asian History,* pp. 133–153.

Sasamoto Shōji. *Nihon no chūsei* 3 *Ikyō o musubu shōnin to shokunin.* Chūō kōron shinsha, 2002.

———. *Sengoku daimyō Takeda shi no kenkyū.* Shikaku shuppan, 1993.

———. "Sengoku jidai no yama no koya." *Shinano* 36 (July 1984): 16–33.

———. *Takeda Shingen.* Chūkō shinkō, 1997.

———. "Yama no koya no shōchō." *Iichikō* 25 (1992): 92–108.

Satō Kazuhiko. *Nihon no rekishi* 11 *Nanboku chō nairan.* Shōgakkan, 1974.

Satō Makoto and Yoshida Nobuyuki, eds. *Shin taikei Nihon shi* 6 *Toshi shakai shi.* Yamakawa shuppan sha, 2001.

Satō Shin'ichi. *Nihon no chūsei kokka.* Iwanami shoten, 1983.

———. *Nihon no rekishi* 9 *Nanboku chō no dōran.* Chūō kōron sha, 1965.

Sawada Goichi. *Nara chō jidai minsei keizai no sūteki kenkyū.* Revised edition. Kashiwa shobō, 1972.

Scheiner, Irwin. "Benevolent Lords and Honorable Peasants." In *Japanese Thought in the Tokugawa Period, 1600–1868.* Edited by Tetsuo Najita and Irwin Scheiner, pp. 39–62. Chicago: University of Chicago Press, 1978.

Seki Akira. *Kikajin.* Shibun dō, 1966.

Seki Yukihiko. "Busō." In *Chūsei o kangaeru: Ikusa.* Edited by Fukuda Toyohiko, pp. 1–71. Yoshikawa kōbunkan, 1993.

Senda Yoshihiro and Kojima Michihiro, eds. *Tenka tōitsu to shiro.* Hanawa shobō, 2002.

Shakadō Mitsuhiro. "Nanboku chō ki kassen ni okeru senshō." *Chūsei nairan shi kenkyū* 13 (August 1992): 27–38.

Shibatsuji Shunroku. "Sengoku daimyō no gaisei to zaikoku." *Sengoku shi kenkyū* 19 (February 1990): 23–25.

———. "Sengoku ki no suiri kangai to kaihatsu." *Minshū shi kenkyū* 11 (March 1973): 79–98.

Shida Jun'ichi. *Chūsei Hitachi no nōson shakai.* Tsukuba shorin, 1984.

Shimada Jirō. *Nihon chūsei no ryōshu sei to sonraku.* 2 vols. Yoshikawa kōbunkan, 1985.

——. *Nihon chūsei sonraku shi no kenkyū.* Yoshikawa kōbunkan, 1966.

——. "Shōenseiteki 'shiki' taisei no kaitai." In Takeuchi, *Taikei Nihon shi sōsho 6 Tochi seido* 1, pp. 275–338.

Shimazu Hisanori. "Chūsei Hitachi no kokuga." *Rekishi* 32 (March 1966): 54–67.

Shimozuma Yasuo. "Kusado mokkan ni miru ryūtsū kin'yū katsudo." *Kokuritsu rekishi minzoku hakubutsukan kenkyū hōkoku* 92 (February 2002): 249–268.

——. "Kusado Sengen ni miru shōgyō katsudō no ichidanmen." In *Chūsei toshi to shōmin shokumin.* Edited by Ishii Susumu and Amino Yoshihiko, pp. 31–43. Meicho shuppan, 1992.

Shinjō Tsunezō. *Chūsei suiun shi no kenkyū.* Hanawa shobō, 1994.

Shinmura Taku. *Nihon iryō shakai shi no kenkyū.* Hōsei daigaku shuppan kyoku, 1985.

Shinoda, Minoru. *The Founding of the Kamakura Shogunate, 1180-85.* New York: Columbia University Press, 1960.

Shryock, Henry, and Jacob Siegel. *The Methods and Materials of Demography.* 2 vols. Revised edition. Washington, D.C.: Bureau of the Census, 1975.

Smith, Robert. *Ancestor Worship in Contemporary Japan.* Stanford, CA: Stanford University Press, 1974.

——. "Japanese Kinship Terminology: The History of a Nomenclature." *Ethnology* 1 (July 1962): 349–359.

Smith, Thomas. *The Agrarian Origins of Modern Japan.* Stanford, CA: Stanford University Press, 1959.

Sonobe Toshiki. "Chūkinsei ikōki sonraku ni okeru miyaza to ie." *Kokuritsu rekishi minzoku hakubutsukan kenkyū hōkoku* 83 (March 2000): 1–24.

Souyri, Pierre. *The World Turned Upside Down: Medieval Japanese Society.* New York: Columbia University Press, 2001.

Sugiyama Hiroshi. *Nihon no rekishi* 11 *Sengoku daimyō.* Chūō kōron sha, 1965.

Suzuki Kunihiro. "Chūsei no shinzoku to 'ie.'" *Rekishi hyōron* 371 (March 1981): 31–49.

——. "Chūsei no 'uji' to myōjizoku." In *Ie to na tomogara no na,* pp. 63–81. Sanseidō, 1988.

——. "Chūsei zenki shinzoku ron josetsu." *Nihonshi kenkyū* 247 (March 1983): 32–57.

——. "Chūsei zenki no kazoku=shinzoku keitai to sono igi." *Nihonshi kenkyū* 242 (October 1982): 15–48.

Suzuki Kunihiro et al. "Kii no kuni Arakawa no shō chōsa hōkoku sho." *Chūsei shi kenkyū* 5 (February 1972): 1–29.

Suzuki Ryōichi. "Chūsei ni okeru nōmin no chōsan." *Shakai keizai shigaku* 6 (September 1934): 1–20.

Suzuki, Takao. *Palaeopathological and Palaeoepidemiological Study of Os- seous Syphilis in Skulls of the Edo Period.* University of Tokyo, 1984.

Suzuki Tetsuo. *Chūsei Nihon no kaihatsu to hyakusei.* Iwata shoin, 2001.

———. "Kenmu tokusei-rei to chiiki shakai." In *Sōkoku no chūsei,* pp. 166– 190. Tokyo dō, 2000.

Suzuki Tsuruko. *Nihon chūsei shakai no ryūtsū kōzo.* Azekura shobō, 2000.

Tabata Yasuko. "Chūsei no josei." In *Nihon josei shi.* Edited by Wakita Haruko et al., pp. 67–112. Yoshikawa kōbunkan, 1987.

———. *Chūsei sonraku no kōzō to ryōshu sei.* Hōsei daigaku shuppan kyoku, 1986.

———. "Kamakura ki ni okeru boshi kankei to bosei kan." In Wakita, *Bosei o tou,* vol. 1, pp. 143–171.

———. *Nihon chūsei no josei.* Yoshikawa kōbunkan, 1987.

———. *Nihon chūsei no shakai to josei.* Yoshikawa kōbunkan, 1998.

———. "Sengokki no 'ie' to josei." In *Kyoto no josei shi.* Kyoto: Shibunkaku dō, 2002.

Tabata Yasuko and Hosokawa Ryōichi. *Nihon no chūsei 4 Nyonin rōjin kodomo.* Chūō kōron shinsha, 2002.

Taeuber, Irene. *The Population of Japan.* Princeton, NJ: Princeton University Press, 1958.

The Taihei ki. Translated by Helen McCullough. New York: Columbia Univer- sity Press, 1959.

Tajima Hajime. "Minshū no kosodate no shūzoku to sono shisō." In *Iwanami kōza Kodomo no hattatsu to kyōiku 2 Kodomo kan to hattatsu shisō no tenkai,* pp. 2–34. Iwanami shoten, 1979.

Takagi Harufumi. "Kenmei ni ikiru shomin no kodomo." In Yūki, *Nihon kodomo no rekishi 2 Ransei no kodomo,* pp. 173–218.

Takagi Shōsaku. "Ransei." *Rekishigaku kenkyū* 574 (November 1987): 67–79.

Takagi Tokurō. "Chūsei ni okeru sanrin shigen to chiiki kankyō." *Rekishigaku kenkyū* 739 (August 2000): 1–16.

———. "Chūsei ni okeru sonraku keikan no hen'yō to chiiki shakai." *Chihō shi kenkyū* 269 (October 1997): 37–58.

Takahashi Bonsen. *Nihon jinkō shi no kenkyū,* vol. 1. San'yū sha, 1941.

Takahashi Hideki. *Nihon chūsei ie to shinzoku.* Yoshikawa kōbunkan, 1996.

Takahashi Manabu. "Kodai matsu ikō ni okeru chikei kankyō no henbō to tochi kaihatsu." *Nihonshi kenkyū* 380 (April 1994): 33–49.

Takahashi Masaaki. "Hōsō no kami—yaaai." *Nihonshi kenkyū* 324 (August 1989): 97–104.

———. "Nihon chūsei hōken shakai ron no zenshin no tame ni." *Rekishi hyōron* 332 (December 1977): 73–96.

———. "Yogore no Kyoto, goryō-e, bushi." *Atarashii rekishigaku no tame ni* 199 (July 1990): 1–13.

Takahashi Shin'ichirō. "Chūsei no toshi mondai." *Rekishi to chiri: Nihonshi no kenkyū* 557 (2002): 1–13.

Takahashi Takashi. "Chūsei ni okeru natsu mugi o megutte." In *Kawaguchi-shi shi chōsa gaihō*, pp. 23–34. Kawaguchi shiyakusho, 1979.

Takamure Itsue. *Nihon kon'in shi*. Jibundō, 1963.

Takano Osamu. *"Ichirenji kakochō." Fujisawa-shi shi kenkyū* 16 (February 1983): 78–229.

Takeda Shōzō. *Furo to yu no hanashi*. Hanawa shobō, 1967.

Takeuchi Rizō. "Jōei shikimoku no hizuke to kana shikimoku." *Kamakura ibun geppō* 6, 5–6 (April 1974).

———, ed. *Taikei Nihon shi sōsho 6 Tochi seido* 1. Yamakawa shuppan, 1973.

Takigawa Masajirō. *Nihon rōdō hōsei shi*. Publisher unknown. 1928.

Tamura Noriyoshi. "Chūsei jin no 'shi' to 'sei.' " *Nihonshi kenkyū* 388 (December 1994): 106–115.

———. "Chūsei ni okeru zaichi shakai to tenkō." *Minshū shi kenkyū* 55 (May 1998): 23–44.

———. "Chūsei 'zaimoku' no chiiki shakai ron." *Nihonshi kenkyū* 488 (April 2003): 16–35.

———. *Nihon chūsei sonraku keisei shi no kenkyū*. Azekura shobō, 1994.

———. "Tsuibu oboegaki—Heian makki Kamakura ki no hyakusei ie chōsan." *Minshū shi kenkyū kai kaihō* 20 (1991): 1–9.

———. *Zaichi ron no shatei*. Azekura shobō, 2001.

Tanahashi Mitsuo. "Jinshin baibai monjo niten o megutte." *Nihonshi kenkyū* 203 (July 1979): 53–59.

Tanaka Katsuyuki. "Mura no 'hanzei' to senran tokusei ikki." *Shigaku zasshi* 102 (June 1993): 1–36.

Tanaka Migaku. *Kodai Nihon o hakkutsu suru 3 Heijō-kyō*. Iwanami shoten, 1984.

Tanuma Mutsumi. *"Masamoto kō tabi hikitsuke* ni miru kikin shiryō to sono shūhen." In Sasaki Junnosuke, *Nihon chūsei kōki kinsei shoki ni okeru kikin to sensō no kenkyū*, pp. 16–19.

Tanuma Tatsumi. "Chūseiteki kōden taisei no seiritsu to tenkai." *Shoryō bu kiyō* 21 (1969): 1–22.

———. "Muromachi bakufu to shugo ryōkoku." In *Kōza Nihon shi 3 Hōkenteki shakai no tenkai*, pp. 85–116. Tokyo daigaku shuppan kai, 1970.

Tashiro Takashi. "Shimo furudate iseki ni tsuite." In *Zusetsu Nihon no rekishi 9 Zusetsu Tochigi-ken no rekishi*, pp. 125–126. Kawade shobō, 1993.

Toda Yoshimi. "Jū-jūsan seiki no nōgyō rōdō to sonraku—aratauchi o chūshin toshite." In *Chūsei shakaki no seiritsu to tenkai*. Yoshikawa kōbunkan, 1976.

Toire no kōkogaku. Tokyo bijutsu, 1997.

Tokunaga, Mitsuo. "*Shinmin kangetsu shū* no nōgyō gijutsu." In *Seiryō ki*, pp. 223–279.

"Tokushū: Tsu no minato o saguru." *Tsu no hon* 29 (June 1989): 10–57.

Tomizawa Kiyondo. *Chūsei shōen to kenchū*. Yoshikawa kōbunkan, 1996.

Tomobe Ken'ichi. "Jinkō to kazoku—Tokugawa zenki no jinkō zōka to 'ie'=

chokkei kazoku no seiritsu." In *Kazoku e no manazashi,* pp. 65–97. Kōbun dō, 2001.

———. "Tokugawa zenki no jinko zoka to 'ie' no seiritsu." *Keio Economic Society Discussion Paper Series* 00-2 (June 2000): 1–25.

Tonomura Hitomi. *Community and Commerce in Late Medieval Japan.* Stanford, CA: Stanford University Press, 1992.

———. "Women and Inheritance in Japan's Early Warrior Society." *Comparative Studies in Society and History* 32 (July 1990): 592–623.

Tonomura Hitomi, Anne Walthall, and Wakita Haruko, eds. *Women and Class in Japanese History.* Ann Arbor: University of Michigan Press, 1999.

Toshi no kyūshinryoku. In *Chūsei toshi kenkyū,* vol. 7. Shin jinbutsu ōrai sha, 2000.

Totman, Conrad. *Early Modern Japan.* Berkeley: University of California Press, 1992.

———. *A History of Japan.* Oxford and Malden, Mass.: Blackwell, 2000.

———. *Politics in the Tokugawa Bakufu, 1600–1843.* Berkeley: University of California Press, 1988.

———. *Pre-Industrial Korea and Japan in Environmental Perspective.* Leiden: Brill, 2004.

Toyoda Takeshi. *Chūsei Nihon no shōgyō.* In *Toyoda Takeshi chosaku shū,* vol. 2. Yoshikawa kōbunkan, 1972.

———. *A History of Pre-Meiji Commerce in Japan.* Kokusai bunka shinkōkai, 1969.

———, ed. *Taikei Nihon sōsho 10 Sangyō shi 1.* Yamakawa shuppan, 1964.

———. *Za no kenkyū.* In *Toyoda Takeshi chosaku shū,* vol. 1. Yoshikawa kōbunkan, 1972.

Troost, Kristina. "Common Property and Community Formation: Self-Governing Villages in Late Medieval Japan, 1300–1600." Ph.D. dissertation, Harvard University, 1990.

———. "Peasants, Elites, and Villages in the Fourteenth Century." In Mass, *The Origins of Japan's Medieval World.*

Tsang, Carol. "Corpses Clog the River: The Kansho Famine, 1460–61." Paper presented at the Association for Asian Studies, San Diego, March 2000.

Tsubunouchi Tetsushi. "Chūsei ni okeru shōen no kaihatsu to kōkogaku jō no mondai ten." *Nihonshi kenkyū* 310 (June 1988): 35–45.

Tsuchiya Megumi. "Negainushi to ama." In Ōsumi and Nishiguchi, *Shiriizu josei to bukkyō 1 Ama to amadera,* pp. 175–219.

Tsuda Hideo, ed. *Kinsei kokka no seiritsu katei.* Hanawa shobō, 1982.

Tsuji Hiroshi. "Iseki kara mita Muromachi ki Kyoto no kōsei." *Nihonshi kenkyū* 436 (December 1998): 26–42.

Tsujimoto Masashi and Okita Yukuji, eds. *Shin taikei Nihon shi 16 Kyōiku shakai shi.* Yamakawa shuppan sha, 2002.

Uchida Minoru. "Chūsei shoki Kinai sonraku to nōgyō keiei." *Shichō* 91 (March 1965): 1–23.

Uejima Tamotsu. "Harima no kuni Yano no shō ni okeru hyakusei myō no seiritsu to myōshu hyakusei." *Nihonshi kenkyū* 29 (September 1956): 1–25.

———. *Kyōkō shōen sonraku no kenkyū.* Hanawa shobō, 1970.

Ueno Haruo. *Kai Takeda shi.* Shinjinbutsu ōrai sha, 1972.

Ueno Katsuyuki. "Nihon kodai chūsei ni okeru shippei ninshiki no hen'yō." *Kyoto daigaku sōgō ningen gaku bu kiyō* 9 (2002): 99–116.

Umemura Mataji. "Tokugawa jidai no jinkō sūsei to sono kisei yōin." *Hitotsubashi daigaku keizai kenkyū* 16 (April 1965): 133–154.

Usami Takayuki. *Nihon chūsei no ryūtsū to shōgyō.* Yoshikawa kōbunkan, 1999.

Ushiyama Yoshiyuki. "Chūsei no amadera to ama." In Ōsumi and Nishiguchi, *Shiirizu josei to bukkyō* 1 *Ama to amadera,* pp. 221–263.

Varley, Paul. *Warriors of Japan.* Honolulu: University of Hawai'i Press, 1994.

Wakita Haruko, ed. *Bosei o tou.* Jinbun shoin, 1985.

———. "Bosei sonchō shisō to zaigo kan." In Wakita, *Bosei o tou,* vol. 1, pp. 173–203.

———. "Chūsei no kōtsū, un'yū." In *Kōza Nihon gijutsu no shakai shi* 8 *Kōtsū un'yū,* pp. 101–142. Nihon hyōron sha, 1985.

———. "The Formation of the *ie* and Medieval Myth: The *Shinto shū,* Nō Theater, and Picture Scrolls of Temple Origins." In *Gender and Japanese History,* pp. 53–86. Osaka: Osaka University Press, 1999.

———. "Ie no seiritsu to chūsei shinwa." In *Jendaa no Nihon shi,* pp. 87–118. Edited by Wakita Haruko and Susan Hanley. Tokyo daigaku shuppan kai, 1994.

———. *Nihon chūsei josei shi no kenkyū.* Tokyo daigaku shuppan kai, 1992.

———. *Nihon chūsei toshi ron.* Tokyo daigaku shuppan kai, 1981.

———. *Taikei Nihon no rekishi 7 Sengoku daimyō.* Shōgakkan, 1993.

———. "Towards a Wider Perspective on Medieval Commerce." *Journal of Japanese Studies* 1 (Spring 1975): 323–346.

Wakita Haruko with Susan Hanley. "Dimensions of Development: Cities in Fifteenth and Sixteenth Century Japan." In J.W. Hall, Nagahara, and Yamamura, *Japan before Tokugawa,* pp. 295–326.

Wakita Osamu. "The *Kokudaka* System: A Device for Unification." *Journal of Japanese Studies* 1 (Spring 1975): 297–320.

Watanabe Akifumi. "Kamakura chūki made no 'akutō.'" *Shisō* 38 (January 1987): 28–41.

Watanabe Hirochika. "Harima no kuni Yano no shō no 'akamai' to 'washi.'" *Gekkan rekishi techō* 22 (November 1994): 4–10.

Watanabe Hisao. "Yamato heiya ni okeru kangō shūraku no keisei to sōson sei to no kankei." *Shigaku kenkyū* 50 (April 1953): 117–134.

Watanabe Sumio. "Nihon no shōen ni tsuite." *Ōita ken chihō shi* 1 (October 1954): 49–63.

Yagi Hironori. *Suiden nōgyō no hatten ronri.* Nihon keizai hyōron sha, 1983.

Yamada Kunikazu. "Chūsei toshi Kyoto no hen'yō." *Chūsei toshi kenkyū* 5 *Toshi o tsukuru*, pp. 90–126. Shinjinbutsu ōrai sha, 1998.

Yamamoto Hiroaki. "Hōka inekari mugikari to sengoku shakai." *Nihon rekishi* 521 (October 1991): 17–36.

Yamamoto Takashi. "Chūsei nōmin no seikatsu no sekai." In *Ikki* 4 *Seikatsu bunka shisō*, pp. 131–166. Tokyo daigaku shuppan kai, 1981.

———. "Kamakura jidai no kannō to shōen shihai." *Rekishigaku kenkyū* 440 (January 1977): 1–13.

———. "Rōnin to chūsei sonraku." *Shichō* 4 (1979): 99–111.

———. "Shōen seika no kōchi nōhō." *Nenpō Nihon shi sō* 2000: 23–39 (2000).

———. *Shōen sei no tenkai to chiiki shakai*. Tōsui shobō, 1995.

Yamamoto Takeo. *Kikō no kataru Nihon rekishi*. Soshiete bunko, 1976.

———. "Rekishi no nagare ni sou Nihon to sono shūhen no kikō hensen," *Chigaku zasshi* 75 (March 1967): 119–141.

Yamamoto Takeshi. *Chōsokabe Motochika*. Yoshikawa kōbunkan, 1960.

Yamamura, Kozo, ed. *The Cambridge History of Japan*, vol. 3: *Medieval Japan*. Cambridge: Cambridge University Press, 1990.

———. "The Decline of the *Ritsuryō* System: Hypotheses on Economic and Institutional Change." *Journal of Japanese Studies* 1 (Autumn 1974): 3–37.

———. "The Development of *Za* in Medieval Japan." *Business History Review* 47 (Winter 1973): 438–465.

———. "From Coins to Rice: Hypotheses on the *Kandaka* and *Kokudaka* Systems." *Journal of Japanese Studies* 14 (Summer 1988): 341–368.

———. "The Growth of Commerce in Medieval Japan." In Yamamura, *The Cambridge History of Japan*, pp. 344–395.

———. "Returns on Unification: Growth in Japan, 1550-1650." In J. W. Hall, Nagahara, and Yamamura, *Japan before Tokugawa*, pp. 327–372.

———. "Tara in Transition: A Study of a Kamakura *Shoen*." *Journal of Japanese Studies* 7 (Autumn 1981): 349–391.

Yamamura, Kozo and Kamiki Tetsuo. "Silver Mines and Sung Coins: A Monetary History of Medieval and Modern Japan in International Perspective." In *Precious Metals in the Later Medieval and Early Modern Worlds*. Edited by J. F. Richards, pp. 329–362. Durham, NC: Carolina Academic Press, 1983.

Yamashita Takeshi. "Sengoku ki ni okeru jōkaku no rekishiteki ritchi." In *Kai chūsei shi to bukkyō bijutsu*, pp. 211–240. Meicho shuppan, 1994.

Yanagihara Toshiaki. "Hyakusei no chōsan to shikimoku yonjū ni jō." *Rekishigaku kenkyū* 588 (December 1988): 1–17.

Yanagita Kunio. *Teihon Yanagita Kunio shū*, vol. 20. Chikuma shobō, 1962.

Yasuda Tsuguo. *Chūsei no Nara*. Yoshikawa kōbunkan, 1998.

Yasuno Masaki. *Ge'nin ron*. Nihon edeitaa sukuuru shuppan bu, 1987.

———. "Jinshin baibai ninjō 'tenkō' bungen no kenkyū." *Hirosaki daigaku kyōyō bu bunka kiyō* 30 (1989): 59–98.

Yata Toshifumi. "Meiō shichi nen Kishū ni okeru jishin tsunami to Wada ura." *Wakayama chihō shi kenkyū* 21 (August 1991): 18–30.

———. *Nihon chūsei sengoku ki kenryoku kōzō no kenkyū.* Hanawa shobō, 1998.

———. *Nihon chūsei sengoku ki no chiiki to minshū.* Seibun dō, 2002.

Yi Tae-jin. "The Influence of Neo-Confucianism on 14th–16th Century Korean Population Growth." *Korea Journal* 37 (Summer 1997): 5–23.

———. "Social Changes in Late Koryo to Early Choson Period." *Korea Journal* 23 (May 1983): 32–44.

Yokoyama Yoshikiyo. "Honchō korai kokō kō." *Gakugei shirin* 5 (1879): 167–175.

Yoshida Takashi. "Ritsuryōsei to sonraku." In *Iwanami kōza Nihon rekishi 3 Kodai 3*, pp. 141–200. Iwanami shoten, 1975.

Yoshida Tōgo. *Ishin shi hachikō.* Fusan bō, 1911.

Yoshida Toshihiro. "Chūsei sonraku no kōzō to sono hen'yō katei." *Shirin* 66 (May 1983): 80–146.

Yūki Rikuro, ed. *Nihon no kodomo no rekishi 2 Ransei no kodomo.* Daiichi hōki shuppan, 1977.

Index

About the Author

William Wayne Farris, who received his doctorate in history from Harvard University, holds the Sen Sōshitsu XV Distinguished Chair in Traditional Japanese Culture and History in the History Department of the University of Hawai'i at Mānoa. In addition to numerous articles, he is the author of three previous books dealing with the social and economic history of pre-1600 Japan: *Population, Disease, and Land in Early Japan, 645–900* (1985); *Heavenly Warriors: The Evolution of Japan's Military, 500–1600* (1992); and *Sacred Texts and Buried Treasures: Issues in the Historical Archaeology of Ancient Japan* (1998). Recipient of numerous grants and honors, he is currently a member of the American Advisory Committee of the Japan Foundation.

Production Notes for Farris / *Japan's Medieval Population*

Cover design by Santos Barbasa Jr.

Interior design by University of Hawai'i Press production staff with display type in Post Antiqua and text in Sabon

Composition by inari information services

Printing and binding by The Maple-Vail Book Manufacturing Group

Printed on 60# Glatfelter Offset B18, 420 ppi